The Habsburg and Hohenzollern Dynasties in the Seventeenth and Eighteenth Centuries

DOCUMENTARY HISTORY OF WESTERN CIVILIZATION
Edited by Eugene C. Black and Leonard W. Levy

A volume
in
DOCUMENTARY HISTORY
of
WESTERN CIVILIZATION

The Habsburg and Hohenzollern Dynasties in the Seventeenth and Eighteenth Centuries

edited by

C. A. MACARTNEY

HARPER PAPERBACKS

Harper & Row, Publishers: New York, Evanston, and London

THE HABSBURG AND HOHENZOLLERN
DYNASTIES IN THE SEVENTEENTH AND
EIGHTEENTH CENTURIES

Introductions, editorial notes, chronology,
bibliography, translations by the editor, and
compilation copyright © 1970 by C. A. Macartney.

Printed in the United States of America.

First HARPER PAPERBACK edition published 1970 by
Harper & Row, Publishers, Incorporated,
New York, N.Y. 10016.

A clothbound edition of this book is published in the
United States and Canada by Walker and Company.

Library of Congress Catalog Card Number: 69-15558.

Contents

Acknowledgments

It is my pleasure, as it is my duty, to express here my most deep obligation to Dr. Ernst Opgenoorth of Bonn University, Germany, for the kindly and expert help he has given me, both in the selection of the documents relating to the Hohenzollerns, and also in the elucidation of many problems connected with them. Without his help I should have been sadly lost in this field. I should, however, emphasize that he is in no way responsible for any errors, insufficiencies, or perversities of judgment either in the elucidations to the documents or in the introductory sketch. He has not seen these; I do not doubt that they would have been greatly improved if he had.

Dr. Peter Wildner, of Vienna University, has also given me valuable help in identifying and supplying Habsburg documents. If my obligation toward him is less extensive than toward Dr. Opgenoorth, this is because I have made fewer calls on him; not that the calls which I did make were less willingly or less competently answered.

All translations in this volume, with the obvious exceptions of numbers 1 and 5-8 of the Habsburg series, are my work.

C. A. MACARTNEY
Hornbeams, Boars Hill, Oxford

*The Habsburg and Hohenzollern Dynasties
in the Seventeenth and Eighteenth Centuries*

I

The Habsburg Dynasty

Introduction: The Expansion of the Habsburg Power in the Seventeenth and Eighteenth Centuries

The opening of the seventeenth century found the Habsburg dominions in central Europe in a state of considerable, and unaccustomed, uncertainty. The founder of the Austrian line, Ferdinand I, had impaired the unity of the *Hausmacht* when, dying, he had thought the imperial dignity, the crowns of Bohemia and Hungary, and the Archduchy of "Austria" (Above and Below the Enns) sufficient portion for his eldest son, Maximilian II while bequeathing to the two younger sons, Ferdinand and Charles, the Tirol and "Inner Austria" respectively. Charles died in 1590 and was in due course succeeded (after a minority of five years) by his elder son, Ferdinand II, while his younger son, Leopold, eventually succeeded to the Tirol. Maximilian's portion passed undivided to his eldest son, but this was the unfortunate Rudolf II, who shut himself up with astrologers and alchemists in his castle of Prague, leaving the government of the Austrias and Hungary to his younger brother, Ernest, and on the latter's death in 1595, to the third brother, Matthias.

The family heritage had been divided before, in similar fashion, but the ill effects of this had been largely remedied by the dutifulness shown by the cadet branches of the family toward the head of the house, and the Tirolean and Inner Austrian branches did not fail in this now; but Matthias fretted against his subordination to his *exalté* elder brother, of whom he hoped to make himself independent. This family disunity was superimposed on a great ideological division which had come to run through all the Habsburgs' dominions, in consequence of the Reformation, which at one time had gained for Protestantism a majority of their subjects in almost every land.

Ferdinand of Tirol had succeeded in reconverting the Tirol (from Lutheranism) without much difficulty, but Charles had been forced to make to his Protestant subjects many concessions that the regents for his son had been unable to retract. When Ferdinand II came of age, he carried through the Counter-Reformation in Inner Austria, although at a heavy cost in human suffering,[1] but the Protestants put up a tough resistance in the Archduchy of Austria and a stouter one still in Bohemia, with its Hussite tradition; while in Hungary, the center of which was under direct Turkish rule, and Transylvania, an autonomous province ruled under Turkish suzerainty by princes, many of whom were Calvinists, the Habsburgs were physically unable to introduce the Counter-Reformation outside the small strip of the country under their direct sovereignty, and even there the Protestants were in a measure protected by support given them by the princes of Transylvania.

It was in almost every respect an unhappy age both for the dynasty and its peoples. The political tension between Catholic rulers and largely Protestant Estates found a counterpart further down the social scale in severe social distress, and to add to all this, 1591 saw the outbreak of a war between Austria and the Porte which lasted for fifteen years, inflicting cruel devastation throughout Hungary.

The Peace of Vienna, signed on June 12, 1606, between the dynasty and the Transylvanian Prince Bocskay, and the Truce of Zsitvatorok, mediated by Bocskay between the Empire and the Porte in the following November, ended this war, but only left the internal situation more acute than ever. Under the Peace of Vienna, Bocskay had not only forced the Habsburgs to recognize an enlarged and near-independent Transylvania, but had also secured far-reaching guarantees for the Protestants of Royal Hungary. In 1608 the Protestant Estates of Hungary combined with those of Austria. Matthias, who was in any case personally not unsympathetic to Protestantism, patronized the movement, and in June Rudolf ceded to him the sovereignty over the Archduchy

[1] See Document 1.

of Austria, Hungary, and Moravia (which had associated itself with Rudolf's opponents). Matthias, who now was crowned king of Hungary, made very far-reaching concessions, political as well as religious, to the Estates of his dominions, and something approaching open rebellion compelled Rudolf, on July 9, 1609, to issue an "Imperial Charter" to give full equality to the Protestants of Bohemia.[2] As he was slow to honor his promises, the Protestants of Bohemia called in Matthias, whom they crowned king of Bohemia on May 26, 1611. Rudolf died in January, 1612, and, the following June, Matthias succeeded him in the imperial dignity.

The replacement of Rudolf by Matthias seemed, on the face of it, a great victory for Protestantism, and for the Estates; but appearances deceived. Matthias was far from enamored of the position of honorary president of half a dozen aristocratic republics to which his various subjects wished to reduce him. He was, moreover, still a Catholic, and on succeeding in Bohemia, retained Rudolf's Catholic advisers there. Further, true Habsburg as he was, he did not question the duty of assuring both the family *Hausmacht* and the imperial dignity for his family. As he was childless, the heritage would have to pass to a collateral branch, and he "adopted" Ferdinand of Inner Austria—in effect, the only possible candidate in the field, since the ages of the other Habsburgs of the Austrian line put them out of the count.[3] Matthias secured Ferdinand's "acceptance" by the Bohemian Estates in 1617 and his actual coronation by the Hungarian in 1618 (in each case under a somewhat ambiguously worded formula that might or might not admit the electoral rights of the Estates). In each case, Ferdinand swore to respect the vested rights and liberties of the kingdom concerned, but his record as the heart and soul of the Counter-Reformation in Inner Austria was not such as to inspire confidence in his sincerity. The Protestant Electors of the Empire were still less reassured, and Catholics and Protestants throughout central Europe girded themselves for a conflict, which the Protestants of Bohemia precipitated by throwing two of Matthias's Catholic advisers out of a window of the Royal Palace in Prague.[4]

Comparatively unserious in its direct effects (two of the three

[2] See Document 2.
[3] Philip II of the Spanish line put in a claim, but Ferdinand bought him off under a secret agreement.
[4] See Document 3.

victims[5] emerged from their ordeal quite unscathed, and the third, although injured, survived) this famous act of ill-temper had enormous secondary results. The Protestant hotheads followed it up with various excesses against the Catholics, set up a provisional government, and appealed abroad for help. Ferdinand, soon after become sole ruler (Matthias died on March 20, 1619), sent troops against the Protestants. They in turn declared his election invalid and offered the crown to the Elector Palatine of the Rhine, who, after some hesitation, accepted it. Throughout Europe, Catholics and Protestants—among the latter, Gabriel Bethlen, prince of Transylvania—sprang to arms, and the Thirty Years' War was raging.

This miserable conflict, the details of which will not be described here, cost the Habsburg lands an almost incalculable price in blood and wealth. Contemporary estimates put the loss to Bohemia at four-fifths of its villages and three-quarters of its population, and later historians regard these figures as not greatly exaggerated. The losses suffered by the German-Austrian lands were less, but still terrible enough, especially in Upper and Lower Austria. The material and intellectual impoverishment was enormous.

But for the dynasty, the end had been triumph. Ferdinand had, after all, achieved the imperial crown, as had his son, Ferdinand III (1637–57) and Ferdinand III's second son, Leopold I (1657–1705),[6] after him; it is true that the Peace of Westphalia of 1648 had reduced the effective power of this office to a shadow, but it remained Europe's most august lay dignity. Ferdinand II had put the "Winter King," as the Elector Palatine was nicknamed from the brief duration of his reign, to ignominious flight, crushed the Bohemian rebels at the Battle of the White Mountain (November 6, 1620), and imposed revised constitutions (*Vernewerte Landesordnungen*) on Bohemia (1627) and Moravia (1628), which left the Estates with only simulacra of power, and no further possibility of electing a non-Habsburg to rule them. The constitutions also established Catholicism as the sole religion. Obdurate Protestants were driven into exile and their estates confiscated and bestowed on creatures of Ferdinand's, many of them of foreign origin.

[5] For good measure, the perpetrators had thrown the governors' secretary after them.

[6] See Document 4.

The German-Austrian lands had not required such severe treatment—the monarch's prerogatives had been so extensive already as to make the issue of new constitutions unnecessary—but the régimes established in them had been as absolute as those in the Bohemian Lands.

Meanwhile, the extinction of the Tirolean line had left all the lands of the Habsburg *Hausmacht* reunited in a single hand.

Ferdinand II carried his work of repression through so thoroughly that Ferdinand III and Leopold I found little to add to it. As at the same time they agreed with its course, the internal political history of the three-quarters of a century of their two reigns is, as regards the German and Bohemian Lands, almost a blank, a long, dreary period in the course of which the active pressure, indeed, relaxed as the need for it diminished, but only to give way to a dull period of routine administration on the one hand and passive submission on the other. And although the spirit of Joseph I was more agile, his short reign (1705–11) was so fully occupied with other problems that he, too, left internal conditions in his western dominions untouched.

It was only in Hungary, of all the Habsburgs' dominions, that the situation was different. Neither Ferdinand II nor his son had dared risk driving the Hungarians into the arms of the Turks, and offending Transylvania, by over-great severity, and although the Counter-Reformation made progress also in Royal Hungary, this was carried through during their reigns chiefly by native Hungarians, with only moderate severity, and the political institutions retained a semblance of reality. The most acute grievance of the Habsburgs' Hungarian subjects, in these years, was that their masters, in order to keep their flank free in their struggle against France for the mastery of central Europe, kept peace with the Turks instead of fulfilling their oath to liberate Hungary from pagan rule.

The end of this period of balance between Vienna, the Porte, and Transylvania came, and a new chapter opened which ended by bringing all Hungary under effective Habsburg rule, but at the cost of elemental clashes, when Prince George II Rákóczy of Transylvania overreached himself in 1657 in an attempt to acquire the crown of Poland and offended the sultan, whose great grand vizier, Mohammed Köprülü (Kuprili), led a force against Transylvania and reduced it to puppet subjection. Both Transylvanians and West Hungarians appealed passionately to Vienna for help, but Leopold, although he sent a small force against the Turks, concluded a humiliating peace with them (Peace of Vasvár, 1664) and left the Hungarians to their fate. Their embitterment was such that a group of the highest magnates in the land conspired against Leopold, entering into negotiations with the Porte, France, and other powers. The conspiracy was betrayed, and Leopold's ultra-Catholic and ultracentralizing minister, Lobkowitz, aided by the cardinal-primate, Szelepcsényi, and his right-hand man and later successor, Kollonics, seized their chance to bring Hungary into line with the Habsburgs' other dominions. Savage personal reprisals were taken against recalcitrant nobles and Protestant pastors.[7] In 1673 the Hungarian Constitution was formally suspended, and Hungary was placed under a Directorate, headed by the Grand Master of the Teutonic Order, who was assisted by a council composed half of Germans and half of Hungarians. Latin and German were declared the official languages, and officials were required to know "Sclavonian" but not Hungarian. These cruel measures produced their inevitable reaction, and a young North Hungarian nobleman named Thököly led a revolt which forced Leopold, in 1681, to restore the Constitution, reconvoke the diet, and remedy some of the worst grievances. But the sultan, encouraged by Thököly's successes, broke the long peace and in 1683 sent a vast army northward, which swept clean through Hungary and laid siege to Vienna itself. Then the tide turned again. The Peace of Nymwegen (1679) had freed Leopold's hands in the west—at the price, indeed, of further losses to the Reich. Reinforcements, including a Polish detachment under Sobieski, reached the beleaguered city just in time. Caught unawares on September 12, the Turkish army was driven back in rout.[8] By the end of the year, all Royal Hungary had been freed, and this time the successes were followed up by a brilliant series of campaigns, directed by the genius of Prince Eugene of Savoy. In 1686 Buda and most of the rest of central and southern Hungary were recovered; in 1687, Transylvania; and in 1699, under the Peace of Karlowitz, the sultan relinquished all Hungary except the Tisza-Maros corner.

The position envisaged by those Hungarian Estates who had

[7] See Document 5.
[8] See Documents 6–8.

elected a Habsburg king of Hungary in 1526 was realized at last, but under conditions very different from those which they had had in mind. The Habsburgs' conception of rule was now that of centralized absolutism, in partnership with the Catholic Church, and as they extended their authority over Hungary they hastened to introduce into it the system already prevailing in their other lands. As early as 1687, Leopold had forced a Hungarian diet to accept the succession of his dynasty in the male line and to re-nounce the nation's old "right of resistance" to illegal actions by the crown. He swore, indeed, to respect the rest of the nation's rights, but as the "liberating" armies advanced, they ravaged the country more cruelly, the Hungarians complained, than the Turks themselves had done. The areas recovered from the Turks were declared to be at the crown's disposal, and a commission allocated them to foreign buyers or to peasant colonists, many of whom now entered Hungary from the Balkans or Germany.[9] Consequently, it took one more conflict yet before a *modus vivendi* could be reached between the Habsburgs and Hungary. In 1703 the young Francis II Rákóczy, a scion of the great Tran-sylvanian house, took advantage of Austria's renewed involvement in the west (over the Spanish succession) to raise the country in revolt. Eight years of fighting passed before a compromise peace was patched up at Szatmár (April, 1711), on the basis of confirma-tion of the political and religious *status quo* coupled with an amnesty and a promise by the new monarch, Charles VI (III of Hungary; Joseph had died on the eve of the signature) to convoke a diet to hear general complaints. At the Diets of 1715 and 1722–23 Hungary promised to regard herself as united "indivisibly and in-separably" with the Habsburgs' other dominions, the union to be valid "for all events and also against external enemies," while Charles again swore to respect the national rights and privileges and to rule Hungary as an independent polity, having its own Constitution, according to its own laws only, and not "after the pattern of other provinces."

As a corollary to this settlement, Hungary also accepted the Habsburg succession in the female line, thereby rounding off a series of transactions in which first Leopold, then Charles, had been engaged to secure the future integrity and indivisibility of

[9] See Document 10.

the Habsburg *Hausmacht* even in the event of the extinction of
the male line of the house.[10] When this prospect became a near-
certainty—Joseph having died without male issue, while Charles's
only son died in infancy—Charles spent much of the rest of his
reign in barren negotiations and struggles with foreign powers to
extract promises from them to recognize the right to the succession of his elder daughter, Maria Theresa. In the course of these,
he lost many of the acquisitions which had come to Austria after
the War of the Spanish Succession (eventually retaining only the
Austrian Netherlands and Milan-Mantua), and his enterprises in
the Balkans were also unsuccessful. He rounded off Hungary by
acquiring the Tisza-Maros corner in 1718 (Peace of Passarowitz)
but failed to penetrate further into the Balkans. Meanwhile, the
internal administration was neglected and the treasury exhausted.

Then, in 1740, Charles died, suddenly and prematurely, leaving
the twenty-three-year-old Maria Theresa, with a disorganized and
largely disaffected *Hausmacht* and an empty treasury, to face a
pack of greedy neighbors, of whom, Frederick II of Prussia, on a
pretext which he himself acknowledged to be untenable, promptly
occupied and demanded the cession of Silesia; while soon after, the
Elector of Bavaria, helped by French troops, marched into Upper
Austria and afterward into Prague, both the Upper Austrian and
the Bohemian Estates acknowledging him as their monarch.

Fortunately for Maria Theresa, the Hungarian diet to which
she appealed for help provided it.[11] The tide of war turned, and
although the long War of the Austrian Succession (1740–47) cost
her nearly all the rich province of Silesia, which she failed to
recover in the Seven Years' War (1756–63) she emerged from
these struggles with her dominions otherwise practically intact,
and later even enlarged them, reluctantly enough, by acquiring
Galicia under the First Partition of Poland (1772). She might,
perhaps, have enlarged them further still at the expense of the
Porte, but refused to do so.[12]

Besides all this, Maria Theresa ended by making her reign the

[10] For the documents relating to this question, Leopold's "*Pactum Mutuae
Successionis,*" Charles's "Pragmatic Sanction," and the Hungarian legislation implementing the latter, see Document 11.

[11] See Document 13.

[12] See Documents 17 and 18.

most solidly constructive, in internal respects, of any in the history of the monarchy.

The difficulties which she encountered at the beginning of her reign from the cumbersome political structure which the monarchy had inherited, with the selfishness and mutual jealousies of the provincial Estates and their advocates at court, led her to carry through, with the help of an adviser of genius, Baron Haugwitz, a great reorganization of the whole political, financial, and military system in her German-Austrian and Bohemian lands.[13] The political and financial (also the judicial) apparatus in these lands was largely transferred from the hands of the Estates into those of a centralized bureaucracy; simultaneously, the financing of the standing army was put on a regular footing. The economic system also was rationalized and strengthened. These changes were initiated chiefly in order to strengthen the monarchy so as to enable it to retain, or later to recover, Silesia but when, after 1763, Maria Theresa abandoned hope of this, she devoted herself to reform for reform's sake, bringing the State's finances into order—this largely by her insistence on a pacific foreign policy—and introducing a large number of reforms in every internal field, cultural and social, as well as economic and administrative.[14] In these years the monarchy in fact achieved a prosperity hitherto unknown, and they also saw the birth—it is true, only so far in restricted circles—of a real "Austrian" patriotism, and attachment to the *Gesammtmonarchie* as distinct from purely national or provisional patriotism.

This sketch will nevertheless not be able to conclude with a picture of the Habsburg monarchy advancing peacefully toward further modernization and consolidation. Maria Theresa's death on November 29, 1780, left her elder son, Joseph, since 1765 already co-regent of the Austrian dominions, and German king and Roman emperor for as long, in sole control. Intensely dogmatic, impatient, and autocratic by nature,[15] Joseph entertained an ideal of a State that should be a single smooth-running machine, obeying only a single will, that of its monarch. He was not at all indifferent to the welfare of his peoples, but he claimed for himself the sole right to determine wherein that welfare should consist, and how

[13] See Document 17.
[14] For examples, see Documents 14 and 15.
[15] See Document 16.

it should be achieved, and all institutions or forces which might obstruct his will were to be swept aside. He had long fretted against the half-measures and concessions to tradition which had marked the last years of his mother's reign, and as soon as her eyes were closed, he plunged into headlong activity. The last effective political rights which the Estates had still enjoyed vanished; the bureaucracy became all-powerful and all-seeing. The landlords' rights over their peasants were further restricted, as were (in the interests of industrialization) the privileges of the guilds. While the Church was left, in theory, supreme *in puris spiritualibus*, the definition of what was "purely spiritual" was severely limited, and, outside the restricted field which remained, the State was to be as absolutely supreme here as everywhere else.

It was not only in depth that Joseph went further than his mother. At her Coronation Diet Maria Theresa had renewed and extended the promises made by her father (and largely disregarded by him) to Hungary to respect its liberties and institutions;[16] and deference to these promises, combined with gratitude toward the Hungarians for the help they had then given her and a realistic appreciation of the difficulties which any other course would entail, had led her to leave Hungary out of most of her measures of reorganization. It is true that even she broke a generous number of promises—thus she convoked only two more diets after that at which she was crowned, again left the office of palatine unfilled, and imposed *jure majestatis* a number of measures on which she should, under any normal interpretation of the documents, have consulted the diet. Nevertheless, when she died, Hungary was still a foreign body within the monarchy, with its intact national tradition, its own self-governing political system, its own social structure, its own language of administration (Latin). In part—to do him justice—the backwardness of many of Hungary's institutions, but still more, the obstacles which they presented to the enforcement of his autocratic will, were thorns in Joseph's flesh, and on accession to the sole power, he simply imposed on Hungary the same measures which he was enacting in Austria, evading the difficulty that a coronation oath would have forbidden this by the simple device of not submitting himself to coronation. Thus the old self-governing institutions were re-

[16] See Document 13A.

placed by an absolutist bureaucracy, for which, moreover, the language of business (as also, in consequence, that of education above the primary level) was German. The land tax which he was preparing to introduce at the end of his reign would have applied, *inter alia*, to noble land in Hungary.

He trampled no less ruthlessly on the traditional liberties and the national prejudices of the Austrian Netherlands.

All this produced a seething discontent, strongest in Hungary and the Netherlands, but not confined to those groups of lands, which Joseph might yet have mastered had he not also been a militarist and an imperialist; another characteristic of his mother's which he did not share was her lack of territorial acquisitiveness. After driving the German princes into the arms of Prussia, and presenting Frederick with at once a pretext and a valid reason for renewed self-assertion, he entangled himself in Catherine of Russia's designs against the Porte. He embarked on a gratuitous campaign in the Balkans, which imposed heavy new sacrifices in blood and money on his subjects—the standing army was enlarged and heavy new taxation imposed—and was, moreover, disastrously ill-conducted. All the chief enemies of his policy took advantage of the difficulties in which he had embroiled himself. In November, 1789, the Austrian Netherlands revolted altogether. The malcontents in Hungary threatened to do the same, and spun threads to Prussia, which moved an army to the Galician frontier. Mortally sick, Joseph at last made a political recantation toward Hungary, repealing most of his edicts in respect to that country, restoring the holy crown (which he had had taken to Vienna), and indicating that he would in future follow the due constitutional path.[17] But this had hardly done more than whet appetites when, on February 20, 1790, he died, leaving his brother and successor, Leopold, until then grand duke of the family secundogeniture of Tuscany, to cope with a situation replete with danger, international and domestic.

Leopold II was a very different man from his brother. He was as anxious for reform as Joseph had been, but he did not believe in "trying to impose even good on the people if they are not convinced of its utility" and even believed that a monarch's powers ought to be constitutionally limited.[18] He had, moreover, a sane

[17] See Document 13B.
[18] See Document 20.

and healthy appreciation of realities. In a swift series of emergency operations, he placated the Hungarians[19] by accepting coronation on terms which, while safeguarding the dynastic position,
removed their genuine constitutional grievances, and liquidated
the international crisis (at the cost, indeed, of the alliance with
Russia) by concluding peace with the Porte and agreeing with
Prussia on the restoration of the *status quo* in central Europe. In
his further transactions with the rest of his subjects, he again
retracted what had been indefensible among Joseph's measures,
while contriving to salvage most of what had been salutary. He
failed to recover the Netherlands, except for a period of a few
months; but for the rest, he had succeeded in laying foundations
which were, indeed, not altogether secure—Joseph's bulldozing had
been too drastic for that—but on which he would probably have
been able to build had he not died with tragic suddenness on
March 1, 1792. In the storms which the French Revolution now
unleashed, the monarchy did indeed hold together, losing at times
very important parts of its territory, but only to recover them, or
their equivalents, in 1815; but its internal institutions were subjected to a prolonged deep freeze, which cracked only in 1848.

The selection of documents which follows is, of necessity, highly
eclectic. It does not pretend to constitute a compendium of the
most imporant pieces of the period—who shall say exactly which
these are?—but to illustrate the trends with examples from each.
The history of the Habsburgs during the early part of the period
with which they are concerned was inseparably bound up with
that of the Counter-Reformation, to which, accordingly, the first
five of the series relate; and as the most famous developments were
those occurring in Bohemia, three of the five (2, 3, and 4, which
form a connected series) refer to that country; but to keep the
balance, one (1) is drawn from the history of German Austria, and
one (5) from that of Hungary. Document 9 relates to the more
general economic problems of the day. The Siege of Vienna (6, 7,
and 8) speaks for itself, but it is not easy to find pieces which deal
adequately with the subsequent recovery of Hungary and do not
run into volumes. We give in 10 one example of the methods used

[19] See Document 13C.

by Vienna in dealing with the problem, while the top-level constitutional issues emerge from the documents connected with the general regulation of the Habsburg succession (11). We have let Maria Theresa describe in her own words the problems which faced her at the opening of her reign, and how she dealt with them (12). The chief internal constitutional issue was thereafter the relationship with Hungary; the main documentation on this point is given in 13. The domestic activities of Maria Theresa and her two sons covered so many fields that it would be quite impossible even to touch on them all, so that we have picked two of the most important, their handling of Church-State relations (14) and the peasant problem (15). Document 16 illustrates the differences which not infrequently troubled the relationship between Maria Theresa and her elder son; Documents 17 and 18 show the different spirits in which they approached the question of the monarchy's foreign relations. Document 19, from an old travel book, may give the reader an inkling (if he needs it) of the problems confronting the ruler of a multinational state so variously composed as was that of Joseph II. Finally, we give, in Document 20, the "profession of faith" of the wisest of all the Habsburgs, whose reign was also the shortest of all.

1. The Counter-Reformation in German Austria

This pamphlet may be found, *inter alia*, in the Bodlean Library, Oxford, and many others. Both parts of it are self-explanatory. The word *Dutch* on the title page means *German (Deutsch)*.

TWO VERY LAMENTABLE RELATIONS:

THE ONE,
THE GRIEVANCES FOR RELIGI-
ON, OF THOSE OF STIRIA, CARINTHIA,
AND CRAYNE, UNDER FERDINAND
THEN DUKE OF GRATZ, NOW
EMPEROUR.

THE OTHER,
THE NOW PRESENT MOST HUMBLE SUP-
PLICATION, OF CERTAYNE OF THE STATES OF
LOWER AUSTRIA, UNTO THE SAID
EMPEROUR.

WHEREIN IS SHEWED THE MOST TERRIBLE, INHU-
MANE, AND BARBARIAN TYRANNIES, COMMITTED BY
THE EMPEROURS SOULDIERS, SPECIALLY THE
CASOCKES AND WALLONS, IN THE
SAID COUNTRIE.

DONE OUT OF THE DUTCH
AND PRINTED

1620

The grievances for Religion of those inhabiting in the Provinces of *Stiria, Carinthia*, and *Cragne;* not onely in their Bodies outwardly, but also in their Consciences inwardly, for the Testimonie of the true Gospell; most cruelly persecuted, by the enemies of the Truth, and their Commissaries; Under Ferdinand, now Emperour, then Duke of *Gratz* etc.

To declare to the World the hourely and minutely griefe of Conscience and grievances for the Religion which wee have had, were almost impossible and also unnecessary, since it is, alas, too well knowne to this Land, to the Empire, and to a great part of the World; yet neverthelesse we will rehearse a few.

1. First, by priviledge, and good will of the illustrious Arch-Duke *Charles* of *Austria*, of famous memory, our gracious Lord and Prince, was granted to the professors of the Gospell, many special Ministers in principall Townes as in *Gratz, Indenburgk, Clagenfourt*, and *Labach*.

2. *Item*, their Colledges and free Schooles of learning, for instructing Noblemens, and others Children, were admitted and granted them, in the foresaid Townes of *Gratz, Clagenfourt*, and *Labach*, all which priviledges are most violently taken from them.

3. Item, in the Countrey of *Stiria*, were many Cathedrall and other Parish Churches also violently taken from them.

4. Also many privileged Churches, pulled downe, and blowne up with Gunpowder.

5. One hundred Preachers and Ministers commanded upon · paine of death to depart the province of *Stiria*.

6. A great many more Schoole-masters, and Teachers of the Youth, most pittifully banished.

7. *Item*, many Church-yards, and resting places for the dead bodyes of the faithfull, being walled and paled about, were most barbarously pulled downe, and made levell with the ground.

8. The bodies of the faithfull digged up, and given to the devoured by Dogs and Hogs; as also the Coffins taken and set by the highway side, some burnt with fire; a worke both barbarous and inhumane.

9. Also upon the burial-places of the faithfull, were erected Gibets and places for execution of malefactors. Also upon those places where Protestant Churches stood, or where the Pulpit stood, or the Font-stone, were erected alwaies most filthy spectacles most ugly to behold.

10. *Item*, many thousand of godly and religious bookes, among which were many hundred Bibles, the witnesses of Gods most holy Word, utterly burnt with fire.

11. Moreover, (a griefe above all griefes) many thousands that professed the Gospell, were most cruelly and shamefully tormented and tortured, and by the same torments compelled shamefully, to denie and renounce the truth of Christs Evangell.

12. Compelling those of the Religion to sweare upon their saluation never to renounce that damnable Popish Idolatrie, the which they were now forced to by torments.

13. The poore distressed people, were also compelled to their extreame cost and charges, to uphold and maintaine a strong gard of Souldiers, for those cruell Commissaries owne obedient *mancipia* and *evotoria*.

14. The constant Confessors and Professors of Christs most holy Word and Gospell, together with their Wives, and innocent Babes, were most cruelly compelled to leave their dwellings and habitations (whether it were in Cities, Townes, or Villages) at the pleasure of those barbarous Comissaries; and the longest terme of their abode was, six weekes and three dayes, sometimes but eight dayes, and sometimes they must be gonne before Sun-setting, and sometimes in the coldest time of Winter, in Frost and Snow:

although it be manifest by the peace of Religion, granted in the yeere of God 1555[1] (as appears by the *Formalia*) that all Subiects or Tenants under Prince, or Noble-man, who were persecuted for Religion, might freely choose the time of their departure out of the Countrie.

15. They were not admitted time and leisure, to make sale of their Lands and Goods, but (as may appeare by that cruell *Edict specialis*) they were constrained shamefully to sell them, to their unspeakable losse, yea, and sometimes compelled to give them; not withstanding, that it most manifestly appeares also, by the foresaid peace of Religion, that there should be no compulsion, in selling or giving of Goods or Lands, excepting only, in *amore Christianae Religionis*.

And if they did sell their Goods or Lands, they were compelled to give the tenth Penny thereof, as by way of taxation; alledging that in Electorall Princes and States Lands of the Empire they did the like. But, as it appeares plainely by the aforesaid peace of Religion, it is said, those Countries shall pay the tenth Penny, who formerly did doe the same; but these our Countries have ever beene free of those taxations. We omit to remember that those Iewes who were iustly expelled not long since, were freely pardoned this taxation.

16. Notwithstanding, those Iewes were bound by bond, to pay the tenth Penny, at their departure out of the Land *per modum Compensationis;* but those poore Christian Exiles must be banished & troubled, and forced not only to quit their Countrey, Friends, alliance & acquaintance; not only debarred the fruits of their labours, but also must be bereft of that little money apointed for their maintenance, in this their wofull banishment.

17. And this was not a banishment with moderation to those devout and most faithfull Christians and our beloved Patriots, but they were exiled under paine of death never to returne. A banishment most infamous and most lamentable, that a man must bee contrained never to returne to the place of his nativitie, there, where so many yeeres he had dwelt with honor and respect; there

---

[1] The agreement concluded in 1555 at Augsburg between the Emperor Charles V and the imperial diet. This laid down, *inter alia*, the principle "cujus regio, ejus religio," and also provided that no form of Protestantism but Lutheranism was to be tolerated. But Lutheran subjects of Ecclesiastical States were not to be forced to renounce their faith.

where are the sepulchers of his dead predecessors. Although it be expresly set downe in the often spoken of peace of Religion, that it shall not be preiudiciall for any man, freely to visite his Countrie, and friends, from whom hee is banished for Religion.

18. Also the Noble-men, and others of those Provinces being Protestants, were not exempted this infamy, but were put by their hereditary offices of State, onely because they were of the Religion; and others were placed in their offices, being men of no qualitie or merit, and only because they were of Romish Religion. Our Protestant Noble-men, were also hindred from being Administrators, or exequutors to their friends or their children, althoug[h] they deale never so faithfully: Which shewes most plainely, that these wrongs done unto them, was not for the insufficiencie of their persons, births, or qualities, but only because they were Protestants.

19. Also the Noble-men and Gentrie of those Provinces being Protestants, were most grievously taxed and caused to pay great and grievous summes of money, over & above the tenth penny; not withstanding that they had quitted their Churches, Schooles, Preachers, and Schoole-masters: yea, even those that willingly would sometimes goe out of the Countrey for devotion, to heare a Sermon, or communicate, were constrained to pay the tenth penny, being out of his Highnesse Countries; although it be manifest *de iure*, that *nemo extra territorium suum* can punish any man.[2] All these iniuries are directly against his Highnesse (now Emperour) owne Edict, given to those of the Religion the last of April, 1599.

20. These great and grievous troubles and tyrannicall vexations, which wee have beene and are plagued withall, were not so much to be pittied, if there were any hope of our ease, or reliefe. But alas! the unmerciful answer and resolution of his Highnesse (now Emperour) given to the Protestants the eighth of December 1609 which was plainely told those of the religion, That he would never yeeld to their demandes, and that hee would continue in this his resolution even till his grave; and that before he would yeeld for any of the least of their demands, concerning their Religion, he would rather adventure the loss of all that ever he had of God, and with a white Staffe, goe barefooted out of all his Coun-

---

[2] I.e. it is the plain law that no authority can impose any penalty for an act committed outside its jurisdiction.

tries. Also his Highnesse (now Emperour) did threaten mightily
the Protestant Estates, vowing that he would be revenged on
them, for seeking any tolleration; alleadging that it was against his
princely Authoritie.

21. To conclude, this last is the worst of all, that his Highnesse
(now Emperor) will not heare his Nobility & Gentry, nor one of
those of the Religion, but he oftentimes comanded them upon paine
of their lives to keepe perpetuall silence: as in Anno 1598 the
thirtyeth of September; the fifth of May 1599 the fifth of March
1601 and this last time, the eighth of December 1609. Also it is
most manifest in that Edict, in the yeere 1599 hee absolutely forbids
under the paine of death, that no man of what degree or qualitie
whatsoever, should entertaine any Preacher or Minister of the
Gospell; vowing also that hee will not heare any more of their
grievances: Which is, *dura et acerba vox regnantis, non velle audire
et scripta accipere, contra qum Vetula illa obyciebat Regi Mace-
donum* Philippo *audientiam recusanti: Si non vis audire, noli ergo
Regnare.*[3] The abuses in Religion is no new thing, especially of the
spiritual sort, but if the Spiritualite did commit any excesse, or
gave any evill example, it was to be seene into by their temporall
Princes and Lords, as we have a fine example in the History of
Stiria (fol. 81,) in the yeere of God 1518. When Doctor *Luther*
had gotten the upper hand, he gave in a long *Catalogue* of Complaints and abuses of the Clergie to the Emperour *Maximilian,*
complayning of the abuses of their Benefices, their neglect of Gods
Service, the insolencies committed in their Diocesse, the carelesnesse
of their salvation, of the evill governing of Church listings, and of
the too many idle persons, that were maintained to the heavie
burthen of the Countrey, as sundry sorts of *Abbots, Canonicats,
Prebendes, Commendats,* and many others: his Imperiall Maiestie
graciously did promise a redresse, giving command to all Dukes and
Lords, to see a reformation. But at this time there is greater cause
of redresse of abuses, since it is to bee plainely seene, that wicked-
nesse hath gotten the upper hand, and alas! there is no hope of
helpe, or redresse.

---

[3] A hard and bitter voice from a ruler, to be unwilling to hear and
receive submissions against which that old woman objected to Philip of
Macedon, when he refused her audience: "If thou wilt not hear me, then,
don't be king."

If this Prince deales so hardly with his owne, much more cruelty is to be looked for at his hands, if he can have the upper hand of others.

The most humble Supplication of certaine of the States of lower *Ausria* made unto the Emperour: Wherein is shewed the most terrible, inhumane, and barbarian tyrannyes, committed by the Emperours Souldiers, by the *Casockes* and *Wallons* in the said Countrie.

Most gracious Prince, the unspeakeable spoyling, destruction, miserie, trouble, calamitie, and subiection of these countries, wrought and effected by the accursed Cosackes and others your Maiesties Souldiers brought into the same, together with the robbings, murtherings, sackings, burnings, massacrings, and other barbarian cruelties used and committed therein, mooveth and provoketh us in the name and behalfe of our principall Lords & the whole Countrey, to take and have our recourse, next unto God, to your Emperiall Maiestie, with sighes and teares to renew our former complaints. In regard that the same (in the least degree) are not yet redressed, neither hath your Imperiall Maiesty, nor you[r] Generals granted any message, nor Mandate in writing for their safe conducts; and to obtayne some reliefe therein for your poore subjects. For although your Maiesty hath heretofore oftentimes beene certified and advised, how and in what manner the Countrie in generall is spoyled and destroyed, both the Gentil-men and Commons rob'd and ransackt, some of the Pesants kild, and some of them driven from house & home into the Woods, and Mountaynes; Vines and earable Lands spoyled and laid waste, humanitie set aside; vertue, modestie, honestie, policy, law and right hindred and neglected, and an innumerable company of sinnes, and shamefull and horrible actions are daily committed, and cruelly exercised by the Souldiers. Your Maiestie having most graciously granted and promised, to take speedy order for the redressing and prevention thereof; and to that end vouchsafed your Gracious Commission to the Generall of your army, for the ceasing and stay of the same: being compelled thereunto by meere necessitie and force, your poore and humble Subjects are againe united to renew their said complaints, and to let your Maiesty know, that the said insolencies are not by any meanes ceased, nor yet lessened, but rather from day to day, and continually, are still committed, and more and more encreased and wax stronger, yea, and in such barbarian, unchristian, and inhumane manner, that we are astonished and abashed to thinke thereon, and in a manner have a detestation to name them to certifie your Majesty thereof. Therefore sith the unruly Souldiers, specially the Cosackes, stil persist in such their strange, feareful, and detestable actions, and that there is no forbearance nor distaste thereof in any sort, as also being certified, that the same is to be continued and practiced by others of your Maiesties troops. Wee, being upon more than a sure ground, for that we are certainely perswaded in our consciences, that it cannot be answered before God, together with the States, whose Officers are respectively to maintaine the Countrie, moved with no small griefe and inward vexation of mind to behold the miserable state of the country-people, & being governours and fathers of the same, (as the duty of every Governor and State-man bindeth him) most heartily and earnestly desiring and wishing to see a remedie therein. Hoping that your Imperiall Maiestie, will not in any wise be offended, nor take it in evill part, that in some sort we make the same knowne unto your Maiesty, only to the end, that your said Maiesty, as a Christian Potentate, and a most gracious Prince of the house of Austria, may the rather with all speede seeke to remedy, and take ayde for the diverting of these great, most enorme, and mischievous proçeedings.

So it is, and it pleased your Imperiall Maiesty, that for as much, as the *Wallons*, and other strange Souldiers, brought into this Country, cease not continually, to make a common practise to waste, spoyle, burne, murther, and massacre the Countrie and the Commons thereof, whereby there is not any fearefull, unspeakeable, and inhumane action whatsoever, which they, and other of your Maiesties souldiers with al cruelty, and bloud-thirstinesse, have not effected, exercised, and committed; sparing not to burne whole Villages, Hamlets, and Market-townes, and in them Storehouses for the provision of Widdowes and Orphans, (among the which we also that are Ambassadors, and have a speciall protection from your Maiety for our defence against all oppressions, are not spared) seised upon, spoyled, and burnt their Castles, houses, and their provision for their houses, being taken from them, the poore subiects that are employed about necessary defences, cannot get a bit of bread to relieve themselves withall, but are constrained to starve and die for hunger. Boys and Women being fearefully violated & ravished, are carried prisoners away, both young and old men and women, most cruelly and terribly martired, torterd, prest, their flesh pinsht, and pulled from their bodies with burning tonges, hangd up by the necks, hands, feete, and their privy-members, women, gentlewomen, and young wenches under yeeres ravished till they die, women great with child, layd so long upon the fire, untill which time as that men may see the fruit in their bodies, and so both mother and child die together, old and young, high and low states, spirituall and temporal persons, without any difference, oppressed, and many thousands of innocent people fearefully murthered. Some in their castles (and yet such as have deserved wel at your Maiesties and the house of Austrias hands, as being old & good friends to the same) not withstanding their Letters Pattents of assurance and protection, (because they professe the Lutheran Religion) pitifully murthered. Some of them with their wives and children brought forth in their shirts and smocks, and wholly bereft of all reliefe, and such as flie out into the fields, not suffred there to be free from their cruelties, but running after them, have beene most pitifully slaine, and hewed to peeces. And many men of great account have beene glad to take Pasports from their owne servants, with many other such like unspeakable and inhumane insolencies, and horrible, and cruel actions that are practiced; which although, now (as loth to make them knowne unto your Maiesty) we forbeare to write it as much as in conscience we can, and wil answere for the same before God, we wil hereafter not spare to declare.

Therefore, sith we know, that your Maiesty takes no pleasure in these feareful and horrible excesses, and intolerable abuses, & much more in respect of your Christian charitie & Princely minde, cannot but conceive a great disliking thereof; and that it is to bee feared, that your Maiesty hath not yet, or may for a long time refraine from resolving upon an answer to be made, & order to be taken touching these our obedient & humble supplications, and therefore the same will have no end nor be restrained, whereby the whole Country will bee in danger to bee laid waste, the Lords and subiects of the same brought and reduced into extreme miserie and affliction, to the great preiudice, not only of your Maiesty, but also of the whole famous and worthy house of Austria, and an unrecoverable damage unto the Empire. Wee most humbly, once againe beseech your Maiesty, in the name of our principall States, for the mercy of God, in the bleeding wounds of our Lord and Saviour *Iesus Christ*, that you would be pleased, according to your naturall commendable Austrian, and Imperiall clemencie, to have compassion upon the necessitie, miserie, and pitifull estates of your faithfull States, Subjects, and inhabitants, whereby your Maiesty shall not only bee a furtherance to your owne desiring of peace, quietnesse, and prosperitie, and procure your most gracious satisfaction, but also obtayne immortall commendation of all posteritie. Which your faithfull and bounden subjects will endeavour with all dutie and obedience to deserve at your Maiesties gracious hands, wherewith we referre our selves to your most Princely pleasure and disposition.

THE TRUE NEATHER AUSTRIAN EVANGELICALL
COMMITTEES AND AMBASSADOURS

2. Rudolf II's Imperial Patent (*Majestätsbrief*)
of July 9, 1609

The "Imperial Patent" was the document wrung from the reluctant Rudolf by the Bohemian Protestants, violations of which and of the supplementary "Treaty" signed the same day between the Catholic and Protestant Estates, led to the defenestration of Prague recorded in Document 3. The background situation which resulted in the issue of the Patent is described by all historians of Austria and Bohemia, and the immediate preliminaries are the subject of a special detailed study by A. Gindely, in his *Geschichte der Ertheilung des böhmischen Majestätsbriefes von 1609* (Prague, 1868), from which the two texts below are taken (pp. 182–9 and 190–2). We need not take this introductory note further back than the Diet of 1575, to which the opening lines of the Patent allude. In that year the then Emperor, Maximilian II, was badly in need of the Bohemian Estates' goodwill, both because he was asking a big contribution from them for his campaign against the Turks and also because he wanted them to crown his son, Rudolf, king before his own death (which occurred the following year). He was also genuinely anxious to prevent religious dissension in his dominions from becoming overacute. The Bohemian Protestants were themselves divided at the time into various sects, of which the two largest were the old-style Bohemian Brethren and the "neo-Utraquists," who followed Luther more closely. After long negotiation among themselves, these factions had succeeded in adapting an agreed statement of doctrine, containing elements from all the various Protestant creeds, which they presented to Maximilian at the diet under the name of the "Bohemian [Czech] Confession," with a demand that its adherents should enjoy complete freedom to practice it. Maximilian did not commit himself formally in writing, neither did he sanction the establishment of a regular new Constitution for the Bohemian Confession, but he gave the authors of the document a verbal promise that they should not be persecuted on account of their faith, and allowed them to appoint fifteen "Defenders" (*Defensores*) of it, not subject to the jurisdiction of the consistory. After Maximilian's death, however, Rudolf again favored the Catholics, while the Protestants, on their side, were encouraged by the support given to the Protestant cause in Hungary and elsewhere by Rudolf's ambitious brother, Matthias, who in January, 1608, was openly demanding the abdication of Rudolf.

When, in the spring of 1608, Matthias actually invaded Bohemia, Rudolf convoked a diet to meet in Prague to appeal for help. This met on March 10, but as only the Catholics appeared at it, Rudolf adjourned it to meet again in the following June. The Bohemian Protestants were not entirely inclined to go over to Matthias, whose Hungarian and other troops were making themselves unpopular in the country, but they saw their chance to press their demands, which they formulated and presented to Rudolf in writing on May 28. Rudolf returned an equivocal answer, and when the adjourned diet met again, said that he could not give the question his full consideration until the negotiations with his brother were completed. These ended on June 27, with a settlement which was humiliating enough for Rudolf, who had to cede to his brother, among other things, the direct rule over Moravia; but it was impossible for the diet to continue its sessions until Matthias's troops had left the country. Meanwhile, Rudolf conceded everything the Estates had demanded except the "Article on Religion," and he promised to discuss this as the first item on the agenda of the next diet, which was convoked to meet in Prague on January 28, 1609. It did so meet, in an exceedingly stormy atmosphere, both Catholics and Protestants assembling in armed camps; the discussions were prolonged and heated, for Rudolf put up an obstinate resistance. In the end, however, he was forced into complete surrender, and accepted the demands of the Protestant Estates verbatim, with the single modification that the word "Utraquist," or an equivalent, was to be sustained for their "evangelical." With this one modification he granted all their terms in an Imperial Patent, which he issued on July 9. On the same day the parties concluded a supplementary Treaty covering certain omissions or ambiguities in the Patent.

The Patent

We, Rudolf, etc., make known this Patent to all men, to be kept in mind forever:

ALL THREE Estates[1] of Our Kingdom of Bohemia who receive the body and blood of Our Lord Jesus Christ in both Kinds, Our beloved and loyal subjects, have at the Diets held in the Castle of Prague in the past year of the Lord 1608 on the Monday after Exaudi and on the Friday after the Feast of John the Baptist in the same year, humbly and with due submissiveness besought Us, as Kings of Bohemia: that the general Bohemian Confession, called by some the Augsburg Confession, which was codified at the general Diet of 1575[2] and submitted to His Majesty the Emperor Maximilian of glorious and honored memory, Our most beloved father (and which, as We have deigned to ascertain from reliable information on the subject, and from letters written in his own hand by Our most beloved father and which is also plain from certain credible documents preserved in the Estates' archives, was at once agreed by His Majesty) and the settlement between them[3] contained in the foreword to the same Confession, and also the other requests relating to religion expressly added by them at the same Diet, may be confirmed, the free practice of the Christian religion in both Kinds permitted without let or hindrance, and sufficient assurances be given to the Estates by Us; all of which is on record, including the request at the said Diet [of 1608] and the negotiations at the Diet itself, a verbatim record whereof is contained in the registers of the General Diet of 1608, for the Monday after Exaudi, under letters K 8.

Since, however, We were prevented by other very important and urgent business, on account of which the Diet of that year had been convened, from conferring the confirmation at that time, We most graciously asked for a postponement of the decision on all these questions until the following Diet, fixed for the first Thursday before Martinmas, assuring the Utraquist Estates meanwhile that pending the complete settlement at the general Diet they were

---

[1] The Estates of Bohemia were at this time only three in number: the Lords (spiritual and temporal), the Knights, and the Burghers.

[2] See introductory note.

[3] I.e., between the Bohemian Brothers and the neo-Utraquists.

entitled to practice their religion as they would, and that until a dcision had been reached on the temporarily adjourned points, We would not issue or accede to any further dispositions, or submit any proposals of any kind to the Estates, nor should they be required to enter into any negotiations.

Since then We were obliged, for certain reasons, to postpone the Diet fixed for the Thursday before Martinmas and to convene another in the Castle of Prague, by Royal mandate, for the Tuesday after the Conversion of St. Paul, and the said Utraquist Estates again submitted to Us their Confession and the agreement concluded between them, and did not cease to pray Us, their King and Lord, both in their own repeated humble supplications and also by invoking sponsors of high standing and repute, graciously to accede to the request of the said Utraquist Estates, Our loyal subjects: We gave to all this Our careful Imperial and Royal consideration, in consultation with the supreme functionaries, judges and councillors of Our Kingdom of Bohemia, and resolved, on the submissive petition of the said Lords, Knights, Burghers of Prague and other cities from all the three Estates of this Our Kingdom of Bohemia who receive the Body and Blood of Our Lord Jesus Christ in both Kinds, and belong to the said Confession, to convoke by Our Royal mandate Our well-beloved and loyal subjects of all three Estates of this Kingdom to a general Diet on a Monday after Rogation Sunday, otherwise called Holy Week, in this year 1609, in the Castle of Prague, and expressly to add in the same general notification that at this Diet We would submit for decision in the Proposals of the Diet the adjourned Articles of Religion and would also provide sufficient assurances that all of them, both the party which receives the Holy Communion in one Kind and also those who receive it in both Kinds and belong to the above-mentioned Confession, may practice their religion without any let or hindrance from any person, spiritual or temporal, as laid down in Our Mandates on this point, given in the Castle of Prague on the Saturday after Jubilate of this year 1609. When, then, all three Estates had assembled obediently and submissively at this general Diet convoked by Us, and We, in accordance with Our gracious assurance, included in the said Mandate, deigned first to propose this article on religion in Our Proposals to the Diet, for debate, the said three Estates of both Kinds renewed their former request to Us and humbly begged for sufficient safeguards, and for official registration thereof in the records of the Diet.

Since, then, it is Our wish that all love and concord, peace and good understanding shall prevail in this Kingdom, now and in the future, between all three Estates, both of the Catholic party and of the above-mentioned Utraquist, and between all Our dear and loyal subjects, for the promotion and maintenance of the general welfare and peace, that each party shall practice the religion in which it hopes for its salvation freely and without let or hindrance, and that satisfaction be thereby given both (as is equitable) to the conclusions of the Diet of 1608 and also to the general enactments issued by Us (in which We have publicly declared the united Utraquist Estates which profess the above-mentioned confession to be what they have always been, namely, Our loyal and obedient subjects under Our gracious protection, beneficiaries of all ordinances, rights and liberties of this Kingdom and subject to Our royal duty, right and authority, and now also do so declare them), and taking into account the weighty promises recorded above, the repeated assiduous requests of the Utraquist Estates themselves, and finally, the many true and important services rendered at all times by them to Us during Our happy rule; for all these and many other causes, We, after mature consideration, with Our serious knowledge and will, by virtue of Our Royal prerogative in Bohemia, with the agreement of the supreme officials, judges and Councillors, do at the present general Diet in the Castle of Prague, with all three Estates of the Kingdom, order and enact this Article in respect of religion, and are minded to confer this Our Royal Patent on them, the Utraquist Estates and do hereby expressly confer it.

Firstly, as it is already laid down in the Bohemian Constitution in respect of the faiths of one or both Kinds, that no man shall vex another, but rather that all shall hold together as good friends, and the one party shall not vilify the other: so now, too, this article of the Constitution shall be constantly observed, and both parties shall be held in future to respect it, under pain of the penalties provided by law. And seeing that the Catholics in this Kingdom are entitled to practice their religion freely and unimpeded, and the Utraquist Party belonging to the above-mentioned Confession may do the former no prejudice nor impose rules on them; so, in order that full equality may prevail, We permit, empower and authorize that the above-mentioned united Utraquist Estates, with their subjects, and in general all persons of any quality, without exception, who have professed and do profess the Bohemian Confession submitted to the Emperor Maximilian of glorious memory, Our beloved father, at the Diet of 1575 and now again submitted to Us, may practice their Christian religion in both Kinds, according to the above-mentioned profession of faith and the agreements and compositions concluded between them, freely and at their pleasure, in any place, and shall be left undisturbed in their faith and religion, and also in their clergy and liturgy as they now have it or may introduce it, this pending the achievement of a complete general settlement of the religious question in the Holy Roman Empire. Likewise they shall not be bound, either now or in the future, to conform to the Compacts dropped at the Diet of 1567 and those cancelled in the Provincial Privileges and elsewhere.[4]

Furthermore, We wish to show the Utraquist Estates Our especial favor, and to restore to their authority and keeping the lower Prague Consistory,[5] and We also most graciously concede that the Utraquist Estates may renew the said Consistory with its clergy according to their faith and associations, and also have their preachers, both Bohemian [Czech] and German, ordained accordingly, or may accept and install those already ordained at their collations without any hindrance from the Archbishop of Prague or any other person. Furthermore, we convey to the keeping of the said Estates the University of Prague, Utraquist since ancient times,[6] with all its appurtenances, that they may staff it with efficient and learned men, make good and praiseworthy dispositions and may place over both reliable persons from among themselves as Defenders.[7] But in the meantime, before all this has been put into

[4] At the 1567 Diet the neo-Utraquists had asked, and obtained, that the famous "*Compactata*" accepted in 1437 by the Council of Basel should no longer be regarded as possessing legal validity.

[5] The Estates had enjoyed the right of nominating members to the Utraquist Consistory until 1562, when Ferdinand I withdrew it from them.

[6] The University of Prague, founded in 1348 as a Catholic institution, had soon passed into Protestant hands, and in 1417 had declared communion in both kinds to be necessary for salvation. Later, however, it had fallen into decadence, and the Jesuits, allowed in 1561 to settle in Prague, had been gaining increasing influence over it.

[7] In 1575, Maximilian, while retaining the crown's control over the consistory, had allowed the Protestants to appoint fifteen "Defenders" (*Defensores*) not subject to the consistory's jurisdiction.

effect, the Utraquist Estates shall nevertheless be left in enjoyment of all the rights set out above, namely, the right to practice their religion freely and unimpeded. Whatever persons they shall select from their midst to be Defenders of the said Consistory and University of Prague, according to their mutual agreement—an equal number from each of the three Estates—and present to Us, as their King and Lord, lists of their names, We will, within two weeks from the day of submission of the lists, confirm all persons thus nominated, without any exception, and pronounce them Defenders without imposing on them duties or instructions beyond the duties prescribed to them by the Estates. Should We, however, on account of Our business, or for any reason whatever, be unable, or fail, to confirm them within the said period, they shall nevertheless continue to be Defenders of these two institutions and have full powers to direct and administer them in all respects, as though they had already been confirmed and recognized by Us. Should one of them die, the Estates shall elect another in his place and add him to the survivors, at the next Diet. And this procedure shall in the future always be followed, as laid down and to be observed by Us, Our heirs and successors to the throne in Bohemia, and also by the Estates and Defenders.

Further, should any member of the Utraquist Estates of the Kingdom wish, now or in the future, to build further places of worship or churches in any town, market center, village or elsewhere, in addition to the churches and places of worship which they now possess and which have been recognized as theirs (in the undisturbed possession of which they are to be left and protected) both the Lords' and Knights' Estates and also the City of Prague and the mining towns and other Royal Boroughs shall all, jointly and severally, be allowed to do this freely and openly, at any time and in any way, without hindrance from any quarter. And because many of Our Royal Boroughs, and also those belonging to Her Majesty the Empress, *qua* Queen of Bohemia,[8] contain adherents of both parties, Catholics and Utraquists, We do will and particularly enjoin that, for the preservation of amity and concord, each party shall practice its religion freely and without restriction, subject to the governance and direction of its own clergy, and that neither party shall impose any rules on the other in respect of its

[8] Six towns in Bohemia, known as the *"laibgeding"* towns, had under an earlier decree been set aside as the appanage of the queen of Bohemia.

religion or usages, neither prevent the practice of its religion, interment of bodies in churches or graveyards, or tolling of bells.

As from today, no person, neither of the higher free Estates nor the inhabitants of unfree towns and villages, nor the peasants, shall be forced or compelled by any device by the authorities over them or by any person, spiritual or temporal, to foresake his religion and accept another religion.

Since all these dispositions set out above have been honestly intended and enacted by Us for the maintenance of amity and concord, We therefore promise and swear on Our Royal word that all these three Estates of Our Kingdom of Bohemia who profess this the Bohemian Confession and their issue, in being and future, shall evermore be left and protected by Us, Our heirs, and future Kings of Bohemia, in complete and undisturbed enjoyment of all the rights set out above, as We do entirely comprehend and confirm them in the Religious Peace of the Holy Empire, whose supreme member We are, and they shall in no wise be infringed, now or ever in the future, either by Us, Our heirs and future Kings of Bohemia, or by any other person of estate spiritual or temporal. And no enactment against the said religious peace, and against the firm assurance given by Us to the Utraquist Estates, no edict or any similar measure which might impose on them the slightest obstacle or any change in their position shall be issued to them either by Us, Our heirs and successors as Kings of Bohemia, or by any other person, nor accepted by them. Should, however, anything of the sort occur, or be undertaken by any person whatsoever, it shall be invalid, and no judicial sentence or edict on this point shall be of any effect. We therefore revoke entirely, and declare to be null and void, all earlier edicts and mandates issued from any source against the said Utraquist party and adherents of the said Bohemian Confession, in such wise that nothing in this Article, nothing asked by the Estates from Us, now and previously, and confirmed to them by Us, and nothing that has occurred since, shall be reckoned against them, the united three Estates of this Kingdom, collectively or as individuals, to their disadvantage or ill repute or as cause for any complaint, nor in any way remembered against them by Us or by future Kings of Bohemia, nor shall it be altered, now or evermore.

We therefore command the supreme functionaries, judges and Our Councillors, and also all Estates, the present and future inhabitants of this Kingdom, Our loyal and beloved subjects, that they shall support and protect them, the Lords, Knights, Burghers of Prague and of the mining and other towns, yea, all three Estates of this Kingdom; with all their subjects and in general, all persons of the Party belonging to the said Bohemian and Utraquist Confession, as assured by Us in this Imperial Patent, all its articles and its tenor; they shall in no wise molest them nor allow others to do so, under pain of Our wrath and displeasure. And should any person whosoever, of spiritual or temporal estate, venture to infringe this Patent, We regard Ourselves bound, with Our heirs and sucessors to the throne of Bohemia, and the Estates of this Kingdom, to regard any such person as an offender against the general weal and disturber of the peace, and to protect and defend the Estates against him, as laid down and provided by the Constitution in the article on the defense of the land, order and law.

Finally, We command the higher and lower officials of the registry of Our Kingdom of Bohemia that they insert and enter, for future remembrance, this Our Imperial Patent in the records of the Diet at the session at which all three Estates of the Kingdom are now to meet and thereafter bring the original to Karlstein,[9] to be deposited with the other Liberties or Privileges of the Kingdom; in faith whereof We have ordered Our Imperial Seal to be affixed to this Imperial Patent. Given at Our Castle in Prague on the Thursday after Procopius in the year 1609, the thirty-fourth year of Our Imperial, the thirty-seventh of Our Hungarian and the thirty-fourth of Our Bohemian, reign.

RUDOLF
ADAMNE DE STERNBERG, Supreme Burgrave of Prague
For the affixing of the Royal Seal, PAULUS MICHNA.

*Agreement Between the Catholics and Protestants, Concluded
Without Prejudice to the Imperial Patent.*

As to the Article on Religion, consideration of which at the Diet of 1608, the Monday after Exaudi, was at the gracious request of H.M. the Emperor, *qua* King of Bohemia, postponed to the following Diet and until all other business had been concluded:

[9] The fortress founded by Charles IV, twenty miles southwest of Prague, where he kept the regalia and the archives.

the substance thereof—seeing that H.M. has debated the said Article through at the Diet with all three Estates of the Kingdom and by his Royal Patent has empowered the Utraquists to practice their religion, according to the Bohemian Confession submitted to His Royal Majesty and in accordance with the treaty and agreement concluded between themselves, freely and without pressure or impediment, on which occasion he also transferred the Lower Consistory and the Academy of Prague, with all appurtenances thereof, to the authority and keeping of the Utraquists, as shown in greater detail in the Imperial Patent which was registered in the Diet records and the special session of the Diet under the date of Thursday after Procopius—is hereby maintained.

Firstly, the Catholics (Communion in one Kind) have discussed with several representatives of the Utraquists and have agreed that the Utraquists shall leave the Catholics their Churches, Divine Service, collations, cloisters, privileges, endowments, tithes, perquisites, reversions, and all usages—in a word, their faith—unaltered, and shall submit them to no violence and no hindrances, even as the Catholics shall and must leave the Protestants the churches now in the possession of that party.

Secondly, should H.M. the Emperor, *qua* King of Bohemia, or any person, Catholic or Utraquist, belonging to the higher Estates, wish to install on his lands for himself or his subjects, on a living in his gift, an Utraquist priest who has been ordained by the Archbishop, he shall be entitled to do so. As regards Prague and the other Royal Boroughs, since the Congregations of Prague and their clergy, and the other urban Congregation, have adhered in large numbers to the Utraquists and that Confession, and most of them wish to follow the order that either has been or is to be established among the Utraquists, according to that Confession, the following agreement is established, for the avoidance of later dissensions and disputes in any commune or parish: should there be in any commune or parish a person who wishes to sit under a Utraquist priest who has been ordained by the Archbishop of Prague and not in accordance with the said Confession, he may apply to any such priest ordained by the Archbishop and have him conduct Divine Service, but without putting impediment in the way of the commune, the parish or the Consistory to be established by the Estates, or causing confusion.

As to the interment of bodies and the tolling of bells, this shall not be permitted to the Utraquists in the churches and parishes of the Catholics, nor *vice versa,* unless with the knowledge and consent of the collator and the incumbent.

If Utraquists are parishioners of a Catholic parish and pay it tithes or any other dues, they can be buried in it without special permission from the patron [collator], and *vice versa:* if Catholics are parishioners of a Catholic parish and pay tithes or other dues in it, they can be buried in it without special permission from the collator. Should the collator or any other person wish to prevent the interment of bodies, the persons in question are not bound to pay tithe or other dues. The person in authority over them may direct them to any parish he pleases and they can carry through their interments there.

Should the Utraquists possess no churches of their own, or graveyards of their own, or shared with Catholics, in any village or town or even on an estate of the King or the Queen, the wording of the Imperial Patent allows them to build churches and lay out graveyards for themselves.

If prior to this agreement any person was at issue with another before the ordinary Courts over a collation, and the legal decision is still outstanding, he shall wait until it is delivered. Should any person wish to acquire a collation from another by process of law, he shall not possess himself of it arbitrarily but wait for the legal verdict, as provided in greater detail in the treaty between Catholics and Protestants.

Since the Imperial Patent given by H.M. the Emperor to the Utraquists is not to prejudice this treaty, nor this treaty the Imperial Patent, and the assurance of the one does not invalidate the true sense of the assurance of the other, H.M. the Emperor leaves the Catholics in enjoyment not only of the safeguards assured them under the Imperial Patent, but also of those secured under this treaty, so that just as the Imperial Patent does not weaken the force of the treaty, so the treaty shall in no way diminish that of the Imperial Patent, and graciously permits that both the Catholics and the Utraquists shall be furnished with a copy both of the Imperial Patent and of this Article of the Diet, from the Dietal Archives, with the seal of this Kingdom attached. Given on the Thursday after Procopius, 1609.

      (signed)

[The Treaty was signed for the Catholics by five members of

the Estate of the Lords, five Knights, and five burgesses of Prague; for the Protestants, by the thirty Directors.]

3. The Defenestration of Prague

This famous outburst of physical violence, commonly regarded as the spark which set off the Thirty Years' War, itself detonated in the atmospheric pressure of hostility and mutual suspicion which brooded over Bohemia during the years of Matthias's reign. As Matthias's advisers committed, and countenanced, act after act which obviously violated at least the spirit of the Imperial Patent of 1609, the resentment of the Protestants grew apace, and although they had voted, on June 17, 1617, to elect Ferdinand king, they had done so only in return for his promise to guarantee the Imperial Patent, and it was not long before they were doubting (with full justice) whether he had meant his promise sincerely, and wishing they had chosen a Protestant instead.

The atmosphere became more heavily charged than ever when Matthias left Prague for Vienna, leaving behind him as "governors" a group of extreme Catholics, including the two later victims of the defenestration, Martinitz and Slavata. The immediate cause of the conflict was the refusal by the governors to allow the inhabitants of two small localities to build Protestant churches. The burghers protested strongly, and Matthias, before leaving Prague, apparently told the governors to resist, if necessary, by force. The governors even had some of the recalcitrants imprisoned. In March, 1618, the more extreme of the two Catholic leaders, Count Thurn, called a meeting of protest, but this proved ineffectual, whereupon he called on the defenders of the Imperial Charter to assemble again for a second, larger meeting. This assembled on May 21. Suddenly alive to their danger, the governors sent to Vienna for help, but it was too late, and on the twenty-third the scene described below took place.

The best-known and most immediately contemporary account of the defenestration is that which Slavata himself afterward committed to paper; but besides being written in Czech, and thus not readily available to most readers,[1] it contains several details which not everyone finds it easy to believe; among others, a report from various burghers of Prague that they had seen the Virgin Mary herself appear and parachute Martinitz down softly. The account which follows is taken from Khevenhüller's *Annales Ferdinandorum* (Vienna, 1722) Vol. IX, pp.

[1] It is reprinted in the *Monumenta Historiae Bohemiae* (Prague, 1869), Vol. II, pp. 182–3. An extract in German may be found in the *Quellenbuch zur oesterreichen Geschichte*, ed. Otto Frass (Vienna, 1959), Vol. II, pp. 108–9.

32 ff. There is an excellent modern account of the incident and the
background, in Miss C. V. Wedgwood's *The Thirty Years War* (1957
edn.), pp. 68ff.

On the twenty-third of May, after the Governors had attended
the procession in the Palace Chapel, and had then repaired to the
Bohemian Chancellery, the Utraquists appeared there, without
warning, a great body of men, armed with pistols and muskets, and
Paul von Titschin addressed the Governors present as follows:

> That report had come to the Estates that the Council of the Old
> Town of Prague had called to them the eldest of the parish and
> others of the citizens and had tried to convince and prevail on them
> that the men of Prague should send no representatives to the Estates,
> nor adhere to them, and that to this end they had locked the City
> Hall, which plainly showed—since no man knew what charge was
> being made against the prisoners—that the whole thing was an anti-
> Protestant move, and that the Prague Council would not presume to
> act so without orders from above.

Thereupon the Supreme Burgrave[1] declared that the Governors
knew nothing of this, and to prevent things from getting worse
they were willing to enquire further into the matter, and if there
was anything amiss, to send down into the Old Town. Thereupon
Count Henrich Matthias von Thurn replied that there was no
need of further information, a burgher from the Old Town
was present, and further, the Estates had already informed themselves exactly. Then von Titschin stepped forward and made a long
speech, the gist of which was as follows:

> They had learned that His Imperial Majesty had sent a severe
> message to the Governors to the effect that the recent meeting had
> been directed against His Imperial Majesty's own person and the
> Kingdom, and that the Estates had gone further than was permitted
> under the Imperial Charter, because they had tried to enlist the
> help of foreign subjects against His Majesty's lawful resolution
> and to use them for their rebellion against His Imperial Majesty.
> His Majesty was therefore intending to act against the authors of
> the meeting, as was appropriate in each case, and consequently the
> Protestants were in fear for their lives, and since no one except
> the Governors could have advised His Majesty to write this severe
> letter, they wished to know from them whether they admitted hav-

[1] The official title of the king's chief representative in Bohemia.

ing done so or not. And although the Governors excused themselves, arguing elaborately that their office forbade them from giving this assurance, nothing of this helped, and the Utraquists pressed their question, one shouting this and the other that;[2] it was Slavata and Schmeissansky,[3] above all, whom the Utraquists accused of wanting to rob the Protestants of the Charter and privileges, to bring over their subjects by improper means and force them from their own to the Catholic religion, and even of harboring designs against the lives of the leaders of the Estates. The Governors repudiated such accusations, appealed to the regular law and to the provisions of the Bohemian Constitution, and earnestly begged their accusers to give them time to consider their defense and then to proceed according to the recognized process of law. None of this helped, and Count Heinrich Matthias von Thurn, Lienhardt von Weels, and Wocabat Werkha stepped forward from among the raging mob and conducted two of the Governors, the Supreme Burgrave Adam von Steinberg (the representative of the King's person) and the Grand Prior of the Order of the Knights of Malta, Leopold Popel, through the rebellious mob out of the Chancellery to their homes, shouting and mocking at them. When these two Governors had been led out of the Chancellery, Wilhelm Popel von Lobkowitz, Hans Lidtian Ritzeham, Ulrich Khintzky [Kinsky], and Paul Kopliers feloniously seized upon Jaroslaw Schmeissansky von Martinitz and Wilhelm Schlawata, His Imperial Majesty's Governors, widely respected citizens, Councillors and Chamberlains and the highest dignitaries of the Kingdom of Bohemia, whose innocence the Utraquists had only a week before recognized in writing, and against all human and divine law, against all tradition of the Kingdom and Provinces, and against all usage even of heathen peoples, cast them, unconfessed and denied Confession and the Holy Communion (which is not denied to the vilest criminals and is often permitted under the Turks) unmercifully out of the window, 28 fathoms down into the fosse, and as if this were not enough, cast Philip, the secretary, down after them. But the Almighty condemned all the miscreants, except Popel, to everlasting imprisonment, casting them into the pit they had designed for others, so that they perished miserably, whereas the other three, in token of His divine mercy and in proof

---

[2] The meeting in March (see introductory note).
[3] Martinitz.

of their innocence and integrity, He made to escape not only with
their lives but without great injury. Martinitz fell on the earth in
a sitting posture. Schlawata fell head downward, striking against
the cornice of a window and injuring his left side severely, and
when writhing about in the fosse got his head so entangled in his
cloak that he would beyond doubt have been choked in blood,
had von Martinitz not rolled over to him, helped him up and wiped
him. As they lay and writhed about, two shots were fired at von
Martinitz, of which the one shot off his sleeve, while the other only
left two bruises on his left hand. And soon after, when the raging
mob had dispersed, shouting "The dogs have had it now", certain
servants of the said lords arrived, of whom one first let down a
ladder out of a window and climbed down it alone. Then two of
them took von Martinitz to the wife of the Supreme Chancellor
Stenekho Popel, a von Bernstein by birth (who on this occasion
showed herself merciful and pitiful towards the injured men and
most valorous and determined towards their attackers). And after
he had confessed to a Canon, he remained in the servants' chamber,
first lying down and then walking about a little, until evening.
And when it grew dark, the servants conducted him out of the
Chancellor's wife's house to his own, and then, accompanied by a
surgeon and servants, but disguised, he went up to the White Hill,
where he was placed in a waiting coach and taken out of the country. Schlawata was lifted by his servants and also arrived at the Chancellor's wife's house, where he was laid on mattresses and given all
necessary treatment by surgeons and doctors, but then arrested in
the same house, but in the end, after being forced to sign a vexatious and shameful recantation, he was allowed to go to his own
house, and when his wife fell at the feet of the Countess von Thurn
and begged for mercy for her husband, the Countess (who had
never liked these proceedings) assured her, "What you are begging
now for your husband I shall soon have to ask for my husband
and the other persons involved in this"—no bad prophecy—and
although Slavata was then released and allowed to move about
freely, and left in undisturbed possession of his property, he at last
decided, and also persuaded the Burgrave, who was over seventy
years old, to leave the country, saying that they preferred to
abandon their considerable fortunes, which amounted to some
millions of thalers, and the peace and comfort of their native land
and live in poverty and exile with wife and children, but un-

molested in their religion, rather than live sumptuously and well under the rebellious religion, to the scandal of the whole world, the offence of the Catholic religion, and the violation of their own consciences. Therefore they quitted Prague, without especial danger, and took their road to Passau. . . .

4. The Revised Constitution of the Kingdom of Bohemia
(*Vernewerte Landesordnung des Königreichs Bohaimh*) of 1627

As the first of the appended documents shows, it was not only in Bohemia that the Emperor Ferdinand II encountered resistance in his enforcement of the Counter-Reformation; and wherever he met it, he crushed it ruthlessly. Protestants were summoned to abjure their faith, and recalcitrants were punished by exile and confiscation of their goods and not a few of them by loss of their lives. Almost everywhere outside Hungary, Catholicism was declared the sole lawful religion.

In the German Austrian provinces, however, the existing constitutional position left Ferdinand a free hand. He already possessed there the absolute *jus legis ferendae*, the right to enact legislation, so that the announcement of his will was already legally valid. Consequently, he did not need to alter their "*Landesordnungen*," or provincial constitutions. In the Lands of the Bohemian Crown the position was different. Certain ancient "privileges" seemed to give the Estates at least a right to be consulted over laws. And there were other differences: the first, concerning the law of succession. In the Austrian Lands the Habsburgs had long since assumed the right to nominate their own successors, only tying their own hands by family instruments, which laid down that the succession should pass in primogeniture. The Bohemian Constitution, like the Hungarian, contained provisions that, under certain circumstances, the right of electing their king reverted to the Estates; and the rebels of 1618–19 had, as we have said elsewhere, claimed that such a situation had arisen and elected a rival to Ferdinand. In addition, the Protestants possessed solemnly guaranteed rights which could not simply be passed over in silence; there were other features of the country's constitutional structure highly objectionable, on one ground or another, to Ferdinand and his Catholic advisers.

These considerations determined Ferdinand, once he had safely

crushed the rebellion, to issue a whole new *Landesordnung*.[1] Only a
few points in it were new. Covering as it did the entire administrative
and legal structure of the kingdom (it runs to a whole volume), it did
not as a rule alter those structures on the lower levels. The only important change it introduces outside that of the relations between the
king and his subjects is that which places the German language on
an equality with Czech in the Courts of Law (Art. C. IV). On the top
level, however, it laid down fundamental principles, the most important
of which are:

The affirmation that the Estates' assumption in respect of the right of
election has been invalid, and the reiteration of the hereditary right of
succession so long as any heir of the blood, male or female, was in
existence (Art. A. I).

Reservation to the crown of the sole right to convoke the diet and
circle assemblages (Art. A. IV).

The king will present his demands for the "contributio" in due form,
but "does not doubt" that they will always be accepted unconditionally
(Art. A.V).

The king posseses the sole right of initiative in the diet (Art. A. VI)[2]
and the *jus legis ferendae* (Art. A. VIII).

The Catholic religion is reinstated as the sole lawful religion, and
all patents, etc., to the contrary are declared null and void (Art. A.
XXIII).

The Estate of the Lords Spiritual is restored, as the First Estate (Art.
A. XXIV).

The Fourth Estate (of the towns) is restored (Art. A. XXXIV).

Besides these, we have translated the article giving the royal oath
(Art. A. II); that in which the king legalizes retrospectively his grants
to foreigners of the confiscated estates of rebels (A. XX), and part of
the preamble, the opening words of which are interesting as showing
Ferdinand's attitude in issuing the document, while a later paragraph
contains an important (subsequently much-quoted) paragraph in which
the crown reserves to itself the right of "adding to, altering and improving" the Constitution.

Although it remained, with certain modifications enacted by subsequent monarchs, the public law of Bohemia until 1849, and thus served
for more than two centuries as the basis of the whole constitutional life
of the kingdom, the *Vernewerte Landesordnung* has seldom been reprinted in full. The text from which the passages which follow are taken
is that reproduced by C. Jiraček, *Codex Juris Bohemici*, Tom. V,
Pars II (Prague 1888; Czech and German texts).

The best easily accessible analysis of it is that of Ernest Denis, *La
Bohême depuis la Montagne-Blanche* (2 vols., 1903), vol. I, pp. 1ff.

---

[1] A parallel document was issued for Moravia in the following year.
[2] In 1640 the Estates were again allowed the initiative in questions of
secondary importance.

EXTRACTS FROM THE PREAMBLE

We, Ferdinand, etc. . . . hereby make known to all and sundry: since We have, with the help and support of Almighty God, re-conquered Our Hereditary Kingdom of Bohemia with the power of the sword and reduced it to obedience to Our authority, We have made it Our chief purpose to secure that the honor of Almighty God be established in this Our Hereditary Kingdom, that fitting justice—yet not untempered by the mercifulness natural to Us and with moderation of its full rigor—be meted out to those who revolted against Us, the lawful authority set over them by God, and took part in the recent most abominable rebellion (whereby not the welfare of their own fatherland alone, but that of almost all Christian Kingdoms and Lands was disturbed and shaken) according to their deserts and the nature of so shocking an enterprise, for an example to others and to avert the most injurious consequences, not for Ourselves alone but for all Princes, which might follow thereon; but that those persons who showed Us loyalty and steadfastness during the rebellion, and notwithstanding that Our Hereditary Kingdom rebelled *in forma universitatis*, nevertheless, each severally, setting aside all else, left their fatherland rather than act against Us, shall be graciously rewarded with honors, dignities, and estates.

Since, now, all this has taken place, We have duly considered, in Our Royal paternal solicitude, how the said Kingdom, having been conquered by Our expensive armaments of war, shall be restored to a condition in which the subjects' respect and obedience to Us and Our heirs, the Kings to come after Us, as their only rightful and natural hereditary Lords, shall be assured, the subjects jointly administered in peace, calm, and unity under the protection of an impartial law and uniform religion, and everything that is contrary to this abolished. . . .

[The next paragraph explains that it had not been possible for Ferdinand, under the prevailing conditions, to work out the perfect solution for every problem; but he reserves to himself the right "to add to, alter, and improve this Our Provincial Constitution and to take any other step in connection with it deriving from Our right of enacting legislation" (*und was sonst das jus legis ferendae mit sich bringt*). Any such changes, interpretations, etc., will have

the same force as the original document, which must meanwhile
be strictly obeyed.]

A.I   Whereas Our most honored predecessor, both in the Kingdom of Bohemia and in the Holy Roman Empire, the late Emperor
Charles IV, out of paternal solicitude, to prevent all dubious divaga-
tions and future scandals, and solicitous to avert the physical,
spiritual and material loss and emperilment (which the said
Emperor clearly foresaw would occur if the traditional right of
inheritance of the Royal stock and blood was called in question by
dangerous calumnies and treachery, as happened in the recent
rebellion), did issue to the inhabitants of the Kingdom of Bohemia
and the Lands incorporated with it a Golden Bull dated Prague,
April 7, 1348, which was ever after regularly adduced and recognized by the said inhabitants in the controversies arising between
the Provinces[1] as a fundamental law, and also solemnly so admitted
by the Privilege of the Kingdom and included as a main document
both in the Constitution sworn to by Our ancestor of glorious
memory, King Wladislaus, in the Castle of Prague, on the Friday
after Epiphany, 1510, and similarly in the Charter issued to the
Estates by Our beloved ancestor, Emperor and King Ferdinand I,
also in the Castle of Prague, on the Wednesday after St. Aegidius,
1545

But it being notorious and patent into what wretchedness and
misery this Kingdom and the Provinces incorporated with it were
brought through the recent rebellion, in that certain persons ventured unlawfully to contest the hereditary right of the Royal
stock and blood, and to undertake an invalid election; whereas it
appears quite clearly from the above adduced Golden Bull and the
other Fundamental Laws, as understood in their true and undis-
torted meaning, that the right to elect a King becomes operative
only when—and not before—no heir of the Royal stock, birth, seed,
and blood, male or female, is in existence or to be expected, or alternatively, should the said Kingdom be vacant and free through the
spontaneous renunciation and waiver of the last heir or heiress, or
should he or she be unfitted to reign through lack and defect of
reason (through which a person is excluded from the succession in
other Electorates under the Golden Bull likewise promulgated by

---

[1] Moravia and Silesia did not always accept the Bohemian law of succession as binding on themselves.

the Emperor Charles IV in the Holy Roman Empire) and he or she has not, and cannot expect, any other heir, male or female, to the Kingdom

Wherefore, to the end that all occasion for such most abominable rebellions as have recently occurred shall forever be prevented, We enact, ordain, and will that should one or more of Our subjects, of whatever dignity, rank, or nature, now or in the future, again venture to revive, by words or deeds, the pretexts of one sort or another, misinterpretations, and sophistries invented and adduced against Our hereditary right by the rebels, in unlawful attestation of their invalid election, they shall be deemed ipso facto and thereby to have committed the felony of *lèse-majesté* and open rebellion, and shall forfeit their life, honor and goods.

[Article A.II lays down the form of homage to be sworn to the king by his subjects.]

A.III   Of the oath and pledge of the King
Whenever it shall occur in the future that one of Our heirs shall be consecrated and crowned King, the Archbishop of Prague, or should that see be vacant, the Bishop of Olmütz, shall before the consecration administer to him this oath, and he shall truly take and repeat it, word for word, as follows:

"We, ..., swear by Almighty God, by the Blessed Mother of God and all Saints, that We will hold firmly to the Catholic faith, manfully administer justice, and maintain the Estates in their time-honored privileges, as confirmed by Our predecessors. Also We will alienate nothing from the Kingdom, but rather enlarge and extend it as We are able, and do everything that is conducive to its welfare and honor. So help Us God, the Blessed Mother of God, and all Saints."

A.IV   Of Diets, and how they are to be held
But whereas the right and duty of convoking and holding the general Diet of this Kingdom, and also assemblages in its Circles,[2] belong to Us alone and to Our successors on the throne and heirs to the Kingdom, therefore shall no man or men in this Our Hereditary Kingdom of Bohemia, whatever their dignity, rank, or estate, venture to convoke, or in any manner or fashion whatever, organize or hold any Diet or assemblage in one or more Circles without

[2] The circles were the administrative subdivisions of the kingdom.

Our previous gracious leave; and if any man is proved or convicted of so doing, he shall be deemed to have committed thereby the offense of *lèse-majesté* and to have forfeited his body, life, honor, goods, and chattels.

A.V   And in respect of the Contributions,[3] We have graciously resolved for Ourselves and the Kings and heirs to the Kingdom who shall succeed Us, that We will put the demand for them to the Estates at the Diets and not otherwise than according to the customary procedure.

As We then do not doubt that Our loyal Estates will always take due note of the needs of Ourselves and the Fatherland, nor can we permit or will that the Contributions desired by Us be made conditional on or delayed by improper conditions incompatible with Our Royal status, majesty, and dignities, e.g., by requests for new Privileges and liberties or similar objections not dependent on Our Proposition, as has happened in the past.

A.VI   And since at such general Diets no one except Ourselves and Our successors and heirs to the Kingdom or, in Our absence, Our Royal Commissioners appointed by Us for the occasion, has power or authority to make Proposals to meet the needs and requirements of this Land; so shall no man, whatever his dignity, rank, or estate, venture, without the special gracious command of Ourselves or Our successors and heirs to the Kingdom, himself to submit to the Estates, or to initiate by word of mouth or in writing, a debate among them on any proposal of any kind whatever. . . .

A.VIII   We expressly reserve to Ourselves and to Our heirs and successors in this Our Hereditary Kingdom the power to enact laws and decrees, and everything devolving from the legislative power *(jus legis ferendae)* which belongs to Us, as the King, alone. . . .

A.XX   Although no foreigner was hitherto allowed to buy himself into this Our Hereditary Kingdom of Bohemia[4] except ac-

---

[3] I.e., the assessment for the tax to be paid by the province into the central exchequer.

[4] Membership of the provincial estates was confined to persons possessing "noble" properties in the kingdom, a list of which was kept in a special register. Such estates could be owned only by persons possessing local "*indigenat.*" A foreigner buying a registered estate thereby acquired "*indigenat,*" but could do so only with the permission of the existing landowning nobles.

cording to a fixed measure and procedure, and the record of the
purchase of the estate had to be inserted and entered in the old
registers of the Visitation; yet since We have recovered possession
of this Our Hereditary Kingdom of Bohemia, after the rebellion
against Us, with strong force and armed hand, and thereafter have
sold or given for sale the estates of certain rebels, which We have
confiscated, partly to foreigners and partly to natives; We now
enact, ordain, and will that in respect of the registration and entitle-
ment of estates the new registers shall have the same force and
validity as the old, and any person venturing to dispute or query
the above purchases and contracts entered in the new registers, to
whomsoever they relate, native or foreigner, on the ground that
they have not been entered and incorporated in the old registers,
but only in the new, shall be severely punished. Similar proceedings
shall be taken against any person disputing any such contract on
the grounds that the foreigners had not yet been admitted into
the country at the time when the contract was drawn up. . . .
[The rest of the article provides that in future cases a foreigner
may not buy or otherwise acquire an estate in Bohemia except with
royal consent; failing which the transaction shall be void and the
purchase price forfeit.]

A.XXIII   Of Religion

In respect of religion: whereas it is plain and apparent that not
alone did religious division, from the time when it arose in this
Our Hereditary Kingdom, give rise to great wars and devastation,
but also that the persons calling themselves Utraquists [*Stände sub
utraque*], under the pretext of the peculiar Privileges and statutes
obtained by them at various times, have been the authors and initi-
ators of the most damnable rebellion against Us; We, after We have
reconquered this Our Hereditary Kingdom by costly and
heavy campaigns, have most graciously resolved what dispositions
to take in respect of religion, for the better constitution of the
Kingdom and the prevention of similar most malignant secessions
and imperilment of Our said Hereditary Kingdom: We therefore
enact, ordain, and will that not only shall all orders graciously
enacted by Us in matters of religion, by various Resolutions, since
the victory given Us by God in this Our Hereditary Kingdom, be
continuously and strictly observed, but also that all earlier Letters
Patent, Dietical Resolutions, Reverses, Resolutions, Privileges, or
other ordinances and institutions, however entitled, contrary to the

same and damaging, detrimental, and prejudicial to Our Holy
Catholic religion, such as were enacted, adduced in their favor,
received, or resolved, at any time whatever, by the so-called Utraquist Estates, shall now and forever be and remain cancelled; and
further, any person attempting to raise and promote the same
shall be deemed ipso facto to have offended against the public
order and to have forfeited his life, honor, and goods. Neither shall
any person be received henceforward into the land, or in its towns,
except he be an adherent of Our Holy Catholic religion.

A.XXIV   Of the Estate Spiritual

Although for long past, since certain non-Catholic doctrines and
opinions began to prevail in this Our Hereditary Kingdom, the
Prelates have no longer been admitted among its Estates;[5] yet
since it is common knowledge and undeniable that in the days of
Our predecessor, the Emperor Charles IV, and many years earlier
still, the Estate of Prelates existed in this Kingdom, and the
Prelates must also pay taxation with and beside the other Estates,
We thereby enact, ordain, and will that henceforward the Archbishop of Prague, with and beside his Prelates and the whole Clergy
of this Our Hereditary Kingdom, shall not only be counted for
all time as an Estate thereof, but further, that the Estate Spiritual
shall, as is customary in other well-ordered Christian lands, be
the first and most honorable of the Estates, yet in such wise that
only the Archbishop and such clergy as are entitled, by Privilege
or ancient custom, to wear an insul or episcopal miter, and further
own estates registered in Our Visitation (whereby no one else who
is not already established in the land shall be admitted to the Diet)
shall be called or summoned to the said Diets, at which they shall
represent the whole clergy. Mitered clergy, and especially the
said Archbishop, shall then take precedence over the Dukes and
Princes in the Diets and on other public occasions, and cast their
votes before them and before the Lords, and the Archbishop shall
be entitled Primate of the Kingdom, and the highest place shall
be his, and after him, if no Bishop be present, the Grand Master
of the Order of the Knights of Malta in the Kingdom of Bohemia
shall be entitled to the next place, above all other Prelates. . . .

---

[5] Up to this time the Lords Spiritual had in fact not ranked as a
separate Estate in Bohemia, where the Estates consisted of the Lords,
the lesser nobles (knights), and the Boroughs.

A.XXXIV Of the Fourth Estate of the Kingdom of Bohemia, namely, the towns

As regards the Royal Boroughs, We have pardoned them all inasmuch as We have most graciously readmitted them to be an Estate, viz., the Fourth. All of them, however, except the towns of Pilsen and Budweiss (which We have exempted from this burden and tax, because they always remained loyal to Us in the late rebellion) shall be strictly bound to pay and deliver to Our Royal Exchequer, to be at the disposal of Us and Our Royal heirs, the sum of 1 gulden of 60 kreuzer on every barrel of beer brewed in them or imported from elsewhere and drunk in them.

C.II And whereas it is Our will that the German and Bohemian tongues shall be equally maintained and preserved in Our Hereditary Kingdom of Bohemia: written bills of indictment may be submitted in either the German or the Bohemian language, so that if it transpires that the defendant does not know German, the indictment shall be in Czech, and if he does not know Czech, then in German, and, if the defendant is not a born Czech or German, he shall be indicted in one of the two languages and the case conducted to the end in the same language, and in the conduct of the case, no submission, transaction, etc., in any Court shall be in any other language.

[Article C.III provides that the staff of the *"Landestafel"* or register of landed property shall contain at least three persons acquainted with German; and C.IV, for the keeping of two registers, one in each language. C.V provides for the appointment of sworn interpreters where the parties to a case are of different languages.]

5. The Sufferings of Hungarian Protestants Under the Counter-Reformation

The pamphlet (now in the British Museum and other libraries) from which the following extracts are taken was published in London in 1676 under the title "A short Memorial of the most grievous sufferings of the Ministers of the Protestant Churches in Hungary by the instigation of the Popish clergy there and of the release of such of them as are yet alive, nineteen of them having died under the Cruelties of their Persecutors and obtained the glorious Crown of Martyrdom." The passages omitted are a preamble, addressed "To All that truly *Love* the Protestant religion in England"; a polemic arguing that the documents on which the charges against the victims were based were not authentic; and a list of the victims. With these exceptions, the pamphlet is reproduced complete. The atrocities related here were among the causes which led to Thököly's revolt (see the narrative section) and thus, indirectly, to the Turkish assault on Vienna and, more indirectly still, to the eventual expulsion of the Turks from Hungary.

The Michael Abaffi (Apafi) mentioned in the concluding paragraph of the appendix proved in the event to be the last autonomous prince of Transylvania. When Leopold's troops occupied the principality in 1686–1687, Leopold at first confirmed Apafi's rank, although he now acknowledged Leopold as his suzerain, but in fact, the country, was ruled despotically by the Austrian "Imperial Commissioner," General Caraffa. Apafi retired in practice, into private life and died in 1690. Under the *"Diploma Leopoldinum,"* issued in 1691, Leopold promised to allow the election of a successor to him; and this should by all precedent have been Apafi's son, Michael II, who, however, was then still only a child. Leopold had him taken to Vienna for safekeeping, and he died there in 1713, whereafter the Habsburgs themselves assumed the title of Princes of Transylvania.

A Short Memorial of the Sufferings of the Protestant Ministers in Hungary

THE PRELATES and the Jesuites in *Hungary* having designed the setting up the Doctrine of the *Roman* Church, over the whole Kingdome, (which they commonly call the Reformation) they have now for a great while with great care and diligence, watched all opportunities that might be improved, for carrying on their ends, but chiefly since the year 1659 in which and in the following year, they attempted great things in the *Lower Hungary*.

And the Tumults that were raised in *Hungary*, in the year 1670 though the chief in those were of the Popish Nobility,[1] seemed to furnish them with a very fit occasion, for executing what they had projected; therefore they contrived how they might fasten, the crime of Rebellion, or at least of being complices of it, on all the Protestants without exception, had they been

---

[1] The participants in the conspiracy to which these words refer were in fact all members of the highest Roman Catholic aristocracy.

never so free of it. As first, they used many arts against those of the Nobility (who were the chief Patrons of the Protestants) and divers others, and by the snares, and other vexations they studied to draw them in, did force them to leave their homes, and to think of means for their preservation, from the violence of their persecutors: and at the same time (to wit in the years 1671, and 1672) they did by violence, not without many tumults, drive away a great number both of *Calvinist* and *Lutheran* Ministers, (but many more of the former sort than of the latter) out of their Parishes, and from their Churches in the Counties of *Zemplin, Aba, Vivar, Torna, Ugocsa, Beregh, Comarom,* and some others. At length, lest those proceedings should have occasioned farther disorders, the *Roman Catholick* Bishops, ordered a general Citation of all the Ministers and School-Masters of those Counties that continued still under his Imperial Majesties obedience, to appear at *Presburg,* and be tried as *Complices of the Rebellion.*

But they thought fit to proceed in that citation with this caution not to fall upon both *Lutherans* and *Calvinists* at once, nor to cite all at the same time, and therefore at first there were but few cited, and those were chiefly of the *Ausburg* Confession [Lutherans], that they might make an essay on those, if they would yield to what they intended to propose to them; and if they prevailed in this attempt, they resolved to go on and cite all the rest over the whole Kingdome, with more hopes.

The Demands or Propositions they offered both in the first and second appearance were these three. First, that the Ministers of both Confessions, *Lutherans* and *Calvinists,* and the Masters of Schools, with the Students, Clerks, and Sextons, should under their hand renounce their Ministery, or Imployments, for avoiding the Tryal and Sentence that was then Imminent, and should never exercise their Minestery or Imployment, either in publick or private, within the Kingdome of *Hungary,* under the pain of Death, and the confiscation of all their Goods; these were also obliged to live still within the Kingdome, as private Subjects. Or, Secondly, they were under their hands, to oblige themselves to depart the Kingdome within thirty days, never again to return under the pain of Death, and confiscation of Goods, and they in both these subscriptions were to declare, they did it of their own accord, and uncompelled, and that they did it, as being guilty of the Crime charged on them, for avoiding the sentence they feared. Or,

Thirdly, That they should embrace the Roman Catholick Religion, the chief thing that was driven at by their Adversaries.

Upon the first Citation of those few, in the year 1673 there appeared at the day appointed, being the 25th of *September*, two and thirty Ministers of the *Ausburg* Confession, and one of the *Helvetian* Confession [Calvinist], and those being much pressed by the Kings Sollicitor, or *Fiscal*, and the Archbishop of *Strigonium* [Esztergom] (then Lord Lieutenant of the Kingdome) to consider the Three forementioned propositions, that by their accepting one of them they might prevent any farther mischief; they alass being overcome with the fear of so severe a Sentence, which they knew would be pronounced against them; and not having sufficiently considered the importance of them, as they ought to have done, did yield to them, and some did renounce the Sacred Ministery, others did subscribe to a voluntary banishment, among whom was he of the *Helvetian* Confession, and one of them changed his Religion.

The Enemies of the Religion finding this first attempt succeed as they had wished, were from thence incouraged to proceed farther, and soon after a general Summons was issued out against all the Ministers of the Reformed Churches, of both Confessions, all Masters of Schools, Clerks, and Sextons where ever they could be found, (some few only excepted, who were in the County of *Borsod* and other places very far distant from *Presburg*) and all this under the pretence of their being Complices of the Rebellion; the Summons was in the name of the Archbishop of *Strigonium* (or *Gran*) and their Priests guarded by Souldiers did every where make these citations. But the Protestants that lived in those places, which are delivered up to the Turks, were forbid by the *Visier Bassa* of *Buda* to appear, and he kept them for some time in *Sicambria* [Buda] that they might not go. All the rest of both Confessions did appear at *Presburg* on the day prefixed in the Summons which was the fifth of *March* 1674. There appeared upon this General Citation above two hundred and fifty in all: among whom there were many more of the *Ausbourg*, then of the *Helvetian* Confession; there being about two hundred of the former, and the rest of the latter sort. The reasons why there were so many of the one, and so few of the other, were these; Before the first Citation, they had driven away a far greater number of Ministers of the *Helvetian* Confession, from their Parishes, than of the others; so that there were not now so many of them remaining, as of the others. The *Visier Bashaw* had also most severely forbidden those under their Contribution, (who were almost all of the *Helvetian* Confession) to appear as hath been already said.

No sooner had they appeared there, than they were much sollicited, and pressed to yield, as their Brethren had done to one of the Three Propositions that were made to them; and all the while they were at *Presburg*, both before and after the Sentence had passed upon them, they were continually assaulted one way or other, to choose one of them; sometimes they threatened them with the Gallies, and perpetual Imprisonment, at other times they made them great offers and promises of rewards, if they would comply with their desires.

Amidst such severe Tryals, it is not much to be wondered at, if humane Infirmity, the fears of the Cross, and the love of this present World, prevailed with many, to abandon this good Cause, by a shameful defection.

The Primitive Church, under the Persecution of the Heathens, had the same ground of regret and sorrow, and so it ought not to be thought strange, if some renounced their Ministry, or subscribed to a voluntary exile, and acknowledged themselves guilty of a Crime, of which they were most Innocent; those who gave this compliance, were of the *Ausburg* Confession, but their fall did not draw the rest to follow their Example, for God by his Grace did confirm others of both Confessions, whom he had chosen to be the Witnesses of this his Cause and Truth, who resolved patiently and willingly to bear the Cross, and therefore gave themselves wholly to Prayer and Fasting, that God might enable them to suffer any thing, that the Malice of their Enemies could contrive and do, rather then forsake him, who gave himself for them. This their Adversaries knew well to be true, who were amazed at the Constancy and Cheerfulness they expressed in all their Sufferings, which made them often say, that the Devil was in them, and that they were the *Devils Martyrs*.

Their Adversaries, that they might seem to proceed according to the Forms of Law, and Rules of Justice, ordered an Inditement to be put in against them, the Heads whereof were, *That the Ministers and Masters of Schools of both Cofessions* [sic.] *now accused, did call the King and Kingdome Idolaters; did in their*

Sermons Inveigh against the Blessed Virgin, and the Saints departed, and their Images; That they had assisted the Rebels by their Counsel and Help, and supplied them with Provisions, and had been making way for the Turks to come in and waste the Kingdome. They did not insist much on the particulars that relate to Religion, but great endeavours were used to prove them Complices of the Rebellion, which their Advocates, and Council did manifestly disprove, and the Honourable D. *Hamell Bruynincx*, the Resident of the States of the *United Provinces* at *Vienna*, did afterwards in a Memorial to the Emperor, fully and solidly refute; the Reader will find a little at the end of this Memorial, to shew their innocence: all that shall be said here, is, they have often, and do still appeal to God, Angels and Men as their witnesses, that there was no evidence or proof brought against any one of them in particular, to prove them guilty, otherwise it is not to be imagined, that they had escaped the punishment due for such a crime, had any sort of proof been brought against them, and the Ministers did often and openly declare, that they were ready and willing to undergoe the severest sentence, if they should be duely convicted of the Crime laid to their charge; nor was their [sic] any evidence brought, but only some presumptions, which as they were of no force in Law, so there was no colour in them, to convict them before any Impartial Judge.

After all the arts used in private and publick, had prevailed nothing to terrifie or shake them, at length on the 4*th* of *April*, 1674 the Sentence of Death and Confiscation of Goods, passed upon all the Ministers, and on the 7*th* of that instant, the same Sentence was passed upon all the Masters of Schools.

When this was done, then their Adversaries begun afresh with them, hoping that the fear of death then imminent, would make them more tractable, and (though it was not desired by any of them) they gave them the free liberty of the Town and Suburbs to lodge, and go up and down as they pleased for eight weeks; nor was there any Guard appointed to wait on them, only there was a strict charge laid on themselves, not to leave the Town. This was thought very strange by all people, since it was against all the course of Law, to set condemned persons at such liberty. But the design of it was generally believed to be, to leave them to this freedom of making their escape, that if they did it, they might have a colour for saying, they took the guilt on them, and upon that pretence, justifie any further cruelties they might execute on all the Protestants of the Kingdom; and it is not to be doubted, but if any of them had been conscious to themselves of guilt, they had made their escape; but those servants of Christ, that they might give the Adversaries no advantage, nor occasion further suspition, and that they might shew what was the quiet and courage of a good conscience, did commit themselves to God and his Grace, and stayed still in *Presburg*, till they might see what should be the issue of this business.

On the 29*th* and 30*th* of *May*, the last attempt was made upon them, and they not yielding to what had been so often pressed on them, were ordered to be sent into several prisons, and then the pretence of their being Complices of the Rebellion was not so much mentioned; but the Prelates did publickly profess, it was because they rejected the Propositions had been so often made to them. This was executed upon some immediately, and upon the rest a week after, and they were put in Irons, and sent with Guards to some of the Citadels of *Hungary* (*Comarom, Leopolstadt, Brencs, Kapuvar,* etc.) to be perpetual Prisoners and Slaves, the number of those upon whom this Sentence was executed, was Forty six of the *Ausburg* Confession, and Forty seven of the *Helvetian* Confession, and in all Ninety and three: but afterward five of the latter (a sixth who was liberated out of the Castle of *Eberhard,* is also suspected) and Twenty eight of the former, in all Thirty three, did faint under their bondage and changed their Religion, but the rest of both the Confessions, were by the Grace of God so strengthened, that they continued faithful to the end, and some of them did dye under the persecution of their Adversaries, and obtained the Victory and the Crown of Martyrdom: the rest who are yet alive, were by the good providence of God afterwards set at liberty.

When they were thus dispersed, they first stript and robbed them of any money they had, then they did put them in stinking prisons, they were also forced to serve perpetually, both in the hardest and the filthiest tasks that could be invented, such as the cleaning of privies and all other work about the Town-walls, or Ditches. They fed them with black course Bread and Water, this last being often denied them in any abundance, none were suffered to give them Alms, or so much as to speak to them: and which was more bitter than all the rest, they were daily forced, (sometimes dragged by the hair of the Head, and sometimes driven violently with Pikes and Musquets) to be present at the *Popish*

Worship, which was chiefly done at *Leopolstadt*, and yet God so strengthened them, that they would never joyn in their Worship. In a word the cruel usage they met with was such, that none but Inhumane, or Savages, could so torment the brute Beasts, as their Persecutors did those faithful Servants of Christ.

But when their enemies saw that they could not gain their end from those Witnesses, neither by the miseries of their Prisons, nor by the hard labour they put them too, or the ill usage they gave them, but that thereby the Truth was more confirmed (for sharing all their Trials, they were so wonderfully supported by the grace of the Holy Ghost, that they were never so much as cast down, but rejoyced and sung *Psalms* continually) then they resolved on the last Trial, which had been long threatened, and that was to send them to be Gallie-slaves; therefore in *March* 1675 nine and forty of them, of whom Thirty five were Ministers, and six Masters of Schools, were by the Orders of the Archbishop *Strigonium*, the Lord-Lieutenant of *Hungary*, and the Bishop of *Leopolstadt*, taken out of *Leopolstadt*, *Comarom*, and *Brencs*, and delivered to a Guard of Soldiers, who did drive them like Sheep, through *Moravia*, *Austria*, *Stiria*, *Carmili* [Carniola], and *Istria*, into *Italy*, during which journey, they endured much hardship, hunger, thirst, nakedness, and many grievous stripes, besides the reproaches were everywhere cast upon them. And indeed the miseries of that journey can hardly be imagined, many of them were barefooted, and so going through such rugged waies, were much cut, and marked their steps with their Bloud, they got nothing to eat all day long, and sometimes at night they got nothing, or when they threw three or four farthings a piece to them to buy bread, it was at so unseasonable an hour, that they could hardly get any. They did also drive them with great violence, for whoever fell last, was severely beaten; nor did they deal more gently with some antient men, who to escape their cruel blows, were forced to do violence to Nature, and with unexpressible difficulty, to haste on, rather than receive a beating; and it was no wonder that it was very uneasy to them, when not only the younger persons, who were their companions in Bonds, were scarce able to hold out, or fetch their breath, by reason of their long journies, their hunger, and the many lashes they received, but even their very tormenters were grievously wearied with the hard usage they put them to.

During their journey to *Italy*, two got to the end of their miseries, by a Glorious death, and six more were quite spent, by so long and grievous marches, and being half dead, they were left in prison at *Theatin*, of whom four did soon after receive the Glorious reward of their long sufferings, the other two were afterwards sent to the Gallies, and three of the *Ausburg* Confession, made their escape: the remaining 30 were driven on to *Naples*, where being arrived, they were on the 8*th* of *May*, put into the Gallies, where they were used in a sort, that cannot be expressed, sometimes when they were at sea they were put to row, being quite naked, and when they were in Port, they were put to work halfe naked, carrying great Cables, and Timber, in which they were unmercifully set to tasks, far beyond their strength, their cruel overseers lashing them most severely, and thus for many months did they suffer as much misery as can be imagined, so that six died in that slavery, and all that while did they continue patient under the Cross, never repining against the Holy Providence of God, nor making shipwrack of the Faith, or a good Conscience.

But after God had thus tried them so long in the furnace, and had got so much glory to his great name, and to his Gospel by their sufferings, he at length had compassion on their miseries, and heard their cry, and sent a Deliverer, who broke off their chains, and changed their Captivity into a welcome Liberty. For Admiral *de Ruyter* of blessed memory, coming with the *Dutch* Fleet to assist the King of *Spain* in the wars of *Sicily*, and having got Orders about them, from the High and Mighty Lords of the *United Provinces*, and having been informed where they were, by the Honourable D. *Hamell Bruynincx* from *Vienna*, he did so carefully sollicite their cause, that on the 11*th* of *February* 1675 Twenty six of them, (all that were alive) were delivered to him, who sent them over into *Holland*.

In *July* 1675 there were twenty more Protestant Ministers, 13 of the *Helvetian*, and 7 of the *Ausburg* Confession, taken out of the Castles of *Sarvar* and *Kapuvar*, and driven to other Countreys, two of those in *August* following, were let goe, a ransom being by a strange providence of God given for them, the rest were still grievously handled in the Prisons in *Triest* and *Bucari*, on the Gulph of *Venice*, they having sent them thither, that it might not be known what was become of them. For the Minister of the

United Provinces continued still to press the Emperor on their behalf; at length he procured an Order for setting them at liberty, which was accordingly done on the 2d of *May*, 1676.

But of the 18, ten made defection, and changed their Religion, seven were of the *Ausburg* Confession, and three of the *Helvetian*, so there remained only five, for three died, and one of those was so weakened with the miseries he had suffered, that soon after he died.

In summ, during the persecution, nineteen of those faithful Servants of Christ died under them, and do now triumph in Heaven, over the enraged cruelty of their enemies, and of those, eleven were of the *Helvetian*, and eight of the *Ausburg* Confession. And Thirty of those who loved not their own lives, but resisted unto Bloud, and were blessed Confessors of the Faith, are yet alive, twenty four of these are of the *Helvetian*, and six of the *Ausburg* Confession, but are yet exiles from their Countrey, and separated from their Families and Parishes; (some of the rest that lay in prison in *Hungary*, are also set at liberty,) eight of them are now in *England*, Humbly intreating the Royal Favour of His Majesty, and that he would joyn his Interposition with the Lords of the *United Provinces*, at the Imperial Court at *Vienna*, that their business may be again examined before just and impartial Judges, that so their Innocence being cleared, they may be restored to their Countrey and Churches, and that the Laws of *Hungary* for the freedom of the Reformed Religion may be observed, and the Churches, which to the number of above Twelve hundred their enemies have taken from them, be again restored, which His Majesty has been pleased Graciously to take to heart, and to send Orders to His Minister on their behalf. *All Honour, Praise and Glory for ever, be ascribed unto God, who through Jesus Christ did thus strengthen and comfort by His Holy Spirit, these His Servants, to give so Glorious a testimony to His Truth, and in the end to be more than Conquerors*, Amen.

AN APPENDIX OF THE STATE OF THE PROTESTANT CHURCHES IN HUNGARY AND TRANSILVANIA

When the Reformation broke out in the former Age, as it did soon find a way into most of the States and Kingdomes of *Europe*, so it got into *Hungary*, and was received by the greatest part of that Kingdome, both of the Nobility and Communalty, and thus it continued without any setled form, till the year 1567. That at *Debrecin*, in a Synod of many Ministers that were on both sides of the *Tibisc*, the *Helvetian* Confession was received, and all subscribed to it; for though the chief Reformer there, *Stephen Szegedinus*, an *Hungarian* born, had been one of *Luthers* Disciples, yet he departed from him in those points that were controverted between him and the Divines of *Helvetia*, yet at that time, all that received the Reformation, went under the common name of *Lutherans*. But afterwards the distinguishing Names of *Lutherans* and *Calvinists* got in among them, the chief of the former being one *Stekeliusi;* but few of the pure *Hungarians* were *Lutherans*, most of them being either *Slavonians* or *Germans* that live in *Hungary*.

The Protestants of both Confessions have full and free Liberty for the Exercise of their Religion, by the Laws of that Kingdome, and the publick Churches were for the greatest part theirs, and now for a great while, their Kings in their Coronation Oaths, have sworn to maintain and preserve their Liberty of Religion to them, which his Imperial Majesty, when he was Crowned King of *Hungary*, did swear, as divers of his Predecessors had done before him.

The numbers of the Protestants were very great over all *Hungary*, so that before the late Persecution, scarce the ninth or tenth Man was of the Church of *Rome*, and all the great Towns of the Kingdome (one or two only excepted) were either for the *Ausburg*, or the *Helvetian* Confession. The Papists begin to build Churches or Chapels, in many of those Towns, but in divers places they could not get above ten or twelve to come to them.

The number of the Protestant Churches of both Confessions, was at least Two thousand and five hundred, and those of the *Helvetian* Conf. made more than three parts of that number. This did inflame the rage of the Jesuits, and other Papists, when they saw themselves so much neglected, and their pains so unsuccessful, therefore they betook themselves to other methods, and began in the years 1659, and 1660 to make great changes in the *Lower Hungary*, and then they laid hold on the Rebellion, that has been of late years, wholly on civil Motives, without any pretence of Religion, to charge all the Ministers as Complices of the Rebellion, by which means most of the Ministers were either driven from their Churches, or suffered in the persecution, so that now in those Dominions that are under the Emperors obedience, and not on the Frontiers, where they are under Contribution to the *Turks*, those of the *Helvetian* Confession, have no Churches but at *Papa*, *Weszprim*, *Szendreo*, *Szathmar*, and *Nemethi*, and in *Filck* and *Leva* the Masters of the Schools continue to Preach and say Prayers, the Ministers of those places being now Exiles; there are also five or six Villages in the County of *Szathmar*, which were not disturbed, and this is all the publique exercise of that Religion in those Countreys, that are entirely under his Imperial Majesties obedience; those of the *Ausburg* Confession have also three or four Churches for the exercise of their Religion. As for the Frontier Countries that remain firm under the Emperors obedience, but pay Contribution to the *Turk;* there are near 200 Churches of the *Helvetian* Confession, but these are under daily and great fears, for they have been allarmed by many threatnings, and in divers of them, their Ministers are driven away, so that the people are left destitute of all Instruction, yet there not being a sufficient number of the Popish Priests, to possess these Churches, many of them likewise being afraid to live so near the *Turks*, by which the Churches continue still void, the Ministers have in divers places, returned to their Parishes.

In the more *Southern* parts of *Hungary*, that are now under the Grand Signior below *Buda*, *Agria*, and about *Waradin*, there are reckoned to be about six hundred Churches, all of the *Helvetian* Confession, for there were never any Churches of the *Ausburg* Confession in those parts.

And this is all that remains of those Churches that were once so numerous and flourishing; there are divers publick Schools over *Hungary*, both for Philosophy and Divinity, but their chief seat of their Learning at this day, is *Debrecin* under the *Turk.*

The Churches of *Transylvania* are reckoned to be at least a thousand of both Confessions, but there be many more of the *Helvetian* than of the *Ausburg* Confession. *Socinians* have also publique Churches allowed them there; for their number being very great, they procured a Law to be made, for the free and publick Profession of their Religion, yet their numbers abate much, and compared to the Protestants of either Confession, they are not at all considerable, they have likewise lost divers of their

Churches, for by the Law there, the publique Churches are to be given to those (of any of the Religions that are tollerated) who are the most numerous, and by this means many Churches have fallen out of their hands, and are now possest by the *Calvinists*. There are no *Socinians* at all in *Hungary*, except one or two Churches, nigh the Town of *Quinque Ecclesie* [Pécs], under the *Turk* in the Southern parts. Some few Papists there are in *Transylvania*, but they are not considerable, neither for Power, nor Interest. And the Prince is almost always a *Calvinist*, such is Michael *Abaffi*, the present Prince, who beside his other great Qualities, is a zealous Assertor of the Protestant Religion, and is a great example of Piety and Virtue to all his People, and has made his Dominions a Shelter and Sanctuary to all the persecuted Protestants in Hungary.

6. The Sultan's Declaration of War on the Emperor, 1683

Given without comment. The text which follows is taken from a broadsheet now in the Bodleian Library, Oxford.

THE GREAT
TURKS DECLARATION
OF
WAR
AGAINST THE EMPEROUR OF
GERMANY
(AT HIS PALLACE AT ADRINOPLE, FEBRUARY 20, 1683)

Mahomet Son of Emperours, Son to the famous and glorious God, Emperour of the *Turks*, King of *Graecia*, *Macedonia*, *Samaria*, and the Holy-land, King of Great and Lesser *Egypt*, King of all the Inhabitants of the Earth, and of the Earthly Paradise, Obedient Prince and Son of *Mahomet*, Preserver of the Towns of *Hungaria*, Possessour of the Sepulcher of your God, Lord of all the Emperours of the World, from the rising of the Sun to the going down thereof, King of all Kings, Lord of the

Tree of Life, Conquerour of *Melonjen, Itegly,* and the City *Prolenix,* Great Pursuer of the Christians, Joy of the flourishing World, Commander and Guardian of the Crucified God, Lord of the Multitude of Heathens.

We Command you to greet the Emperour Leopold (*in case he desire it*) *and you are our Friends, and a Friend to our Majesty, whose Power we will extend very far.*) *Thus,*

You have for some time past acted to our prejudice, and violated our Frendship, although we have not offended you, neither by War, or any otherwise; but you have taken private advice with other Kings, and your Council's how to take off your Yoke, in which you have acted very Indiscreetly, and thereby have exposed your People to fear and danger, having nothing to expect but Death, which you have brought upon your selves. For I declare unto you, I will make my self your Master, pursue you from *East* to *West,* and extend my Majesty to the end of the Earth; in all which you shall find my Power to your great prejudice. I assure you that you shall feel the weight of my Power; and for that you have put your hope and expectation in the strength of some Towns and Castles, I have given command to overthrow them, and to trample under feet with my Horses, all that is acceptable and pleasant in your Eyes, leaving nothing hereafter by which you shall make a friendship with me, or any fortified places to put your trust in: For I have resolved without retarding of time, to ruin both you and your People, to take the *German* Empire according to my pleasure, and to leave in the Empire a Commemoration of my dreadful Sword, that it may appear to all, it will be a pleasure to me, to give a publick establishment of my Religion, and to pursue your Crucified God, whose Wrath I fear not, nor his coming to your Assistance, to deliver you out of my hands. I will according to my pleasure put your Sacred Priests to the Plough, and expose the Brests of your Matrons to be Suckt by Dogs and other Beasts.

You will therefore do well to forsake your Religion, or else I will give Order to Consume you with Fire. This is enough said unto you, and to give you to understand what I would have, in case you have a mind to know it.

LONDON, Printed by G. C. for John Mumford, 1683.

7. The Raising of the Siege of Vienna, 1683

This lively contemporary account of the raising of the siege of Vienna (taken from a pamphlet preserved in the Bodleian Library, Oxford) again calls for little comment. The places mentioned in the early part of it are all in the immediate vicinity of Vienna. "Bruckam of Ceytha" is presumably Bruck an der Leitha, on the Austro-Hungarian frontier. "Greekish Weissenberg" is Belgrade. "Stuhlweissembourgh" is Székes-fehérvár in West Hungary.

There is a comprehensive bibliography of the siege of Vienna in Reinhold Lorenz's *Das Türkenjahr, 1683* (Vienna, 3rd edn., 1944). An excellent recent account of the siege in English is J. W. Stoye's *The Siege of Vienna* (London, 1964).

A True and Exact
Relation
Of the Raising of the
Siege
of
Vienna
And the Victory obtained over the
Ottoman Army,
The 12th of September 1683

After a Siege of Sixty days, accompanied with a Thousand Difficulties, Sicknesses, Want of Provisions, and great Effusion of Blood, after a Million of Cannon and Musquet Shot, Bombs, Granadoes, and all sorts of Fire Works, which has changed the Face of the fairest and most flourishing City in the World, disfigured and ruined most part of the best Palaces of the same, and chiefly those of the Emperor; and damaged in many places the Beautiful Tower and Church of St. *Stephen*, with many Sumptuous Buildings. After a Resistance so vigorous, and the Loss of so many brave Officers and Souldiers, whose Valour and Bravery deserve Immortal Glory. After so many Toils endured, so many Watchings and so many Orders so prudently distributed by Count *Staremburgh*, and so punctually executed by the other Officers.

After so many new Retrenchments, Pallizadoes, Parapets, new Ditches in the Ravelins, Bastions, Courtins, and principal Streets and Houses in the Town: Finally, after a Vigorous Defence and a Resistance without parallel, Heaven favourably heard the Prayers and Tears of a Cast-down and Mournful People, and retorted the Terror on a powerful Enemy, and drove him from the Walls of *Vienna*, who since the Fifteenth of *July* last early in the Morning, to the Twelfth of *September*, had so Vigorously attacked it with Two hundred thousand Men; and by endless Workings, Trenchings, and Minings, reduced it almost to its last gasp.

Count *Staremburgh*, who sustained this great Burden, assisted by so many Gallant Officers, having given Notice to the Christian Army, by Discharge of Musquets from the Tower of St. *Stephen*, of the Extremity whereto the City was reduced, they discovered on the Twelfth of this Month, early in the Morning, the Christian Troops marching down the Neighbouring Mountains of *Kalemberg*, and heard continually the Discharges of their Artillery against the *Turks*, who being advanced thither, were fortified with Parapets of Earth and great Stones, to hinder the Descent of the Christian Army from the Mountains, who notwithstanding did advance. The Vanguard of the Horse and Foot, seconded by the Polish Horse, had a long Skirmish with the *Turks*, disputing every Foot of Ground; but seeing themselves totally vanquished by the Christian Forces, who had surmounted all the Difficulties of the Mountains, and drawn down their Cannon in spight of them, they retired Fighting, leaving to the Christians all their Camps full of Pavillions, Tents, Barracks, and Eight Pieces of Cannon (with which they had raised a Battery on that side Four days before) and retreated towards their Principal Camp, between the Villages of *Hernalls*, *Haderkling* and *Jezing;* but as they passed by the Bastion of *Melck* they fired their Cannon furiously on them: The Christians being ravish'd with the Victory, pursued them with so much heat, that they were not only forced to leave their great Camps, but likewise all their others; flying towards *Hungary:* And it is certain, had not the Night come on, they had totally defeated and routed the *Ottoman Army*.

During these hot Skirmishes on the Mountains, the Christians lost near 100 Men, among whom the Serjeant Major of the Regiment of *Schultz*, Prince *Maurice* of *Croy*, Captain of the Regiment of *Grana*, the Prince his Brother, Mareshal Lieutenant of the Field, was wounded there in his Shoulder: They fired then continually against the Approaches and Batteries of the *Turks*, with the Artillery from our Bastions and Ramparts; the Besiegers, animated by the presence of the *Grand Visier*, answered vigorously from theirs, and great Vollies of Musquets were discharged from both sides, intermingled with great quantities of Granado's. The *Grand Visier*, who was in the Approaches, gave them hopes of carrying the place; Prince *Lewis* of *Baden* and Collonel *Heusler* entred their Trenches, at the same time Count *Staremburgh* sallied and seconded them, and repulsed the Janizaries, who saved themselves, with the *Grand Visier*, whose Son was either killed or taken Prisoner, and himself wounded, as 'tis said. Of late the Enemy had not shot so many Bombs nor Stones, nor Fire-works, as they did that Sunday Morning when our Men descended from the Hills towards the *Scotch* and *Melk* Bastions, upon which there stood a great many People to see from a-far our Descent and the Combat; but they observed the Enemy did but little Hurt. Towards the Evening the *Turks* seeing the Christians Masters of their Camp over against the *Scotch* Bastion, and that our Cavalry had entred it, planted Two Pieces of Cannon and shot against them, a while after, seeing themselves surprized, they quitted their Approaches and all their Artillery, consisting of Seventy five Pieces of Cannon, Fourteen Cannons for Battery, and some Mortar Pieces being comprized therein. At the same time there happened a Skirmish in the Camp with the Janizaries, who were come out of the Trenches, but they made no great resistance, and like Cowards ran away.

In the Night the Christians made themselves Masters of all the *Turks* Camp. Afterwards Four Companies of our Foot entred into the Enemies Approaches with Torches and lighted Straw, but found nothing but Dead Bodies; they took possession of the Enemies Artillery, some whereof were brought into the City. All the night long we saw Fires at a distance, the *Turk* having fired as many of their Camps as so sudden a flight would give them leave, and retreated from the *Island* by favour of a Bridge which they had made below the River, upon one of the Arms of the *Danube*, the Christians having seized the Bridge above, on the same River.

On Monday Morning we saw all the Camps and Fields covered with Souldiers as well *Poles* as *Germans*. The *City* was relieved on

Sunday about Five of the Clock in the Afternoon, and every bodies curiosity carried them to see the Camp, after they had been shut up above two Months.

The King of *Poland* having in the mean time with the greatest Vigor repulsed the Enemy on his side and put them to flight, leaving the Plunder of their Camp behind them, which consisted of a very Rich Tent of the Grand Visier, his Colours, Two Poles with the Horse Tails, their usual Signal of War, and his Guidon or Standard, set with Diamonds, his Treasure designed for the Payment of the Army, and in short, all his Equipage was possess'd by the *Polanders*. As for the rest of the Tents, Baggage, Artillery, Ammunition, and Provisions enough to load Eight thousand Waggons, was divided among our Army.

Night coming on, we could no longer pursue, having followed the Enemy about a Mile from their Camp, and our Army having been all that time without Eating and Drinking, we were forced to found a Retreat to refresh them. We had all that Night to rest in, and the Enemy to save themselves. The next day being the Thirteenth we continued not the pursuit for the same reason, which without doubt we might have done with great advantage, since they fled in much disorder toward St. *Godart* to get over the River *Raab*. We are building a Bridge at *Alltemburgh* in *Hungary*, and our Armies will march very suddenly. On Sunday Night, after the Battle, his Imperial Majesty came to *Cloister Nuburgh*, Four hours from *Vienna*, from whence he sent the next day to compliment the King of *Poland* and the Electors upon their good success the day before.

On the Fourteenth, Count *Staremburgh* came to his Imperial Majesty (who received him with all manner of demonstrations of Affection and Esteem) and gave him a Relation of several considerable passages during the Siege: A short time after the Emperour embarked on the *Danube*, and landed above the Bridge before the Town, and entred the City at the *Stuben Gate*, at Landing he was received by the Electors of *Bavaria* and *Saxony*, who were attended by their Guards and a great many Noble Men. It being impossible to remove in so short a time such a number of Dead Bodies, both *Turks*, *Christians*, and *Horses*, whereof the stench was so great on the Road, that it was enough to have caused an Infection.

We saw the Mines of the *Turks* which had made so great Breaches, one in the Bastion of *Leb* and the other in that of the *Palace*, each about Six Fathoms long from bottom to top: There were also Five Mines under the Courtin, which would have been ready to spring in two days, when they designed a general Assault; which would have been dangerous, as well for the greatness of the Breach, as the diminution of the Strength of the Besieged: As His Majesty passed over the Bridge erected on purpose at the Bastion of *Stuben-Tower*, he was harangued in Latin by the Magistrate, and thence he went to the Cathedral of St. *Stephens.* Three Royal Vollies were made by all the Artillery, the first at his Majesties arrival near the Town, the second at his landing, the third during the *Te Deum;* which being ended, he returned to his Palace, and gave Audience to several Publick Ministers, and after dined with the two Electors.

Towards Night arrived the D[uke] of *Lorrain*, who was received with great Joy and Satisfaction (having behaved himself to Admiration) for his Care, Valour and Conduct, during the whole Action. On the fifteenth the Emperour, Electors, and D. of *Lorrain*, went to Visit the King of *Poland* and take a View of his Army, which was Encamped upon the High-way as far as *Ebersdorf.* The Elector of *Bavaria* was at the Head of his Troops with his Sword drawn, with which he made a most profound Reverence to His Imperial Majesty; who came and embrac'd him, saying a Thousand obliging Things of him, desiring him to put up his Sword; Whereupon his Electoral Highness told him that it was the same Sword which had been given him by His Imperial Majesty at *Alten Oettinghen* Two years since, and which having promised to wear for his Service, he was now come to perform his Duty: but since his Majesty commanded him to put it up, he obeyed. And then he asked his Majesty whether he should March or Retreat with his Troops: He likewise asked the same of his Highness of *Lorrain*, who stood by the Emperours side, and then follow'd the Emperour to *Ebersdorf*, and from thence to *Schwechet*, where was the Head Quarters. As soon as the King saw the Emperour coming, he advanced towards him, accompanied with the Prince his Son, the great Mareschal *Jablonowsky*, Palatin of *Russia*, with several other Persons of Quality, very bravely attended; and as we marched likewise in a great Body, we made a

Demi-circle on both sides, and drew so near to one another that we made a perfect Circle, that no body could enter.

Their Majesties being on Horse-back, complimented each other upon the Victory, which the one attributed to the other; the King of *Poland* had the greatest share of the glory of this day which he best deserved: for he may be truly stiled one of the Greatest Kings of Christendom, and the most Valiant. After half an hours Conversation, the Emperour was desired by the King of *Poland* to see his Army, which he accepted of, and was conducted by his Great Mareshal. In effect never any thing could be seen more Great and Heroick than the Four thousand Hussars, who were all well-armed with Coats of Male, and all the rest of the Army very bravely accoutred.

Having viewed the whole Polish Army, the Great Mareshal commanded the said Hussars to make the Course which they are used to make when they go to invest the Enemy, wherewith His Imperial Majesty was highly pleased.

Afterwards His Imperial Majesty returned to Court, where we learn every hour so many particulars of this happy Success, that the Victory and the Loss which the Enemy has suffered, is greater than can be imagined.

We have taken all the Tents of the Enemy, about One hundred and twenty Great Guns, all their Baggage, and a very great Quantity of Ammunition.

It is confirmed likewise, That the King of *Poland*, has (besides the Tent of the *Grand Visier*) his Horses with their rich Harness. It is also said, That besides all the Treasure in Silver, which was designed for the payment of the *Ottoman Army*, there were two Cabinets with Jewels; so that the Booty was so great, that it is not well to be express'd.

Last Night Forty Janizaries having saved themselves upon the Battlements which are call'd Pavillions, with a great number of Christian Children of both Sexes, whom they had made Slaves, and the Poles having summoned them to surrender, they begg'd that they might be received into the Janizary Guards of the King of *Poland*, and unless that might be granted, they would kill the Children and defend themselves to the man: Whereupon the King of *Poland* granted their request.

Yesterday the King of *Poland* began to march in pursuit of the *Turks*, and was to be this Night at *Wischa*. Our Army is to follow too Morrow. One Part is already past the *Danube* in quest of the Rebels.

His Imperial Majesty makes account too morrow to return to *Lintz*.

September 19th

The Emperour is gone this day to Lintz: We are now beginning to cleanse the City of its Rubbish, and carry off the Dead Carcasses of Man and Beast. The *Turks* had a *French Ingineer* in their Camp, who hath done very much hurt to this City, and ruin'd us 50 Pieces of Cannon: There was also a great many *French* among the *Janizaries*, and many were found among the Dead with *French* Silver and Gold in their Pockets. There are daily brought in a great number of *Turks* Prisoners since the flight of the Grand Visier. It is intended to set the *Turks* that are already, and shall be hereafter taken, at Work on the reparation of our *Bastions* and *Courtins*. The Sieur *Kaunitz*, the Emperours Resident at the Port, who was found in the *Grand Visier* Tent, is now in this *City*.

This moment comes the News that *Friday* last the 17*th*, a part of the *Turks Army* fled away in such haste, within sight of *Raab*, as if ours were at their backs; the Officer who brought it, added that in his way from *Raab* he met with but two *Turks*, whom he brought Prisoners to *Bruckham* of *Ceytha*, where he sold them for four Pecks of Oats. All the Enemies or Rebels who had got into the Isle of *Schut*, are retired thence. There are gone down from hence some Boats full of Infantry towards *Hungary*. We are in hopes to hear shortly of some great Enterprize on the *Turks*. Here are daily brought in abundance of young Children whom the *Turks* had taken Captive; they ravish'd the young Maids and Women, and cut off the Heads of the old Men and Women.

Here is News from *Gratz*, That Count *Budiani* (who hath desired Count *Strasoldo* to intercede for him to the Emperour) had commanded 8000 *Hussars* of his Troops, under the Command of his Son and the Count *Nadasti*, to fall on 2000 *Turks* encamped near *Canisa*, and that they have put them all to the Sword. *Baron Buroni* is dead, and his Son revolted from the Rebels, and begs the Emperours Pardon. The *Turks* who are Prisoners, unanimously affirm, That the Grand Visier hath caused *Ibrahim Bassa* Visier of *Buda* to be strangled for first giving Ground at the Battle before *Vienna*. Part of the *Ottoman Army* is arrived near *Greekish Weissenburg*.

Since this Signal Victory obtained by the Christian Army (who some days had refreshed themselves) we are certainly informed they passed *Presbourgh* the 23th of *September,* in pursuit of the scattered Forces of the Ottoman Army, who fled to *Stollweissembourgh;* so that a few days will bring us an Accompt of what has passed between them. This Victory hath already given this advantage to our Affairs, that the Count of *Trausmondorse* [Trautmannsdorf] had taken and confiscated the Castles and Revenues of those who had done Homage to the *Turk;* and it was resolved to do the like in *Hungary.*

Finis

London,
Printed for Samuel Crouch at the Corner of Popes-Head Alley next
Cornhill, 1683.

8. The King of Poland (John III Sobieski) on the Raising of the Siege of Vienna

We cannot resist supplementing the preceding document by the following, if only for its psychological interest. The share of the author and his men in the great victory was, indeed, somewhat more modest than his own account of it would suggest. It is true that the belated arrival of the Polish contingent of 20,000 men (40,000 had been promised) tipped the balance and enabled the imperial forces to go over to the offensive; true, also, that Sobieski was given the supreme command for the decisive battle. But the Polish troops made up less than one-third of the imperial armies, which, with them, numbered something over 70,000 men. The garrison of Vienna, although hard pressed, had, under the heroic generalship of Count Rüdiger von Starhemberg, inflicted such heavy losses on the Turks during the siege that the janissaries were already disaffected. Finally, the rout of the Turks would have been more complete still had the victors pursued them at once, as recommended by Charles of Lorraine; but Sobieski insisted on waiting while his troops plundered the abandoned Turkish camp.
This plamphlet is to be found in various libraries, including the Bodlean Library, Oxford.

A
LETTER
FROM THE
KING OF POLAND
TO HIS QUEEN.
IN WHICH IS INCERTED
MANY PARTICULARS RELATING TO THE VICTORIES OBTAINED
AGAINST THE TURKS. WITH A PRAYER OF THE TURKS AGAINST
THE CHRISTIANS.
(TRANSLATED FROM THE COLOGNE GAZETTE, OCTOB. 19. 1683.
NUMB. 84.)

THE IMMORTAL God, (to whom Honour and Glory be Ascribed for Ever) has Blest us with so Signal a Victory, as scarce the Memory of Man can Equal: The Enemy was not only content to Raise the Siege of *Vienna*, and Leave us Masters of the Field; But also of all their Cannon, and Tents, with Inestimable Treasure, and clim'd over Mountains of Carcasses made by their own Body's in the Flight. My Eyes were never Blest before with so delightful a Prospect as to see my Soldiers follow here a great Drove of their Sheep and Oxen, and there a much greater Herd of *Turkish* Captives; Nor my Ear's e're Charm'd with so pleasing Musick, as the Howlings and Dying Groans of these Miserable Wretches: So great was their Hast, that the Prime Visier almost alone and forsaken of all, was forc't without the Ceremony of his Turbant, to take his Flight; But yet he left me Heir to his Tent and Riches whith were shewn me by a Renegado of his own Retinue.

I have Presented the *Turkish* Standard to His Holyness, who was Instrumental no less by His Money, than His Prayers, to their Overthrow. The Prime Vizor's Horse with all his Trappings, I reserv'd for my self; And tho he was so Fortunate in his Flight to Escape us, yet his Caymecam, or Lieutenant-General, with some of the most Considerable Bassa's [Pashas] fell by our Swords; But the approaching Night put a Stop to our Pursuit, and their Slaughter. Those Janizaries which were left behind in the Mines and Trenches, we thought not worth the dulling of our Swords, therefore we made but one Funeral Pile for 'em all, and Burnt 'em.

In that Action there were about Thirty Thousand *Turks* kill'd; besides *Tartars*, and One Hundred Thousand Tents taken. Our

Souldiers, and the Burghers of *Vienna*, were Two whole Nights, and One Day, in Rifling their Tents and Body's, and I believe a Week would scarce suffice to finish it.

The Rarities which were found in the Prime Vizor's Tent, were no less Numerous than Strange and Surprising, as very curious Parrots, and some Birds of Paradise, with all his Banio's [baths], and Fountains, and some Ostriches, which he Chose rather to Kill, than let 'em fall Alive into our Hands; Nay his Dispair and Jealousy transported him so far, as to Destroy his very Women for the same Reason.

The whole Army Attributes the Glory of this Victory to God, and Us, and all the Princes of the Empire, with the Great Officers, as the Dukes of *Bavaria* and *Lorrain*, Prince *Waldek*, etc. were so far transported with my Valour and Success, that their Thanks and Praises were more Numerous, than was their Fears before; and Count *Staremberg* the Governour, Saluted me with the Title of his Mighty Deliverer. The Common People in my going to and from the Churches, pay'd their Veneration even to my very Garments, and made their Cry's and Acclamations reach the Sky, of *Long Live the King of* Poland.

In the Battel we Lost some of our Friends, as Prince *Halicki*, and the Treasurer of our Household. The Reverend *Marinus Daviano*, heapt on me his Pray'rs and Blessings, and told me he saw a White Dove fluttering o're the Army, which he look'd upon as an happy Augure of our Victory.

We are now on our March towards *Hungary;* taking the Advantage of their Distraction, to Defeat the Remainder of their scatter'd Troops, and Surprize *Gran* or *Newheufell*. I have all the Princes of the Empire my Companions in this Enterprise, who tell me they are ready to follow such a Leader not only into *Hungary*, but to the End of the World.

The Prime Vizor being unable to put a Stop to our Pursuit, told his Eldest Son *Mahomet Han*, That he must now bid Adieu to all his Greatness, and never expect to be in Safety, whilst their Lye's one Stone upon another in the Walls of *Vienna*, but withal bid him hasten to the Grand Seignor and Demand a Speedy Succour, to whom his Son Reply'd, That he knew him too well for that, and there was nothing for 'em now to Rely on but their Flight.

I am just now going to take Horse, and all my way for Two *Hungarian* Miles together, are so strew'd with the Carcasses of

Men, Horses, and Camels, that the Stench of 'em would be insupportable to any but a Soldier.

I have sent several Dispatches to Forein Princes to give Notice of this Action, but the King of *France* was forgotten.

I Rejoyce to see our Son *Alexander* of so Clear and Undanted a Courage who always stuck to me in my most iminent Dangers: and made the first onset on a Body of *Turkish Spahn*, with that Courage that he put 'em soon to flight, and Receiv'd the Applauses of the whole Army. He has Contracted a very Intimate Friendship with the young Duke of *Bavaria* with whom he equally devided the spoyl, This Prince has been very Assiduous in his Services to me; therefore I have presented him three of my Horses, the Bassa of *Egypt's* Tent and Standard, and ten Pieces of Cannon. To his Sister the *Dauphiness*, a Locket of Diamonds. Yet there Remains such heaps of their Colours and Symeters in our possession as are not to be numbred.

All my Countrey men March't with the same Bravery to the Relief of *Vienna*, as the Souldiers of *Godfrey* of *Bullein* did to the *Holy Land*, and the miraculous Cross that you presented me with (which was his Companion in that Expedition) I Believe Contributed no less to our Victory.

Thanks be to Heaven, now the Half-Moon Triumphs no longer o're the Cross, And 'twas thrown down from St. *Stephen's* Steeple in *Vienna* (whom it had o'retopt so long) immediately on the Defeat: Neither have the *Turks* any occasion to upbraid us with their Blasphemous Mahometan Proverb. *Ye Christians where is Your God?*

The *Turks* Prayer against the *Christians*

Eternal God and Creator of all things, and thou O Mahomet his Sacred and Divine Prophet. We Beseech Thee let us not dread the Christians, who are so mean and silly to Rely on a Crucifyed God. By the Power of thy Right Hand, so strengthen ours that we may surround this Foolish People, on every side, and utterly destroy 'em. At length fulfill our Prayers and put these Miscreants into our hands, that we may Establish thy Throne for ever in Mecha, and Sacrifice all those Enemies of our most Holy Religion at thy Tomb. Blow us with thy mighty Breath like Swarms of Flies into their Quarters, and let the Eyes of these Infidels be Dazl'd with the

Lustre of our Moon. Consume them with thy fiery Darts, and Blind them with the Dust which they themselves have Raised. Destroy them all in thine Anger. Break all their Bones in pieces, and Consume the Flesh and Blood of those who defile thy Sacrifice, and hang the Sacred Light of Circumcision on their Cross. Wash them with Showers of many Waters, who are so stupid to Worship Gods they know not: and make their Christ a Son to that God who ne're Begot him. Hasten therefore their Destruction we humbly Intreat thee, and blott out their Name and Religion, which they Glory so much in, from off the Face of the Earth, that they may be no more, who Condemn and Moch at thy Law. Amen.

London, Printed for R. Baldwin, in the Old-Bailey. 1683.

9. "Austria Over All, If She Only Wills It"
(*Oesterreich über Alles, wenn es nur will*)

Philip Wilhelm von Hörnigk was born in Frankfurt am Main in 1640 but came to Vienna in or about 1665 and spent the rest of his life, until his death in 1712, in Austrian service, a large part of it as secretary to Count Johann Philipp von Lamberg, imperial minister at the court of Brandenburg, from 1680 to 1684, and prince bishop of Passau from 1689 to 1712. In the course of these years he came to look on Austria as his true fatherland.

Hörnigk's various duties took him on extensive travels throughout the western parts of the monarchy and the German Empire. One of these journeys was especially important for him: a tour of inspection of the Austrian and Bohemian provinces on which he was sent in 1673 to collect material which should serve as basis for a proposed tax on handicrafts. Meanwhile, he had formed an economic creed that was strongly influenced by the well-known "mercantilist" economist, Johann Joachim Becher. The special application which Hörnigk made of Becher's ideas is due largely to two events to which frequent allusions appear in his book: the Treaty of Nymwegen (1679), which left France mistress of central Europe, and the liberation of Vienna from the Turkish danger (1683).

His book, which was first published (anonymously) in 1684 (under the above title), deserves attention for many reasons. It constitutes perhaps the clearest exposition to be found anywhere outside France of the fashionable mercantilist doctrines of the day. It gives a vivid (although perhaps unduly rosy) picture of the economic resources of "Austria" in the 1670's and is perhaps remarkable above all in its geographical conception. The "Austria" which Hörnigk wishes to see developed into an economic autarky is the Habsburgs' *Hausmacht* of the day, the so-called Austrian Hereditary Lands, the Lands of the Bohemian Crown, and Hungary. While France is the enemy in chief, everything outside this unity is foreign territory.

The book had an instantaneous success. It was reprinted in a revised edition in 1703, and fourteen more editions appeared in the following century. Meanwhile, its doctrines had strongly influenced Austrian economic policy, and continued to do so up to the nineteenth century. Many measures enacted by Charles VI, Maria Theresa, and Joseph II were inspired, at least indirectly, by Hörnigk.

In the nineteenth and twentieth centuries Hörnigk's title was still quoted by all historians, but the book itself had fallen into forgetfulness. After 1784 it was not reprinted until 1964, when a new edition appeared (as Vols. 249 to 251 of the *Oesterreich-Reihe*, Vienna), with a biographical introduction, annotations and bibliography by G. Otruba.

Chapter 1

I HAVE set myself to prove that Austria can be over all, if she only wills it. . . . Under my "Austria" I understand not only the world-famed Archduchy of that name on the two sides of the Danube, but also the whole hereditary Kingdom and Lands of the German Archducal House of Austria, whether lying inside or outside the Roman Empire, thus including Hungary. . . . The excellence in question I find in that superfluity, either existing or potentially existing, of human necessaries and amenities, independent of other nations, in respect of gold and silver, which has perhaps hitherto been little recorded and is therefore unsuspected, which I ascribe to our Austria and put, so to speak, at her disposition. . . .

And would to God it were as easy to inspire Austria with the will to draw the proper benefit from her natural gifts and advantages as it is to prove the manifest fact that her salvation and recovery truly depend—after God's help alone—solely on her own will. . . .

[When I look who should lead Germany to cast off its economic dependence on France], . . . no one is able to do so with more confident prospect of success than his Roman Imperial Majesty, in view not only of his supreme Imperial dignity and prerogatives, but especially of his far-flung Hereditary Kingdom and Dominions so blessed by God and nature, all subject in the same dependence on a single head, all mutually contiguous and thus forming, as it were, a single body, of which the one part can out of its superfluity supply the shortages and needs of others, and is thus so amply endowed with abundance beyond all wishing of raw materials and great domestic consumption thereof that they can rightly boast, more than any other land in Europe, to constitute almost a little world in themselves and to be supplied, without help from abroad, not only with necessaries but with luxuries, if only assisted with the right institutions. . . .

Chapters III–VI

[The development of these lands into an economic autarky is the more necessary because of the changed political situation] . . . . A hundred years ago, when pressed by the Turks and others, our forefathers could still rely on the Roman Empire and its other Princes. But in our days, the guile of France has thrown all into such confusion that man can place his confidence only in God and in himself, and hardly anyone will give another the smallest neighborly help, unless it is also in his own interest, without payment in cash. Therefore every man is well advised to look to himself. For he fares well who in time of need has money in his own purse, let him who has it not at once resolve to be the abject servant, not only of the enemy but of friends and helpers. Against such misfortune Austria can at any time guard herself, if she but will, with a third of the money that now goes out of the country, mostly to France, for quite unnecessary things. . . .

If, then, the power and excellence of a country lie in its superfluity of gold, silver and all other things necessary and desirable for its subsistence, all, as far as possible, from its own stocks, without dependence on others and further, in the proper cultivation, use and application thereof, it follows that a national economic system has to see how such superfluity, cultivation and enjoyment can be brought into being out of native resources, without dependence on others or, where this is not completely possible, then with as little dependence as possible and with all possible economy of the national finances. To which end the following nine rules must chiefly serve.

First: the nature of the country must be exactly observed and surveyed, every corner, every clod of earth examined to see whether it be cultivable. Every useful plant under the sun shall be examined to see whether it could flourish in the country and how well, since the proximity of the sun, or its reverse, is not everything. In all that concerns gold and silver, no labor or expense should be spared to bring them to light.

Secondly, all commodities in a country which cannot be used raw are to be processed at home; since the cost of manufacture usually exceeds that of the raw material by twice, thrice, ten, twenty, sometimes a hundredfold, and a sensible economist must shudder to throw this away.

Thirdly, men are necessary to put these rules into effect, both to produce and transport, and to cultivate the raw materials and to process them. Regard must therefore be had to populating a country with as many men as it can support—the business, alas! often neglected, of a well-ordered State. And all possible ways and means must be found to bring these men out of idleness into productive employment, to teach them and encourage them in all inventions, arts, and handicrafts, and, if necessary, to have instructors brought in from abroad.

Fourthly, gold and silver, once in the country, whether home-produced or brought in from abroad through industry, are in no way or fashion, so far as is at all possible, to be allowed to leave it again, nor allowed to remain buried in chests and strongboxes, but always kept in circulation; nor are they to be allowed to be fashioned into forms where they are, as it were, made useless and unserviceable. For so it will be impossible for a country which once acquires a considerable stock, especially one which has its own gold and silver mines, to fall into poverty, impossible, indeed, for it not to increase continuously in wealth and property. Therefore,

Fifthly, the inhabitants are to be most strongly enjoined to content themselves with their domestic products, to limit their indulgence and display to these, and as far as possible, to renounce foreign ones (except in case of absolute necessity or if not necessity, irremediable bad habits which have crept in, such as the use of Indian spice). And,

Sixthly, what is indispensable, of necessity or through irremediable bad habit, should wherever possible not be bought directly from abroad for gold or silver, but be exchanged against other domestic products.

Seventhly, such foreign products shall then be acquired in their raw state and processed at home and the cost of manufacture earned there.

Eighthly, day and night watch must be kept that surplus home products be sold abroad in manufactured form, so far as this is necessary, and for gold and silver, and to this end consumers must be sought out, so to speak, from the ends of the world and exports promoted in every way.

Ninthly, failing important reasons to the contrary, products available domestically in sufficient quantity and of adequate quality should never be allowed to be imported; no sympathy or pity for the foreigner should affect this policy, whether he be friend, kinsman, ally, or enemy. For all friendship stops when it conduces to my own weakness and destruction. And this applies even when the domestic product is worse in quality or even more expensive. For, strange as it may appear to ill-informed minds, it is better to give two thalers which remain in the country for an object, than one thaler that goes abroad. . . .

Chapter X

[The author now turns to enumerating the natural resources of Austria. We omit his somewhat particular description of its resources in gold, silver and salt. He then points out that for food and drink, man needs cereals, fruit, milk products, vegetables, meat, fish, etc., and goes on:]

Anyone who knows the common saying that the Hereditary Dominions were really made for eating and drinking can easily imagine that all these things are present, not only in abundance but in superfluity. Hardly one of all the Provinces lacks sufficiency of any of them (saffron excepted). And if one, such as Silesia, lacks wine, it can get it from the nearest co-Province, so that the money spent on this, too, remains, so to speak, at home. Only the Tirol draws its supplies of bread from some foreign neighbors, but more for convenience than of necessity; the barns of other Austrian Provinces could assuredly supply its needs. And for the rest, most products, such as salt, wheat, wine, cattle, swine, fish, vinegar, brandy, fruit, etc. are present in such abundance that the only complaint is where to dispose of them all. As it is, the inhabitants are almost driven to knavery to get rid of the surplus to prevent its going bad. Austria and Bohemia lead the way in this superfluity, but above all, Hungary, which should really be regarded as

Europe's Promised Land. Its soil is so fruitful that ordinary seed yields the finest wheat flour in the second crop and the grass almost covers the backs of the grazing cattle. The water is so full of fish that it is hardly an extravagance to say that the Tisza in Upper Hungary carries between its banks two parts of water and one of fish. The wine of some districts, such as Tokay, can vie with the best in the world. The fields resound with the voices of beasts, great and small. The farmyard practically overflows with poultry, the air teems with its feathered denizens—in a word, Hungary is a real mine of bread, fat, and meat. I will say no more, lest I be held a hired panegyrist.

After the fruit comes the shell, or the clothing, and what appertains thereto. For this, the provinces yield wool, flax, and hides. Bohemian wool, especially the long wool of the district of Pilsen, is the best for making good stuffs, Silesia comes next after Bohemia in quantity and quality, then Moravia. Austria and Hungary have enough, but of poor quality. Linen manufacture is truly at home, as it were, in Silesia, Upper Austria, and parts of Inner Austria, whence many neighboring lands and some further afield used to supply themselves, and still do; and they still have ample for the Hereditary Provinces. It is obvious that the stock raising of which I spoke and the abundant game preserves must necessarily produce a superfluity of hides of all kinds (except the expensive fine furs). There are even tame "kinglets" and beaver fur. After the shell comes the husk, viz., the housing, for which earth and clay, timber and stone are required. Of these there is no shortage, in respect either of quantity or quality. I need not dwell on it. There is even excellent marble and other valuable stone for the labor of quarrying and carting them. The Caplier Castle of Milnschau in Bohemia is built on a rock of pure jasper. Finally, all the other necessaries of human existence are there; all kinds of tools and furniture and ornaments, of which many are fashioned out of the stone, earths, gold, silver, wool, linen, leather, etc., mentioned above. Others are made of the lesser metals, of which, with the exception of one not found to my knowledge elsewhere in the known world except China, not one is lacking in our Provinces. For copper and iron are present in nearly all of them. Bohemia has long supplied Schlackenwald tin, without which even English tin cannot be properly worked. And now Geyersberg is producing such quantities of it that it looks as though soon half the world could be supplied with it; it is not a hairsbreadth worse than the English. There is lead in Carinthia, near Villach, some in Bohemia, sufficient in Hungary, and allegedly in Schlamming, near Admont in Upper Styria, an ore, not yet exploited, contains 60 lb. of lead to the hundredweight. Idria produces quicksilver so lavishly that if it were fully exploited and properly marketed it could supply the whole world, hence it is regarded as a jewel of the Monarchy. Under this heading come also minerals, the most important of which—sulphur, coppers and antimony—Hungary alone, not to speak of the others, produces enough to supply the world. All the others again, are present in abundance and superabundance, one here, the other there; Hungary has a practical monopoly of mountain green. In Tirol there is cadmium, out of which some brass is prepared. Where, then, a place possesses all metals and minerals, the materials for metallic coloring cannot be far away, if the trouble to look for them is taken. Of the salts, there is rock salt or salt pans enough everywhere, an abundance in Hungary; Bohemia seems like the very father of alum, since there is an incredible mountain of this near the Meissen frontier, if only a market for it could be found. Of timber, the principal constituent of all sorts of implements needed for human existence, there is in places so much, such regrettable superfluity, that he would be doing a great service who showed a way to be rid of it at a profit. There is plenty of it also for ships' masts and hulls, not to mention other purposes. Precious stones, too, come under this heading as the chief adornments. Of these, Hungary gives us opals and jade, Bohemia the finest garnets, though small, and also lapis lazuli, diamonds, amethysts, sapphires, topazes, cornelians, aquamarine, agate, jasper, all kinds of colors, pearls—although of somewhat inferior quality—and the agreeable serpentine.

Of wax, tallow, horns, glass, bones, pitch, horsehair, buck's hair, feathers, and other similar products which serve human needs no less than the objects listed above there is nothing further to say beyond this: that seeing the superfluity of the bees, cattle, linen, etc., of which these are the by-products, there can be no shortage of them either. But neither should we forget that very efficent living instrument of human labor, the horse, for which Hungary, above all, is famous, then Bohemia; but there is no shortage in any of the other Provinces—in most, a superfluity, and equally little shortage of other necessary European beasts of burden. . . .

Chapters XI–XV

[Hörnigk goes on to argue, with some repetition, that there is practically no commodity necessary for human existence in which "Austria" is not self-sufficient and that she could easily do without practically any imports if she would consume her native products instead of running after foreign ones. Neither is it the case that her inhabitants are stupid—many of her products have long enjoyed high reputations. Silesian cloth, in particular (he comes back to this point several times) is bought cheaply by Dutch traders, processed in the Netherlands, and sold back expensively as a Dutch product. These final processes could just as easily be carried out at home, as could the processing of silk.] It is true, some districts in Austria are more industrious than others; the inhabitants of the wine-growing districts are not only commonly accused of themselves caring more for their own glasses than for work, but within a few years they make the foreign artisans, who are imported like themselves, idlers and good-for-nothings. The beer-producing districts work much harder. And if in some places, as in the flat parts of Bohemia, where the land laughs for abundance of corn and cattle, and where it is worth while producing wine, the industry and application of the inhabitants leave something to be desired, the mountains [of German Bohemia] are, on the other hand, full of stout, hard-working men. In Vienna itself, where indulgence and love of gay living has become, as it were, a general tradition, neither skill nor application would be lacking for manufactures, given only the will, encouragement, and leadership. . . .

Chapters XVI–XVIII

[Hörnigk then discusses how far his "nine rules" are observed in Austria, and after giving, with reason, examples to show how each one of them is habitually broken, he writes:]

There is a saying: If one is good, they are all good; but I say now: If one of these rules were ever properly observed among us, so would they all be. But in fact, no one of them is observed. Nothing is sound with us, from head to foot. And is it any wonder that the lands are poor in money, or is the cause far to seek? Rather, things are in such a condition that it is something like an

Austrian miracle that everything has not yet gone to total ruin long ago. . . .

Yet I would fain believe that we are not yet so far rejected by God that no hope more should remain. I rather comfort myself that Heaven will yet bring us some men who will help our unhappy Fatherland to acquire these blessings as the chosen implement of God. Blessed Imperial realms and blessed day when we shall experience this salvation! Most dear, ever most glorious Emperor, who shall thus, by firm resolution and unshakable institutions, console the sad and distressful land and peoples entrusted to him by God and help them out of the present slough of penury and want. Yes, blessed Turkish affliction, blessed devastation of Austria, welcome flight from Vienna, if the effect of you is that at last eyes are opened, hands set working, and through you, as when part of a cargo is jettisoned, the whole decrepit ship of our common life, nigh to foundering in the storm, is snatched to safety from the violent tempest and from destruction. . . .

Chapter XX

Yes, I say, the salvation must come from the Princes of our people, for the people can do nothing without them. . . .

[The rest of Hörnigk's remarks do not lend themselves to extracts; we will say here only that the first and chief step advocated by him is an absolute prohibition on the importation of all manufactured woolens, linen goods, silks, and all other commodities known as "French manufactures." The money saved on these imports, estimated by Hörnigk at ten million gulden yearly, is to be spent on establishing local manufactures. It is also interesting that he recommends that the guild system should, at least at first, not be allowed "in the manufactures which are not yet established in the dominions, but are still to be introduced."]

10. The "Serb Privilege" of 1691

Austrian armies, having taken Belgrade in 1688, penetrated into the Balkans in the following year, and their commander called on the local Slavs to rise against the Turks. In 1690, however, the tide of the

campaign turned; the imperial forces were driven back, and to escape the vengeance of the Turks, the Serbian patriarch of Ipek led a great body of his countrymen, estimated at 36,000 fighting men, or some 200,000 persons in all, across the Danube and Save (Száva), where they were settled provisionally in empty spaces in southern Hungary. The Emperor Leopold granted them the Privilege, the translation of which follows. This was, as will be seen, issued on the assumption that the imperial armies would reconquer the northern Balkans, whither the Serbs would return; but the campaign failed, and the Peace of Passarowitz (1699) established the Danube and the Save as the frontiers between the monarchy and the Porte. The Serbs were unable to return to the Balkans, and made their temporary homes in Hungary permanent.

In spite of the altered circumstances, the Privilege was never revoked. It was, indeed, never extended as the Serbs wished; for they repeatedly petitioned to be allotted an area of their own, in which they should enjoy complete corporate self-government, political, under a "voivode" elected by themselves, as well as ecclesiastical. The territory was never granted them, and they were never allowed a voivode —only once, a vice-voivode. Instead, they came under various political dispensations, some in civilian Hungary and Croatia, others in the Military Frontier and the Bánát of Temesvar. The patriarch's ecclesiastic authority (which, it may be remarked, extended also over the Orthodox Rumanians of the kingdom of Hungary) was, however, left intact, and this gave them a large measure of national cohesion. Bitterly hostile, on national, religious and social grounds alike to the Hungarian State and the Magyar people, they remained in fact a foreign body. The Serbs of the Military Frontier and the Bánát were militarily organized, and a valuable instrument in the hands of the Austrian authorities, for use both in the monarchy's foreign wars and as a counterweight to Hungarian national aspirations.

The text from which the following translation is made is taken from H. Marczali (Ed.), Enchiridion Fontium Historiae Hungarorum, Budapest, 1902, pp. 596ff.

LEOPOLD, BY the Grace of God by election ever august Emperor of the Romans and King of Germany, Hungary, Bohemia, etc., to Our honorable, faithful and well-beloved Arsenius Csernovich, Archbishop of the Rascians[1] of the Greek rite of the Eastern Church, and to the Bishops and all other ecclesiastical and secular captains, vice-captains, and to the whole community of the said Greek rite and nation of Rascians in Hungary, Slavonia, Illyria, Moesia, Albania, Greece, Bulgaria, Herzegovina, Dalmatia, Pod-

---

[1] Serbians.

goria,[2] Jenopolis,[3] and other places attached, and to all others who shall receive, read or hear these Our presents, Our Imperial and Royal grace and all good things. Not only from the humble memorial sent in the name of you all by your delegate to Us, Isaia Diakovich, Bishop of Jenopolis, but also more plainly from his oral exposition, We have most graciously taken note of your humble thanks that We have snatched you out of the jaws of the barbarous tyranny of the Turks and restored you to your former liberty, and of the perpetual obligation toward Us under which you have averred yourselves and your descendants to stand for this great benefit conferred on you, which is, indeed, due from you, but gives Us the greater satisfaction because, acknowledging Our right, and casting yourselves on the bosom of Our grace and clemency, you declare with laudable fortitude of soul your intention of living and dying under the shadow of Our protection.

In favorable consideration of which entreaties and representations from you, We not only most mercifully receive you, all and singular, under Our Imperial and Royal protection but, in order that Our lofty proposal be fixed in your minds and perpetually inculcated into your sons and confirmed ever more and more in all relevant documents, We do accordingly paternally exhort you to take up arms against the most inveterate enemy of the name of Christian, your persecutors, under Our auspices and the direction of Our generals, to avenge the injuries, calamities and miseries most unjustly and cruelly inflicted on you. In return, that ye may feel at the very outset the gentleness and sweetness of Our Empire and rule, We, assenting with the piety native to Us to your petitions, have most graciously decreed that ye shall freely retain the custom of the Eastern Church of the Greek Rite of the Rascians according to the rule of the old Calender, and as hitherto, so henceforward, ye shall not be submitted to molestation from any Estates, civilian or secular; and that ye be permitted yourselves to appoint autonomously an Archbishop of the Rascian nationality and language, to be elected by your ecclesiastical and secular Estates, and he, your Archbishop, shall have the free right of disposition of all churches of the Greek Eastern rite, of consecrating Bishops, of disposing priests in monasteries, of building churches, where needful, at his own discretion, of subordaining Rascian priests in cities and towns: in a word, he shall continue to be in authority, as

---

[2] The district of Karlstadt in the Military Frontier of Croatia.
[3] Jenö, a small town northeast of Arad, then a Serbian bishopric.

hitherto, over the churches of the Greek rite and the community
of the same profession, of his own ecclesiastical authority, in virtue
of the privileges granted to you by Our predecessors, former kings
of Hungary, in all Greece, Rascia, Bulgaria, Dalmatia, Bosnia,
Jenopolis and Herzegovina, and likewise in Hungary and Croatia,
Moesia and Illyria, wherever they are now to be found, and shall
be authorized to hold charge over them insofar and so long as all
and singular shall be true and loyal to Us. And the ecclesiastical
Orders, the Archbishops, Bishops, monks, and priests of all kinds of
the Greek rite, shall continue to be assured autonomy in their monasteries and churches, in such fashion that no man be authorized
to do violence to your said monasteries, churches and residences;
but in respect of tithes, taxation, and quartering [of soldiers] they
shall enjoy their ancient exemption, nor shall any secular authority
except themselves have power over their Church to arrest or
imprison any man, but the Archbishop shall be entitled to punish
according to his own canonical law such ecclesiastics under him as
may incur any penalty. We also confer and confirm that the
churches and monasteries of the Greek rite, with what appertains
thereto, and also all property of any sort belonging to the Archbishop and Bishops, are to be possessed by them as ordained by
Our predecessors; and as for the churches taken from you by the
Turk, the enemy of Christianity, we have charged that when they
are recovered they, too, are to be resigned into your hands. And
should your Archbishop, or Bishops, find it necessary to visit
churches or monasteries in cities or in the countryside, We will not
suffer them to be molested by any man, ecclesiastic or secular.
And We will also make every possible endeavor to return the
said Rascian people, through Our victorious arms, with the help
of God, as speedily as possible, into their former territories and
habitations, and to expel enemies therefrom. And it is Our will
that the said Rascian people shall continue under the direction and
disposition of its own authorities [*magistratus*] and enjoy unmolested the ancient privileges graciously granted to it by Our
Majesty, and its customs. We furthermore agree that should
any person of the Greek rite die without the consolation of issue
and blood kin, all his substance shall pass to the Archbishop and
Church; similarly, should the Archbishop and any Bishop die, all his
substance shall pass to the Archbishop. Finally, We most graciously
will and command that all shall be subject to the Archbishop, as
their ecclesiastical head, both in spiritual and secular respects [*tam*

in spiritualibus, quam secularibus dependent]. Which Our most
munificent and most merciful concession to you, We firmly assure
Ourselves will be rewarded by your loyalty and devotion, to be
continuously observed, unshaken by any tempest. And for the rest
We most graciously assure you, all and singular, of Our Imperial
and Royal grace. Given in Our City of Vienna in Austria, on the
twentieth day of the month of August, in the year of the Lord one
thousand six hundred and ninety one, the thirty-fourth year of Our
Roman reign, the thirty-seventh of Our Hungarian and the thirty-
fifth of the Bohemian.

LEOPOLD
BLASIUS JACKLIN, BISHOP OF NITRA
JOHANNES MAHOLANY

11. The Habsburg Succession, 1687–1722/23

The documents which follow show the various enactments concluded
round the turn of the seventeenth to eighteenth centuries to regulate the
succession in the Habsburg monarchy. The situation when they open
was the hereditary succession in the male or female line was already assured in the German-Austrian provinces under the fifteenth-century
Privilegium Maius, and in the Bohemian, under the *Vernewerte Landesordnungen* of 1627–28 (see above, pp. 37–45). The Hungarian Estates
had, however, continued to maintain their right to elect their king, and
not to crown him until he had sworn in due form to respect and maintain the national liberties, etc., his coronation oath still admitted the
validity of the famous *"jus resistendi"* granted by King Andrew II in
his Golden Bull of 1222, authorizing the country to resist an illegal
measure by the king; the participants in the "Wesselényi conspiracy" (a
group of Hungarian magnates, headed by the palatine) had in fact
proposed to invoke this clause in 1666–1667 as justification for raising
Hungary against Leopold I.

In 1687 Leopold then convoked a Hungarian diet, which he forced to
accept the hereditary succession in the male line, and to renounce the
"jus resistendi." Leopold's elder son, Joseph, was then duly crowned
and took the oath to the Constitution, thus emended, and with the additional stipulation that "the King and assembled Estates were to agree
on the interpretation and application of the laws." The essential legislation enacted at this diet follows here as Document A.

On November 1, 1699, Charles II, the last reigning Habsburg of the
Spanish line, died without male issue, and Leopold then claimed the

Spanish throne. The maritime powers were willing to support the candidature of Leopold's younger son, Charles III (VI), against his French rival, but only on condition that the crowns of Spain and Austria were never united, and Leopold consequently renounced the crown of Spain for himself and Joseph; nevertheless, he had drawn up, and read out to a select body of privy councillors, the *"Pactum Mutuae Successionis,"* which follows below as Document B, laying down that if the male line of either of his sons became extinct, the male issue of the other son should succeed to the possessions of both, the inheritance passing in primogeniture. Female issue was to succeed in default of male, but the Josephinian line was always to take precedence of the Carolean.

Leopold died on May 5, 1705. Joseph succeeded him in Austria (and Hungary), while Charles was still fighting, although with small and ever-diminishing prospects of success, for the Spanish crown. On April 17, 1711, Joseph also died, leaving only two daughters. Charles now returned to Austria, where he succeeded unquestioned to the family dominions, and was also elected emperor, but the Spanish crown passed definitively to the Bourbon candidate when the Peace of Rastatt was concluded in 1714. Meanwhile, Charles had determined that his possessions should pass undivided to his own issue, and therefore, on April 19, 1713, had read out to another assemblage of privy councillors the so-called "Pragmatic Sanction" (Document C), decreeing that they should so pass, in primogeniture, first to his male issue, and in default thereof, to his female issue; in default of these again, to Joseph's line, in primogeniture, and then to the lines of Leopold's daughters.

The compatibility of the Pragmatic Sanction with the *Pactum Mutuae Successionis* is questionable, but some Austrian historians, at least, regard Charles as having been within his rights—a view which seems to have been Charles's own, since in issuing the Sanction he made explicit reference to the *Pactum*. No problem would, however, arise if Charles had a son, and in this hope he, for the time, kept the Pragmatic Sanction a secret. But the son, Leopold, whom his wife bore to him in 1716, died in infancy, and after this the only issue of his marriage consisted of two daughters, Maria Theresa (b. 1717) and Maria Anna (b. 1718). In 1720, therefore, Charles made the Pragmatic Sanction public, communicating it to his various dominions. When Joseph's daughters married, he made them renounce any claim to succeed in preference to his own daughters.[1]

All the extra-Hungarian dominions successively took cognizance of the Pragmatic Sanction.[2] Some of them attempted to lay down conditions, but were told that they were not entitled to do so.

---

[1] The elder daughter's husband, Frederick Augustus of Saxony-Poland, made a similar renunciation; the younger daughter's husband, the Elector of Bavaria, refused to do so.

[2] In 1720, Upper Austria, April 19; Lower Austria, April 22; Carinthia, June 5; Styria, June 10; Carniola, June 19; Gorizia, August 5; Gradisca, August 8; Trieste, September 9; Bohemia, October 16; Moravia, October

The Lands of the Hungarian Crown were still only bound to accept the male succession, for at the Diet of 1712 to 1715 held by Charles after the liquidation of the Rákóczi rebellion, at which he was crowned, he had not raised the question of the female succession and had in other respects only sworn to maintain the position established in 1687, with the exception of the assurance reproduced as Document D. Acceptance of the female succession could be given only if the diet in session passed a law to that effect; and in 1720 Charles accordingly announced the convocation of another diet, before which he proposed to lay the Pragmatic Sanction for its acceptance.

Meanwhile, there had been developments in the country itself. As early as 1712 the Croat diet, assembled to elect its representatives to the Hungarian diet, had resolved to accept whatever person, male or female, should succeed to rule over Inner Austria (these three provinces had traditionally supplied the Austrian garrisons of Croatia) and was thus able to provide forces for the defense of Croatia against the Turks. The Croatian diet had sent a deputation to Vienna conveying its wish and threatening to secede from Hungary should the kingdom insist on election. Charles had replied that he would try to get the Hungarian diet to accept the proposal. The Hungarians had, in 1712, decided on somewhat different conditions. They were willing to accept the female succession, provided that the lands of the putative ruler of Austria were linked "indivisibly and inseparably" with the Lands of the Hungarian Crown, and that their ruler undertook obligations to defend Hungary with her other resources—a necessary precaution, since a female could not be Holy Roman emperor and thus could not command the resources of the Empire for this purpose.

When the diet assembled (before its formal opening by the king) it sent a deputation to Vienna to convey its wishes, and as Charles accepted them, the diet passed the appropriate legislation, reproduced here as Series E.

It will be remarked that, owing to the stipulations made by the Hungarians, the provisions for the succession in Hungary were not, after all, absolutely identical with those of the Pragmatic Sanction: not only did the Hungarian law provide that Hungary recovered her right of election in the events of the extinction of both Charles's and Joseph's lines, but it also laid down that the ruler must be "an Archduke or Archduchess of Austria." Originally intended only to ensure that the monarchy possessed sufficient resources to defend the country "against foreign aggression" (the emphasis thus being on the word "Austria"), it acquired in the twentieth century a different significance, when the situation arose that the heir presumptive to the throne (the Archduke Franz Ferdinand) had made a morganatic marriage, under which his issue did not rank as archdukes.

17; Upper and Lower Silesia, October 25; Tirol, December 20. In 1721, Eger, July 23, followed by the Vorlande. In 1722, Transylvania; in 1724, the Netherlands; and in 1725, Lombardy and Fiume.

The Pragmatic Sanction, with accompaniments, is rightly considered one of the most important documents of its time. Charles VI spent much of the rest of his reign in trying to secure international recognition and guarantees of it from the powers. The wars which broke out while he was still hardly cold in his grave did little honor to the good faith of those who pledged themselves; but even internationally, the Sanction was not without its effect in preventing the dismemberment of the Habsburg monarchy. Internally it was very important. In itself it brought nothing new to the mutual relationship of Charles's various dominions: the constitutional link between them remained purely dynastic. Nevertheless, the proclamation of their indivisibility not only averted the danger of any further partition of them between various members of the dynasty, such as had so weakened the Habsburg power in the fourteenth to fifteenth and again in the sixteenth to seventeenth centuries, but also, naturally, strengthened in very great degree the centripetal forces in the monarchy. Particularly important was Hungary's pledge to accept the female succession and its admission, in connection therewith, that the unity should apply "also against foreign aggression," an admission originally made in Hungary's own interests —the diet was thinking of Turkish aggression against Hungary—but one in virtue of which Hungary, in 1741, actually provided the forces to which Maria Theresa owed the maintenance of her throne. Out of this grew the centrally controlled army that was afterward the mainstay of the further unity of the monarchy.

The fullest studies on this subject are in a series by G. Turba, *Geschichte des Thronfolgerechtes in den habsburgischen Ländern 1156– 1732* (Vienna, 1903); *Grundlagen der Pragmatischen Sanktion* (Vienna, 2 vols., 1911–12); *Die Pragmatische Sanktion, authentische Texte mit Erläuterungen* (Vienna, 1913). For the Hungarian aspects, see H. Marczali, *Ungarisches Verfassungsrecht* (Tübingen, 1911).

A. EXTRACTS FROM THE LAWS OF THE HUNGARIAN DIET OF 1687*

Law I, Paragraph 2.[1]
(Joseph's Coronation oath)[2]

WE, JOSEPH, by the Grace of God King of Hungary, etc., swear by the living God, by His most holy Mother the Virgin Mary, by all the Saints: that We will keep the Churches of God, the

---

* From *Magyar Törvénytár* (*Corpus Juris Hungarici*), Ed. K. Csiky and D. Markus, Budapest, 1907, Vol. I, pp. 233ff).

[1] Para. 1 is a preamble.

[2] This oath afterward became the regular form and was repeated in identical terms, *mutatis mutandis*, by all Joseph's crowned successors.

Prelates, barons, nobles, free cities, and all inhabitants of the country in their immunities and liberties, laws and privileges, and in their old, good and approved customs, as the King and the assembled Estates shall agree on the interpretation and application thereof; We will do justice to all, we will observe the Decree of His Majesty Andrew of blessed memory (excepting and excluding Article 31 of that Decree, from "but should We, etc.," to "license forever"[3]); We will not alienate nor diminish the frontiers of Our Kingdom of Hungary, nor of anything that belongs to it by whatever right or title, but rather increase and extend them so far as We are able; and We will do all else that We can justly do for the general good, honor, and increase of all the Estates and of all Our Kingdom of Hungary; so help us God, and all Saints.

[Law II begins with a preamble expressing in extravagant terms the gratitude of the Estates to Leopold for his victories over the Turks, and especially for the liberation of Buda, and continues:]

And in commemoration of these great and ever-memorable benefits, and in ever-visible token of their gratitude and humble devotion, the said Estates of the Realm of this Kingdom of Hungary and of the territories attached thereto[4] declare that in future they will for all time recognize as their legitimate King and Lord none other than the male heir in primogeniture truly and lawfully begotten by this His Imperial and Royal Majesty (as already determined by Law 5 of 1547 and other laws relating thereto) and will therefore always, and whenever the occasion of such inauguration recurs, after reception of articles contained in the above-mentioned diploma, or Royal assurance thereon, and oath taken in the form used by His predecessors, crown him in assembled Diet within this Kingdom of Hungary.

[3] These words ran in the Golden Bull: "But should We, or any of Our successors, at any time try to violate this Our disposition, both the bishops and other lords and nobles, collectively or singly, present and future, shall have the right to resist and oppose Us and Our successors, without imputation of treason, and We hereby grant them such licence forever." In Law IV the diet again expressly declared the words "excluded and deleted."

[4] The *"Partes adnexae"* or *"adjunctae"* were those territories not forming part of the Kingdom of Hungary proper which were nevertheless regarded as subject to the Hungarian Crown. Chief among them was Croatia; the usage varied in other respects.

Law III

If, however (which may Divine Providence be pleased to avert for all time), the male line of His Imperial and Royal Majesty should die out, then the subsequent succession to the throne shall (again after precedent Royal assurance in the form detailed above, and after acceptance of the articles of the Diploma and confirmation thereof on oath) pass and revert in like manner to the male line of the King of Spain, H.M. Charles II, and consequently, only in such case (which may Divine Providence avert) that the male line both of His Sacred Imperial and Royal Majesty and of the said King of Spain should fail, will the ancient and honorable prerogative of the said Estates of the Realm to elect and crown their Kings again apply.

B. The "Pactum Mutuae Successionis" (September 12, 1703)*

Following on Our renunciation of the Spanish Monarchy and on the agreement which forms the central point of that renunciation, We establish and declare with the will, consent and agreement of both Our sons, as a law valid, with God's help, for all time, that both in the Kingdoms and Provinces belonging to the Spanish Crown and in Our other Hereditary Kingdoms and Lands, the right of succession of Our male issue, born in the male line in lawful wedlock (not legitimized) shall always have precedence before all female issue and their issue, male or female, of whatever line or degree, and among that issue the right of primogeniture shall always prevail, so that in those realms which remain in possession of Our first-born son, his sons, and in those which have been ceded to Our second son, Charles, his male issue, shall be first in the succession, and thus in both lines, so long as God grant that male issue, born to the male line in lawful wedlock, survive.

But if—which may God forfend!—either our well-beloved son King Charles III dies without male issue begotten in lawful wedlock, or their legitimate male issue, in the male line, should die out, whether or not there exist female descendants or the children, male

* From Edmund Bernatzik, *Die oesterreichischen Verfassungsgesetze*, 3rd edn. (Vienna, 1911), pp. 5ff.

or female, of such, then, according to the Law of Succession established in Our House and now confirmed, the whole Spanish Monarchy and all Kingdoms and Lands belonging and subject thereto shall immediately revert to Us and Our first-born son and after him to his lawful (not legitimized) children and descendants; yet provided that should there be surviving legitimate daughters of Our son Charles III or of his issue, provision shall be made for them in the manner hitherto customary in Our House; but they too shall, after the extinction of Our male line and of the female issue of Our first-born son, which everywhere and always takes precedence of them, be assured the right of succession in virtue of primogeniture, where this becomes applicable.

If, however—which, again, may benign Providence avert— Our first-born son Joseph, King of the Romans, should die without sons begotten in lawful wedlock, or there should be among his issue in the male line no legitimate male descendants, then Our son King Charles or his lawful (not legitimized) male issue in the male line shall succeed, also according to primogeniture, also in those of Our other Hereditary Kingdoms and Lands which were at that date in possession of Our first-born son or of his lawful male issue, and in respect of the surviving Princesses the principle laid down above shall be observed, that their right of succession and that of their male descendants of both lines in all Kingdoms, Provinces, and Lordships belonging to Us and Our descendants shall always come after that of all legitimate male descendants in the male line of either line.

C. THE PRAGMATIC SANCTION*

His Imperial Majesty summoned all his Privy Councillors present in Vienna to appear at the usual place at ten o'clock on the nineteenth of April, 1713. When, then, the designated hour arrived, His Imperial Majesty took his place in His Privy Council Chamber, under the baldaquin, at the customary Imperial table, whereupon his Privy Councillors and Ministers were called in, these entering in their order of precedence and each standing in his place: Prince Eugene of Savoy, Prince Von Trautsohn, Prince von Schwarzen-

---

* Bernatzik, *op. cit.*, pp. 6ff.; G. Turba, *Die Pragmatische Sanktion,* Vienna, 1913, pp. 48ff.

berg, Prince von Traun, Land Marshal, Count von Thurn, Lord High Steward of Her Imperial Majesty Eleonore, Count von Dietrichstein, Master of the Horse, Count von Seilern, Court Chancellor, Count von Stahrnberg, Cameral President, Count von Martinitz, junior, Count von Herberstein, Vice-President of the Military Council, Count von Schlick, Supreme Court Chancellor in Bohemia, Count von Schönborn, Imperial Vice-Chancellor, the Archbishop of Valencia, Count von Sinzendorf, Head Chamberlain, Count von Paar, Comptroller of the Household of Her Imperial Majesty Amalia, Count von Sinzendorf, Vice-President of the Military Council, Count Nicolaus Pálffy, Chief Justice of the Kingdom of Hungary, Count Illiesházy, Hungarian Chancellor, Count Khevenhüller, Governor of Lower Austria, Count Gallas, Count von Salm, Master of the Horse to Her Imperial Majesty Amalia, Manches Romeo, Royal Spanish Privy Secretary of State, Count Kornis, Transylvanian Vice-Chancellor. Secretary, von Schlickh.

When all these Privy Councillors and Ministers were assembled, His Imperial Majesty stated that the reason and purpose of calling them together was to make known to them that certain dispositions, orders and Pacts of Succession had been concluded by and between His gracious and most honored father, the Emperor Leopold, now with God, and His well-beloved brother Joseph of glorious memory, then Roman King and afterwards also Roman Emperor, and His Imperial Majesty, at that time declared King in Spain; to which they had sworn in the presence of sundry Privy Councillors and Ministers. Since, however, few of those Councillors and Ministers were now still living, His Imperial Majesty had thought it necessary not only to make this communication to His assembled Councillors and Ministers, but also Himself to inform them and have read to them the said agreement and Pacts; His Imperial Majesty then graciously commanded His Court Chancellor, Count von Seilern, so to read them.

Thereupon the said Chancellor read out loud and clearly first the Spanish introduction to the original Deed of Acceptance signed by His then Royal Majesty, as King of Spain, now Imperial Majesty, confirmed by the attached Royal seal; then, the full contents, from beginning to end, of the Instrument of Succession signed by the Emperor Leopold and the Roman King Joseph and confirmed with the two seals, Imperial and Royal, attached, with the attached notarial appendix; and finally, again out of the Royal Spanish instrument, the acceptance and the confirmation from that side, to the end, also with the notarial appendix; which instruments are dated Vienna, September 12, 1703.

After this had been done, His Imperial Majesty made the following announcement: that the instruments which had been read out showed the true and attested disposition and the Pact of Mutual Succession, concluded for all time, between the two lines, the Josephinian and Carolean; accordingly, that besides and in addition to the Hereditary Kingdoms and Lands inherited by His Imperial Majesty from His late Imperial Majesty Leopold and Joseph of blessed memory, now, after the death of His late Majesty, His beloved brother, without male heirs, all His Hereditary Kingdoms also fell to His Imperial Majesty and all had to remain undivided in the hand of His legitimate male heirs, according to the law of primogeniture, so long as such existed.

On the extinction of the male line, which may God be pleased to avert, they come similarly undivided to His legitimate daughters, again according to the law and order of primogeniture. Further, in default or extinction of all legitimate descendants, male or female, of His Imperial Majesty, this hereditary right to all Kingdoms and Lands undivided devolves on the daughters of His Imperial Majesty, His Majesty's dear brother Joseph and their legitimate descendants, again similarly in primogeniture, and by the same right and order their Archducal wives must enjoy all other advantages and precedences of their rank.

It being always understood that after the two lines, the Carolean now ruling and thereafter, the female representatives of the Josephinian line, all rights of succession and all that appertains thereto devolve, belong, and are reserved to the sisters of His Imperial Majesty and all other lines of the most august Arch House, according to the right of primogeniture, in the order dictated thereby.

And seeing that this perpetual Disposition, order, and Pact, regarded and established to the honor of God and the preservation of all Hereditary Lands, was also affirmed by His Imperial Majesty's bodily oath, beside and together with that of his late father and his beloved brother; so will His Imperial Majesty constantly observe it, and His Majesty has also been pleased to instruct His Privy Councillors and Ministers and also graciously warned and commanded them that they shall no less be mindful and diligent to observe, maintain and defend the said Pact and Disposition; as then His Imperial Majesty has to this end released His Privy Councillors and Ministers from the obligation of silence on this point.

Whereupon His Imperial Majesty withdrew, as did the Privy Councillors and Ministers after him.

That this is a true record of these events and proceedings I testify with the signature of my own hand and my customary seal.

Vienna, April 19, 1713
(signed) GEORGE FRIEDRICH VON SCHLICKH, Lower Austrian Privy Secretary and Recorder of His Imperial Majesty, the Roman Emperor, appointed for this purpose Notary Public by Imperial and Archducal authority.

D. EXTRACT FROM THE HUNGARIAN LAWS OF 1712–15*

Law III, 2

By which most gracious Royal declaration on the clause "as the King and the assembled Estates shall agree on the interpretation and application of the laws" he [the king] has given the said Estates of the Realm sufficient assurances against any truncation of the country and against submitting it to a form of government akin to that of other Provinces.

E. THE HUNGARIAN IMPLEMENTING LEGISLATION, 1721–22†

[Law I, after the usual preamble dilating on the Estates' gratitude and devotion to the king, goes on to express their especial thanks:]

1. Because, when the female line also of the most august House of Austria, up to the extinction of it and its posterity, was by the unanimous and free suffrage of all Estates of the Realm of Hungary and its attached Parts declared entitled to the Royal Crown of Hungary and to all Parts, Kingdoms and Provinces appertaining

* *Magyar Törvénytár*, Vol. I, p. 480.
† *Magyar Törvénytár*, Vol. I, pp. 526ff.

thereto, and this was conveyed by a Deputation to His Sacred Imperial and Royal Majesty in Vienna

2. He not only deigned to accept so benevolently, courteously and graciously this offer, and the respectful and salutary wishes of His faithful Estates

3. But also declared His will that this order of succession in respect of the Holy Crown of Hungary and the Parts, Kingdoms, and Provinces attached thereto should be regulated, kept, and assured by the same law of primogeniture as for the male sex and according to the order determined, fixed, proclaimed, and accepted by His Majesty in His Hereditary Lands and Provinces in and outside Germany, indivisibly, the male sex enjoying precedence within the same grade of affinity,

4. So that that female or her male heir who shall succeed to the said Kingdoms and Provinces of the most august House of Austria shall, according to the said order of primogeniture accepted in the most august House of Austria, according to the same hereditary right of succession, for this and for all future cases, be recognized and crowned as undoubted King of Hungary and of the Parts, Kingdoms, and Provinces appertaining thereto, which are equally to be understood as indivisible.[1]

Law II

[This Law again begins with a preamble, followed by a number of introductory paragraphs expressing the correct sentiments of the Estates. These lead on to the substantive paragraphs, 5 to 7, as follows:]

5. In case of the extinction of the male line of His Most Sacred Imperial and Royal Majesty (which may God be pleased to avert), the succession in Hungary and the Parts, Kingdoms, and Provinces appertaining thereto, already recovered or, with the help of God, to be recovered in the future, shall pass also to the female line of the august House of Austria; in the first place, to the line of His august Imperial and Royal Majesty now ruling,

6. Thereafter, should that line fail, to that of the Emperor and King Joseph, of blessed memory

7. And should that fail also, to the issue of the loins of Leopold

---

[1] An important phrase, by which the Hungarians safeguarded themselves against any separatist moves, especially from Croatia.

of blessed memory, Emperor and King of Hungary and to their successors of either sex, being legitimate, Roman Catholic and Archdukes or Archduchesses of Austria, conformably with the order of primogeniture laid down by His Sacred Majesty now ruling for his other Kingdoms and Hereditary Provinces inside and outside Germany, according to the above rule and order, to be possessed of hereditary right, ruled and administered indivisibly and inseparably, mutually and simultaneously and together with the Kingdom of Hungary and the Parts, Kingdoms, and Provinces annexed thereto.

8. And they approve the said order of succession.

9. And they establish the female succession, as described above, as it has been introduced and recognized in the most august House of Austria (now extending it thereto, and thereby replacing Laws II and III of 1687 and also Laws II and III of 1715) according to the above order.

10. And they lay down that it is to be accepted and ratified by the Archdukes or Archduchesses of Austria, deriving through the female line of the most august House of Austria, which shall be declared heirs and successors in the aforesaid manner, on the occasion of the coronation, to be observed for all time, together with the aforesaid Diplomas, likewise most graciously confirmed in the aforesaid manner by His Most Sacred Imperial and Royal Majesty, and other Liberties and Prerogatives, previously recited, of the Estates of the Realm and of the Parts, Kingdoms, and Provinces annexed thereto, according to the sense of the Laws quoted above.

11. And only in the case of the complete extinction of the said line do they reserve the inherited, ancient, approved, and recognized right of the Estates in respect of the election and coronation of their Kings.

Law III

1. His Most Sacred Imperial and Royal Majesty hereby graciously confirms all charters and other rights, liberties and privileges, immunities, prerogatives, laws already enacted, and recognized customs (in accordance with Laws I and II of the present Diet, which are to be understood in the sense of Laws I, II, and III of 1715 and the form of oath contained there) and will observe them.

2. Similarly His Majesty's successors, lawfully crowned to be Kings of Hungary and its annexed Parts, will preserve the Estates of the Kingdom and its annexes in the same privileges and said immunities and laws, inviolate.

3. Furthermore, His Sacred Imperial and Royal Majesty will secure enforcement of all these things in respect also of His other subjects, without regard to Estate, rank, or position.

12. Maria Theresa's Political Testament

The document which follows, popularly known as "Maria Theresa's Political Testament"—and obviously intended as such—was discovered by the historian Alfred Von Arneth in the Austrian archives and published by him in 1871 in the *Archiv für Oesterreiche Geschichte*. It was reprinted in book form in 1962, with an introduction by J. Kallbrunner and linguistic explanations by C. Biener.[1] The document bears no date, but internal evidence shows it to have been composed around the turn of the year 1749/50.[2]

According to the pundits, the document is not by the empress's own hand, "but composed at her orders, with her most direct participation, by a person most close in her confidence."[3] If this is so, the work of the other hand, except in respect of the appendices to which occasional allusion is made,[4] can have amounted to little more than taking down the empress's dictation, for the whole document is essentially personal —not only, it may be said, in its psychology, but also in its highly individual vocabulary and syntax.

It is, indeed, the self-portrait that emerges from its pages which gives them their unique human interest and much of their importance, since Maria Theresa's personal character was, after all, one of the major determining factors in European history for a long generation. Her piety, her common sense, and her resolution, to all of which the document bears speaking testimony, governed her actions and thereby the fate of the monarchy and of Europe. But the document is also one of great historical importance. The reforms which she describes are, of

---

[1] *Maria Theresias Politisches Testament* (Vienna, 1952).

[2] See p. 126. "My greatest difficulties are at present with Italy, but Count Pallavicini still hopes, etc." Pallavicini was appointed governor of Lombardy in October, 1750.

[3] Kallbrunner, p. 21.

[4] These are not reproduced here. They were not attached to the document when discovered by Arneth, although two of them have since come to light.

course on record elsewhere, more fully and sometimes more accurately —for her recollection was not always faultless—but only here do we get an entirely faithful account of the motives which impelled her to carry through those reforms, and an uniquely unvarnished picture of the conditions that confronted her on her accession.

A full annotation of the document, sufficient to make every allusion in it clear to persons unacquainted with the history of the period, would require a volume in itself, and in the following pages we have confined ourselves to the indispensable minimum of exegitical notes; but readers may find it convenient to be reminded most briefly of the political and financial organization of the monarchy when Maria Theresa ascended the throne.

The earlier understanding had been that the crown "lived of its own," financing its own requirements out of the crown lands and other revenues collected and administered by the "Camera," or "Hof-kammer." The provinces, which were organized in "Estates," looked after their own needs. This system had, however, ceased to be workable with the introduction of standing armies, thereafter administered by the central Hofkriegsrat, which made superfluous the local militias with which earlier sovereigns had carried on their wars. In lieu of this service (incompletely in Hungary, the Tirol, and the Military Frontier) the Estates now provided a "contributio," or war tax, the bulk of which was levied on the villein peasants. The Estates were, however, still nominally entitled to query or even refuse the "contributio," and although pressure could be put on them, they were, as the document shows, often reluctant and inadequate payers. The monarchical authority was further weakened by the fact that it possessed no unified political machinery. It transacted its affairs with the Estates through chancelleries, of which there were four: the "Austrian" (only recently created by the amalgamation of several smaller bodies, but now responsible for all the "German-Austrian" Lands); the Bohemian (for the Lands of the Bohemian Crown—Bohemia, Moravia, Silesia; the head of this office bore the title of "Supreme Chancellor" [*Oberster Kanzler*]); the Hungarian, and the Transylvanian.[5] Foreign affairs were in charge of the Austrian court chancellery until 1742, when Maria Theresa (she does not refer here to this reform) established a separate Court and State Chancellery, reducing the Austrian Court Chancellor's agenda to the internal affairs of his group of provinces, and thus depriving him of the *de facto* precedence that he had previously enjoyed; without, however, conferring on the new court and state chancellor any powers outside his own field. The monarch had thus no effective prime minister whatever.

Although by the end of 1749 Maria Theresa had carried through a number of reforms, she dwells in this document chiefly on two, both, indeed, of the first importance, and both due to the genius of Count

[5] The Netherlands and Lombardy corresponded through sections of the Austrian chancellery.

Haugwitz. One was to persuade the Estates of her Austrian and Bohemian Lands to accept a fixed "contributio," determined decennially, and unalterable for that period. This involved a substantially higher payment than had previously been exacted, and in order to meet it, the nobles agreed that their demesne lands should be subject to taxation (this was not imposed on Hungary, where Maria Theresa had, on her coronation, sworn to accept for all time the nobles' exemption from taxation). In return, they were relieved of various expenses to which they had previously been subject in connection with the billeting, provisioning, etc., of troops quartered in their provinces. The second was the amalgamation of the Austrian and Bohemian court chancelleries, the transference to them of the Cameral agenda for those groups of provinces, and the parallel establishment, for both groups of provinces, of an *"Oberste Justizstelle,"* serving at once as Ministry of Justice and Supreme Court of Appeal. The judicial and administrative services were thus separated, but the financial was united with the latter. It may be remarked that this last measure was, in spite of Maria Theresa's injunctions to her descendants, revoked by herself some years later.

Fuller descriptions of these reforms may be found in the biographies of Maria Theresa, the best of which are the old but exhaustive life by Alfred von Arneth (10 vols., Vienna, 1863–79) and the shorter but excellent work of H. Kretschmayer (Vienna, 1925, 2nd edn., 1938); also in F. Walter, *Die Geschichte der oesterreichichischen Zentralverwaltung unter Maria Theresia*, II/1/1 (Vienna, 1938) and in a brilliant short account by the same writer, *Die theresianische Staatsreform von 1749* (Munich, 1950).

There are, in fact, two of these "Testaments," of which the second, composed a few years later, is more coherent and although shorter in some respects, more complete, because less repetitive. We have, however, chosen the earlier of the two to translate, in spite of its diffuseness and frequent repetitions, because it is, of the two, the more personal (the hand of the collaborator is more apparent in the second) and because most of the famous passages quoted by later historians come from it. It must be admitted that the translator's work is not easy: there are sentences that run to whole paragraphs, most loosely strung together, and some passages, even one or two words, have defeated the two latest editors, although one is a historian, the other a linguist, and both Viennese. In a few cases the present translator has been reduced to guessing the exact purpose of some clause, although he believes himself always to have given the general meaning.

First Memorandum

INSTRUCTIONS DRAWN up out of motherly solicitude for the especial benefit of my posterity. I have thought well to divide these in sections according to their importance.

The first describes the situation of the Monarchy, both internal and international, as I found it when I began my reign.

The second, the abuses which had gradually crept into the said Monarchy under my predecessors.

The third, the measures introduced during the nine difficult years of the recent war, and the reasons which induced me to take them.

The fourth, the changes effected after the conclusion of general peace[1] in the internal constitution of the Ministries and the Provinces, in accordance with the system established for the preservation of the Monarchy.

The fifth, the benefit that will accrue to my posterity from this reorganization, this being the only means of consolidating the Monarchy and preserving it for my posterity.

The sixth, the necessity of maintaining the institutions so established, to avert ruin, and what maxims my successors must follow to achieve this end.

When the unexpected and lamentable death of my father of blessed memory occurred,[2] this being especially painful for me because I not only loved and honored him as a father, but, no less than the least of his vassals, looked on him as my lord, and thus felt a double loss and grief, and was at the time the more devoid of the experience and knowledge needful to rule dominions so extensive and so various because my father had never been pleased to initiate or inform me in the conduct of either internal or foreign affairs, I found myself suddenly without either money, troops, or counsel.

I had no experience in seeking such counsel, and my natural

[1] The "general peace" concluding the War of the Austrian Succession was that of Aix-la-Chapelle, October, 1746, by which Austria concluded peace with France and Spain. Peace with Prussia had, however, been concluded under the Treaty of Dresden, signed on December 25, 1745, under which Maria Theresa acknowledged the cession to Frederick of Prussia of the parts of Silesia occupied by him, in return for his promise of recognition of Maria Theresa's husband, Francis Stephen, as emperor. Peace with Bavaria had come even earlier (April 22, 1745) after the death of the elector (later emperor) who had joined Maria Theresa's enemies in 1741; his son then renounced his claims to the throne of Austria, promised his vote to Francis Stephen in the forthcoming imperial election, and in return, was given back Bavaria.

[2] Charles VI, Maria Theresa's father, died suddenly on October 20, 1740, aged only fifty-four.

great timidity and diffidence, born of this inexperience, itself made the choice of this most necessary advice and information particularly difficult; as in the last ten unhappy years of His Majesty my father's reign I had only heard, like any other private person, the distress and laments which reached the public without knowing whence and why they came, since at that time everything was not, as it is today, put on the Ministers. I therefore resolved not to conceal my ignorance, but to listen to each in his own department and thus to inform myself properly. Count Sinzendorff,[3] the Court Chancellor, was a great Minister, and later I came to feel his loss more deeply, but he did not possess my confidence. Count Starhemberg[4] possessed it completely, and I venerated him greatly, although he had not so much political insight as the other. The former initiated me and informed me of all matters from the outset, but the latter possessed my full confidence. This went on quite smoothly and well until the arrival of Kinsky,[5] who, with the best intentions, so distracted me and led me into such unrest and confusion that I quite lost this tranquillity and brought much chagrin on myself.

At this juncture I got to know Bartenstein,[6] who was brought to my notice by the Counts Starhemberg and Herberstein.[7] At first I was strongly prejudiced against him, but then found him to be—as all who really know him must agree—a great statesman. Afterward I made much use of him to smooth out my tangles in the Ministry and to speak to one and the other, which, however, led me ever and again into fresh mazes and obscurities, so that presently I often became, contrary to my nature, undecided and mistrustful, and had God Himself not drawn a line by their all dying,[8] I should never have been able to remedy this, for I pre-

[3] Ludwig Philipp, Graf von Sinzendorff, b. 1671, was from 1706 Austrian court chancellor, and thus in charge of foreign policy.

[4] Gundacker Thomas, Graf Starhemberg, b. 1663. President of the Hofkammer from 1703, founder (1703) and subsequent manager of the "Wiener Stadtbank."

[5] Philipp Josef Graf Kinsky, b. 1700, Bohemian court chancellor in 1738.

[6] Johann Christian Bartenstein, b. Strasburg 1689, of bourgeois origin, a convert to Catholicism, from 1726, privy secretary of state and confidential adviser to Charles VI.

[7] Ferdinand Leopold, Graf Herberstein, b. 1695, from 1735 comptroller of the household of Maria Theresa.

[8] Sinzendorff died in 1742, Starhemberg in 1745, Kinsky in 1749, Herberstein in 1744, and of persons mentioned below, Khevenhüller in 1744, Harrach in 1749.

ferred to suffer myself rather than to take violent decisions injurious to the honor and reputation of others—easily understandable, for these were all simply individual unpleasantnesses for me and they themselves all meant honorably; only they would not agree with each other, mostly out of ambition and because each wanted to have the bigger hand and voice in things. This mentality of theirs did affect policy, but never stopped me from deciding against them on central issues, in which Bartenstein gave me invaluable support and knew how to work on men's minds, which was why I depended very greatly on his advice and presentation of affairs and how he came to enjoy so much credit in my eyes, which he never abused, so that he was really my adviser in chief when I came to the throne.

From the outset I decided and made it my principle, for my own inner guidance, to apply myself, with a pure mind and instant prayer to God, to put aside all secondary considerations, arrogance, ambition, or other passions, having on many occasions examined myself in respect of these things, and to undertake the business of government incumbent on me quietly and resolutely— a principle that has, indeed, been the one guidance which saved me, with God's help, in my great need, and made me follow the resolutions taken by me, making it ever my chief maxim in all I did and left undone to trust only in God, Whose almighty hand singled me out for this position without move or desire of my own and Who would therefore also make me worthy through my conduct, principles, and intentions to fulfill properly the tasks laid on me, and thus to call down and preserve His almighty protection for myself and those He has set under me, which truth I had held daily before my eyes and maturely considered that my duty was not to myself personally but only to the public.

After I had each time well tested my intentions by this principle, I afterwards undertook each enterprise with great determination and strong resolution, and was consequently tranquil in my spirit in the greatest extremity as though the issue did not affect me personally at all; and with the same tranquillity and pleasure, had Divine Providence so disposed, I would instantly have laid down the whole government and left it to the enemies who so beset me, had I believed that in so doing I should be doing my duty or promoting the best welfare of my lands, which two points have always been my chief maxims. And dearly as I love my family and children, so that I spare no effort, trouble,

care, or labor for their sakes, yet I would always have put the
general welfare of my dominions above them had I been convinced in my conscience that I should do this or that their welfare demanded it, seeing that I am the general and first mother
of the said dominions.

I found myself in this situation, without money, without credit,
without army, without experience and knowledge of my own
and finally, also without any counsel, because each one of them
at first wanted to wait and see what way things would develop.
This was my position when I was attacked by the King of
Prussia.[9] This King's sweet words and vehement protestations misled even my Ministers, because they were unable and unwilling to
believe that the King of Prussia would act as an enemy. The
confidence of my Ministers, especially of Sinzendorff, and my
own inexperience and good faith were the reason why the defensive
preparations in Silesia, and the reinforcement of the garrison there
by neighboring units, were largely neglected and the King in
Prussia was thus left a free hand to overrun the Duchy of Silesia
within six weeks.

Cotter[10] was sent here by the King of Prussia when the latter
had already reached Glogau, and soon after actually took Breslau.
He proposed that I should cede all Silesia to his master, when he
would immediately guarantee his help against all other claims to
the succession, and also to secure the election of my dear husband
to the Imperial Crown. Some of my Ministers—Sinzendorff, Harrach[11] and Kinsky—advised treating with the King; the other
Ministers, Starhemberg and Bartenstein, with whom I agreed,
argued that the cession of any territory, even if only of a few
Principalities, would be the more prejudicial to the dispositions
of the Pragmatic Sanction because all the other Powers, as guar-
antors, would regard themselves as the less obliged to give a
further guarantee because we should ourselves have broken the
indivisible succession by concluding the treaty with Prussia, while
the King, as soon as he had received part of Silesia by agreement,
would probably claim the rest, or at least the greater part of it,

---

[9] Frederick made his first démarches immediately on Charles's death; his
invasion of Silesia began in December, 1740.

[10] Prussian minister to Vienna.

[11] Friedrich August, Graf Harrach, b. 1696, viceroy of the Netherlands in
1712, succeeded Kinsky in Bohemia in 1745.

as proportionate return for his help. The event proved that we were right and that the King's object was to acquire the whole of Silesia.

The misfortune was that after I had resolved to repel the impact of Prussia's unjust force with just counter-force, dissidence and faction at once struck root among my Ministers, due exclusively to my own excessive goodness of heart and wish to do the best for all and to believe the best. And would to God I had been alone with Sinzendorff and Starhemberg, with Bartenstein; then much would have been avoided and averted. I must put this rather more fully. Sinzendorff was a great statesman, far superior to Starhemberg, but not always without *arrières pensées*, prejudices, and passions; I was never able to prove anything against him so long as he was serving me, yet his conduct with regard to Prussia was not always regular, and warnings against him which I received were the reason why I put my whole confidence in Starhemberg, who was a great man and a straightforward German. But he could never forget that under my father Sinzendorff had edged him out, and he tried to recover his old place under me, although never in a way that was dishonest or smacked of intrigue. He and Herberstein, who was at that time the Comptroller of my Household, and a thoroughly honest and capable man, introduced Bartenstein to me, against whom I had been strongly prejudiced when I came to the throne, but must in justice acknowledge that I owe to him alone the preservation of the Monarchy. Without him everything would have been lost, for Starhemberg was no longer active enough by himself, and I learned only long after that it was Bartenstein alone who prevented my Spanish marriage,[12] which Sinzendorff favored; he alone devised and championed the co-Regency, advised my sister's marriage, and sought to procure everything conducive to the unity and consolidation of this dynasty, which was the foundation stone of all its being. I will not say that he had no faults: these arose out of his temperament, certainly not out of any lack of loyalty and zeal, nor out of ambition; for that I can vouch, and it is my duty toward him and his for all time to do so, as a duty, not a grace. I have had to set this down for my own satisfaction,

[12] The plan, long favored in court circles, of marrying Maria Theresa to the infante of Spain, Don Carlos. Maria Theresa had insisted on marrying the husband of her choice.

to do these three Ministers justice, seeing that all evil arose solely out of their dissensions.

In the first, difficult years of my reign it was quite impossible for me personally to investigate the conditions and resources of the Provinces, so that I was obliged to follow my Ministers' advice not to ask any more help from the Provinces, either in money or men, especially since the Ministers constantly pretended that any such demands would make my reign deeply detested at its very outset. Consequently, there was no money to mobilize the few regiments earmarked for use against Prussia. And when I found myself forced to ask for this purpose for some hundreds of thousands as loans or urgent grants in aid from private persons, I could not but see that the big men, and even the Ministers themselves, were plainly trying to spare their own pockets.

In general, the man chiefly responsible—in all innocence—for the sluggish and lukewarm defense arrangements was Kinsky, Supreme Chancellor of Bohemia on my accession, who especially set himself to persuade me, and did convince me, because it was undeniable, that the Bohemians were always overreached by the Austrians; and he made such an impression on me by his arguments and by many old documents and proofs which he produced, that I took him into the Ministry, against everyone's advice, with the laudable intention of proving myself the true mother of all the peoples under me.

Hardly had this been done when the vehemence of Kinsky's temperament became entirely uncontrollable. And although at first I flattered myself that my move would have good results, it presently became clear that all my hopes had been vain, for Kinsky was openly prejudiced in favor of his own nation, devoting all his efforts to getting advantages for it, and consequently simply acted as advocate of the Provinces in his charge and attacked all the others, alleging that his object was to establish an ideal proportion between the Bohemian and Austrian Provinces, under which the latter should pay more, and the former less.

This produced a deep enough split between Ministers, services, and peoples, which I did not notice early enough, and later, when it became very acute, did not deal with resolutely enough, because I was too good-hearted—moreover, the situation was very ticklish —but only applied palliatives, which only made matters worse. This was, in fact, the beginning of the trouble, for although I must pay all tribute to Kinsky's honesty and loyalty, it is certain that his temperament, vehemence, passions, and local feeling were the real sources and causes of the whole calamity, and carried away Kinsky himself, contrary to his own intentions, because when the war was carried into the Bohemian Provinces he refused to allow them to be flooded by too many troops, always expecting that we should be too much for the Prussians; moreover, the movement of the weak regiments quartered on the Turkish and Transylvanian frontiers proceeded very slowly, as the whole dispositions in those Provinces were extremely sluggish.

Matters got worse and worse, and owing to the division between the Provinces, none of the Ministers was really trying to rescue me and the State from this terrible embarrassment. At first, all proposals of nature to inflict the smallest hardship on any Province were immediately rejected by the officials in charge of that Province, and everyone cared only for his own interest, and I was not able to oppose this, knowing too little of the situation.

Khevenhüller[13] and Neipperg[14] were proposed for commanders of the force to be sent against the Prussians, but the former asked for many regiments and assured money for their pay. Neipperg's appointment was canvassed by the Supreme Chancellor of Bohemia, that is, the man who had undertaken to supply the army, and he refused to have anything to do with Khevenhüller. I therefore decided for Neipperg, especially as no one questioned his experience in the field.

Neipperg contented himself with a few very weak regiments, which he picked himself, as he did the Generals, with the result that some regiments were ordered up from very long distances, while others, much nearer at hand, were left in their stations.

I flattered myself that the good relations between the General commanding and the Chancellor in charge of provisioning the army would be very profitable, but this good understanding was very quickly broken.

It is true that Neipperg had no more than 14,000 combatant troops under him, but he thought that would suffice, and on the one hand, there was no money to mobilize more regiments, since

---

[13] Ludwig Andreas, Graf Khevenhüller, b. 1683, field marshal in 1737.
[14] Wilhelm Reinhard Neipperg, b. 1684, general in 1735. Had actually been impeached and imprisoned for his unfortunate conduct of the campaign against the Turks in 1738/1739, but was released and rehabilitated.

no demands at all were to be made of the Provinces, the Chancellor, by an unbelievable error, believing that the Provinces could not provision a larger number of troops without ruining themselves; on the other hand, although Count Uhlfeld,[15] in Turkey, assured me that no danger threatened from that quarter, the Ministers were not entirely satisfied that the very recent peace would prove quite stable, and for that reason, and also out of mistrust of the Hungarians themselves,[16] thought it inadvisable to take too many troops away from the Turkish frontier.

The general opinion was that this small force would be a match for the inexperienced Prussian army.[17]

Some of the Ministers made no concealment of their wish to sit down and reach agreement with Prussia at any moment, at the first opportunity that presented itself, whether things in Silesia went well or ill. The hope of defeating Prussia was the more reasonable because we had good grounds for hoping that we could gain the assistance of Saxony and Hanover, and there was still a possibility of getting that of Russia.

The former hope would probably have been realized if the campaign in Silesia had been undertaken at the outset with larger forces, and more caution. But the factors mentioned above made the Ministers lukewarm. My notes on the later campaign in Bavaria will be found in the annexe.[18]

I was beginning to appreciate the mistakes which the Ministry had made in my father's lifetime; nevertheless, although I made every effort to read the mind of each of them, I yet did not venture to oppose them directly on such important issues, especially since I knew how inexperienced I was. I rather tried to reconcile the differences and to achieve the greatest measure of common agreement possible. I did not always succeed in this—sometimes the opposite—but this was what I tried to bring about in the most important deliberations.

---

[15] Corfiz Anton, Graf Uhlfeld, b. 1699, appointed in 1738 ambassador to the Porte (made head of the Geheime Haus und Hofkanzlei on its creation in 1742, thus in practice succeeding Sinzendorff as foreign minister).

[16] The editors of the 1952 edition interpret this sentence as meaning that "the Hungarians, too, mistrusted the Turks," but the parallel passage in the second Testament shows the meaning to be as I give it.

[17] The Prussian army was spendidly picked and drilled, but had in fact hardly seen active service since 1735.

[18] Has not been found.

But these difficulties proved insurmountable because, under the Constitution as it then stood, each Minister played, as it were, the lord and master in the department under his charge, used his power to thwart any opposition and followed only the course which seemed good to him or agreed with his preconceived opinion.

I did, indeed, at once perceive this long-standing and deep-rooted abuse, which was present in practically every department, but hard as I fought against it, all my efforts were vain, and the situation at the time forbade me from forcibly remedying it at once.

Most of these Ministers had acquired great prestige, at home and abroad, in my father's day, and their long service and their own merits had brought them much experience and had also won them the respect and confidence of the public. I needed their experience, and most of them were Ministers of long standing, of undeniable merit, and honorable men. I could not do without them in those critical days without making matters worse still, and was consequently unable to rid myself at once of their excessive ascendancy, so that I had perforce to leave matters as they then stood, until times should become easier.

This brings me to

Section II

viz., to the abuses in the Government of Austria which had gradually crept in under my predecessors.

Seeing that piety is that basic principle in virtue whereof a Prince may hope to receive God's blessing, which my forbears had also most diligently pursued to the immortal glory of their memories—and so visibly was God's grace and His mighty support manifested in the extreme dangers which threatened the Monarchy with ruin, that the greater the danger, the more marvelous was the help that came from God, and I myself manifestly owe to it my whole salvation, and have further perceived, in the many quite extraordinary tribulations which pressed on me, how, trusting faithfully in Divine Providence I was in no wise left unaided— I cannot therefore do otherwise than enjoin my successors, for their good, to follow most carefully the example of their forbears, and consequently on every occasion, above all else and at all times to set their whole confidence on God and on the hope of His mighty support, and in all things to keep a pure and uncorrupt mind.

By this I do not mean Pharisaicalness and hypocrisy unaccompanied by true diligence, work and care for the State and for the general good.

Here I will say a few words about my predecessors. Their great piety led them to donate many—most—of the Cameral estates and revenues, which at that time served good purpose in supporting religion and improving the position of the clergy. Since, however, God has now so blessed us in the German Hereditary Lands that both the Catholic religion is most flourishing and the condition of the clergy is good and assured, this principle no longer holds good.[19] And it would not merely not be laudable, but would in my view rather be culpable to give and cede more to the clergy, for, firstly, they do not need it, and secondly, they do not— alas!—apply what they have as they should, and moreover, they constitute a heavy burden on the public. For no monastic House observes the limitations of its statutes, and many idlers are admitted; all of this will call for a great reform, which I propose to carry out in good time and after due consideration.[20]

I except, however, from such measures the Kingdom of Hungary, where much still remains to be done for religion, in which task I shall require the clergy there to cooperate, but not work with them alone, but concert chiefly with laymen on the principles to be followed, the chief aim of which must be to introduce seminaries, colleges, academies, hospitals for the sick and injured, conservatories, as in Italy, for unmarried women, for the better instruction of the young, etc., taking careful pains to support and develop what is useful to the public, and not what profits the private advantage of the clergy, monks, and nuns in any Province, it being well understood that even this salutary intention cannot be realized until the military has been put completely on the footing necessary to secure the preservation of the Monarchy and the welfare of its Provinces and subjects.

I must also say something of the Crown revenues, out of which

---

[19] A justly famous passage. The Catholic Church was in fact in possession at this time of enormous estates in Austria.

[20] Maria Theresa never got down to carrying through any very radical reforms in this field; very drastic reforms were, however, enacted immediately after her death by her son (see below, Docs. C–H)

the requirements of the Court and the Embassies have to be met as is proper and necessary, and also of the public debt,[21] on which the preservation of the Monarchy also depends, and without which no State can exist. When these necessities of State have been met, it is a Prince's duty to devote all his resources to the welfare and relief of his lands and subjects, and of the poor among them; not to waste the money coming in on frivolities, pomp and display.

And although I shall probably not live to see that happy day, yet I hope by constant laborious effort, care and toil to set affairs in such a state that in fifty years, or perhaps even earlier, the results will, with God's blessing, be showing themselves;[22] and I rely confidently on my successors to continue in this path, adhering faithfully to the principles of virtue, piety, justice, and fatherly love, mercy and care for their lands and subjects, which I have tried to inculcate in them in their youth. Should—which God forbid—this not occur, I would wish and earnestly pray to God that if foreigners and even enemies were more deserving and cared better for their lands, it were a thousand times better they should have them.

But to come back to my forbears: not only did they give away most of the Crown estates, but on top of this, they took on themselves the debts of the properties confiscated in times of rebellion, a burden from which the exchequer is still not yet free. The Emperor Leopold found not much left to give away, but owing, presumably, to the large-scale wars of his reign, such Crown estates as remained were pledged and farmed out, and there came no improvement under his successors, so that the yield of the Crown revenues when I came to the throne hardly amounted to 80,000 gulden; moreover, under my forbears the Ministers received big emoluments from the Emperors themselves and from the Provinces, because not only did they succeed in making flattering appeals to the well-known liberality, grace, and Austrian munificence, representing to each what fame his predecessors had acquired thereby, but also, since they usually possessed the ear of the Prince and of the clergy, got everything

[21] This amounted in 1740 to 101 million gulden, largely owed abroad.
[22] For a convenient short description of these measures by a modern writer, see G. Otruba, *Die Wirtschaftspolitik Maria Theresias* (Vienna, 1963), pp. 21ff.

that they wanted. Their prestige became such that they were more feared and honored in their Provinces than the Prince himself. And when, in the end, the Crown's resources began to dry up, these Ministers turned for remuneration to the Provinces, in which they achieved enormous authority. And when at last complaints reached the Princes, yet they, out of goodness of heart and patience, let the practices go on awhile unchecked.

And although the possibilities of big donations had in this way been largely exhausted, yet under Joseph and Charles the Ministers took advantage of every opportunity to enrich themselves or their kinsfolk through donations or concessions.

Under all these Emperors, the position and prestige of these Ministers was unshakable because each Minister in practice played the sovereign in the department assigned to him. Such Ministers almost always, in any Province, enjoyed a free hand in dealing with the Estates; the Minister in charge of a Province was usually the biggest landowner in it and thus enjoyed the greatest respect and authority among the Estates, and for that reason, many of them received large annual remunerations from the Estates. If then the sovereign wished to obtain from the Provinces the subsidies necessary for the maintenance of his armies and the assurance of the general welfare, he was forced to grant the Ministers, who alone were able to secure these for him, whatever grace and favor they required.

This chance now gave the Ministers such prestige that the Monarch himself thought it expedient in his own interests to support them, having learned by experience that the greater the prestige enjoyed by the men at the heads of the Provinces, the easier it was for them to get their demands accepted by the Provinces.

The merciful and gracious disposition of the House of Austria, which forbade the removal of anyone from his post unless he had proved himself totally unworthy of it, emboldened many of them actually to oppose the Monarch and his interests in the Provinces, and so the Ministers enjoyed such authority that they flattered themselves that they were to be regarded not as mere "Ministers," as at other Courts, but as co-regents or at least as *pares curiae*.[22a]

[22a] This seems to be an allusion to the position of the French "*paires du Royaume*"; but the phrase is obscure.

The Emperor Leopold was the first of my forbears who kept a firm grip on his sovereign authority and insisted on maintaining it against all comers, which considerations led him often to change his Ministers and, under certain circumstances, disgrace them. But this only made the Ministers more cautious, and, since he did not change the old Constitution, he was unable to assert his authority to remedy the abuses which had crept in.

When a Minister was replaced, his successor had not, perhaps, the same prejudices, but always maintained the old main principles both of maintaining his own authority and securing advantages for his Province, so that such changes often only made matters worse. I myself have experienced cases in which such changes neither enhanced my own authority nor led to diminution of the abuses.

Such abuses really derive from two main causes: the first, the egotism and craving for power innate in most men, inasmuch as the Ministers were large landowners in their own Provinces, and for that reason even the new men followed the same principles of self-preservation and looked more to their own interest and that of their families than to the general welfare.

The other reason is that these Ministers and heads of Provinces represented the Provinces' acquired privileges and liberties to the Monarch in so formidable a light that the latter were often left powerless to safeguard the general welfare. In order somehow to get what was indispensably necessary out of the Estates, the Prince was forced to utilize the credit and prestige of his Ministers and to grant their demands with a good grace, if he was to save himself and the State from the threatened ruin.

These vaunted privileges are, when one looks at them closely, mostly founded on customary rights which were in fact only conceded tacitly and then confirmed by earlier Monarchs, which customs, in respect of their periodical confirmation, are attributable solely to the credit, prestige, and power of the Ministries, which ordinarily consisted exclusively of Estates. And since the formula of confirmation speaks expressly of "honorable, ancient customs," the maintenance of them is rightly to be understood only as applying to those ancient customs which are good, not to the bad.

It is certain that in no country would the Estates ever have developed their freedoms so far, had they not been powerfully

supported by the Ministers, since their authority and credit depended exclusively on this, and the Court was most to blame for
this, for they brought it on themselves, and were willing to give
and do anything to get money quickly; whereas, if the Prince had
not felt himself dependent on the arbitrary *yes* or *no* of the Estates,
he would not have needed to appeal to the prestige and authority
of the Ministers to get his way.

This is the real reason why the authority and prestige of the
Ministers became so inordinately high under my forbears, to the
detriment of the Princely authority, and why, so long as this central Constitution was in force, it seemed inadvisable to impair or
diminish it.

These Ministers also utilized the preferential influence which
they had acquired over the Prince to secure such favors for the
Province which was governed by them, and in which their own
estates lay, that the other Provinces were treated unfairly and
regarded, so to speak, as though they were foreign lands and
not subjects of the same lord.

This was the sole reason why, as soon as my eyes were opened,
I gradually took my steps to make a complete change in the form
of government.

The perpetual and unintermittent envy, ill-feeling, and calumnies among the Ministers led to the most injurious animosities and
consequently gave rise to incurable prejudices whereby the most
salutary measures were thwarted, or when advice was given, it
was usually colored by innumerable arbitrary prejudices, so that
the Prince was often placed in a situation of extreme embarrassment.

And while many of my forbears have been accused of dilatori-
ness and indecision in the governance of their Provinces and
State, the sole true reason for this was the constant disharmony
between the Ministers and the obstinate insistence of each on his
own opinion, which naturally could not fail to make the Monarch
the more undecided, because he might suppose his own opinion
to be mistaken.

This constant disunity of the Ministries, in every reign, has
often plunged the whole system into extreme danger of collapse,
from which only Divine Providence has extricated and saved our
House.

After Ferdinand had crushed the Bohemian rebellion[23] and lavished gifts and benefits on the Ministers who had remained true to him, and on others, the beneficiaries used their prestige in the new Constitution imposed on Bohemia more for the advantage of the Province than in the interest of the Monarch, although the country had been conquered by force of arms.

The office of Supreme Chancellor brought with it, in respect of the Bohemian Lands, the greatest embarrassments and the most detrimental effects for the Crown service, for the sovereign found himself hardly able to effect or enforce any measure in those Lands which seemed good to him or was advised by his other Ministers, unless the Supreme Chancellor was agreed. The natural consequence of this abuse was that the whole Chancellery showed itself readier to obey the orders of the Supreme Chancellor of the day than those of the Monarch, so that the power of the Bohemian Supreme Chancellor gradually became quite illimitable—and it was very obvious how incompatible this was with the authority and the service of the Crown.

This was exclusively the result of the indulgence and grace shown by my forbears to the great and mighty in those Provinces, although it was the same leniency and benevolence that had brought them to their high estate, especially since certain families pushed matters so far that so long as one member of them was there, these high offices always reverted to him, and thus these excessive powers were transmitted from father to son. The complete suppression of this office of Supreme Chancellor is thus most advantageous to the advancement of the service. It is true that the Bohemian Chancellery kept much better order than the Austrian, and did not lightly allow the Estates to encroach on its authority, but it itself had no scruples about keeping the internal government of the Provinces a secret from the sovereign, and seeing to it that he was not too exactly informed of it. This veil had to be drawn to prevent the Crown's financial services from interfering in the administration. And thus it was impossible to secure respect and obedience for the Crown's authority and orders without the consent of the Chancellor, and so the Supreme Chancellors were able continuously to strengthen their own influence and authority, and

[23] In 1622. The "New Constitution" is the famous *Vernewerte Landesordnung* (see above, Doc. 4).

often to exercise it to the disadvantage of the other Provinces, which applied conversely to the Austrian Provinces when their heads were more influential than the men governing Bohemia.

And since the Ministry was usually composed of more Austrian Ministers than Bohemian, the former usually predominated over the latter.

These circumstances led to a deep-rooted and unremitting hatred between the two nations, which reached such a pitch that everyone in each national Ministry, down to the lowest member or Councillor, invariably used every possible lawful device to surpass the other. The Austrian team, however, got the better of all the others and were the most overbearing of all.

This was felt especially by the Hungarians, whom the others tried to keep in permanent subjection, and also excluded members of that nation from all services. The excuse given was the disorder and rebellions which prevailed in Hungary up to the time of Charles VI. But equity and fair policy require that the black sheep should be segregated from the rest, and thus those deserving of reward should not be kept in the same condemnation as the undeserving, which must necessarily drive them to depression and despair.

Such are the proofs that the Ministers of my predecessors in no wise followed a wise policy, conducive to the advantage of the service, but only used the power-positions which they had achieved to serve their own interests, to transmit the Ministerial offices to their families and friends, and to follow the old, deep-rooted practices of their forbears.

Another abuse, very detrimental to the service, was that the heads and Presidents were paid and remunerated by the Estates at their pleasure. They consequently remained in a state of constant dependence on the Estates, the more so because they were always trained up in these false principles.

It is surprising that under these conditions my ancestors were able to entrust the preservation of the Monarchy to them.

For proof of this it is only necessary to consider the condition of the Austrian Provinces on my accession. They had always governed themselves as they pleased, the Chancellery paying little or no regard to their interests, and the secret documents and Provincial accounts show that any threat of control, however minor, was often averted by lavish remunerations and donations, a share of which was often allotted to the Prince.[24]

The chief evil was that at that time many Ministers were regarding each only the welfare of his own Province, and none of them had the courage or the will to draw down odium on himself, which aggravated the calamities that befell in the Italian and Hungarian wars the more because no Minister dared make further demands of the Province in his charge; and thus the others seized the occasion to attack him and hold him up to public contempt. So credit was hampered in every Province, and yet credit was necessary to cover requirements of the State: the exchequer had no more funds or resources to draw on or pledge, so that everything had to be raised on the credit of the Provincial war tax, which brought little or no profit to the Prince or the paying common man,[25] but great profit to a few private individuals. The long period of peace was used only to mislead the sovereign, to multiply factions, and to seek opportunity to realize the wretched Spanish plans,[26] which were brought up again and again and were strongly favored by very many Ministers and also, assuredly, were not displeasing to the generous sentiments of the Monarch.

Thus when war broke out, all was in the greatest confusion, without any system or idea of inner or foreign policy, and this Monarchy was consequently exposed to the most extreme danger, especially as the internal domestic debt of the Austrian Provinces then amounted to over twenty-four million, the interest on which alone came to 1.2 million, which had necessarily to be deducted from the sum paid into the war chest; and this was the more irresponsible because, to spare the landowners, most of whom paid nothing at all, the earlier contributions to the Treasury had been paid out of borrowed capital.

These disturbing conditions justified me in deciding to be more cautious in how I trusted my Ministers and Councillors.

But all my caution was in vain until I found myself forced to alter the central constitutional structure.

[24] "Often" is perhaps an exaggeration, but at least one case is on record of a *douceur* finding its way into the monarch's privy purse.

[25] As mentioned above, the demesne lands of the nobles were then untaxed, and almost all taxation was borne by the villein peasants.

[26] See above, p. 101, fn. 12.

The paralyzing disharmony between all departments was so great that I, like my predecessors, had to spend most of my time in smoothing over these wretched disputes. The Ministers were always particularly embittered against the Hofkammer, against which they made a common front, however much they disagreed between themselves.

That organ was itself a lifeless body, forsaken by everyone. It always had to procure money, while the Chancelleries most often blocked every avenue through which it could obtain it. The progressive and unmanageable indebtedness of the Treasury and the extraordinary confusion prevailing in the Hofkammer, which was often intentionally aggravated out of ulterior motives, led the Hofkammer to take various false steps, against which the Ministries and the public appealed. Yet hardly ever was a Ministry itself prepared to supply the means of covering necessary expenditure, and it seemed likely that the incessant inter-Ministerial warfare would perpetuate itself until the Monarchy collapsed, unless I tried to grasp the evil by the root. I enlarge on this subject in the following

Section III

viz., on the measures which I took during the late nine years' war and the reasons which led me to act as I did.

In my first section I described the most unhappy situation at my accession, my inexperience, and the various factions, and in the second, how I was at first unable even to see the great and long-standing weaknesses which had crept into the system, much less remedy them completely, with the result that matters reached a state of chaos whence they could never have been extricated without visible miracle and the special help of God. I have already written that I would gladly have renounced all and become Grand Duchess of Tuscany[27] had I believed such to be God's will. Since, however, He had chosen to lay on me the great burden of government, I resolved that so long as there was any help to be found, or any resources available, I would apply them, and that it was my

[27] Francis Stephen, on marrying Maria Theresa, had renounced his own patrimony of Lorraine, but had been given instead the reversion of Tuscany. This Maria Theresa afterward conferred on her second son, Leopold, as a family secondogeniture.

duty to do so. This gave me such spiritual tranquillity that
I watched my own fate as though it had been a stranger's, and
felt so little hate against my enemies that I grieved for the unhappy
fate and death of the Bavarian Emperor[28] and for the cold and
discomfort endured by the French at the siege of Prague, and
equally for the Prussians, but not for the King of Prussia, whom
I did not, indeed, hate, but felt no sympathy for him since he never
needed it, but always detested his false character.

Such was my state of mind during the war, up to the Peace of
Dresden.[29] I have made Bartenstein draw up a careful account of
the whole development of affairs during this time, both political
and internal, and have gone through it carefully, both for my
own future justification, and for the instruction of my successor,
that he may know the real history of events, about which there
has been and still is so much discussion and search, and scrutiny
of the records of the time will show why such and such was done,
often necessarily. For every government is criticized by its successor.

Up to the Peace of Dresden I acted boldly, shrank from no
risk, and spared no effort, for besides my motives of principle, as
set out above, I had another spur, to wit, the conviction that no
more unhappy fate could befall my poor dominions than to fall
into Prussian hands; indeed, had I not been nearly always *enceinte*,
no one could have stopped me from taking the field personally
against my perjured enemy. But God willed it otherwise and it is
easy to imagine, seeing with what love and tenderness I cared for
my dominions, even placing them above myself and my children,
how intolerably painful it must be to me to bear their—I will not
say hatred, but—ingratitude.

And when I saw that I must put my hand to the Peace of
Dresden, my state of mind suddenly changed, and I directed my
whole attention to internal problems and to devising how the
German Hereditary Lands could still be preserved and protected
against two so mighty enemies, Prussia and the Turk, lacking
fortresses and ready money, and with weakened armies.

The high policy of this House changed completely;[30] formerly

[28] See p. 97, fn. 1.
[29] *Ibid.*
[30] An allusion to the famous *"renversement d'alliances,"* advised and subsequently carried through by Kaunitz, under which Austria abandoned

it was directed toward holding the balance of power against France. Now there was no more thought of that, only of internal consolidation, so that the Netherlands and Italy were no longer a reason to prolong the war; the objective had to be get well out of it, at any cost.

This was the reason why I concluded the Peace of Aix-la-Chapelle so quickly. And after the Peace of Dresden my one endeavor was to inform myself of the situation and resources of each Province, and then to acquire a thorough understanding and picture of the abuses which had crept into them and their administrative services, resulting in the utmost confusion and distressfulness. Those who ought to have enlightened me on this were either unable or unwilling to do so.

Here, too, I am all-indebted to Bartenstein, who helped me greatly and lighted the true candle, following which I found certain individuals who brought me much material through the channel of my private secretary, Koch,[31] who entered my service at the same time; he also took all pains to procure me privily secret information here and in the Provinces. Koch's equal for discretion would be hard to find, and he is also uncommonly honest, Christian, and free from intrigue. He stood on the same footing with me as Tarouca,[32] who succeeded Herberstein when he died as my special confidant and adviser; furthermore, since he knew German, I made him summarize and report to me on military and Chancellery agenda and also on Provincial affairs, and also draft the decisions for me to see and approve.

In affairs of State I seldom used anyone else but followed Bartenstein alone, but I also availed myself of his counsel in all other questions, particularly my private affairs, troubles, and cares,

---

her traditional policy of hostility to France. At the council at which Maria Theresa assented to this policy, Kaunitz advised following it even if it should prove necessary to buy France's friendship with Austria's possessions in Italy and the Netherlands. At the Peace of Aix-la-Chapelle she in fact ceded Parma, Piacenza, and Guastalla to the Infante of Spain.

[31] Ignaz Koch, b. 1707, of bourgeois origin. After serving under Prince Eugene of Savoy and Charles VI he became secretary of the cabinet to Maria Theresa in 1740.

[32] Emanuel Tellez, Graf Sylva Tarouca, b. 1696 of Portuguese origin, entered the imperial army as a volunteer in 1715, created president of the Netherlands Council in 1740. Comptroller of the imperial household from 1744 to his death in 1771.

and always profited by it. My chief maxim was: if man is not true to God, what can he expect from him? He shall not be blessed.

Bartenstein and Haugwitz[33] gave me what I needed for the State and the preservation of the Monarchy. Tarouca and Koch supplied me with consolation, counsel and private information for my own knowledge and correction; and so long as I live I shall be mindful of them, their children, and their children's children for the services which they rendered to me and the State.

And I also enjoin those who come after me, ever to be mindful of their kinsfolk for all time, so long as there be any such in this world, since my chief motive in composing this record, besides that of informing my successors, is that their names should be preserved after them and their offspring receive the mede which I could not render them sufficiently.

But to come back to the true course of events, I turn to

Section IV

which shows the constitutional changes, in the Ministries and the Provinces, which I carried through after the conclusion of general peace in accordance with the system which I established for the preservation of the Monarchy.

In the preceding section I have already described the defects and abuses of the Constitution then in effect, and felt myself the more compelled to abolish it, because Divine Providence had shown me clearly that the measures essential for the preservation of the Monarchy could not be combined with these old institutions, nor put into effect while they existed.

Each one of my Ministers readily agreed that if the Crown and scepter were to be preserved, it was most necessary to keep a standing force of over 100,000 men, and consequently indispensable to bring new system and order into the extreme confusion into which the finances had fallen.

To this end, I instructed the Ministers to put their views to me in writing, and to work out such a system as speedily as

---

[33] Friedrich Wilhelm, Count Haugwitz, b. 1700, son of a Saxon general, entered Austrian service in Silesia in 1725. Remained in Austrian service after the seizure of Silesia by Prussia, first in Austrian Silesia, of which he became practically the dictator. Afterward the main author of the reforms described by Maria Theresa in the following pages. In 1760 he was, however, supplanted in most of his offices by Kaunitz. Died in 1765.

possible. When, however, no constructive idea emerged, my repeated reminders notwithstanding, and when I saw that the
Ministers were more inclined to spread themselves in controversy
and argument than genuinely to take the problem in hand—
urgent as it was—that the work dragged on and on, and that no
one was willing, or able, to attack the problem seriously, then,
however, by the especial intervention and Providence of God,
and to the salvation of these lands, I became acquainted with
Count Haugwitz, who, out of loyalty and devotion, had left all
in Silesia and stood by my side in time of trouble. He was presented to me first by H. M. the Emperor, and after him, Count
Tarucca, who was always my consultant in private affairs, as well
as in matters concerning the Italian Provinces and the Netherlands,
and from whom I received much good advice and counsel in my
inexperience; also, he brought me to a true understanding of
affairs and men, without, however, ever interfering in Provincial
and State affairs, only pointing out my course to me and showing
me where I went wrong, which is most necessary for a ruler;
yet there are very few willing to do it, most men refraining out
of respect or self-interest. I should therefore wish that all my
children might find his like, to give them such help, and I owe
Tarucca a great debt, which I will always seek to repay to his
children and enjoin my successors to do likewise.

But to come back to Haugwitz. He was truly sent to me by
Providence, for to break the deadlock I needed such a man, honorable, disinterested, without predispositions, and with neither ambition nor hangers-on, who supported what was good because he saw
it to be good, of magnanimous disinterestedness and attachment to
his Monarch, unprejudiced, with great capacity and industry and
untiring diligence, not afraid to come into the open or to draw
on himself the unjust hatred of interested parties—indeed, Count
Harrach, who, as I shall presently show, was his greatest opponent,
often himself said to me that without Haugwitz things could
never have been brought into order, that a man like him was
necessary for this, and that no one but he alone would have
ventured to undertake the task—and, verily, the special blessing
of God's mighty hand has been over him in all and everything.

The situation had reached the very desperate pitch which I have
described when, with the Emperor's approval, I instructed Koch
to have Haugwitz draw up a plan for the maintenance of a force

of 100,000 men, with all possible economy, eliminating all excessive demands by the military and providing all possible relief for the Provinces. Haugwitz carried out this commission in a way which earned my and His Majesty's special approval, because on the one hand it ensured that the Provinces were unmolested and protected against all exactions by the military, and on the other, it provided for the greatest possible economy in the military budget, while yet allowing sufficiently for all essential expediture.

I had Haugwitz communicate this confidentially to the Supreme Chancellor, Count von Harrach. The latter actually told me that he entirely agreed with the main principles, and all the Ministers approved them almost entirely, except that some of them said that they must first examine the capacity of their Provinces to raise the necessary sums, a reasonable reservation which was generally met by drawing up complete balance sheets, which showed that when all forced levies, Provincial contributions, and other demands on the State and private individuals were added together, the total would infallibly exceed what was required for the system. This gained the proposals further adherents.

The first big difficulty arose over the allocation of the payments among the different Provinces. Some Councillors appealed to an alleged traditional quota, which would have laid quite disproportionate burdens on the Inner Austrian Provinces,[34] the poorest and most heavily burdened of all. The Supreme Chancellor, Count Harrach, who insisted on this most strongly, produced the idea of abolishing all Cameral and consumption surcharges in the Provinces—a sum amounting to many millions—in return for which the Estates were to be asked to vote all expenditure beyond what the few remaining Cameral resources could supply, both for the systematic upkeep of the 108,000 men and for the covering of the entire debt and the regular Cameral expediture.

I found, however, no one agreeing with this.

Some thought it was completely impracticable, and must lead to the collapse of the "Banco"[35] (which I was always most anxious to avoid), to expect the lands, even given these tax remissions, to produce increased revenues amounting to some twenty-seven million, especially since, if the consumers bore no share of the increased prices, the burden on the direct taxpayers would be

[34] Styria, Carinthia, and Carniola.
[35] The Vienna City Bank (see above, p. 98, fn. 4).

impossibly heavy. On the other hand, neither I nor my other Ministers could take on ourselves the responsibility before posterity of
letting the surcharges which my predecessors had already imposed
and actually collected slip again out of my hands altogether, and
thus leave Provincial revenue, the whole essence of the Prince's
authority, the whole material condition of its existence, dependent
on the pleasure and arbitrary disposition of the Estates. This change
would greatly have limited the power of the Crown, and while the
Estates or some private persons might have profited from it, it would
certainly not have promoted the general welfare; for strongly as I
have asserted my authority where I have believed this necessary and
salutary, so gladly and unhesitatingly would I have limited it or
even renounced it altogether for myself and my successors if justice
and equity and the general welfare would have been better served
under the administration of the Estates. Since, however, I was
entirely convinced of the contrary, and sure that even highly
placed persons were only seeking to increase their advantage and
repute on both sides by playing off the Crown against the Estates
as they pleased, I could not possibly accept the idea.

It is true that Count von Harrach proposed to introduce far-
reaching economic reforms which, he argued, would make it possible for the taxpayers to raise these huge sums, but since it would
have taken more than ten years before these became effective, they
could not have brought the taxpayers any perceptible immediate
relief.

A conference accordingly rejected Count von Harrach's proposal by a unanimous vote, which I had specially recorded,[36] and
since no one present was able to suggest anything different or better
than Haugwitz's draft plan, on which I had already decided, after
private consultation with Bartenstein, I resolved to send Count
Haugwitz to Moravia and Bohemia to sound the Estates there,
whether they were prepared to adopt the principles of his plan as
in their own best interest.

The Ministers, and particularly the Supreme Chancellor Count
Harrach, had firmly convinced themselves that the Estates would

---

[36] Maria Theresa is far from accurate here. At the great Crown Council
convoked (on January 28, 1748) to discuss the two plans, only Haugwitz
himself supported his own plan, while Khevenhüller agreed to it under a
misunderstanding. The rest rather favored Harrach's, but were simply
overruled by the empress and her husband (see Walter, *op. cit.*, pp. 45 ff.).

never accept any such proposals; even wires were pulled, great efforts were made from Vienna to foment ill will among the Estates, which was the more to be feared because the Estates had been sent very misleading interpretations of the proposals.

Yet even as I had commended to Divine Providence, with sincere confidence, the execution of my idea for preserving the Monarchy, so I was now made visibly aware of the Divine help which I had expected, for in spite of all the obstacles put in his way from Vienna, Count von Haugwitz was successful in obtaining the consent of the Moravian Estates to the proposed military system and to the financial obligations involved. I therefore instructed him to make the same proposals in Bohemia. Here, it appeared, more difficulties were to be anticipated, since the Estates had been affected by the talk and minework from Vienna.

Nevertheless, the business was carried through quite successfully in Bohemia also, and the Deputies of the Bohemian and Moravian Estates arrived for the close of the Recess. Count von Harrach and some other Ministers maintained that the Estates in these two Provinces had been hurried into their decisions, or even corrupted (although I had neither given nor promised the smallest consideration in any Province, nor had any been asked), or ought at least to have stipulated other conditions on the lines of Harrach's own opinion.

I thereupon personally asked the Deputies of both Provinces to say on their consciences whether they thought Harrach's ideas preferable for their Provinces; and they assured me unanimously that Harrach's plan was quite impracticable, a simple chimera which could neither exist nor be realized, especially as most of the advantages Harrach was dangling before their eyes were only hypothetical and lacked any real basis.

Haugwitz, however, agreed with the Supreme Chancellor, and all the other Ministers concurred, that this military system would not advance the welfare of the Monarchy unless the debt and the Camera were, at the same time, put in order.

The Cameral funds were insufficient for these two purposes, and Count Harrach himself was the less able to deny this because he had himself undertaken to draw up an estimate of what was needed for the Cameral expenditure and the debt.

Even here, however, I was unable to fall in with his ideas, which would again have involved robbing the Bank of the greater part of

its funds, which would have ruined it completely, since the hypo-
theses on which he based his speculations were, by universal consent and most plainly, nonexistent and incapable of realization.

I was therefore forced to apply to Count von Haugwitz again,
to work out the system for the debt and the Camera, and this he
finally succeeded in doing, in spite of the unimaginable confusion
reigning in both departments. His conclusion, however, was that,
after allowance had been made for essential Cameral expenditure,
for the service of the existing debt at 6 per cent (5 per cent interest
and 1 per cent amortization) and for obligations to the Bank, a
deficit of about 2.5 million would be left. This sum, which was
necessary for the consolidation of the main system, had to be asked
of the Provinces, and since the Bohemian and Moravian Deputies
were in Vienna, I myself approached them and explained the situation to them in detail. I thus persuaded them to undertake themselves to put my proposals before their colleagues, and they did
so in the subsequent Diets, with the effect that Bohemia, Moravia,
and Silesia granted the Cameral quotas needed for the debt.

Count von Harrach was acting Landmarschall in Lower Austria.[37] He could not bring himself to ask the Estates to grant the
two million that fell to them under the plan, so I was forced to
appoint Count von Haugwitz Commissioner and Count von Bräuner the new Landmarschall.[38] Here, too, there was success; the
Lower Austrian Estates most readily accepted their quota of two
million, and a ten years' Recess was agreed with them, as with the
Bohemian Provinces.

I had rather more difficulty in obtaining its million from Upper
Austria, where I was unable to send Count von Haugwitz. When,
however, its Deputies appeared for the closure of the Recess, the
matter was eventually settled satisfactorily.

The greatest difficulties came with the three Inner Austrian
Provinces. All the Austrian Provinces, but particularly these three,
had managed their affairs in so irresponsible and unbusinesslike a
fashion that the Court—that is, the Chancelleries of the day—had
allowed them to accumulate a so-called domestic debt of twenty-
four million, the interest on which amounted to 200,000 gulden.
It was the financial weakness of these lands that involved them in

[37] His brother Ferdinand was actually titular Landmarschall (governor)
but was then in Milan, as Governor; Friedrich was replacing him.
[38] Karl Adam, Graf Bräuner, 1689–1777. Held many important offices.

this big debt, and was also the reason why the quotas allocated to them were regarded in advance as impossibly high, and in certain cases could really be regarded as such.

The Inner Austrian Provinces had been treated with particular indulgence by my Government, and had often been allowed to give IOU's for sums due from them; they consequently found it much harder than any others to submit to the proposed orderly system. It was thus only possible to obtain from Styria a Recess of three years, and that with the utmost difficulty.

In Carniola we had to wait a whole year before we could achieve a three years' Recess, and that after remitting the sum due on the debt.

There was no doing anything in Carinthia, and after failing to bring the Estates to any kind of reason, I was compelled to collect the tax *jure regio*, although in order to help them I had, a year before, at Count von Haugwitz's suggestion, sent two Commissioners, to the latter of whom, Rudolph Count von Chotek,[39] they gave their written consent to the Recess but withdrew it three weeks later. They were constantly lamenting that they could not raise the State tax, but refused to make any economies in their local or supplementary administration, and proposed—out of ignorance or malice—to increase the burdens of the unfree population. That is the reason why I had the sum collected myself, *jure regio* (i.e., by virtue of my supreme prerogative).

The Estates' persistent representations that the burdens were too heavy for them, which were not without their force, although the fault lay in their own unbusinesslike methods, naturally led me to make provision for a better and more equitable management of the local finances. And I must insist that it is generally true that the prime cause of the decay of my Hereditary Lands lies in the over-great freedom the Estates had gradually usurped; for the Estates seldom behaved justly, their Presidents usually simply doing as their predecessors had done and furthering their private advantages, while refusing or rejecting any help that justice demanded should be given to the poor oppressed classes, and thus as a rule letting one Estate oppress another.

The final purpose of most of the so-called prerogatives of the Estates was simply to secure an arbitrary free hand for some of their

[39] Rudolph, Graf Chotek, 1701–71; was Hofkammerpräsident in 1759, Oberster Kanzler (when the title was revived) in 1761.

members, who claimed an inordinate authority over the rest.

It was formerly the easier for all this to go on because the said overpowerful members of the Estates, who usually made common cause with the Ministers in charge of the Provinces, generally had in their hands the fortunes, both of the Crown and of the Estates themselves, and thus disposed of them according to their pleasure, for which very reason the Ministers here in Vienna gave every support to the prerogatives which brought them so much advantage.

And although the result was only detriment to the public interest, yet the Estates insisted on these prerogatives the more stubbornly because most of them failed to understand the position and easily allowed themselves to be hoodwinked by these their own representatives.

Neither do I myself wish, nor do I advise my successors, to encroach on the useful and legitimate privileges of the Estates, seeing that the welfare of my dominions is inexpressibly dear to me, and I cannot repeat often enough that if I had found their privileges so clear, or if they had conducted the administration more justly than I or the Crown, I should not merely not have hesitated to submit and abrogate my authority entirely to them, I should rather myself have diminished and renounced or limited it for my successors, because I should always have placed the welfare and prosperity of the Provinces before my own or that of my family and children.

But neither my own interest nor that of my successors, and least of all the public interest, can be sacrificed to illegitimate abuses which have taken root with the connivance of the Ministers; wherefore such alleged privileges as are founded on abuse and an evil tradition should not be confirmed without extreme caution and careful consideration, and I have often observed that Crown rights which have fallen into desuetude through the connivance of the Ministers are questioned with the object of tying the Monarch's hands in these respects also; this applies above all to the supervision of the Estates' domestic funds and the management of them, and also to the equalization and adjustment of taxation, which should be conscientiously undertaken in the interest of justice and of the general welfare.[40]

The Austrian Provinces in particular have made every endeavor

[40] The practice had been for the Crown to demand a global total from a Province, and for its Estates to partition this among their own members.

to exclude my supervision and disposition on these cardinal points.

For this purpose, I began with the Inner Austrian Provinces and insisted, the more firmly because their conduct of their own affairs had been so unbusinesslike, both on dictating to them their allocations for local expenditure and also, for my own satisfaction and that of the Provinces, on adjusting the taxation in accordance with the principles already observed, and have continued to give the completion of the operation my most careful attention.

In Upper Austria my opportunity to intervene more closely in the internal constitution and to establish there the principle of adjustment presented itself, since that Province, its credit being weak, had often appealed to me for a remission of its Recess quota. I gradually reached the decision to carry through a reform there also, and to reduce the Domestic Fund substantially.

My greatest difficulties were with the Lower Austrian Estates here, which had been particularly spoiled by the Ministers, who were especially well disposed toward them because they had advanced large sums on credit to the Court and in earlier emergencies had been exceedingly generous in every way.

The Austrian Provinces knew excellently how to turn this to their own advantage. Nevertheless, I was not to be deterred from reaching my goal here also, and consequently from limiting the domestic expenditure for the benefit of the poor taxpayers, and also from carrying through and regulating equitably the adjustment —more necessary here than anywhere—and the extension of taxation to properties formerly exempt. I hope thereby not only to consolidate the uniform system—since I wish these principles to be observed equally in all Provinces—but also to attract the blessing of God on this my salutary intention.

As to the Tirol and the Vorlande,[41] I had, indeed, had Count von Chotek carry through an enquiry here, but when the new system was introduced, the whole arrangements had to be entirely recast; there, too, however, I succeeded in obtaining the quota allocated to them under the system, which I also achieved in Transylvania and the Banat of Temesvár. Only in the Kingdom of Hungary did I think it better not to introduce any change, because it would have been inadvisable to attempt anything of the sort except at a legally convoked Diet, and special considerations apply in the

---

[41] I.e. the territorial enclaves in the Reich under Habsburg sovereignty.

case of the Hungarians, who are extremely sensitive on such points.[42]

The system established for my German Hereditary Lands in respect of the defense forces, the Camera, and the public debt covers the Hungarian Lands, as well as the Bohemian and Austrian, and makes it possible for me, after deduction of Cameral expenditure and service of the debt, to maintain in them 110,000 men, and also gradually to economize a certain sum each year with which to keep my army ready to march immediately in case of enemy invasion, and thus to avoid a recurrence of the situation which—unfortunately—confronted me at the outset of my reign and was the real origin of all the subsequent trouble.

Twenty-four thousand are to be kept in the Netherlands and at least 26,000 in Italy, so that the grand total amounts to 150,000. My greatest difficulties at present are with Italy, but Count Pallavicini[43] still hopes to get the plan through to my satisfaction.

I have also been at pains to have the Varasdin, Carlstadt, and Croat frontier districts divided into regiments and organized regularly.[44] And although these troops rendered excellent service in the last war, I can hope for even better results in the future now that they are better organized, and the Ban of Croatia has established new regiments. The tables and inventories are attached.

Thus 24,000 men of these peoples are constantly ready to move anywhere at a word, while in peacetime, when they are at home, they cost my exchequer little more than 400,000 a year.

All this shows how greatly I labored to organize and put on a firm footing the military force which is so indispensable for the preservation of the Monarchy and, further, to put the artillery, with the expert help of Prince von Liechtenstein,[45] on a proper footing, the object of this military system being to ensure that the Provincial contributions come in regularly every month, so that the forces are paid punctually, while extreme care is also taken to see that no ex-

[42] In fact, Maria Theresa had, at the famous Diet of 1741, confirmed the Hungarian nobles' right to exemption from all taxation.

[43] Johann Lucas Pallavicini, b. Genoa 1697, entered the imperial service in 1731, general commanding the forces in Milan in October, 1744, governor in November, 1749.

[44] The reorganization of the Military Frontier was carried through between 1742 and 1744.

[45] Joseph Wenzel, Prince Liechtenstein, b. 1696, with Daun (below) chief reorganizer of the Austrian army.

tortions or exactions are practiced on the taxpayers and not even the smallest bribes or *douceurs* permitted, however gladly the Provinces would pay them or however much the military demand them, for this would only throw the whole system into confusion and open the door to the old exactions, which are generally beyond the capacity of the peasant at the present level of taxation, while certainly no lord would ever open his own purse. Beneficial and easy as this appeared, and strictly as I have forbidden the military to allow such exactions, yet it is most important to insist that not even everything that appears good can be put into effect without careful consideration. Finally, a two-volume manual on military discipline, drill and regulations, for which I am indebted to the wise and industrious efforts of General Daun,[46] has been drawn up and is appended.[47]

In order to put all this on a firm and lasting foundation, I found myself forced to depart from the old, traditional Constitution, with the detrimental qualities which it had acquired, and to enact such new measures as could be harmonized with the new system.

And to make it more solid still, I decided that I would myself, with H.M. the Emperor, attend the weekly sessions concerned with the establishment of the system, and thus personally control and enact the orders to be sent out to the Provinces. I had the material prepared by a Committee meeting under the chairmanship of Count von Haugwitz, and including a Councillor of the Bohemian Chancellery, another of the Austrian, a Councillor of the Hofkammer and someone from the General War Commissariat. In each of the Provinces I appointed a Deputation whose sole business it should be to collect and report on all material relevant to the system, whether financial or non-technical military.[48]

But I soon saw that this still would not bring me realization of my main objective, especially as both Chancellors, besides the Hofkammer and nearly all the Ministers, were very hostile to this institution, to the great detriment of its authority and standing, and were only looking for a chance to think up suggestions and difficulties and so, sooner or later, to put things back on their old, bad

[46] Leopold Joseph Maria, Graf Daun, b. 1705, major general in 1748, later full general; defeated the Prussian armies at Kolin in 1757.

[47] Not reproduced.

[48] "*Militaria mixta*," i.e., questions relating to the quartering, supply, etc., of the army.

footing; especially since those Ministers and the Councillors under them who should, owing to their positions, have been the chief supporters of the reform, were its greatest enemies, avowing their intention both openly and privately to destroy it, and poisoning public opinion against it. And always thinking as I was to provide not only for the present, but also the future, solidly, so that my children should not fall into the same labyrinth as I, I was for that very reason sometimes too precipitate and undertook too much at once, and thus set everyone against me, particularly those who were sitting at the fleshpots. And since it was impossible to grant any help or relief to the poor and oppressed, because of the urgency of the emergency, there was general discontent, which brought on me much unpopularity.

Consequently, after long and mature thought, having perceived that the root cause of my Monarchy's troubles lay in the fact that each Minister and his staff was always satisfied to play the advocate and protector of the Province in his charge—often with only halfhearted regard to the general welfare and to the interests of the Crown—and to shift all burdens onto other Provinces, and next after this, to discredit the Cameral services so as to make them incapable of serving the public interest by gradually reducing their activities to the keeping of balance sheets and manipulation of figures—in spite of which, whenever a crisis arose, the Ministers always expected the Hofkammer to produce the money to meet any requirement, although they must have known how empty were its hands and how extremely limited its competences; furthermore that, instead of promoting the service by good agreement between the branches, they wasted time unconscionably in arguments and disputes to the neglect of any constructive work, with the result that practically every opportunity was always missed, having become alive to all this, I determined to alter the whole rotten Constitution, central and Provincial, completely and to set up new institutions of nature to put the system on a firm footing.

To this end I abolished altogether all the Cameral agenda of the former Hofkammer in the Austrian and Bohemian Provinces and limited its activities to Hungary and to the Court finance, the latter only for the lifetime of the present President, and abolished both Chancelleries and transferred all administrative and Cameral agenda, with the non-technical military, to the newly established Directorate.

For justice in the Bohemian and Austrian Provinces I established a single supreme instance[49] (the staff lists, instructions, and plans of these two offices are attached[50]), thus ensuring that the uniformity at which I was aiming should not be interrupted, nor any opportunity be left to look back at the harmful old Constitution.

To this end I abolished the title of Chancellor: the heads and deputy heads of the Directorate and Supreme Court were entitled Presidents. In the Provinces I set up everywhere "Representations"[51] in charge of the administration, Cameral finance, and non-technical military business. The Provincial Military Comissioners were, in the interests of efficiency and uniformity, attached to the Representations. These bodies are responsible exclusively to the Directorate in Vienna, and similarly, the judicial instances in the Provinces report to the Supreme Court, which body is competent to decide any case according to its conscience, without reporting elsewhere.

Lists of all proposed decisions of the Directorate must, on the other hand, be drawn up weekly and submitted to me, and matters of importance are considered every Friday in a conference in the presence of myself and H.M. the Emperor. In general, I have laid down the rule that all business coming in each week must be dealt with immediately and nothing held back unless it needs much work, when it must be kept constantly under review.

I have, indeed, set up a separate Department of Commerce,[52] subordinate to the Directorate, but this is composed chiefly of Councillors from the Directorate, and has also been instructed to concert most closely with that body in all matters involving administrative action, to which end its President attends a weekly meeting of the Directorate, and is also invited by me to the conference on internal policy.

I am convinced that these fixed institutions are the true foundation on which I can support the Monarchy entrusted to me by God, with the strong help which I hope, He will continue to give me, and

[49] The "Oberste Justizstelle" (see headnote to the document).
[50] Not reproduced.
[51] These "Representations" were the predecessors of the full-fledged provincial "Gubernia" of later decades. In fact, they now took over most of the work of the old Estates.
[52] *Kommerzdirectorium.* The functions of this body were wider than the word "commerce" would indicate; it was more like a modern Ministry of Economic Planning.

preserve it to the best interest and profit of my successors. Seeing that such institutions give a Monarch the opportunity of acquiring personal knowledge of the nature of his dominions, discussing and examining their grievances and withal promoting a just relationship, such as is pleasing to God, between lords and their subjects, but especially of watching closely that the poor, and particularly the unfree population, be not oppressed by the rich and by their masters.

And as the system closely restricts the old excessive authority of the Ministers and higher officials, it may easily be appreciated that most of them, and also the great figures in the Provinces, regard these measures as intolerable and will only gradually learn to admit the truth; meanwhile, they try to incite public feeling against the system, and launch stupid and angry attacks against it—which ought, indeed, to be severely censured. But thinking that these grumblings would gradually die away and the people be brought to a better frame of mind by seeing that the measures are all for their good, I generally disregarded and ignored such offensive utterances, even at the time; but it may well be necessary in the future to put some check on them, because I have observed only too plainly that they exercise a most harmful influence on the public and may therefore gradually lead to harmful consequences.

The military, on which this new system imposed orderly and proper restrictions, at first complained against it especially bitterly, because the officers found their opportunities of taking bribes in the Provinces cut off, yet every reasonable officer must admit that they have no cause to complain now that they receive their pay regularly every month. My chief worry was that the malpractices which had taken root among the troops would be very hard to eradicate, and I had decided to proceed here with the utmost severity. To my extreme relief, however, I managed things so that the Provinces made no complaints of excesses by the troops, but rather begged for more regiments to be quartered on them, who would buy what they had to sell.

I was also, indeed, at pains to introduce a uniform drill and proper military discipline everywhere among my troops. To that end they were to be concentrated in camps for two months each year. Who would believe that no sort of rule was in force among my troops? Each unit had a different order of marching, a different drill, etc. One practiced rapid fire, another slow. The same words of command were differently interpreted in each unit, and it is really no wonder that ten years before my accession the Emperor was defeated every time, and the subsequent state of the army beggars description.

In order to show my successors with what real care and motherly love I applied my whole heart to their welfare, allowing no difficulties to daunt me and overcoming every obstacle with patience and resolution . . . [sentence incomplete]

My

Section V

shows the benefits accruing to posterity from the reorganization, which was the only way of consolidating the Monarchy and preserving it for my successors.

It is the less necessary to expatiate on this because I have described so fully the evils now passed, and the advantages of the present Constitution are as clear as day. For just as—everyone must agree—only a miracle was able to save the Monarchy in its previous condition of disintegration, confusion, and malpractices, so that I myself was constantly anticipating its end, so my successors will themselves understand that the measures and dispositions which I then took were the only way to preserve the Monarchy and transmit it to those who shall come after me. And here, in

Section VI

follows the necessity of maintaining these institutions, in self-preservation, and as for the maxims my successors have to follow to this end, I can give them no other counsel than not to allow themselves to be misled by anyone, for most people's advice is governed by their private ends and interests. I myself, when taking these most salutary measures, would have been led into confusion by the many insinuations and misleading accounts given me, had I not taken the utmost pains to acquaint myself through firsthand observation with the real nature of affairs, and this is why I feel myself obliged to enjoin my successors, for their own good and for the sake of the preservation of the Monarchy and its dominions, to alter nothing in the arrangements and Constitution laid down by me, but rather to preserve them as the apple of their eye, lest evil recur. And to this end they have especially to endeavor to seek out honorable and efficient servants and, no less, to train up young men diligently, that from their youth up they may form a right picture of the work and through their zeal and application may fit themselves to render salutary, ample, and effective service according to the systematic order described above to their sovereign and to the public.

13. The Habsburgs and Hungary, 1741–91

The general course of the Habsburgs' relations with Hungary during this half-century has been indicated in outline in the narrative section. For documentary illustration, we begin with the main laws enacted at the famous Diet of 1741. The constitutional issue was not openly raised again during Maria Theresa's reign, for which, accordingly, we confine ourselves to a single piece from a different field. Joseph II's irruptions into public affairs were, on the contrary, so numerous that we can find space only for two or three of them, but we give his famous recantation. Finally, we give the most important laws which constituted Leopold's settlement.

THE HUNGARIAN DIET OF 1741

This diet is best known for the famous scene of September 11 at which assembled representatives of the kingdom shouted their willingness to offer "life and blood to our King, Maria Theresa," and the other (often confused with it but actually taking place nine days later) when Maria Theresa exhibited her infant child to the cheering magnates. But these two episodes actually took place at a comparatively late stage in the proceedings of the diet, which had met in the preceding May for the coronation ceremony.

The coronation of each ruler was, by usage, the great occasion when the constitutional relationship between ruler and nation was restated, and since Charles, once he had gained his point over the succession,[1] had practically ignored Hungarian affairs, convoking the diet only once again (in 1734), dismissing it when it refused to accede to his wishes, and leaving the office of palatine unfilled on the death of its holder in the same year, the diet, when it met in 1741, was very insistent that the restatement should on this occasion contain substantial further guarantees for the nation.

[1] See above, pp. 87–88.

The queen and her advisers had realized from the first that some concessions would be necessary, and although they succeeded, with difficulty, in persuading the diet to agree to an unaltered wording for the Coronation Diploma, they consented not only to reaffirm the essential promises made by Charles in 1722–23 (including the regular appointment of a palatine), but to add certain new ones. The most important of these were those contained in Law VIII, which not only laid down that certain laws, privileges, etc., of the Estates were "fundamental," to which the clause in the Diploma on the joint inter-pretation of the laws by the king and diet should not apply (thus robbing the clause of half its sting), but also specifically included among such rights the exemption of Hungarian nobles from all forms of taxation, which it declared to be "fundamental" and perpetually irrevocable. Other important laws excluded the possibility of leaving the office of palatine indefinitely unfilled and provided for the inde-pendence of the Hungarian administration.

The diet's chief counter-concessions were contained in Law IV, which accepted Maria Theresa's husband as co-regent for his lifetime (this was a late concession by the diet, which had refused it for many months) and Law LXVIII, which records the diet's consent to provide the military assistance for which Maria Theresa had appealed.

The texts of some of the most important of these laws, and the substance of some others, the textual reproduction of which would be otiose, follows. The texts are taken from the *Corpus Juris Hungarici*, Vol. II, pp. 7ff.

[THE PREAMBLE records the Diet's recognition of Maria Theresa's right to succeed to the throne in virtue of the legislation of 1722–23, implementing the Pragmatic Sanction.

Laws I to III give the texts of Maria Theresa's coronation oath and Diploma. There are identical with those of her predecessors[1] and therefore need not be reproduced here.

Law IV records the diet's recognition of Maria Theresa's hus-band as co-regent for his lifetime.

Law V records the election of the new palatine, Count János (John) Pálffy.

Law VI records the names of the new Keepers of the Holy Crown.

Under Law VII the queen promises to reside in Hungary "in-sofar as the administration of other Provinces, and business, permits it."

Law VIII follows:]

[1] See above, pp. 85–86.

On the clause in the Diploma, "as shall have been agreed in respect of their use and interpretation by common agreement between the Crown and the Estates assembled in Diet": that this is by no means to be stretched to cover the fundamental rights, liberties, immunities, and prerogatives of the Estates of the Realm.

It is laid down, by gracious declaration of Her Sacred Majesty, that the fundamental rights, liberties, immunities, and privileges of the Estates of the Realm of Hungary and of the Parts annexed thereto, and particularly those laid down in Para. 9, Part I, of the *Tripartitum*[2] and Law VI of 1723, exempting them in perpetuity from payment of the *contributio;* with the principle, confirmed in privileges based on immemorial customary right, that no public charges shall be attached to the land (as they are also safeguarded and assured by Law III of 1715, to the effect that they shall not be governed after the manner of other Provinces) shall be regarded as covered by the Diploma [*sub sensum diplomati insertae*] and the clause on the use and interpretation of laws can in no wise apply to them.

[Law IX relates to "the office of Palatine." Its first clause runs:]

Whenever in future the office of Palatine and the Vice-Regal office legally connected with it shall become vacant, it shall not be left vacant for more than one year.

[Law XI runs:]

On Hungarian affairs and business: that these are to be conducted through Hungarians.

1. Her Majesty has further graciously resolved that She will conduct, and have conducted, the affairs and business of the country, both inside and outside the country, through Hungarians.

2. Consequently, also in Her august Court, in matters dependent on the supreme power enjoyed by Her, She will, in accordance with Her august judgment and royal prerogative, make use of the assistance and counsel of Her loyal Hungarian Councillors.

3. Further, when matters of great import arise, She will cause

---

[2] The codification in three parts of Hungarian law compiled in 1514 by the jurist Werböczi. Never formally promulgated (owing to the disorders of the time) this work was ever after treated as possessed of legal validity, and authoritative.

to be summoned to Her august presence the Primate of the Kingdom and the Palatine and other dignitaries of the Kingdom, and
also the Ban of the Kingdoms of Dalmatia, Croatia, and Slavonia
when the business and security of those Kingdoms is especially at
issue, and will take council with them over these questions.

4. And She will deign to take men of Hungarian nationality into
the Ministry of State itself.

5. And inside the Kingdom She will in the future also duly
conduct all administration and matters concerning the public affairs
of the same Kingdom in the manner determined by the laws of the
land, through the channel of the Vice-Regal Council (which is to
be preserved in the sphere of competence and independence laid
down in Law CI of 1723).

6. And in cases of future vacancies in the said Vice-Regal
Council She will appoint suitable landed Hungarians from all parts
of the Kingdom, men acquainted with the business and constitution
of the Kingdom.

[Law XII defines the jurisdiction of the chancellor in certain
cases. Law XIII, on the Royal Hungarian court chancellery, provides:]

Since the supreme authority and dignity of Her Royal Majesty
would not permit Her gracious Resolutions, issued through the
Royal Hungarian Court Chancellery, to be interfered with, or the
execution of them impeded, by other authorities, Her said Royal
Majesty has graciously declared that She will not permit this to
occur.

1. And that She will in the future also, of Her august authority
and supreme judgment, provide for the appointment to the said
Hungarian Court Chancellery, as an immediate Court organ of
government, on a footing of complete equality with the other immediate Court organs of the same Crown, of suitable and competent landed Hungarians from all parts of the Kingdom, following
the same procedure when vacancies occur.

2. And She will also show friendly regard to the reverend clergy.

[Law XIV promises to retain the Hungarian Camera as an independent organ, reporting immediately to the Crown and with
jurisdiction also over the mines and salt mines of Hungary.

We may add here three more laws, relating to other fields:]

Law XVIII. Of Transylvania, and of the restoration to and rein-
corporation in Hungary of the counties, districts, and areas belonging to Hungary:

Her Royal Majesty has further graciously resolved to have in-
scribed in the public laws of the Kingdom:

1. In respect of Transylvania, which belongs to the Holy Crown
of Hungary, that both She and Her successors will possess and rule
it *qua* Kings of Hungary.

[Paragraph 2 provides for the transfer of certain areas from
Transylvania to Hungary, and also for the re-extension of civilian
authority to districts of South Hungary and Slavonia.

Law XXI provides for the liquidation of the "Neo-acquistica
Commission."[3]

The preamble to Law LXIII relates how, in the extremity caused
by the invasion of the archduchy of Austria by the Elector of
Bavaria (with French assistance) and of Silesia by the King of
Prussia, Maria Theresa]

. . . Not only begged the said Estates of the Realm, appealing
to the traditional valor of the Hungarian people, to take up arms
against the said enemies of Herself and Her hereditary domains,
but also most graciously deigned to commit Her sacred person and
Her august royal issue to the loyalty and prudence of Her most
loyal Hungarians; as also the said Estates of the Realm have received with the deepest loyal devotion the confidence and motherly
affection and propensity shown by Her Sacred Royal Majesty,
lady and Queen, toward Her most faithful hereditary subjects, and
have promised with unanimous acclamation that they will devote
life and blood[4] to the defense of their most legitimate sovereign
and realm, and its Holy Crown and of the rights adopted, confirmed and established in Laws I and II of the Diet of 1723—thus
being diligent with most willing hearts to devote all cares, pains
and means in their power to repel the unjust enterprises of the said
Elector of Bavaria and other monarchs. Since the shortness of time
did not permit the recruitment of the necessary force by the
ordinary methods, they have, in view of the magnitude of the
imminent danger, spurred on by the example for their forebears,
determined, for the purpose designated, and for this especial occa-

---

[3] See above, p. 7.
[4] *Vitam et sanguinem.* The "formula of acclamation" was "*Vitam et sanguinem pro rege nostro* [sic] *Maria Theresia.*"

sion and emergency, and subject to conditions and safeguards—
that no prejudice be done thereby to the fundamental laws of the
Kingdom and the ancestral noble prerogatives, rights, and liberties
(on the preservation whereof Her said Royal Majesty has, on this
occasion also, most graciously deigned to give assurances to the
Estates of the Realm)— and stipulating that this shall not be allowed
to serve as precedent to any future occasion—to proclaim the national *levée en masse* [*generalem regni insurrectionem*].

[The rest of the law sets out the number of troops Hungary was
to provide, and the way in which the burden was to be distributed.
Besides the *levée en masse*, estimated to yield 15,000 to 20,000
horsemen, the diet offered 21,622 foot-soldiers to be recruited
from among the unfree population. It was calculated that the whole
of the Lands of the Hungarian Crown would yield about 100,000
soldiers, although it is probable that the figure was not in the event
reached.]

Joseph II's Recantation

While the broad statement is true enough that Joseph II's assaults on
the national liberties and traditions of Hungary provoked a resistance
which forced him to retract them, the chief of the immediate grievances
which in 1789 drove the Hungarian Estates to the verge of revolt was
financial—the threat of increased taxation, including taxation on noble
land, arbitrarily imposed—and the lever which they operated against him
was financial: the threat of sabotaging the supplies of men and money of
which Joseph was in urgent need, unless he limited his demands to
what he was constitutionally entitled to ask, and made them through
constitutional channels. This involved, indeed, going back to the
starting point, for men and taxes could constitutionally be voted only
by a diet, legally convened, in agreement with a king, legally crowned;
but the Hungarians' constitutional case was irrefutable, and in the
autumn of 1789, when matters were working up to a climax, with the
Netherlands setting the precedent of open revolt and the king of
Prussia moving armies to the Galician frontier, those Hungarians who
were most loyal to the crown besought Joseph to yield to it. Joseph
had (illegally) left the office of palatine vacant, but those Hungarians
who, in the absence of a palatine, were at the head of the national
administration—the Lord Chief Justice and acting president of the
"*Consilium Locumtenentiale,*" Count Károly Zichy, and the court
chancellor, Count Károly Pálffy—repeatedly warned Joseph that he
could not hope to get his supplies by force, and Pálffy further urged him
strongly also to remedy Hungary's other main constitutional grievances

—to submit himself to coronation (with the Holy Crown, which must be returned to Hungary), take the traditional coronation oath, restore the regular administrative and judicial system, and convene a diet.

On January 24, 1790, Joseph instructed the imperial chancellor, Kaunitz, to send a representative to a session of the Hungarian court chancellery, to take place on the following day. The upshot of this was that Kaunitz wrote to Joseph on the twenty-eighth, strongly urging him to accept Pálffy's advice, repeal immediately his more objectionable measures, and convoke a Coronation Diet, to meet not later than the following June. Now Joseph, who was already mortally sick, yielded at last. He answered Kaunitz that he was prepared to make the concessions, except that the state of his health precluded the immediate convocation of a diet, and that he was sending instructions (a copy of which he enclosed) to that effect to the chancellery. These, slightly amended, appeared over his signature on January 30 (antedated to January 28).

Kaunitz to Joseph II*

January 28, 1790

Thue Hungarian-Transylvania Chancellery has, in view of my having attended their session, communicated to me the result thereof through the report to Your Majesty, dated the twenty-sixth of this month.

I see that this ventures to give Your Majesty approximately the same advice as I felt it my duty to give Your Majesty verbally before the meeting, through Privy Councillor Spielmann.

I consequently agree entirely with the substance of this report and only hope that the immediate execution of its proposals will suffice to produce the effects which it anticipates, since feeling is so exceedingly exacerbated and confidence has been so completely lost that the contrary would be quite possible, and I therefore fear that it may not be accepted as sufficient unless simultaneously the Diet is convoked for this year, say, for June 1, and meanwhile efforts are made to obtain from the nation, through good words and good representations, all that urgent assistance which will afterwards have, if possible, to be obtained legally from the Diet.

Your Majesty will remember that You have already lost the Netherlands, perhaps irrevocably, simply and solely because You

---

* Reproduced from the State Archives, Vienna, in H. Marczali *Magyarország Történelte* II. *József korában*, 3 Vols., Budapest, 2nd. Ed., 1885–1888, Vol. III, p. 605.

not only took in ill part my considered representations of June 20, 1787, but since then have thought fit to enact the exact contrary in every respect.

It is only too possible that should my present advice meet with no better fate than my previous counsels, the same misfortune will overtake the Monarchy, first, from the side of the Hungarian nation, which will probably not lack foreign help.

I therefore beseech Your Majesty, as an honest man who has his Sovereign's interests at heart, at least to enact without delay all the measures, without exception, that the Hungaro-Transylvanian Court Chancellery has had the honor to advise.

May God grant that Your Majesty steel Himself to this resolve, and with this earnest wish I commend myself to Your Majesty's gracious goodwill, which I have endeavored to merit from Your Majesty's House during fifty years of service.

KAUNITZ, R.

Joseph's Reply to Kaunitz (written on the above)*

From the attached copy of My Resolution you will see that I have tried to grasp the nettle by the root. Should this prove ineffectual, the die has been cast for rebellion. I am deeply grateful to you for your loyal advice, which I value as it deserves. I have the greater need of it in this exceedingly critical situation and in view of my miserable health, which renders me absolutely prostrate.

Joseph's Own Draft Resolution (as sent by him to the Hungarian Chancellery)†

In such circumstances half-measures are useless. Consequently, in order to meet at one stroke all imaginable grievances, possessed of even a shadow of justification, of the Hungarian and Transylvanian Estates, I wish to cancel all general rescripts and enactments issued during my reign and restore the situation as it was at the death of Her late Majesty the Empress. I except only the Toleration Patent, the measures relating to the new Church livings, and those relating to the unfree populations. The Crown and the other

* Ibid.
† Ibid., pp. 564ff.

national insignia are to be taken to the Castle of Buda as soon as a place is ready for them there.[1] Since these measures will remedy the grievances, the Estates will not press so urgently for the Diet, the holding of which is impossible in the present situation and in my state of health. I hope that the Estates will see my disinterestedness and my wish for their best, and I feel justified in expecting them to furnish the State with recruits in the meantime, and the army, with the necessary supplies. The survey[2] is to be interrupted in such fashion that the existing surveys and valuations, which have already cost so much money and are, after all, necessary, can still be used.

The Rescript is to be drafted in this sense. I wish with all my heart that through these measures Hungary may gain as much happiness and good order as I wished to procure for it through my enactments in all fields.

The Final Resolution*

[The final draft, as edited by the Chancellery, omitted the sentence on the survey but added after the words "ready for them there":]

The Counties and Free Boroughs are reinstated in their previous competence but the public administration is not to be disorganized and no arbitrary changes made. The Estates retain their right of collaborating in legislation.

C. Leopold II's Settlement with Hungary, 1790–91†

The settlement achieved by Leopold II with the Hungarian Estates took place in three stages. The first was played entirely behind the scenes, for privy negotiations were necessary to overcome the resistance of the Hungarian extremists to accepting Leopold as king at all or, at any rate, as king of hereditary right, and denied his right even to convene a diet. On this point Leopold won the day, and the diet was convened for Buda on June 10, 1790. There it agreed to accept and crown Leopold as legitimate king and heir to the throne, in virtue of the law of succession as regulated under Laws I and II of 1722–23.

---

[1] They were in fact returned to Buda on February 18.
[2] The land survey on the basis of which the planned new land tax was to be levied.
* Viktor Bibl, *Kaiser Josef II* (Vienna and Leipzig, 1943), p. 280.
† *Magyar Törvénytár* (Corpus Juris Hungarici), Vol. II, p. 144ff.

Like its predecessor of 1741, it also agreed, after a struggle, that the Inaugural Diploma should again be in the form that had become traditional since 1711, while stipulating that this should be recorded in the form of a law. Laws I and II record these agreements. In return, Leopold promised, under a resolution dated September 21, 1790, to negotiate laws calculated to remove the just grievances of the Estates. These were worked out in subsequent debate (in the course of which the diet moved to Pozsony). The most important of them follow:

Law III: That the Inauguration and Royal Coronation Shall Take Place Within Six Months After Each Change of Ruler

[This law was framed to prevent recurrence of Joseph II's device of escaping the obligations of the coronation oath and Diploma by not submitting himself to coronation at all.]

In order to eliminate any doubt that might arise out of certain words in the Inaugural Diploma, accepted and promulgated by His Most Sacred Royal Majesty, on the Coronation to be undergone by the hereditary Kings of Hungary, such as has been or might in the future be raised against the fundamental laws of the realm, His Imperial and Royal Majesty has graciously consented that on every change of rule the Royal inauguration and coronation shall without fail take place, in the form prescribed by law, within the space of six months, counted from the day of death of the deceased King, without detriment in the meantime to all rights of the hereditary King in respect of the public and constitutional administration of the Kingdom or to the obligations of loyal obedience due to the said King; the legitimately crowned Royal Majesty being, however, in the future also, solely competent in respect of the conferment of privileges.

[Law IV records the election of the palatine (the king's brother, the Archduke Alexander Leopold). He is to reside in the center of the kingdom, at the seat of the central administrative offices. He is to be the supreme commander of the national armed forces (Law V). The Holy Crown is to be kept in Buda (Law VI). The most important of the next laws are contained in the following series, the first of which thereafter ranked in Hungary as "fundamental":]

Law X: On the Independence of the Kingdom of Hungary and of the Parts Annexed Thereto

In reply to the humble proposal of the Estates of the Realm, His Most Sacred Majesty has further deigned to recognize that although the succession of the female line of the august House of Austria, established in the Kingdom of Hungary and the Parts annexed thereto by Laws I and II of 1723, relates to the same Prince as in the other Kingdoms and Hereditary Possessions, inside and outside Germany, to be possessed inseparably and indivisibly according to the established order of succession, nevertheless Hungary with its annexed Parts shall be a free Kingdom and independent in respect of its entire lawful administration (including hereunder its Dicasteria),[1] that is, not subject to any other Kingdom or people, but having its own political entity and Constitution and consequently to be ruled and governed by its own lawfully crowned hereditary King, and thus also by His Most Sacred Majesty and his successors, according to its own laws and customs, and not after the fashion of other Provinces, as is laid down in Law III of 1715 and Laws VIII and XI of 1741. . . .[2]

Law XII

On the exercise of the legislative and executive power, His Most Sacred Majesty recognizes, freely and spontaneously, that the right of enacting, rescinding, and interpreting legislation in the Kingdom of Hungary and its annexed Parts is vested (without prejudice to Law VIII of 1741) jointly in the lawfully crowned Prince and the Estates of the Realm, lawfully assembled in Diet, and cannot be exercised outside it, and has graciously declared that He will preserve this right of the Estates uninfringed, and as He has inherited it from His ancestors of blessed memory, so He will transmit it inviolate to His successors, assuring the Estates of the Realm that the Kingdom and the annexed Parts are never to be governed through Edicts or so-called Patents, which in any case can never be accepted by any jurisdictions in the Kingdom, reserving only the right of issuing a Patent for cases where the law is unaffected, and publication cannot be effectively realized otherwise than by this method.

The form of the judicatures, as lawfully established or to be established, shall not be altered by Royal authority, neither shall the execution of sentences lawfully enacted be impeded, nor the impediment of them by others be permitted, by mandate, nor

---

[1] The autonomous counties and municipalities.
[2] See above, p. 91 and pp. 134–135.

shall the lawful sentences of Courts of Law be altered or submitted to revision by the Crown or by any administrative instance, but shall be carried out in conformity with the laws hitherto enacted, or to be enacted in the future, and the acknowledged custom of the realm, judicial enactments by judges to be chosen without discrimination on the score of religion, while the executive power shall be exercised by His Royal Majesty, in the sense of the laws only.

Law XIII: On the Periodical Sessions of the Diets

Every third year, or even earlier should the public welfare of the Kingdom make it advisable and necessary, His Royal Majesty will, as required by the laws enacted on the subject (sc., 1655, Law XLIX, 1715, Law XIV, and 1723, Laws VII, X, which are hereby renewed), convoke a general Diet of the Kingdom, at which the Estates of the Realm are to appear, being in no wise impeded from doing so, and are to be suffered to discuss the business of the Realm with lawful liberty. And His Royal Majesty will also at all future times ensure by the force of His Royal authority that after due discussion of the Royal proposals, all just complaints of all Estates of the Realm shall at every Diet be dealt with effectually and in full, and the laws passed at each Diet shall be exactly executed and caused to be executed.

Law XIV: On the Royal Hungarian Vice-Regal Council

In order that, in accordance with the fundamental laws of the Land, His Sacred Majesty may conduct the business and affairs of Hungary and its annexed Parts, as provided by Laws X to XIV of 1608 and LXI of 1714, through Hungarians, and may be duly advised by them, His Sacred Majesty has most graciously ordained that the Royal Hungarian Vice-Regal Council—which in virtue of its very foundation is equipped with all necessary authority to execute the law and to see to its observance, and is politically the highest organ of Hungary, which, under the existing laws, is in any case independent of all other organs and directly subordinate to His Sacred Majesty—shall be bound in its loyal duty to the King and the country, should by any mishap unlawful commands reach the country, to make the appropriate representations; while His Majesty shall, in accordance with His Royal prerogatives and His promise to maintain the law, pay due heed to such representations, the legal form and competences of the counties and of the other jurisdictions remaining intact. . . .

Law XVII: On the Realization of Law XI of 1741

Since Law XI of 1741 has here been reaffirmed in its full compass, His Sacred Majesty has graciously deigned spontaneously to declare that He will see that the said law be put into effect in all its parts, and in this connection will both take Hungarians into the Ministry of State and will also order that such Hungarians as, provided they possess the necessary intellectual gifts and abilities, are prepared to accept diplomatic posts, are to be offered every opportunity in the Privy Chancellery to undergo a thorough training. His Majesty has also declared Himself ready to satisfy the wishes of the Estates in that internal affairs shall be conducted by Hungarians, and foreign affairs, with the participation of Hungarians, and then submitted directly to His Majesty's decision, and in future His Majesty will provide that the laws enacted in connection with the conclusion of a peace with the Turks be submitted to the Realm.

[Law XVIII lays down that officials must take an oath to observe the Constitution.]

Law XIX: On Subsidies and Contributions

His Majesty has also deigned to assure the Estates of the Realm of Hungary and its annexed Parts that no subsidies, however designated, whether in cash, kind, or recruits, shall be levied by Royal Edict either on the Estates or on non-nobles, even under the pretext of a voluntary offer, or any other similar term, except from the Diet, except as provided under Law VIII of 1715, defined more closely under Law XXII of 1741,[3] and that the size of the Contribution laid down for the maintenance of the military shall always be fixed at the Diet, for the period of one Diet to the next, the remaining provisions of the above-mentioned Law VIII of 1715 being declared to be legally valid and hereby reaffirmed.

---

[3] This law allowed some extraordinary expenditure in connection with the expenses of Turkish embassies.

[The other laws enacted at this diet were not of such prime constitutional importance. The only real concession in them was contained in Law XVI, which provided that "a foreign language" (sc., German) should not in the future be used in any business. Latin remained the language of all official transactions, but instruction in the Magyar language and literature was to be introduced in secondary and higher educational establishments, including the national university. Other laws legalized, sometimes with some modifications, those of Joseph's Patents which he had not retracted, or gave effect to other reasonable wishes put forward by the Estates.]

14. The Habsburgs and the Churches, 1740–92

It is possible to speak of a certain continuity of line in the religious policies of the three Austrian rulers whose reigns bridged the last half century of Europe's *ancien régime*, insofar as all of them rejected, far more resolutely than their predecessors, the complete subservience of the lay arm to the spiritual; but beyond this, the policies of each of the three differed widely. Maria Theresa was far too conscious of her monarchic rights to hesitate to exercise them where she thought this necessary, and, as the reader will have gathered from her remarks on the subject in her "Political Testament,"[1] too clearheaded not to perceive that the gap between the Church in theory and the Church in practice often called for her intervention. She never got down to the sweeping measures of reorganization which she once envisaged, but she more than once exercised the *Placetum Regium;* she instituted a censorship which extended to works on theology; she forced the Holy See to concede, most reluctantly, a drastic diminution in the numbers of public holidays; she limited the *jura stolae;*[2] subjected the administration of Church properties to State supervision; consented to the expulsion from her dominions of the Society of Jesus, and confiscated its property.

But Maria Theresa was personally a devout, even a bigoted, Catholic. It was only with reluctance that she challenged the authority of the Holy See, and she long resisted the expulsion of the Jesuits. Above all, she adhered rigidly to the point of principle that Austria was a Catholic State, holding tolerance toward non-Catholics to be wrong in principle

---

[1] See above, p. 96.
[2] The *"jura stolae"* were the free-will offertories, etc., which formed part of the customary stipend of the parish priest.

and detrimental in practice, and she did not shrink from very extreme measures to enforce this principle. As late as 1752 the profession of Protestantism was declared a capital offense in Bohemia, equal to treason and rebellion, and later still, unmasked crypto-Protestants in Upper Austria, Styria, and Carinthia were forced to emigrate to Transylvania, or to leave Austrian territory altogether. As she grew older, she became less harsh in her practice toward heretics, but up to the end of her reign, a Protestant in the western Lands, even where transmitted law permitted him the private practice of his faith, could not own real property, nor practice a number of callings. The disabilities to which the Jews (whose long-established community in Prague she was only with difficulty dissuaded from expelling early in her reign) were subjected were still heavier. In Hungary her hands were tied by stipulations in her coronation oath and Diploma, but she got round these where she could, and even there her reign was popularly known as the "Babylonian captivity."

Joseph II's attitude and policies were very different. He always professed that he, too, was a good Catholic; that he was not attacking Catholicism, but purifying it. But he was deeply imbued with the fashionable rationalist philosophy of his day, and in any case, was as bossy and autocratic in this field as in every other. It is with justice that the Erastianism that characterized Church-State relations in Austria from 1780 to 1848 and reasserted itself (in a different form but with great obstinacy) after 1861 is known as "Josephinism." While his mother asserted the authority of the secular arm over the spiritual only occasionally, in connection with some special problem, Joseph did so systematically and exhaustively. He did not simply veto the publication of some particular papal bull: he forbade the entry of any such communications without previous sanction from himself. He took the seminaries out of the hands of the bishops or superiors of orders and replaced them by "general seminaries" under State direction. He personally laid down an "Order of Divine Service," which went into such details as how many candles might be used on altars. More holidays, processions, etc., were forbidden. He dissolved almost all the contemplative Orders, whose members he regarded as idle parasites, "useless and not pleasing to God," and even a certain number of other Orders, confiscating their properties. Above all, he made a complete breach with his mother's principles in respect of the "toleration" of non-Catholics, and after failing to convert her to his views during her lifetime, hastened as soon as her eyes were closed to issue a patent granting members of the Lutheran, Calvinist, and Greek Orthodox religions freedom to practice their religion anywhere unmolested in private and, with certain restrictions, also in public, and admitting them to full equality of civic rights with Catholics in almost every respect. This was followed by less far-reaching but still very extensive concessions to the Jews.

Some of Joseph's measures could in fact be regarded as beneficial to true religion: thus the confiscated monastic funds were to be used to improve the education and status, and increase the numbers, of the parochial clergy (it is true that this purpose could only be partially achieved, partly because many of the Houses turned out to be heavily indebted and their creditors had to be satisfied, partly owing to bad management of the remaining proceeds). But many of them naturally evoked great resentment and even produced the sensational effect of bringing the pope himself (Pope Pius VI) to Vienna in an attempt to persuade Joseph to retract some of them. The pope met on the whole with little success; Joseph went on his self-willed way, convinced, as always, that he was right. But the political discontent provoked by his policies was a major element in the seething discontent in which he left his dominions when he came to die, and his successor, Leopold, found it prudent to make a measured and limited retreat on this front, as on most. His own views on Church-State relations were probably not very different from his brother's, and he made no essential concessions to Ultramontanism, nor on the principle of toleration, but he did repeal, or modify, a large number of Joseph's more unpopular enactments.

In the selection of documents that follows we have included little from the pen of Maria Theresa because, pragmatist as she was, her enactments were usually of particular rather than of general interest. We reproduce, however, a few characteristic *mots*, or decisions, of hers and also an exchange of letters between her and Joseph in which mother and son argued with fervor and conviction the cases for and against toleration as a State policy. Joseph's main enactments are of wide enough application—over-generalization was one of his characteristic and besetting faults—but a complete collection of them would fill fat volumes. We give here what are usually regarded as the six most important: those relating respectively to the *Placetum Regium*, the seminaries, the dissolution of the monasteries, the formation of new livings, and the Toleration and one of the Jewish Patents.

We have not included anything from Leopold, most of whose documentary utterances in this field are simply assents to, or refusals of, requests. His personal profession of faith is given elsewhere (below, pp. 204ff.

The policies of the three Habsburgs can be studied conveniently in the longer biographies of them: Arneth's *Maria Theresia*, especially Vol. IX; P. von Mitranov's *Joseph II* (K. V. von Demelič, Vienna, 1910, 2 vols.); and A. Wandruszka's *Leopold II* (Vienna, 1965, 2 vols.). See also C. Wolfsgruber, *Kirchengeschichte Oesterreichs* (Vienna, 1909), G. Loesche *Geschichte des Protestantismus in Oesterreich.* (Vienna, 2nd. edn., 1927); and the *Jewish Encyclopedia*. A lively older appreciation can be found in Vol. I of I. Beidtel's *Geschichte der oesterreichischen Staatsverwaltung* (Innsbruck, 1896–98). See also K. Ritter,

Joseph II und seine kirchlichen Reformen (2 vols., Regensburg, 1867). The special studies on some of Joseph's patents are given in the introductory notes to these.

A. MARIA THERESA IN A NUTSHELL

The dicta which follow are taken from a collection in H. Kretschmayer's *Maria Theresia* (2nd. Ed., Gotha, 1938, pp. 330 ff.).

On Pilgrimages

[Answer to the Hofkriegsrat, which had forwarded to her a request from an officer for permission to go to Rome; date, April, 1765.]

I set no store by pilgrimages, God is with us everywhere, ask the General's opinion, I believe that he is a *mauvais sujet*, anyway.

On the Control of Education

[Answer to Cardinal Migatti, who protested against proposals to put the schools under the supervision of laymen; date, 1770.]

The school is and remains a politicum [i.e., an administrative question].

On the Jews

[Answer to a private request from the supreme chancellor that a family of Jews in whom he was interested should be allowed to settle in Vienna; date, 1777.]

In future no Jew, as they are called, is to be allowed to be in Vienna without My written permission. I know no worse public plague than this people, with their swindling, usury, and money-making, bringing people to beggary, practicing all evil transactions which an honest man abhors; they are therefore to be kept away from here and avoided as far as possible.

B. MARIA THERESA AND JOSEPH II ON TOLERATION

The question of toleration (i.e., of non-Catholics in the public life of the State) was that on which the views of Maria Theresa and her son probably differed more fundamentally than any other in the field of public policy towards religious questions. It was also undoubtedly one of the most important for the lives of their subjects; few of Joseph II's enactments had effects more widespread or far-reaching than the Toleration Patent (reproduced below, pp. 154–157), which Joseph hastened to issue only a few weeks after his mother had closed her resolute old eyes. The correspondence reproduced below thus relates to matters of great historical importance, besides being highly interesting for the arguments with which each of the writers states and defends his or her case. When it took place, Joseph was traveling in western Europe; it was started by an apparently casual remark made by him at the end of an otherwise not particularly interesting letter written from Rochefort on June 19, 1777 (Doc. A). He followed this up a few days later with a fuller and more considered statement of his views (Doc. B), in which he refers to a serious outbreak of heresy where sixty-odd villages suddenly went over to open Protestantism in Moravia, which had seriously perturbed Maria Theresa, causing her to apply very strong repressive measures, including arrests and removal of children from their parents' charge. To this Maria Theresa replied with a reasoned profession of her own views on the subject (Doc. C), to which again Joseph answered (Doc. D), and she once more (Doc. E). The correspondence closed without either party's having converted the other. The breach between them caused by the incident was however, one of the most serious of all their many disagreements.

The correspondence is reprinted in full in Arneth's *Maria Theresia und Joseph II. Ihre Correspondenz* (Vienna, 1867–68, 3 vols.), Vol. II, pp. 140ff., and almost in full, in German translation, with comments, by the same author in his *Geschichte Maria Theresiens*, Vol. IX, pp. 139ff.

A. Joseph to Maria Theresa
(June 19, 1777)

. . . In politics, difference of religions in a State is an evil only insofar as there exist fanaticism, disunity, and party spirit. It disappears automatically when one treats members of all sects with perfect equality and leaves the rest to Him Who alone rules hearts.

B. Joseph to Maria Theresa
(late June, 1777)

What Your Majesty writes me on the open professions of irreligion in Moravia convinces me more and more of my principles: liberty of belief, and there will remain only one religion, which will consist of guiding all inhabitants equally for the welfare of the State. If one does not accept this method, not only will one save no more souls; on the contrary, one will lose far more useful and necessary bodies. To take only half-measures does not agree with my principles: either one must allow complete freedom of worship, or you must be able to expel from your lands everyone who does not believe the same as you and does not accept the same forms of worshipping, the same God and serving the same neighbor. But if, in order that their souls shall not be damned forever after death, one expels excellent workmen and good subjects during their lifetime, and thereby deprives oneself of all the profit that one could derive from them, what power is one arrogating to oneself thereby? Can one extend it so far as to pass judgment on Divine mercy, which will save men against their will, order their consciences? So long as the service of the State is cared for, the law of nature and society observed, Your person not dishonored but respected and revered, what business have you temporal administrators to interfere in other things? The Holy Ghost is said to illuminate hearts; your laws will never be able to do anything more than weaken its effects. Those are my views; Your Majesty knows them, and I fear that my complete conviction will make it impossible for me to change them all my life long.

C. Maria Theresa to Joseph, July 5, 1777

This letter will reach you in Switzerland; those people do not appreciate the value of your presence. An asylum for all debauchees and criminals, it also shelters some of our women, whom you will not, I hope, see. They were shameless enough to try to arrange this, and to my great grief I have to say that there would be nothing more to corrupt in respect of religion if you intend to insist on that general toleration of which you maintain that it is a principle from which you will never depart. I hope it all the same, and I will not cease from praying myself, and causing those who are worthier than myself to pray, that God may protect you from this misfortune, the greatest which would ever have descended on the Monarchy. In the belief of having workers, keeping them, even attracting them, you will ruin your State and be guilty of the destruction of so many souls. What would it profit you to possess the true religion, when you appreciate it and love it so little, when you care so little to preserve and propagate it? I do not observe such indifference among the Protestants; I wish, on the contrary, that one might imitate them, since no [Protestant] State allows such indifference in itself. You will see this in that ugly Switzerland; there they watch and experiment daily with what is allowed in the German Empire, in England, Saxony, Baden, Holland, etc., with the exception of Prussia, but is the country the happier for it? Does it possess those workers, those people who are so necessary to make the State flourish? There are no lands less happy, none more backward in this respect than those provinces. One needs good faith and immutable rules; where will you find them or keep them?

D. Joseph to Maria Theresa, July 20, 1777

In answer to your long and gracious letter, you must permit me to tell you that the picture and conclusions which Your Majesty draws from what I ventured to write to you about the Protestants who were unmasked in Moravia so astounded and moved me that I cannot at this moment at all recollect whether anything of the sort escaped from my pen in error, whereas I am very far from thinking so. Fortunately, the word "toleration," which you were good enough to repeat to me, dispelled my doubts and transformed my whole fear into a tender and lively gratitude for the truly moving, heroic, manly, and powerful goodness with which you revealed to me the conclusions you draw from it. But it is only the word "toleration" which has caused the misunderstanding. You have taken it in quite a different meaning. God preserve me from thinking it a matter of indifference whether the citizens turn Protestant or remain Catholic, still less, whether they cleave to, or at least observe, the cult which they have inherited from their fathers! I would give all I possess if all the Protestants of your States would go over to Catholicism.

The word "toleration," as I understand it, means only that I would employ any persons, without distinction of religion, in purely temporal matters, allow them to own property, practice trades, be citizens, if they were qualified and if this would be of advantage to the State and its industry. Those who, unfortunately, adhere to a false faith, are far further from being converted if they remain in their own country than if they migrate into another, in which they can hear and see the convincing truths of the Catholic faith. Similarly, the undisturbed practice of their religion makes them far better subjects and causes them to avoid irreligion, which is a far greater danger to our Catholics than if one lets them see others practice their religion unimpeded. If the Protestants do not generally adopt this method in their States, this is because their governments lack the clarity and perceptiveness of ours, and because it is harder for Republicans to undertake such changes. Finally, if I had the leisure that a letter does not allow, I should be able to prove that, as I see the question, I could stand on my view before the awful judgment seat which will pronounce on my eternal destiny. Certainly no one would then turn Lutheran or Calvinist; there would be fewer unbelievers in all religions, the State would profit greatly thereby, and I cannot believe that all this together would make me appear guilty in the eyes of God. To me, at least, this would seem hardly compatible either with His all power, or with the office which He has conferred on me, in making me the servant of fifteen million human beings.

E. Maria Theresa to Joseph
(late July, 1777)

Without a dominant religion? Toleration, indifference are precisely the true means of undermining everything, taking away every foundation; we others will then be the greatest losers. It is not the Edict of Nantes that has ruined those provinces; there was never any such edict in Bordeaux, and the place is none the richer for it. What has ruined that land, with all its natural advantages, has been the ill-advised farmings out (*i.e.* of Crown resources), the bad administration, the weak or revengeful Ministers, the lack of religion among the officials, who are concerned only with their own interests or passions; this has ruined everything. What restraints are left for that sort of person? None, neither, the gallows nor the wheel, except religion, or cruelty against them. He is no friend of humanity, as the popular phrase is, who allows everyone his own thoughts. I am speaking only in the political sense, not as a Christian; nothing is so necessary and salutary as religion. Will you allow everyone to fashion his own religion as he pleases? No fixed cult, no subordination to the Church—what will then become of us? The result will not be quiet and contentment; its outcome will be the rule of the stronger and more unhappy times like those which we have already seen. A manifesto by you to this effect can produce the utmost distress and make you responsible for many thousands of souls. And what are my own sufferings, when I see you entangled in opinions so erroneous? What is at stake is not only the welfare of the State, but your salvation, that of a son who since his birth has been the one purpose of all my actions, the salvation of your soul. Turning your eyes and ears everywhere, mingling your spirit of contradiction with the simultaneous desire to create something, you are ruining yourself and dragging the Monarchy down with you into the abyss, destroying the fruits of all the laborious care of your forefathers, who at the cost of the greatest pains bequeathed these lands to us and even greatly improved their condition, because they introduced our holy religion into them, not, like our enemies, with violence and cruelty, but with care, pains, and expense. No spirit of persecution, but still less any spirit of indifference or tolerantism [sic]; in this I hope to maintain myself so long as I live, and I only wish to live so long as I can hope to descend to my ancestors with the consolation that my son will be as great, as religious as his forebears, that he will return from his erroneous views, from those wicked books whose authors parade their cleverness at the expense of all that is most holy and most worthy of respect in the world, who want to introduce an imaginary freedom which can never exist and which degenerates into license and into complete revolution.

C. The Placetum Regium

The Patent which follows is Joseph's central ruling on this subject, but it was afterward supplemented by a number of subsidiary enactments, e.g., a decree (January 1, 1782) annulling the jurisdiction of an official person, such as a notary, protonotary, bishop *in partibus*, etc., appointed by the Holy See; the consent of the government was required even for a purely titular appointment (Decree of March 3, 1782). The Decree reproduced here was in fact invoked within weeks of its appearance to forbid publication of two Bulls: the *In Coena Domini* of April 14, 1781, and the *Unigenitus* of May 5 of the same year. The *De Largitione Munerum* was forbidden on July 7, 1783.

Patent In Spiritualibus* *(March 26, 1781)*

SINCE IT is possible for any Brief, Bull, or other enactment issued by the Papal See to impinge on the sphere of the civic power: the contents of any such document are invariably to be submitted

---

* J. Kropatschek, *Sammlung der Gesetze, welche unter der Reierung Kaiser Joseph II Erschienen sind* (1781), pp. 65ff.

before effective publication for the Royal Assent [*Placetum Regium*] or license to publish [*Exequatur*]. All Archbishops and Bishops of the Imperial and Royal Hereditary Lands, *qua* Ordinaries, and other spiritual Superiors, and all persons, are therefore required (1) before promulgating any Papal Bull, Brief, Decree, Constitution, or enactment of any kind, if it affects the public, ecclesiastical or secular communities or individuals and also the conferment of any benefice, honor, power or personal jurisdiction, or the secularization of a professed member of any Order, whether relating to dogma or to ecclesiastical organization or discipline, always to submit it, together with a copy certified by a Notary Public of the Province, to the competent administrative authority, with a request that it be forwarded for the Royal Assent. The said authority shall then immediately call for a report (to be delivered without undue delay) from the Cameral Procurator or Law Officer, stating whether the said document contains anything relating to the civic power and to the laws of the Province or of any third party or contrary to the enactments of the sovereign power, as defined in the Provincial Constitution, and shall forward these remarks, with the document in question and its own opinion, to the Bohemian-Austrian Court Chancellery and then await further instructions. His Majesty's decision is then to be conveyed in writing, through the Provincial authority, to the Ordinary or the Superior of the Order, with the original. (2) The same procedure is to be aplied to enactments or appointments by foreign Ordinaries whose competences and dioceses extend into Our territories, relating to the above cases and subjects. (3) All Provincial administrators, Procurators, and Law Officers shall see that this law is strictly applied and shall immediately report to the Ministry any infringement of it, failing which any appointment or conferment of a personal dignity, and any action, will be regarded as totally null and void, and punishable.

D. The Toleration Patent

The text which follows of this famous edict, is that finally agreed in the Hofrat on October 20, 1781 (hence the odd-sounding opening; it is a communication addressed to the provincial chancelleries) and reproduced by G. Frank, *Die Toleranzpatent Kaiser Joseph II* (Vienna, 1862, pp. 35ff.), which is still the best general account of the subject.

This replaced a slightly different version, dated October 13, which is that given in Kropatschek (*Sammlung*, 1781, No. 334). The versions issued (in French) for the Netherlands (November 12, 1781) and (in Italian) for Lombardy (May 30, 1782) are identical. That for Hungary (October 26, 1781, printed in Marczali, *Enchiridion*, pp. 209ff.) differs only in inserting, where appropriate, the words "where this is not already permitted under existing legislation." This was fairly often the case, for not only did the Protestants of Hungary and Transylvania still enjoy considerable rights, but the Greek Orthodox Church there also enjoyed far-reaching autonomy under the "Serb Privilege" of 1691 (see above, pp. 78ff.).

The Patent met with a disconcerting success, for an unsuspectedly large number of crypto-Protestants revealed themselves when it was issued, and conversions from Catholicism took place in such numbers that official obstacles were placed in the way of them. Leopold was put under strong pressure to repeal it, but refused to do so.

Order In Spiritualibus *to All Imperial and Royal Provincial Governments*

MY DEAR LIEGES!

Being convinced, on the one hand, that all violence to conscience is harmful, and, on the other, of the great benefit accruing to religion and to the State from a true Christian tolerance, We have found Ourselves moved to grant to the adherents of the Lutheran and Calvinist religions, and also to the non-Uniat Greek religion, everywhere, the appropriate private practice of their faith, regardless of whether it had been previously customary or introduced, or not. The Catholic religion alone shall continue to enjoy the prerogative of the public practice of its faith, but members of the two Protestant religions and the existing non-Uniat Greek shall be permitted the private practice thereof in any place where the number of persons, as defined below, and the resources of the inhabitants make it practicable, and where the said non-Catholics do not already enjoy the right of practicing it publicly. In particular, We allow:

Firstly, non-Catholic subjects, where there are one hundred families, even if they are not all domiciled in the locality of the place of worship or of the pastor, but part of them live as much as some hours' distance away, to build a place of worship and school of their own, and those living further away may attend the nearest place of worship (inside Our Hereditary Dominions)

as often as they wish, also the pastors belonging to Our Hereditary
Dominions may visit the members of their congregations, and may
administer the necessary instruction and spiritual and material
comfort to the sick, but may not, under pain of severest punishment, prevent a Catholic priest from being called in, if any sick
person wishes it.

In respect to the place of worship, We order expressly that it
shall not have any chimes, bells, or towers, unless such already
exist, or public entrance from the street signifying a church, but
otherwise they are free to build it of whatever material they will
and shall be completely free to administer their sacraments and
celebrate Divine service, both in the place itself and conveyed to
the sick in the Chapels of Ease, and to conduct funerals with their
pastor in attendance.

Secondly, they are free to appoint their own schoolmasters, who
are maintained by the parish, but shall be subject to the supervision
of the Provincial Schools Directorate in respect of methods of
instruction and discipline. In particular, We allow:

Thirdly, to the non-Catholic inhabitants of a locality, the choice
of their pastors, if they pay for and support the same, but where
the authorities provide these services they must enjoy the right of
presentation; but We reserve to Ourselves the right of confirmation, in such fashion that where there are Protestant Consistories,
the confirmation is given through them, and where there are
none, granted through the existing Protestant Consistories in
Teschen or Hungary, until conditions call for the establishment
in a Province of its own Consistory.

Fourthly: the *jura stolae*[1] remain reserved to the Parish Ordinary,
as in Silesia.

Fifthly: the jurisdiction in respect of matters affecting the religion of non-Catholics shall be exercised by the administrative officials of the Province, assisted by one of their own pastors and
theologians; this Court shall render judgment in accordance with
their religious tenets, but appeal shall lie from this to Our Chancellery.

Sixthly: the issue by non-Catholics of the reversals on marriage,
hitherto customary, in respect of the upbringing of the children
in the Catholic faith is to cease altogether from now on; where
the father is a Catholic, all children, of either sex, are to be

[1] See above, p. 145, fn. 2.

brought up without question in the Catholic religion, this being to be regarded as a prerogative of the ruling religion; where, however, the father is Protestant and the mother Catholic, the sex of the child shall decide.

Seventhly: non-Catholics are in future admitted under dispensation to buy houses and real property, to acquire municipal domicile and practice as master craftsmen, to take up academic appointments and posts in the public service, and are not to be required to take the oath in any form contrary to their religious tenets, nor, unless they themselves wish it, to attend processions or functions of the ruling religion. The sole criteria in all choices or appointments to official posts are—as has long been the case in Our army, without the least difficulty and with great benefit—to be the candidate's integrity and competence, and also his Christian and moral way of life; difference of religion is to be disregarded. Dispensations to acquire property, municipal domicile, and master craftsmen's licences are to be issued by the Kreis authorities in towns under manorial jurisdiction; in Royal and *laibgeding*[1] boroughs, by the Provincial Cameral offices, where such exist; failing them, by Our Provincial Government. They are to be issued without difficulty. Should, however, the authority find any objection to an application suggesting that it ought to be rejected, a reasoned report is to be sent to the Provincial Government, and thence to the Chancellery, for Our decision.

In cases of the *jus incolatus* of the upper classes,[2] the Provincial Government is to give its opinion, and the dispensation is to be granted by Our Bohemian-Austrian Court Chancellery.

Provincial Governments are to communicate this Our decision to all Kreis offices, magistrates, and manorial authorities through printed circulars, of which a larger number than the usual is to be run off. Further, printers and publishers in the Province are permitted to hand these printed circulars to any person asking for them and thus secure adequate dissemination thereof also in other Provinces.

B. The Monasteries Patent

The document which follows is, again, only one of a long series of enactments in this field for the sentence pronounced here on only a

[1] See above, p. 28, fn. 8.
[2] See above, p. 42, fn. 4.

small number of orders, some of them unimportant enough, was subsequently extended to many more, amounting in all to about one-third of the total of Houses in the monarchy.[1] A large number of supplementary decrees were also issued in connection with the transfer of the monastic property to State hands, the administration of the "Religious Fund" into which the proceeds were paid, and so on. The text translated here is that of Joseph's own "Resolution," as reproduced by A. Wolf, *Die Aufhebung der Klöster in Inneroesterreich* (Vienna, 1871), the best special account of the subject; but all histories of the time devote considerable space to it. The Patent was promulgated on January 12.

Order In Spiritualibus *(January 1, 1781)*

WE HAVE found fit, for good and sufficient reasons, to abolish all Houses of the following Orders in Our Hereditary Lands and to make the following dispositions with respect to their members and property:

1. All Houses, Monasteries, Hospices, or whatever else these spiritual houses of communal life are called, of the male Orders of the Carthusians and Camaldolites and the Eremites or so-called *Waldbrüder*, and the female Orders of the Carmelites, Sisters of St. Clare, Capuchines, and Franciscans are dissolved, and the communal life of the persons in them is to cease.

2. The processes of dissolution shall be as follows: On receipt of this Rescript, the Provincial Government shall send to each House of the said Orders a qualified Commissioner with the necessary instructions and written authority, together with a skilled man from the Cameral accounting office, with the mission of informing the Superiors and all the communities, in the most deferential and kindly fashion, of Our decision, and intimating to them that henceforward no male or female novices or other members of the Order who have not yet taken their vows shall be permitted to do so. The instruction is to be taken down in writing and signed by the Father or Mother Superior and the head of the House, in witness that they have received the order. Next, the Commissioner shall demand the keys of the cashboxes, treasuries, archives, and stores, and shall seal up everything not necessary for daily use in the church and the house so long as the members of the Order

---

[1] According to J. Wendrinsky, *Kaiser Joseph II* (Vienna, 1880), p. 161, the total number of Houses in the monarchy in 1770 was 2,163, of which 738 had been liquidated by 1786.

remain there, leaving unsealed what is necessary for their day-to-day purposes. An inventory shall them immediately be drawn up, and the valuation put in the hands of a skilled and honest lay official, who shall supply the religious with their daily needs until they disperse.

3. The Superiors, the bursars, and all persons officially concerned with the administration of the real and personal property of the Monastery, Church, or chapel of the communities, whether priests or lay brothers or sisters, or secular persons, are to make a sworn statement to the Commission in the enclosed form. . . . The Commissioner shall further warn them to observe their oath, under pain of severe penalty. This is to be recorded in the official minute.

4. The Commissioner's work is not to be hampered by any obstacle, not excluding the Enclosure, which must always be open for the Commissioner. He must carry out his duties with seemliness and dignity, but for precaution's sake, every Diocesan should be asked to order the Cloister to carry out all orders exactly.

5. After the real and personal property has been taken over, an inventory is to be drawn up in duplicate, one copy to go to the Provincial authorities, the other to be sent to Vienna. The administration of the whole property is to be entrusted to the Camera, which has to see that until their discharge and the payment of their pensions the clergy are provided with food and clothing as hereto, but without superfluity or hospitality.

6. All objects in the cells or the Superior's lodgings serving personal use, such as pictures, books, furniture, and utensils, shall be left with their owners; an inventory is to be taken of these objects also, but when their owners leave the House the owners shall be permitted to take these objects with them.

Furthermore, it is to be made known to all, orally or in writing, that: (a) Persons who have not yet taken their vows receive a single gratuity of 150 florins, and must leave the Cloister within four weeks; they may take with them what they brought with them. (b) Religious of either sex may leave Austria and go to religious Houses abroad; in that case they are to be given passports and adequate journey money, but no further pension. (c) Those wishing to transfer to other orders are given, on application, every facility and an annual pension of 150 florins; but if they become Brothers of Charity [*Barmherzige Brüder*] or Piarists, the pension shall be 300 florins, and for women becoming Sisters of Elizabeth, 200 florins, paid out of the Cameral funds. Persons entering the secular priesthood are to receive an annual pension of 300 florins, besides the Princely grant *titulo mensae* until provided with a living. If a Carthusian Abbot [sic] transfers to the secular clergy, he is to receive 800 florins a year until provided with a benefice. (d) The regulation procedure is to be followed in respect of release from religious vows. This applies also, *mutatis mutandis*, to nuns. (e) Monks of Orders whose rules enjoin them to live quietly and peaceably, aloof from all worldly things, may continue to live according to the rule of their Order, but must take up their residence in a House of another Order, to which House the stipend for their maintenance shall then be paid. No one is to remain in the dissolved Houses of the male Orders unless he is too aged and infirm to be received in another House or by relatives. Such cases are to be reported. Professed nuns who do not transfer to another Order may remain together in a designated convent, but the Provincial authorities and the Ordinary shall prescribe to them a way of living and a spiritual Superior.

7. Circle officers shall order the Eremites or *Waldbrüder*, whether serving as Church sacristans or not, to discard their hermit's dress forever within fourteen days. Where foundations exist, they may continue to serve as sacristans or schoolmasters, but must be registered.

8. The church valuables are listed in the inventory. The report is to state whether the inhabitants of the locality wish for Divine Service to continue to be celebrated in the church. The Commissioners are to make sensible and appropriate dispositions.

F. The Seminaries Patent

Before Joseph II's accession all seminaries in the monarchy were controlled by the local bishops or superiors of orders. Joseph's most fundamental objection to this was the ultramontane spirit that reigned in the institutions, which he once described as "nests of the fanatical hydra of ultramontanism," but he also argued, not without justice, that the teaching given in them was usually too academic and left their alumni ill-equipped for parochial duties. It was in 1783 that he attacked the problem, then issuing a series of main patents, province by province; these were followed up by a large number of supplementary enactments regulating administrative details. The text translated here is that of the Patent issued for Bohemia; it is taken from Kropatschek's *Sammlung* for 1783, No. 146, pp. 102–4. The fullest account of the whole subject is in a monograph by O. Wolf, *Kaiser Joseph II und die oesterreichischen Generalseminarien* (Raumer-Diehls Historisches Taschenbuch, Berlin, 1877).

This edict was repealed after Joseph's death by his brother, who liquidated the general seminaries.

Court Decree In Spiritualibus *(March 30, 1783)*

A GENERAL Seminary is to be established, which is to be the common training center of instruction for all future secular clergy and religious. At it all the young men are to complete the entire course of public instruction in theology, after which they are to spend a year in all kinds of practical pastoral ministrations under the supervision of the Seminary staff. Accordingly:

1. All schools of philosophy and theology in all Colleges and Monasteries are closed down.

2. All religious who have already taken the habit are to be sent to the towns in which there are Imperial-Royal Universities, to attend the official schools there. The Colleges or Monasteries must see to their maintenance in the Monasteries or Houses of their Orders, or elsewhere.

3. No person except a candidate already accepted as a lay brother may enter any monastic Order until he has first as a cleric completed six years of theological studies and practical pastoral ministrations, nor may any person be ordained as a secular priest who has not passed the said years in the General Seminary. Exceptionally, in the cases of persons at present attending courses in theology, years already spent, with satisfactory results, in theological study may be counted toward the prescribed term.

4. Any person desirous of being accepted in this Seminary must have obtained from his Bishop a promise of admission to Petrine status, or a promise from the Superior of an Order of admission to that Order, and must produce a duly attested certificate that he has completed a full course of philosophical studies, with satisfactory results.

5. The dress and subsistence of all pupils in the General Seminary shall be the same.

6. Every Foundation or Order, except the strictly mendicant, must

pay for its own clerics; only the members of the mendicant Orders are to be supported out of the Religious Fund.

7. For the maintenance of the clerics accepted by the Ordinaries recourse must be had to all existing Foundations; firstly, to Presbyteries, Seminaries, and other colleges for clergy, and secondly, to the scholarships or other subsidies for students of theology.

8. The Rector of the Seminary shall be a Canon or other secular priest; he shall be in charge of its maintenance and general administration. He shall be responsible for reporting bad clerics to the Orders which have admitted them, or to the Bishop, with a view to their dismissal.

G. The "Livings Patent"

The problem of the shortage of parochial clergy in his dominions, especially by comparison with the abundance of monastic, was one of those which early occupied Joseph. In 1782 he ordered all local authorities to send in lists of localities in which the establishment of new vicarages or curacies was desirable, owing to the numbers of the inhabitants or the remoteness or inaccessibility of the existing places of worship. Patrons were to take steps to build the necessary new churches, or to put small or disused buildings into repair. His main patents were issued land by land, from the end of 1783 on. That for Lower Austria, which is dated October 24, 1783, runs as follows:

Court Decree In Spiritualibus

1. Where the parochial clergy are too few in numbers, or too far from the communes which they serve, either, according to the numbers of the populations, new priests or local curates shall be appointed, or the districts lying too far from their place of worship shall be transferred to other parishes, the principle to be followed being that in future no person shall have to journey more than an hour to his place of worship.

2. Where there is a shortage of churches and vicarages, these, unless built voluntarily by the manorial authority, shall be constructed out of the Religious Fund, in which case the right of presentation shall belong to the Commission for religion, which must, however, make its choice from among candidates presenting themselves, after advertisement. The new churches, or poor old churches, shall be equipped free of charge from the vessels, etc., of the liquidated Monasteries and churches. Under this rule,

3. Lower Austria gets 263 new parish priests, who shall be drawn in part, and for preference, from members of Monasteries and Orders adjudged most suitable after a diocesan examination, on the system that

4. On the domains and dependencies of the spiritual Foundations, the new priests and parish vicars or chaplains are to be taken from among their own members; in other places they shall be selected from among the best-qualified secular clergy or members of other Orders.

5. Incumbents from Foundations, if they pass the Bishop's examination, enjoy parochial rights immediately; but on future occasions all such *simplicia beneficia* shall be turned into *curata*.

6. All persons, from Bishops down, thus including all Foundations, Monasteries, parish livings and incumbencies, retain their existing increments complete. In consequence only the new parochial priests will be paid out of the Religious Fund, as follows: a parish priest to receive a stipend of 600 florins, a curate with a cure, 350 florins, a suffragan curate, 250 florins; but

7. The priests appointed out of the Foundations are to receive from these Foundations and Monasteries only the sum designated for their maintenance, on the above scale.

8. New priests and local curates whose cures have been separated from their former parish are independent of it. They must, however, pay over to it the offertories, in order that the old priests shall suffer no diminution of income.

9. The rule is thus that the old ministers continue to enjoy their stipends as established. Only the sums paid to the former ministers by the communes now separated off and provided with their own priests for the weekly or fortnightly Divine service now cease, because the former priest has no longer to perform the same spiritual preparations for them.

10. All subsidiary churches and other chapels are in future unnecessary in places already provided with a parish church or chapel of ease, for purposes of public worship; but manorial lords and other persons are free, provided the Ordinary permits, to use their private chapels or similar buildings for the reading of the Mass.

11. Monasteries will retain such persons as are necessary either for the charge of their own parishes, or to help in parochial duties, and an adequate number of priests, including a sufficient reserve for emergencies, will be designated for this purpose.

The other Monasteries that are quite superfluous for parochial duties will gradually disappear and be merged in the surviving Houses of their Orders.

Since, however, the monastic clergy not designated as parish priests and curates are not included in the number of clergy to remain in the Monasteries, the Monasteries are allowed, when one of the number of priests allotted to them dies, to take another in his place. The old clergy now past duty are included in the number to be designated, and are to be maintained in the Monasteries of their Orders for the term of their lives.

12. Since the appointment to parochial duties of many monastic clergy will leave sufficient room in the Houses, the larger buildings shall in future be used to house, not only members of their own Order, but any aged and infirm priest from any parish. Such persons continue to receive their pensions; all that the Foundations have to provide gratis is thus the accommodation, which is in any case vacant.

13. A number of deaneries are to be established, proportionate to the increased number of parochial clergy, so that priests who perform their duties with distinction may have an opportunity of worthwhile promotion. And it is further herewith enacted that while all persons, including whole corporations, retain in the future undiminished any right enjoyed by them of presentation or election to Chapters, yet they are not empowered to elect thereto any person, of whatever degree, who has not previously spent at least ten years in parochial duties and attained particular distinction therein.

H. THE JEWISH PATENTS

Joseph II's Jewish enactments constitute an extraordinarily miscellaneous collection. His major legislation in this field is contained in a series of provincial patents, the first of which was that issued for Bohemia (October 19, 1781). Patents for Silesia (December 15, 1781) and Lower Austria (January 2, 1782) followed; then, after a long interval, patents for Galicia (September 30, 1789) and Moravia (October, 1789), the latter being extended in the same month to Hungary and Transylvania. Shorter instruments were issued for Gorizia and Trieste, but none for the Inner Austrian provinces or the Tirol, the Jewish populations of which were minimal, or nonexistent. In addition to the patents, Joseph issued an enormous numbers of enactments and instructions, some applicable to the whole monarchy, others only to individual provinces.

While the patent for Lower Austria is reproduced below, this is given only as a specimen, for although the general purpose of all the patents was the same—to turn the Jews into a useful and productive factor in the life of the monarchy—the great differences between local conditions and existing legislation, besides the development of Joseph's own ideas, resulted in a great variety between the different patents. The linguistic assimilation and connected educational provisions appear in them all, as does the permission to the Jews to engage in a number of occupations from which they had formerly been excluded, and the principle of religious toleration in respect of private worship. Vienna, however, is the only place in the monarchy in which the Jews are not allowed to form their own community, and the detailed safeguards against settlement in Vienna by "foreign" Jews find no counterpart elsewhere. The Bohemian Patent contains no clauses corresponding to Arts. 18 and 24 of the Lower Austrian, and does not formally abolish the "Ghettozwang," which is specifically maintained in Gorizia. The Bohemian Jews are, on the other hand, allowed to engage in agriculture, though only as leaseholders and only employing Jewish labor, although, "as the Jews are not yet competent agriculturalists," they may, for a transitional period, employ Christian laborers, who must, however, sleep in Christian houses.

The *ad hoc* regulations are even more various. Not only is the Jews' religion protected, but the population is forbidden to molest or insult them. But newly born children and juveniles may not be baptized, and adults, only with official permission. They have to take surnames, but these must be generally intelligible, and not ridiculous (the soldiers who had first been charged with providing names for them had sometimes amused themselves by giving them names which were absurd or even obscene). They lost their exemption from military service. Many efforts were made to direct them into agriculture, but they were forbidden to buy State properties or to lease the tithe or the salt tax, etc. All in all, Joseph's legislation brought the Jews many important advantages, but nothing like complete civic equality. For that they had to wait nearly 150 years more.

The patent which follows is translated from J. Wendrinsky, *Kaiser Joseph II* (Vienna, 1880), pp. 152–6.

Edict of Toleration for the Jews of Lower Austria

1. In the future also, the Jews in Vienna shall not constitute their own community, under their own direction; each individual family enjoys the protection of the law of the land; no public worship, no public synagogue, no press of their own for works in Hebrew, for which they must use the press in Bohemia.

2. It is also intended that the number of Jews and the conditions under which they are at present tolerated in Lower Austria and here in Vienna shall remain unaltered, and where no Jews have ever been domiciled, none shall be allowed to settle in the future.

3. Thus, as in the past, no Jew shall be free to come to Vienna from another Hereditary Land, to settle here permanently. Foreign Jews must apply for permission for this to Us personally.

4. A person applying for a permit must state the trade or occupation which he proposes to pursue, and show what are his means, and also show how he proposes to utilize the toleration granted him. The Government will then determine the amount of the protection fee, which it may fix higher or lower as it thinks right.

5. On payment of this protection fee he may reside in Vienna with his wife and minor children, and pursue the calling on his permit. If, however,

6. A son marries and sets up his own household, he must obtain a permit for himself or, if he prefers, pay for a permit to leave. Similarly, a permit is required for a son-in-law, or if the daughter has received permission to marry a foreign Jew, the leaving permit must be paid out of the dowry going abroad.

7. No Jew is permitted to settle in a rural district of Lower Austria, unless he proposes to introduce a manufacture or a useful trade, for which he must apply to the Government for a permit, when he will enjoy the same rights as in the capital. The facilities enjoyed by the Jewish religion under the present regulations, which entirely supersede the last regulations, of May 5, 1761, are, accordingly, as follows:

Since it is Our purpose to make the Jews more useful and serviceable to the State, principally through according their children better instruction and enlightenment, and by employing them in the sciences, arts, and handicrafts:

8. We permit and command the tolerated Jews, in places where they have no German schools of their own, to send their children to the Christian upper elementary schools, so that they shall learn at least reading, writing, and arithmetic, and although they have no synagogue of their own in Our capital, We yet permit them to build for their children, at their own expense, a normally equipped school, with a teaching staff of their own religion, which shall be subject to the same control as all the German schools here, the composition of the moral books being left to them.

9. In respect of higher schools, the permission enjoyed by them to attend these is herewith renewed and confirmed.

10. We permit them henceforward, here and elsewhere, to learn all kinds of crafts and trades from Christian masters, to hire themselves to the same as apprentices, or to work for them as journeymen, without, however, submitting either Jews or Christians to any compulsion.

11. We further permit them to practice any kind of trade, but without right of domicile or master's certificates, from which they are still excluded, and only under permit from the Magistracy in Vienna or the Government of Lower Austria for rural districts. Painting, sculpture, and the practice of the free arts are open to them as to Christians.

12. We also allow them complete freedom of choice between all uncontrolled [*unbürgerlich*] callings, and authorize them to apply for licenses as wholesale traders.

13. We further herewith permit and exhort them to establish manufactures and factories.

14. We further permit them to lend money on real estate and to secure their advances, but not to make the valuation themselves.

15. The use, orally or in writing, of the Hebrew and so-called Yiddish (Hebrew mixed with German) languages in any public judicial or extrajudicial procedures is forbidden henceforward; instead, the locally current language is to be used. A two years' grace from the day of issue of this Patent is allowed; thereafter all documents written in Hebrew or Yiddish will be invalid and null and void.

16. Jews may keep as many Jewish or Christian servants as their business requires, but are bound to submit a reliable register annually, and each head of a family must not only lodge his Jewish servants in his own house, but must also guarantee that they do not engage in any occupation forbidden to non-tolerated Jews.

17. The wives, husbands, and adult children of such Jewish servants who engage in occupations of their own must also be tolerated.

18. We lift the restriction of Jews to specified houses and permit tolerated Jews to lease their own accommodation where they please in the city or its suburbs.

19. We further abolish entirely the so-called personal toll on foreign Jews, and permit them free entry from time to time into Our capital, in pursuit of their business, without being compelled

to find their accommodation and meals only in houses of tolerated Jews or in Jewish restaurants.

20. Since, however, the number of Jewish families established here is not to be increased, foreign Jews arriving here must report themselves immediately on arrival to the Lower Austrian Government, stating their business and the time they need to transact it, must await confirmation, and on expiry of the period must either leave or apply to the Government for an extension. The police is to keep a close eye to see that these foreign Jews really leave, and the Christians or Jews with whom foreign Jews lodge are to report the same day to the Government.

21. Such visitors are accordingly not permitted to trade in objects reserved for specially licensed tradesmen and local tolerated Jews. They, and all others, are also forbidden to peddle in the streets or country districts, under pain of confiscation of the merchandise.

22. Such foreign Jews are, however, permitted to trade at annual fairs in all objects the importation of which is generally permitted and outside the fairs, in objects which can lawfully be sold by any foreign dealer. They are also permitted to buy, accept orders for, etc., permitted objects.

23. The double fees at present paid by Jews on official and judicial transactions are abolished, as are:

24. All present customary distinctive marks and discriminations, such as the wearing of beards, the prohibition on going out before noon on Sundays and holidays, on frequenting public places of amusement, etc., on the contrary, wholesale merchants and their sons, and university graduates, may carry daggers.

25. Since it is Our wish to place the Jewish nation, through these concessions, on a footing of near-equality with the followers of other foreign religions in respect of their occupations and the enjoyment of civic and domestic amenities, We do earnestly exhort them to observe strictly all political, civic, and judicial laws of the land, as applying to them equally with all other subjects, and to submit themseves in their affairs and their public and judicial transactions to the competent Provincial or local authority; and We look to their sense of duty and their gratitude that they do not misuse this Our grace and the freedom deriving from it to cause any public scandal by excesses and loose living, and nowhere to offend the Christian religion, nor to show con-

tempt toward it and its servants; for misconduct of this kind will
be most severely punished and will be visited on the offender,
according to the circumstances, by expulsion from here and from
all Our dominions.

JOSEPH II
Vienna, January 2, 1782

15. The Habsburgs and the Peasant Question, 1740–90[1]

When Maria Theresa ascended the throne, the conditions of the unfree peasants in her dominions—and the great majority of them were
unfree—had been deteriorating perceptibly for a long period. The administrative system of the *nexus subditelae*, which had not been revised
for centuries, left them practically at the mercy of their manorial lords,
who with their officials ordered their daily lives and administered
justice to them through their manorial courts; and their economic
burdens had long been growing increasingly onerous. The landlords,
as their tastes grew more luxurious, had raised the rents which they were
entitled to take from their tenants, and especially, as they began to
engage in farming their own demesne lands for profit, had increased
the amount of compulsory labor service (generally known under the

---

[1] The best account of the peasant question in any part of the monarchy is
that of K. Grünberg, *Die Bauernbefreiung in Böhmen und Mähren* (2 vols.,
Leipzig, 1893). This is often drawn on by writers who generalize its data,
without noticing that many of them are true only for the Bohemian Lands.
For these, see also J. Kerner, *Bohemia in the Eighteenth Century* (New
York, 1932). For Hungary, I. Acsády, *A magyar jobbágyság története*
(Budapest, 2nd edn., 1944) and D. Szabó, *A magyarországi urbérrendezése*
(Budapest, 1932); both works only up to 1765. All the standard Austrian
historians give some account of the development in the German-Austrian
provinces. For Maria Theresa's policy, there is some material, but very
fragmentary, in Vol. III of Arneth's work; a useful short account in G.
Otruba, *Die Wirtschaftspolitik Maria Theresias* (Vienna, 1963). For Joseph
II, the standard histories, especially that of Mitranov; of the shorter works,
the best on this subject are those of Fejtö and the old life of Joseph by
J. Wendrinsky, *Kaiser Joseph II*, eclectic, but with some documents. Some
others are to be found in Kropatschek's *Sammlung*. For further literature
(and also for a very clear short account of the subject in general) see K.
and M. Uhlirz, *Handbuch der Geschichte Oesterreichs* (4 vols., Graz,
1927ff.), Vol. II.1. pp. 36ff.

Slavonic term of *robot*), which was one form of the rental which they might exact. Furthermore, practically the whole "contributio," or direct tax paid by the provinces, was derived from a land tax levied on peasant land, the nobles' demesne lands being at that time almost everywhere tax free, and the demands of the State, too, had been growing heavier. A further abuse, largely the result of the taxation system, had been the growing practice of enclosure (*Bauernlegung*), when a landlord evicted a peasant from his holding and turned it into demesne land.

Maria Theresa approached the peasant problem only rather gradually. The extension of taxation to noble demesne land in the west, and others of Haugwitz's early political reforms, including the extension of the land tax to noble demesne land, were of some benefit to the peasants, but the advantage to them was indirect and only partial, and the reforms did not extend at all to Hungary. The peasants benefited more, but again only indirectly and again only in the west, from the progressive transference of authority from the hands of the Estates, who were the landlords in another capacity, to those of the new State civil service. But Maria Theresa was too greatly occupied, during these first years of her reign, with foreign policy and top-level constitutional questions to have much time to spare for the peasant question; nor, at that time, did she query the necessity, or indeed, the rightness, of the *nexus subditelae*. But in the 1760's and 1770's the economic pressure on the peasants between the hammer of the State and the anvil of the landlords grew intolerable, and serious revolts broke out in several provinces. Maria Theresa set investigations on foot, and these revealed so horrifying a picture of the conditions under which the peasants were living in some provinces, notably Bohemia and parts of Hungary, that she intervened. For the State she established the principle that the demands on the peasant taxpayers were not to be increased, and she issued patents, land by land, laying down in detail the maximum of *robot* that could be exacted. Further alienation of rustical land to demesne was forbidden and, where necessary, surveys (*urbaria*) were carried through to establish the existing position.

The *robot* patents and *urbaria*—especially taken in conjunction with the vigilance which the new State bureaucracy was now required to exercise in respect of landlord-peasant relations—undoubtedly improved the position of the peasants very largely by the veto that they imposed on arbitrary abuse of the law by the landlords—requisition of a peasant's whole time at harvest, failure to allow for journey time, etc. They did not, however, as a rule alter the law itself (and the peasants' own complaints had usually not been against the law, but against the disregard of it by the landlords), which was generally left in each land as it had been established by local law and usage. Similarly, the *urbaria* did not re-rusticalize demesne land, except in cases of proven recent usurpation. In her later years, the empress became more radical and would have liked to abolish the *nexus subditelae* and the *robot* altogether, at least in Bohemia, but was forced to drop the idea by the opposition of the landlords and her councillors, with whom her son associated himself.

She had to content herself with minor reforms, and with introducing on certain crown properties, and recommending to private landlords, a system under which a peasant, while remaining subject to the authority of his manorial lord, who remained the legal "owner" of the land, might buy himself into a position which was, in practice, that of a nonevictable copyholder paying an annual rent in cash.

The position was thus still a tangle of loose ends when Joseph II became sole ruler, and he set himself, with his usual vigor, to tidying them up. He, again, did not tamper with the *nexus subditelae* as such, but he officially abolished the status of "serfdom" (*Leibeigenschaft*, or servitude *ad personam*) wherever it still existed in the monarchy, reformed the procedure of the manorial courts, further improved the peasants' conditions of tenure, and introduced a very large number of miscellaneous reforms, such as limiting the lord's sporting rights over his peasants' land, abolishing various economic "*banalités*" formerly enjoyed by him, etc. He had proposed to go further, for in the last years of his reign he was preparing a really radical change, viz., to raise the whole "contributio" exclusively from a single land tax, to be levied equally on all land in the country: all the peasant's economic obligations to his lord were to be compounded for a fixed rent, to be paid in cash. This measure, indeed, never came into force, for the outcry against it from the landlords was so formidable that Joseph postponed the introduction of it, and died before the second date fixed, and his successor first suspended it, then let it lapse.

Maria Theresa's *robot* patents and *urbaria* do not easily lend themselves to reproduction: they are very detailed documents, full of special local provisions of little general interest. In the following series we therefore present only three texts from her reign: two which illustrate the change in her views on the merits of the *nexus subditelae*, and an extract from the report of the Commission of Enquiry sent to enquire into the causes of the peasant unrest in Bohemia. Joseph's enactments are, as a rule, more manageable, but so numerous that it is impossible to give more than a selection of them; we give here a few of the most important.

A. MARIA THERESA AND THE NEXUS SUBDITELAE

The following quotations show the development of Maria Theresa's ideas on this question. The first (quoted by F. M. Mayer, *Geschichte Oesterreichs*, 5th Ed., Vienna, 1960, Vol. II, p. 427) was written in 1742. The French invaders of Bohemia had promised the peasants their freedom, and it had been suggested to Maria Theresa that she might counter this by a similar proclamation. She replied:

IT CAN never be thought practicable to abolish the *nexus subditelae* altogether, for there is no country which does not make a distinction between lords and subjects; to free the peasant from his obligations toward his lord would make the one ungovernable and the other discontented, and would in any case run contrary to justice.

Our second quotation is taken from Arneth's *Maria Theresia*, Vol. IX, p. 349 and dates from November, 1772. Maria Theresa had introduced her *Robotpatent* in Bohemia, regulating the length, conditions, etc., of *robot*, but was now hoping to get the landlords to follow the example she was setting on certain Crown estates of letting the peasants commute into copyholders paying money rents but doing no other services for their holdings. The abbot of one monastery in Moravia had obeyed her wishes, and the chancellor, Kaunitz, had recommended that he be given a distinction, to encourage others to follow his example. At this moment Maria Theresa was feeling so strongly the necessity of adopting her plan that she was threatening to abdicate if the lords resisted it. She answered Kaunitz:

As to the abolition of serfdom, which would be the only way of keeping me at the helm of the State, I have today ordered Blanc [Franz Anton von Blanc, her chief supporter among her advisers] to raise this on point 5 of the agenda [of the State Council]. If I were alone and *en vigeur*, not only would he [the abbot] have got all this, but I would have created him a Prince, to do honor to the Monastery.

In 1775 she had calmed down a little, but had not changed the view she now held of the desirability of abolishing serfdom altogether, and was still deeply embittered against her son and coregent, Joseph, for opposing her. The following is an extract from a letter written by her to her son the Archduke Ferdinand (quoted by F. Kubin, *Briefe der Kaiserin Maria Theresia*, 2 Vols., Munich and Leipzig, 1914, Vol. I, pp. 239ff.):

THE CARNIVAL takes up little of my time, but Bohemian affairs— the hope of reaching a fixed system at last—much of it. Not that there are revolts or even insubordinations at this moment, but it may be expected in the summer, if the necessary measures have not been taken by then, for the peasants are in despair over the excesses of the lords, and the latter have again succeeded, as they always have during the thirty-six years of my rule, in getting out of things, have never created order, and have always oppressed the subjects. I believe that if the Emperor [Joseph] would, I will not even say support me, but only remain neutral, I should succeed in abolishing serfdom and the forced services; then everything would be all right. But unfortunately, these gentlemen, seeing that they could not impose on me, have put themselves on the Emperor's side. . . . The Bohemian situation is causing me much worry, the more so, since the Emperor and I cannot agree on methods. The oppression of these poor people and the tyranny are known and recorded. What is needed is to establish equitable principles. I was already reaching the stage of action, when suddenly the landlords, to whom, incidentally, all the Ministers belong, succeeded in making the Emperor hesitate, and thus they succeeded in one moment in undoing the work of two years. I hope that the measures now being applied will be sufficient to re-establish order and obedience, but I am much afraid that it will prove necessary to resort to force. People who have no hope have nothing to fear, and are dangerous. I should like to bring the people to obedience and yet at the same time to get them some alleviations.

From the report of the Commission of Enquiry into the conditions of the peasants in Bohemia, presented to the Council of State in June, 1769. The report is in the Austrian State archives, Vienna. A modern writer to quote it is F. Fejtö, *Un Hapsbourg Révolutionnaire, Joseph II*, Paris, 1952, pp. 129ff.

The *robot* gives rise to continual vexations. Even those nobles who have the best intentions are unable to protect their peasants, because their agents are rough, evil, violent and grasping. These burdens are terrifyingly heavy, and it is not surprising that the peasants try to evade them by every means. In consequence of the arbitrary allocation of the *robot*, the peasants live in a condition of real slavery; they become savage and brutalized, and cultivate the lands in their charge badly. They are rachitic, thin and ragged; they are forced to do *robot* from their infancy. In their ruinous huts, the parents sleep on straw, the children naked on the wide shelves of earthenware stoves; they never wash, which promotes the spread of epidemics; there are no doctors to look after them. . . . Even their personal effects are not safe from the greed of the great lords. If they own a good horse, the lord forces them to sell it him, or if their good horse succumbs to the severity of the *robot*, they are compensated with a blind old screw. In many places the serfs are forced to buy sick sheep from their lord at an arbitrarily fixed price. Implements of torture are set up in every village market square, or in front of the castle;

recalcitrant peasants are thrown into irons, they are forced to sit
astride a sharp wooden horse, which cuts deeply into their flesh;
stones are hung on their legs; for the most trifling offense they
are given fifty strokes of the rod; the serf who arrives late for
his *robot*, be it only half an hour, is beaten half-dead. Many flee
into Prussia to escape this reign of terror; there are hundreds of
huts which their occupants have abandoned because they threatened
to collapse and they had not the means to repair them. In other
places the thatches have been taken off to feed the horses for
lack of fodder, because these wretched creatures are forbidden to
gather leaves in the forest for fear of their disturbing the game. Even
when the harvest has been good they are obliged to ask for seed
from their lord, and he sells it them at an extortionate price. The
big landlords drive away the Jews, who make loans on better
terms. . . . The Kingdom of Bohemia is like a statue which is col-
lapsing because its pedestal has been taken away, because all the
charges of the Kingdom are born by the peasants, who are the
sole taxpayers.

B. Peasant Patents Issued by Joseph II

The Penal and Subjects' Patents of September 1, 1781

Joseph II's two first enactments in the field of the landlord-peasant relationship, which were issued simultaneously and were mutually com-
plementary, constituted an attempt to make the system of manorial
courts operate at the same time effectively and justly. The "Penal Patent"
(*Strafpatent*), which is reproduced below, regulated the procedure to be
followed by the courts against a peasant offender, and laid down the
penalties that such courts were entitled to impose. Its counterpart, the
Subjects' Patent (*Untertanspatent*) laid down the procedure to be
followed by a "subject" aggrieved by any action on the part of his manorial lord or the lord's agents. We do not reproduce this, out of considerations of space, noting only that it laid down a very elaborate
procedure, the first stage of which had to be complaint to the court
itself; but if the court did not recognize and remedy the grievance,
the peasant might appeal to the Kreis authorities, and might in such
case avail himself of legal aid. Both Patents are reproduced in Kropatschek's *Summlung* for 1784, as Nos. 365 and 366 respectively; the
text of the Subjects' Patent may be found also in Wendrinsky's *Kaiser
Joseph II*, pp. 221–8.

PENAL PATENT (*Strafpatent*) OF SEPTEMBER 1, 1781

That on the one hand, the general welfare may be promoted and preserved, and the dependence and obedience of the subjects to their lawful lords, which is necessary for tranquility, be established, and on the other hand, that subjects be protected against any abuse by the manorial authority—Be it enacted:

1. Every subject shall obey and submit to the commands of the Crown services and the orders of the manorial lords and their officials.

2. No subject shall be judge in his own case, but shall carry any complaint to the lawful authorities, and act as instructed by them.

3. A person disobeying such instructions is to be punished as ordered by the manorial authority unless a penalty has already been imposed on him by a higher instance.

4. Persons inciting others to disobedience or combining with them to that purpose are to be regarded as principal offenders.

5. Before any subject is punished, his offense shall be recited to him in the local Court in the presence of the magistrate or of two neighbors, and his defense heard. If his defense is untenable, or if his offense is proved by witnesses, the authority shall impose on him a punishment appropriate to the offense.

6. A record must be drawn up stating the offense, indictment and all attendant circumstances, and the sentence. This shall be read aloud and signed by the neighbors convoked for the purpose.

7. Should the subject wish to appeal against the punishment, he is to be furnished free of charge with a copy of this record; but the authority may proceed at once to put the sentence into effect.

8. The punishments which the manorial Court or its officials may award are the following:

   a. Detention in decent circumstances not prejudicial to health; this may include a diet of bread and water.
   b. Hard labor.
   c. Rigorous detention and hard labor in irons.
   d. Eviction from house and land.

In framing the sentence, regard must be had to the age or extreme youth of the offender, and in general, to his physical condition; the severer punishments must be awarded only to individuals

on whom lighter punishments have had no effect; sentences of detention and penal labor awarded at a time when urgent work in the
fields is in progress shall not be served until this is completed.

9. A sentence of a week's detention or of expulsion from house
and land must first be approved by the Kreis office.

10. The Court must send the record of the case to the Kreis
office, which shall confirm it within a maximum of eight days if
approved or else institute enquiries within that period.

11. A subject sentenced to detention does not have to pay for his
keep, neither can a fine, in cash or its equivalent, be imposed on him.
Should he, however, have inflicted damage, this shall be assessed
by qualified persons, and equitable compensation fixed.

12. The manorial Courts and their servants are not to make unreasonable demands on the subjects. If found guilty of this they are
to be punished by the Kreis office. Records of these punishments
are to be sent quarterly to the Provincial authorities.

*The Serfdom Patent of November 1, 1781; the Buying In Patent of
the Same Date; the Hungarian* Jobbágypatent *of August 22, 1785*

Of the three Patents which we now reproduce, the two first were again
issued simultaneously (on November 1, 1781). The title of Serfdom
Patent by which the first of them was, from the outset, generally known
has earned Joseph a reputation which he did not deserve, for it has
created a widespread impression that he transformed the peasants of the
monarchy from serfs into free men. In fact, even before the issue of the
Patent true serfdom had not existed anywhere in the monarchy, except
to a limited extent in Galicia, where it was on its way out, and even such
restrictions as might be held to constitute servitude *ad personam* (such
as are described in the Patent) no longer existed in most of the German-
Austrian provinces, having either been officially abolished there or at
least fallen into desuetude. Since, on the other hand, the Patent did
not make the peasants free men, but left them in a condition of "moderate hereditary subjugation," it made so little difference to the inhabitants of the German-Austrian provinces that in some of them it was
promulgated only because of the reference in it to military service.
It is, however, true that the concessions in it were of real and great
importance for the Bohemian Lands, in which it greatly facilitated the
progress of industrialization.

The Buying-In Patent, an attempt to secure wider application of the
principle that Maria Theresa had already introduced on Crown estates,[1]

[1] See above, p. 171.

again had only small practical effects, less owing to resistance by the landlords than because the peasants rarely possessed the cash to carry through the transaction and where they did, were often reluctant to use it for this purpose.

The two Patents were promulgated in the German-Austrian and Bohemian Lands, Land by Land, in the course of 1782 and 1783, always in identical or near-identical form and in each case separately. In Hungary, promulgation did not take place until 1785, when the two were combined in a single enactment, which also covered (briefly) the ground of the two Patents of September 1, 1781. We give this (slightly abbreviated) as the third number in this subseries. Interesting in this third document is the reference to "liberty" as a "natural right." The Hungarian Diet of 1790–91 (which, of course, denied the legal validity of any of Joseph II's enactments) then re-enacted the substance of it in its Law XXXVI.

The texts of the Serfdom and Buying-In Patents translated here are reproduced in Kropatschek's *Sammlung* for 1781 (Nos. 480, 481); that of the *Jobbágypatent* in Wendrinsky, *op. cit.*, pp. 232–3.

THE SERFDOM PATENT

Patent of November 1, 1781, *in re* Manorial Lords and Subjects. The servile status of subjects is herewith abolished completely and the following dispositions enacted:

1. Any subject is entitled to marry, subject to previous notification and acquisition of a certificate, to be delivered free of charge.

2. He may, provided he observes the regulations governing conscription for military service, leave his present manor and settle or take service on another within the Province; but if he wishes to establish himself as a peasant cultivator or cottager on another manor, he must ask for a leaving certificate, which must also be issued him free of charge, to be shown to the new manorial authority.

3. A subject is free to learn any handicraft, trade, etc., and seek his livelihood where he will. For this no leaving permit is necessary.

4. Subjects are no longer required to perform domestic service for their lords, except orphans, who may be required to do such service for a period not exceeding three years.

5. No services shall be imposed on or required of subjects beyond the *robot* and payments in kind and cash attaching to their holdings.

Subjects are bound to render obedience to their lords in virtue of the existing laws.

THE BUYING-IN PATENT

Patent of November 1, 1781, *in re* Manors and Subjects.

Manors must be prepared to cede to their peasants, on request, the possession of their holdings against an equitable remuneration. The advantages enjoyed by subjects already possessing their holdings, or acquiring possession of them in the future, are defined as follows:

a. As soon as a subject acquires possession of his holding, he may, in virtue of the *dominium utile* now vested in him, but without infringement of the manorial rights, use, dispose of, mortgage, sell, or exchange it at will, except that the land going with the house may not be sold without the house.

b. A subject is not obliged to obtain manorial permission before raising a mortgage on his holding; but shall not mortgage more than two-thirds of his real estate; if he does so, he may be dispossessed of his holding as prescribed by law.

c. Debts are to be registered only if the creditor so desires.

Subjects not possessing their holdings in *dominio utile* are not serfs in respect of their persons, but must, however, subject themselves to the laws of their present *nexus* in respect of their holdings until they have effected the purchase. The manors, however, are strictly forbidden to force their subjects to make this purchase against their wills, or to impose onerous obligations on them in connection with the transaction. The Kreis offices and Provincial authorities must see to this.

EXTRACTS FROM JOSEPH II'S SERFDOM PATENT FOR HUNGARY

We, Joseph II, etc., to all whom it may concern: Whereas from the beginning of Our reign We have directed Our paternal care and Our unremitting endeavor toward promoting so far as possible and establishing on a firm basis the welfare of the peoples subject to Us, without distinction of rank, nationality, or religion:

Having realized and recognized that the improvement of agriculture and the encouragement of diligence are the two most excellent means of achieving this end, but that they cannot be effectual unless personal liberty, which is every man's natural and political right, is generally extended also to the subjects, and the possession of the property possessed by them, insofar as vested in them by the law of the land, is assured to them and established: it is consequently Our most gracious will that it be proclaimed everywhere in the Realm, for all to know and mark:

1. That We do altogether abolish the so-called condition of villein-age [*jobbágystand*], insofar as this has hitherto imposed a perpetual subjection on the subject and has bound him to the soil of his abode, and the word *jobbágy*, which in the Hungarian language means a "subject,"[1] shall no longer be used in this sense; on the contrary, We ordain and command that subjects, without distinction of nationality or language, shall be regarded in respect of their persons as persons free to move about (as which We pronounce them) and shall everywhere be so regarded and treated, as natural law and the public welfare demand, whence it follows that all demands by the subjects or the so-called proceedings "for the recovering of liberty" have for the future to cease altogether.

[Paras. 2 and 3 repeat almost verbatim the provisions of paras. 1 to 3 of the Austrian "Serfdom Patent," while para. 4 allows all subjects the same rights in respect of their holdings as are enjoyed by peasants who have "bought in" their holdings under the Austrian Manorial Patent of 1781. Para. 5 prohibits eviction of a subject or his heir without due cause and formal sentence pronounced by the committee of the country court. Para. 6 summarizes the elaborate provisions of the Austrian Subjects' Patent as follows:]

As for the other questions not covered by these provisions, subjects must submit themselves to Our edicts already issued, but the County is required to grant legal assistance to any aggrieved subject and to secure for him redress for the wrong inflicted on him.

Joseph's Decision in Favor of the Indivisible Peasant Holding
(Communication to the State Council, October 15, 1786)

This document stands somewhat apart from the others quoted here, but is worth reproducing on account of its great importance for the agrarian history of the monarchy. The question of the divisibility or otherwise of peasant holdings was a very vexed one. Strong arguments were brought up on both sides: on the one hand, that too great subdivi-

---

[1] Actually, as then used, it denoted a "rustical" peasant holder, by contrast with a cottager or landless man.

sion resulted in the creation of uneconomic small and dwarf holdings; on the other, that the retention of relatively large holdings in a single hand created a landless rural proletariat. Further, it was argued that the holdings as originally allocated (in days when the density of the population was less and methods of cultivation more primitive) were often too large to be cultivated to the full by a single holder, and that smaller holdings were often economically more profitable, especially in districts where the population had secondary sources of income. The maintenance of the undivided holding (*Bestiftungszwang*) was in fact the usual practice in most Lands of the monarchy.

The question had suddenly been made immediate by the introduction of the new civil code (*Bürgerliches Gesetzbuch*), which laid down the principle of equal inheritance for all heirs of the same degree. The question was then asked, whether this law should apply to real property. Joseph's decision laid down a ruling which was thereafter maintained until 1868, when it was altered by the liberal government of the day, with results which are often considered to have been most unhappy for the Austrian peasantry. Joseph's decision runs:

THE CENTRAL question for the State is whether the peasant holding should be held undivided by a single individual, or subdivided? Strong peasant units, composed of one family of several members, answer all requirements of the State much better than smaller holdings. It therefore appears preferable to declare farms [*Hausgründe*] inalienable and indivisible, so that only one son, whether the elder or the younger, holds it, whereas the so-called outlying fields [*Ueberlandsgründe*] are treated as alienable, whereby the better or wealthier farmer could buy land from the poorer or less efficient. The peasant might also raise mortgages on the farm, but in case of distraint, a single creditor would have to take over the whole property, and this could never be subdivided.

The Taxation and Urbarial Patent of 1789

As last item in this series of Joseph II's enactments on the peasant-landlord question we give the paragraphs dealing with the peasants' obligations in his radical Patent of February 10, 1789, introducing a single, uniform land tax on all land in the monarchy. As we have said above, the resistance to this Patent was so violent that in the end it was (thanks to the intervention of death, which removed its author from the field) never put into force—a fact which does not, however, detract from its interest, nor, indeed, from its importance, for it was by dropping this measure that Leopold succeeded in persuading the Estates to accept the great bulk of his brother's other reforms. The measure was originally issued in the form of a Rescript, dated February 10, 1789, which ordered all provincial governments to promulgate it with an intimation that it would enter into force as from November 1, 1791. Our text is taken from Grünberg, *op. cit.*, Vol. II, pp. 443ff.; the text of the Galician version is given also in Kropatschek's *Sammlung* (1789), No. 283, pp. 110ff. The first chapter (sections 1 to 9), not reproduced here, gives notice that the old provincial "contributions" are to be replaced by a land tax, to be levied equally on all land, irrespective of the quality of its owner, at the rate of 12 florins, 13 1/3 kreuzer per 100 florins of its gross yield, without allowance for seed, labor costs, etc., and not inclusive of any income derived from urbarial dues or from trades (for Galicia, in view of its poverty, the sum was fixed at one-third less, viz., 8 florin, 16 4/5 kreuzer). Every commune was in future to be responsible for the collection and delivery of the tax.

THE TAX

[Chapter II is headed: "On the Manorial Dues from the Peasants" (*von den herrschaftlichen Urbarialforderungen*). It runs:]

The final objective of the State—to establish equality through a proportionate allocation of the land taxes, and thus enable the owners of land to carry out their civic duties without hardship, and not only be capable of maintaining their diligence but also to have an incentive to increase it—could never be attained unless at the same time alleviations were granted to those subjects on whom the burden or demands of their landlords, magistrates, or recipients of tithe weigh too heavily.

10. Far as it be from Us to intervene arbitrarily in the property rights of the manorial lords or to enquire into the causes, customs, or contracts from which the present obligations in service, cash, and kind, and the so-called subjects' dues sometimes levied on death or change of tenure, derive; yet the duty by which We are bound to watch over the preservation of the whole requires, that where the manorial dues exceed the resources which the subject can draw from his land, equitable limits and definitive bounds shall be set. With this object, and considering that under the above dispositions the definition of gross yield has been raised, no deduction being made either for seed or for cultivation, and further that the cultivator, after providing for himself and his family, has also to bear separately the communal expenses and the payments to the minister of religion and the schoolmaster, We lay down as a general rule that the subject shall be allowed to retain, on an average, a minimum of 70 per cent of his gross yield, as declared and controlled, to

provide for these demands, and only the remaining 30 per cent shall be devoted to covering the Provincial land tax and the manorial dues, 12/florins, 13½/kreuzer, for the former and 17/florins, 46⅔/kreuzer, for the latter, this 17/florins, 46⅔/kreuzer, to include everything due from the subject to his landlord and manorial authority, whether in cash, in kind (value converted into cash), or in haulage or hand service, and also the taxes, death duties, and duties on change of tenure customary in some Provinces, which last, insofar—but only insofar—as they affect real property and industries, are to be assessed on a twenty years' average and converted into a fixed annual payment.

In calculating the manorial dues, the same scale, allowing for the different quality of the land of which a subject's holding consists, is to be applied as has been laid down for calculating the State taxation. Thus, the maximum rate for arable and vineyards is fixed at 15 florins, 25 kreuzer per hundred, for leys, gardens and fishponds at 26 florins, 2¾ kreuzer, for rough pasturage and woodlands at 30 florins, 50 kreuzer, and for lakes and rivers at 15 florins, 25 kreuzer, giving an absolute maximum average of 17 florins, 46⅔ kreuzer.

Where, however, a subject has not at present to pay so much, his future obligations are to remain at the lower figure.

11. According to these principles, money is thus in the future the sole, immutable measure for determining all manorial dues; and in future, the manorial authorities are, as a general rule, not entitled to demand anything but money from the subjects. The two parties are, however, free to convert this monetary sum into dues in kind or labor, including wage labor, under agreement *voluntarily* entered into between them; but this agreement must be concluded each time for a minimum of three years, and attested by the Kreis office.

Should the lord and the subject be unable to agree on the value of the service [*robot*], work, or dues in kind previously rendered, the Kreis office, under the chairmanship of the Higher Committee for Tax Regulation . . . shall decide on the valuation of the labor services and work on the model of the State properties in the Kreis, where conditions are similar, on which the labor services have already been commuted for an equitable and reasonable cash equivalent; the dues in kind are to be valued in accordance with local prices.

If a subject is able to prove that the dues, etc., hitherto paid by him amounted to more than the estimated 17 florins, 46⅔ kreuzer per hundred, the Kreisamt, under the chairmanship of the Tax Regulation Committee, shall reduce them to this maximum, and the subject is allowed a maximum of two years to produce the necessary documents, etc.

12. If a case of reduction of previous obligations arises, and if the subject's obligations are towards more than one manorial authority and tithe beneficiary, each must concede a proportionate reduction thereof.

13. The regulations in para. 10 relate only to the so-called rustical lands, which have always been used as peasant holdings and under previous Patents can no longer be reconverted to demesne land, under pain of punishment; this irrespective of whether the tenure is hereditary and bought in, or not. In the case of demesne land no control is exercised over the agreements between the landlords and their tenants or emphyteutical holders.

To avoid undue delays: should any question arise whether any land is demesne or rustical, the existing situation is to be retained, and a peasant who claims as rustical any land now in *de facto* possession of the landlord, or *vice versa*, must bring proof that the land in question fell within the category claimed by him in the "normal years" fixed in each Province for the determination of the demesne and rustical areas in them.

14. Cottagers of all categories and livers-in continue to pay their previous dues, which they may also commute against cash with the agreement of their masters, and, where their obligations consist of payments to be made on death or change of tenure, these are to be commuted for annual payments calculated on the basis of the average receipts over the last twenty years.

Where cottagers hold taxable land besides their cottages, or where livers-in hold such land, they are to be treated in respect thereof in accordance with Our general rules for all landholders.

Millers, brewers, innkeepers, and other owners of assets deriving from a license to trade, if they also possess rustical holdings, are taxed like other rusticalists in respect thereof. The remainder of their obligations, attached to the property as a whole or, more properly, to the trade license, is, where occasional duties and payments on death and change of tenure are levied, commuted into an annual payment calculated on the basis that such payments recur every twenty to twenty-five years, but only on the yield from the real property.

Given in Vienna, February 10, 1789
JOSEPH, LEOPOLD, COUNT KOLLOWRAT, FRANZ KARL, COUNT VON
KRESSEL, JOHANN WENZEL, COUNT VON UGARTE
ad mandatum, etc., JOSEPH VON KALLER

16. "Manners Makyth Man"

Fond as Maria Theresa was of her eldest son and destined successor, she was far too sensible to be blind to his faults. Several writings from her pen which date from his childhood express misgivings over his rudeness and lack of consideration towards his inferiors, and these defects of his did not grow less pronounced as he came to man's estate and began to take part in public affairs. They grew more pronounced still after he had succeeded his father as emperor and co-regent of the Habsburg *Hausmacht*. The letter which follows (which is printed in full in Arneth's *Maria Theresia und Joseph II. Ihre Correspondenz*, Vol. 1, pp. 199ff., and in extract in many other works, including Kretschmayer's *Maria Theresa*, pp. 278–9) was written (in French) on September 14, 1776; it was in answer to a letter written to her by Joseph ten days earlier. Of the two specific points to which it refers, it may be mentioned that Count d'Ayasase, a senior Austrian general, had suggested certain changes in the High Command of the Austrian army. Joseph had written that he was unable to imagine any reason for this beyond d'Ayasase's *amour propre* and desire to discredit and elbow out those senior to him. The "San Remo affair" was a diplomatic tangle in which Austria had become involved with Prussia. Joseph, who was just then suffering from an acute attack of *Schwärmerei* for Frederick of Prussia, described Kaunitz's handling of the problem in terms most wounding to the chancellor, and enclosed the note which he had himself dictated to the German minister, this, again being couched in terms most offensive to his mother's advisers.

It must unfortunately be added that although Joseph in his reply expressed contrition and filial gratitude for the good advice, it in fact ran off him like water off a duck's back. This was immeasurably to his own disadvantage, and also to that of his monarchy, in which he could have put through, as permanencies, many salutary reforms had he set about them with even a modicum of ordinary human courtesy.

Monsieur mon cher fils

   . . . I cannot pass over in silence what you write about Ayasase. Since I have known him, I have never found him so full of *amour propre* or so malicious as to harm anyone out of self-love. I know him to be serious, stiff, but upright and zealous, no intrigant. Why, then, wish to see him in a bad light and to condemn him out of hand? I greatly fear that through having a generally bad opinion of people you will lose even the small number of honest men by mixing and confounding them with the others. It is a most essential point, for a man of good intentions will not suffer himself to be suspected and confused with others; he will rather remove himself, if he can, or he will serve with less zeal. The great moving force is confidence; if that is absent, everything is absent.

   The same with the San Remo affair. I must confess to you that the terms in which the German note was drawn up were such that I found it hard to believe that you could think like that, and find satisfaction in mortifying others and publicly humiliating them. I must tell you that is the exact opposite of what I have done all my life. I have preferred to get people to do what I wanted by kind words, to persuade them rather than force them. This has served me well. I hope you may find as many resources as I have in your States and your servants. . . .

   [Maria Theresa now goes into some small personal details of the way in which Joseph had personally wounded certain ministers, and goes on:]

Do you think that this is the way to keep your subjects? I fear that you will fall into the hands of rascals who, in order to achieve their end, will put up with anything that a soul which is noble and truly attached cannot endure. Judge of my situation *vis-à-vis* Kaunitz! I must do him the justice to say that he was cut to the quick, and said only: "I did not think to have deserved these reproaches." What will Stahremberg think when he sees your thoughts? And what strikes me most, this was no immediate reaction; it was twenty-four hours after having received the dispatches, and thus after ripe reflection, that you pleased yourself to drive the dagger into the heart; ironically and with reproaches against people whom you yourself believe to be the best, and whom you have tried to retain. I was obliged almost to doubt whether you were sincere then. What I fear is that you will never find a friend, a man attached to

Joseph—by which you set such store—for it is neither from the
Emperor nor from the co-Regent that these biting, ironical, malicious shafts proceed, but from the heart of Joseph, and this is what
alarms me, and what will be the misfortune of your days and will
entail that of the Monarchy and of us all. I shall no longer be
alive, but I had flattered myself that after my death I should live on
in your heart, that your numerous family, your States, would lose
nothing by my death, but would, on the contrary, gain by it. Can
I nurse this hope, if you indulge yourself in this tone which repels
all tenderness and friendship? Imitation does not flatter; this hero
who has made so much talk about himself,[1] this conqueror, has he a
single friend? Has he not reason to distrust the whole world? What
sort of a life is that from which humanity is banished? In our religion, charity, above all, is the chief foundation, not an advice but a
precept, and do you think that you are practicing it when you
afflict and bite at people ironically, even those who have rendered
great services and who have no weaknesses save those common to
us all, such as do not harm either the State or us, but only themselves, and who even in this case have only done their duty in pointing out the drawbacks, who have tried to find a compromise way
to reconcile what is past and what is wanted now, with the difficulties which are to be expected—and this is how it is taken! Who
will be willing to risk this experience again? To expose himself, if
only under the imperative necessity of representing the truth to
you, when he is received so?

Talented as you are, you cannot possibly have all the experience,
all the familiarity with the past and the present, to do things alone.
A "yes" or a "no," a simple refusal would have been better than
all these ironical outpourings in which your heart has vented itself
and found satisfaction in admiring the volubility of its words. Beware of taking pleasure in malice! Your heart is not yet bad, but
it will become it. It is more than time to stop relishing all these
bons mots, these witticisms, which are only designed to wound
others and to pour ridicule on them, thereby estranging all decent
people and making one believe that the whole human race is unworthy of respect and affection, because one has by one's own act
repelled all that is good and has only kept and opened the door to
rogues, toadies, and flatterers. Look here at the example of the Sin-

---

[1] Frederick of Prussia.

zendorffs. One cannot deny them wit, talent, a pleasant manner, but no one can endure them; bad family men, bad subjects, good for no employment either in war or in politics. In a sovereign the harm would be greater still, and would be disastrous both to him and to all his subjects.

After this long sermon, which you must pardon me, for it comes from overtenderness of heart towards you and my countries, I will show you a picture of yourself, with all your gifts and attractions. You are a coquette of wit, and run after it wherever you think to find it, without discrimination. A *bon mot*, a witticism, found in a book or uttered by someone, obsesses you, you apply it at the first opportunity without considering whether it is appropriate, like your sister Elisabeth with her beauty: If she pleases the Swiss guard or a Prince, that is enough for her; she asks for no more.

In ending this letter, I take your head between my hands, embrace you tenderly and pray that you may forgive me the tedium of this long scolding; look only at the heart from which it comes. All I wish is to see you esteemed and loved by the world as you deserve.

I remain, ever your good old mother

17. Maria Theresa on Proposals to Partition Poland and Turkey in Europe

The first two of the three documents which follow were written at almost the same stage of the tangled negotiations for the so-called First Partition of Poland. While Austria herself had actually been the first of Poland's three neighbors to deprive her of territory *de facto* in her possession, by occupying and subsequently resuming sovereignty over the Szepes (Zips) area of North Hungary, those actions could be regarded as a special case; she had been invited by a Polish party to enter the area, and it was still technically Hungarian (it had been pledged to Poland by Sigismund, king of Hungary, in 1412, but not formally ceded). But it gave Catherine of Russia and Frederick of Prussia an excuse for planning a far more extensive truncation of Poland, in which Austria could not, of course, be ignored. The negotiations which now opened were complicated, from the Austrian side, by two factors: one, that while the last word still rested with the empress, the actual negotiations were being conducted by her chancellor, Kaunitz, under the auspices of her son, Joseph, and neither man shared her views on international morality, so that Austria was speaking with two voices. Secondly, the Porte had since 1768 been at war with Russia, which in 1770 had occupied and proclaimed a protectorate over the Danubian Provinces. In July, 1771, Austria had, on Joseph's initiative, concluded a treaty with the Porte, under which she promised, in return for subsidies and commercial advantages, not to allow Russia to cross the Danube. In return, she was to be allowed herself to annex "Little Wallachia," i.e., the western end of that province.

The first of the documents which follows (printed in Arneth's *Maria Theresia*, Vol. IX, pp. 353–4; original in French) was written by Maria Theresa, probably for the private eyes of Kaunitz, on January 22, 1772. The situation then was that Russia was making various proposals, some going as far as a complete partition of the Balkans between Russia and Austria (which in that case would make war on the Porte). Another was that Russia, while helping herself to Polish territory in the north, should cede the Danubian Provinces and Bessarabia, the southern portions to Austria, the northern to Poland, in compensation for her losses elsewhere. Maria Theresa was still not only resisting any suggestion of breaking faith with the Porte, but was also opposed, on moral grounds, to Austria's annexing any territory that was lawfully Polish, and was urging that Austria should obtain her compensation by the re-cession to her by Prussia of parts of Silesia (perhaps also other areas of Prussia).[1]

Kaunitz was himself against the Balkan partition, but less opposed to the Danubian; plainly foreseeing that Frederick would never cede back any part of Silesia, he had agreed with Joseph that Austria should then press for a share of Poland as valuable as those taken by Russia and Prussia. Van Swieten was going to Potsdam to discuss the whole problem with Frederick.

A. Memorandum by Maria Theresa (January 22, 1772)

I am so depressed by our critical situation that I am unable even to see it clearly and to look for a remedy which could not be good, but might be the least bad. Our first endeavor must be to bring about peace between the two belligerents[2] as quickly as possible; postponement would only make our position worse. Now, after the false steps which we have taken—I still regard them in that light— since November, 1770, when we decided to bring our troops back out of the Netherlands and Italy, and after the unlucky Convention

---

[1] Another memorandum, written probably on the same day, objected to any solution except that of compensation in the form of Prussian territory.
[2] Russia and the Porte.

with the Turks, it is no longer possible to retrace our steps. The over-threatening tone towards the Russians, our secretiveness towards our allies as well as our enemies—all this resulted from the principle which we adopted that we must try to gain profit from the war between Russian and the Porte, to extend our frontiers and secure advantages of which we never thought before the war. We wanted to act *à la* Prussia and at the same time to preserve the appearance of honesty. This led us to deceive ourselves in respect of the means, as we are now deceiving ourselves about the appearance and course of events. I may be wrong: the course of events may be more favorable than I can persuade myself. But were they to obtain for us even the share offered in the first plan of partition (which I doubt more than ever after Lobkowitz's letter of yester-day), were they to get us the District of Wallachia and even Belgrade itself, I should still think the price too high, for we should have bought it at the cost of our honor, of the good name of the Monarchy, of our good faith, and our religious principles. Since the outset of my unhappy reign we have at least tried always to show a true and just attitude, good faith, moderation, and loyal fulfillment of our obligations. This won us the confidence—I make bold to say, the admiration—of all Europe, the respect and homage even of our enemies. In the past year all this has been lost. I admit that I find this almost intolerable, and that nothing in the world has pained me so much as the loss of our good name. Unfortunately, I must admit to you that we have deserved it. This is where I wish to apply the remedy, by rejecting as evil and destructive the prin-ciple of drawing advantage out of these troubled waters, and seeing how we can get out of this unhappy situation as quickly as we may, and as cheaply, without thinking of conquests, but thinking indeed of our good name, by reinstating loyalty and good faith, and—as far as possible—the political balance.

B. Second Memorandum (February, 1772)

The second memorandum (Arneth, *Maria Theresia*, Vol. IX, pp. 595–6; in German translation, *ibid*., pp. 358–60,) was written a month later, after van Swieten's audience with Frederick. Frederick had, as expected, flatly rejected any idea of ceding Prussian territory and had objected to Kaunitz's proposals as to the share Austria might receive of Poland as excessive. He had suggested that Austria compen-sate herself in the Balkans, and in Wallachia, and in this connection the possibility of compensating Poland in the Danubian Provinces occupies a larger part of the foreground than in the preceding memorandum. The idea does not seem to have struck Maria Theresa as morally untenable (she probably regarded the provinces as lost to the Porte anyway), but she has other objections to it.

I admit that it goes against the grain for me to take a decision on a question of the justice of which I am by no means convinced, even if it were advantageous. But I cannot even see the advantage in any of the three courses between which I am to choose.

The easiest course would certainly be to accept the offer made to us of participating in the partition of Poland. But where is the justice in robbing an innocent party which we have always prided ourselves on defending and supporting? To what purpose are all these vast and costly preparations, all these loud, threatening affirmations of our determination to preserve the balance in northern Europe? The single motive of interest, that we should not remain alone between the two other Powers without securing any advantage, does not seem to me a sufficient or even an honorable pretext for joining in with two unjust usurpers, with the purpose of thrusting a third still further down, without any legal title.

I do not understand a policy which, when two use their superior strength to oppress an innocent victim, allows and enjoins a third to imitate them and commit the same injustice, as a simple precaution for the future and out of present expediency; this seems to me untenable. A Prince has no more rights than any other mortal; the greatness and support of his State will not avail him when the day comes on which we must all give account for our actions. If I can be convinced of the contrary, I am prepared to submit. I ardently hope that I am mistaken.

I have known long and exactly (and often lamented) the critical situation in which we stand, but a man must know when to discipline himself, and this is such an occasion. Whatever might accrue to us will not be half so large or valuable as the others' portions; we must not linger on it and allow ourselves to be tempted by an unequal partition. Our whole aim must be to endeavor to end this war as quickly as possible, honorably, and in such fashion that friends and foes alike are thankful to us and we win their respect through our honor and magnanimity. I will even go as far as to say that to do no man injustice is not an act of magnanimity but an effect of true principles. We have allied ourselves with the Porte; we have even accepted money from it; to find pretexts to make the Turks take a first false step and then enrich ourselves at their expense is in no way consonant with scrupulous honesty and true principles. I would never consent to it; there can, therefore, be no question of Serbia and Bosnia, the only Provinces which would bring us advantage. We are left with Wallachia and Moldavia, unsalubrious, devastated countries, exposed to the Turks, Tatars and Russians, with no fortresses, lands on which we should have to spend many millions of money, and many men, to keep hold of them. Our Monarchy can do without an enlargement of this kind, which would end by ruining it altogether; we should have then to turn back to Poland and assign her Moldavia and Wallachia as compensation. That would be the least evil, the only course to which I might possibly consent; any other would either lead to war with the Turks, which would be unjust, or to taking from a third party that which is his, without compensating him. What would France, Spain, England say if we were now suddenly to ally ourselves with those whom we have tried so hard to keep in check and whose conduct we have declared to be unjust? This, I agree, would be a denial of all that has been done during thirty years of my reign. Let us try rather to reduce the pretensions of others than think of sharing with them under conditions so unequal; let us be held weak rather than dishonorable.

C. Maria Theresa to Count Mercy (July 31, 1777)

While most commentators on these two famous documents have, naturally, been chiefly interested to emphasize the witness they bear to Maria Theresa's high moral principles (in which connection it will come as a surprise to many to observe that her objections to violating Austria's treaty with the Porte are expressed even more strongly than her repugnance to sharing in the truncation of Poland), the second of them in particular, is extremely interesting for its illustration of another feature of her mentality: her indifference to acquisition for acquisition's sake, unless the object seemed to her intrinsically valuable and further, her cavalier dismissal of the Danubian Provinces as possessing no such value.

This continence was another quality which her son did not share with her, and, we have said elsewhere, as soon as his mother's eyes were closed he entered into commerce with Catherine of Russia, concocting with her various schemes, similar to some of those put before Maria Theresa in 1770, for partitioning the Balkans between Russia and Austria. We quote later one document relating to one of these plans,[1] but Joseph was already evolving them before his mother's death, and it is not

---

[1] See below, p. 193.

without interest to add the following extract from another of her memoranda, which expresses in even more forcible terms than those used by her in the documents quoted above her view of such enterprises. This is a communication by her to Count Mercy-d'Argenteau, Austrian Ambassador in Paris, on July 31, 1777. The text is translated from Arneth, *Maria Theresia*, Vol. IX, p. 99.

THE PARTITION of the Ottoman Empire would be, of all enterprises, the most reckless and dangerous. What should we gain, if we were to extend our conquests to the walls of Constantinople itself? Unsalubrious, uncultivated Provinces, inhabited either not at all, or by unreliable Greeks,[1] which would not add to the forces of the Monarchy, but rather exhaust them. This would be an even more critical event than the Partition of Poland. . . . I will never lend my hand to a partition of the Porte, and I hope that my grandchildren after me will see the Turks in Europe.

18. Joseph II and the "Greek Project"

The document which follows forms an appropriate tailpiece to the preceding series. Maria Theresa's opposition did not make Catherine of Russia waver in her designs on Turkey, and Joseph fell increasingly under her spell. The two met in Russia—at Mogilev, on the Dnieper—in May, 1780, then going on to Saint Petersburg, and exchanged confidences. The suggestion made by Catherine—that all the gains in the Balkans should go to Russia, while Austria compensated herself in Rome—did not, indeed, appeal to Joseph, but he nevertheless concluded an alliance with Russia on May 21, 1781. This contained no provisions for territorial aggrandizement by either party, but on September 10, 1782, Catherine wrote to Joseph proposing a grandiose plan, the main features of which were to be the establishment of a Greek empire at Constantinople and a "Kingdom of Dacia" composed of Moldavia, Wallachia, and Bessarabia. Both would obviously have been mere Russian satellites; indeed, the Greek "emperor" was to be Catherine's own grandson, then an infant. Joseph's letter, given below, is his reply to these proposals; of which it may be added that on January 4, 1783, Catherine answered, accepting Joseph's conditions, except that she wanted the Morea and the Greek islands to go, not to Venice, but to her Greek empire.

[1] I.e., members of the Greek Church.

The "Greek Project" remained, indeed, a pipe-dream. The opposition of the other powers was such that it was never even put in treaty form, much less realized. It was, however, in pursuit of the dream that, when war broke out between Russia and the Porte in 1789, Russia having successfully egged the Porte into declaring it, Joseph, acting under the Treaty of 1781, embarked on the campaign that ended in the ruin of all his plans and in his own death.

The text is translated from Arneth, *Joseph II und Katherina Von Russland*, No. XXXIV (Vienna, 1869), pp. 172–3.

LETTER FROM JOSEPH TO CATHERINE (NOVEMBER 13, 1782)

IT WOULD be absolutely impossible to hope for any success failing an agreement with France, whereas if agreement is reached with her, it will be possible, as Your Imperial Majesty has Yourself well perceived, to contain the King of Prussia without the necessity of buying his consent at a heavy price. . . . As to the creation of a new hereditary Kingdom of Dacia for a Prince of the Greek religion, and the establishment of Your grandson Constantine as sovereign and Emperor of the Greek Empire at Constantinople, the fortunes of war alone can decide, and, if they are propitious, there will never be any difficulty from my side in the way of the satisfaction of all Your desires, if they are united and joint with those which suit me. On this latter point, I cannot conceal from You that after having reflected carefully on what might suit us best in one direction and the other, for the present and the future, and what would cause the least inconveniences and difficulties, I think that the following are the only frontiers which would be agreeable to the Austrian Monarchy: the town of Khotin, with a small territory the boundaries of which can be arranged, to serve as bridgehead for Galicia and the Bukovina, a part of Wallachia bounded by the Aluta and thence to Nicopolis inclusive, thence up the Danube to Belgrade, on both banks, three leagues[1] in depth, thus taking in the towns of Vidin, Orsova, and Belgrade, as bridgeheads to cover Hungary; from Belgrade the straightest and shortest line possible, conformably with the terrain, to the Adriatic, taking in the Gulf of the Drina; and finally the Venetian continental possessions such as Istria and Dalmatia would offer the only way of exploiting the products of My States; the Morean Peninsula, the Island of Candia [Crete], Cyprus, and the other numerous islands of the Archipelago could furnish ample

---

[1] Fifteen English statute miles.

compensation for these republicans, who in any case have snatched all that they possess from My State, either by guile, or by profiting from circumstances and moments of weakness. I could then have some vassals, like Venice today, and could consequently be of greater service to Your Imperial Majesty on all occasions. It is understood that Danubian trade remains perfectly free to My subjects, both down to its mouth in the Black Sea and at the exit from the Black Sea through the Dardanelles. The two new Empires of Dacia and Greece must bind themselves never to put restrictions or tolls of any kind on My vessels.

19. Problems for Joseph II

Those of the following descriptions which relate to the Poles and Ruthenes are taken from a work published in Vienna in 4 Volumes, 1804, J. A. Demian's *Darstellung der oe. Monarchie*, an originally conceived but highly entertaining and informative sort of guide to the monarchy as it was in the author's day. The descriptions of the "Vlachs" and gypsies of Transylvania can also be found, in substantially identical form, in the same book, but the author has copied these almost verbatim out of a somewhat earlier anonymous work (which may also be by Demian's hand), *Ueber den Nationalcharacter der in Siebenbürgen befindlichen Nationen* (Vienna, 1792). This little work distinguishes no fewer than twelve "nations" inhabiting Transylvania—Hungarians, Szekels, Saxons, Bulgars and Vlachs (whom he lumps together), "Landler" (Germans from Hanover), Armenians, Greeks, Jews, Moravian Brothers, Poles, Ruthenes or Russians, and gypsies.

One may sympathize with the anonymous author's rueful comment on the inapplicability of Joseph II's philosophy ("which distinguishes only two kinds of people, a good and a bad") to the realities of Transylvania, and the sketches which the two works give of the mores of some of the more backward peoples of the monarchy may give cause for thought to the reader of today, who is too apt to consider the problem of the multinational state as that of adjusting the relations between peoples all more or less on the same level of civilization.

THE POLES

THE GALICIAN noble's manners toward the world are gallant. Nobles touch cheeks in token of welcome; a young noble kisses his elder relatives on the shoulder; girls kiss one another on the neck or the bosom, but one would be greatly mistaken if one deduced from this that the friendship between them was intimate, affectionate, or lasting, for this polish has not reached the interior of their spirits. The Polish noble whose mouth is full of compliments and who is so gallant toward a woman that in five minutes he has bestowed fifty kisses on a lady's ungloved arm, behaves toward his servants with the utmost harshness and brutality, and if he is taking only few steps in the morning out of his house into the village or the fields, does not hesitate to take with him a cudgel with which to visit with instant punishment anything that displeases him. Things have altered only since the days of Joseph II, who expressly forbade landlords to beat or order the beating of their peasants at will. . . .

Polish nobles are very hospitable and entertain strangers, in particular, excellently. They never stint with food and drink, and their tables are often laden with dishes, which, however, are so ill-concocted with honey and brews of mead as to be practically uneatable by anyone but themselves. The dirt of their kitchens and the rags worn by their cooks are, moreover, so exceedingly repulsive that strangers whom curiosity has prompted to look into the kitchens lose their appetites for long periods. The lady of the house and mesdemoiselles her daughters would regard it as far beneath their dignity to keep an eye on the economy or the cooking, as a German does. Altogether, there is perhaps no people where the womenfolk, from the lowest to the highest class, have so little inclination for the domestic virtues as the Polish. For the rest, Polish women possess more agreeable qualities than true charms, more art to attract the eye than to hold it. The many tasteful dresses which one sees in Lemberg and elsewhere cover only coarse contours, and it would be vain to seek a bold, upright stature or blooming femininity in which perfect form is blended with majesty.

The Galician peasant in particular is a peculiar mixture of servility and refractoriness, of stupidity and cunning; in particular, the frequent enjoyment of brandy has become a terrible necessity—no less than meat—for him. When the peasant drives to market, he calls in on the way there at several Jewish taverns, leaves the payment till the return journey, then on that repeats all his visits and drinks away half, sometimes all, the money he has made at the market. He swills down twenty to thirty glasses at a sitting. His wife is not a hairsbreadth behind him. On Sundays and holidays they walk to the church in their best clothes, but barefoot, carrying their boots under their arms. At the entrance to the village in which the parish church stands they put on their boots; after Divine Service they take them off again in the same place and then go into the taverns with their husbands or kinsfolk. There they drink brandy till sundown, without eating so much as a morsel of bread; then they start off, singing, for their villages, which are often a couple of leagues away, and often spend the whole night lying in heaps on the road. Usually it is the Jews who provide this, the Galician peasants' fount of happiness, brandy, which serves him as means to drive away all cares, tonic, as medicine, to cheer him up and even to appease the pangs of hunger. At their frequent meetings the Jew enters into intimate conversation with him, listens to his complaints and often gives him sound advice. In these frequent conversations he learns what each peasant possesses, what he has to sell, what he is short of and what he can do without. Now the Jew is already master of the poor helot's property. Very soon the peasant drinks himself into indebtedness to the Jew, and this does not worry the creditor. He does not recite his sins to the peasant until he knows that the latter is no longer able to purge them with money. Then a composition is made, and the Jew takes everything the peasant offers in lieu of payment in cash, and renews his credit. The Jew knows all sorts of ways of shutting the mouth of the peasant's wife, too. Now the peasant enjoys a few happy days in careless tranquillity, and does not mind hungering so long as he is not athirst. But before long the time arrives when he has to pay dues to his landlord, buy supplies, and pay his taxes, and he can find no means of producing money. Again, he resorts to the Jew, who pays his debts and magnanimously contents himself with the peasant's mortgaging him his growing corn, assigning him his still unborn calf for a mess of pottage or making this or that journey for him, doing this or that job. The peasant feels only his immediate need, and immediate relief of it is all he wants. So his household remains eternally in the same state of wretchedness, and the peasant's continued habit of regarding the Jew as his friend gradually engenders an unlimited confidence in the Jew which is infinitely advantageous to the latter. To remedy this evil the Austrian Government has prohibited Jews from leasing the taverns in the country and the towns, and in 1780 ordered that Jews might reside in villages only as agriculturalists or craftsmen, because they had so corrupted the peasants as tavern-keepers. But this wise measure was relaxed. A decree of 1792 permitted Jewish distillers of brandy and all persons gaining their livelihoods from permitted trades, whether Jews or Christians, to continue to reside in the villages. The Jews have therefore gone on living in the villages, calling themselves distillers, while putting in a Christian as nominal licensee of the inn, but in reality continuing to practice the forbidden trade, and continuing to constitute a great danger for the population.

THE RUTHENES

The Mountain Ruthenes or Pokutians are a branch of the Russian people, who inhabit in particular the Circles of Zaleczky, Stanislav, and Stry. They all belong to the Greek Church. On their heads they wear a soft cap of black lamb's wool, round their necks a leather strap greased black with fat, on which are hung a quantity of larger or smaller brass crucifixes and often other ornaments of similar material and value. The more a youth—men hang on fewer or even only one—is decked with this ornamentation, the higher is his prestige with the girls. Round their bodies the Pokutians wear a short sheepskin jacket, Hungarian fashion, over it a short outer jacket and long white ankle-length trousers; both articles are dyed brick-red with alder bark, which in time becomes a brownish yellow. Their shirts, especially the herdsmens', are, as in Hungary, usually steeped in fat to drive off insects. Round their waists they wear a leather belt on which is hung a powder horn, also a small leather case with flint and steel, etc. A Pokutian, like the other inhabitants of the Carpathians, is never without his axe, which is so sharp that it can cut the smallest object. Even at entertainments and dances he always wears this weapon. When he leaps and pirouettes, holding his partner round the waist, he holds his axe in the air with his other hand, over the girl's head, often throwing it high into the air and catching it with great adroitness.

The character of the people is none of the best; not only are they sly and thievish, but exceedingly licentious. Few of them cohabit with their wives, but with one or more stepsisters or neighbors. Jealousy is unknown among them. For the rest, they are industrious, and, poor as they are, they are hospitable with the little they possess. If they were not so intemperate in love they would know little of ill-health. The women, who are as licentious as the men, also have their special dress. Unmarried girls go bareheaded, with their hair plaited, while the men let it hang loose. They [the girls] weave into their locks a strap studded with small coins, buttons, and mussel shells. Married women cover their heads with a linen kerchief. Round their necks they wear collars with glass beads of every color, alternating with brass crucifixes; the girls also wear armlets of fine thread studded with gaiter buttons. The blouse, embroided with bright wools, Wallach-fashion, is open in front so that the men's breasts are always naked. Round their waists the women tie an apron of wool, dyed in various colors; both sexes wear laced slippers on their feet or else high boots. Round their loins they wear a belt of blue wool, from which two tassels hang down behind.

The "Wallachs" (Vlachs, Rumanians) of Transylvania

. . . The Wallach is still a quite peculiar type of humanity, extraordinarily neglected by niggardly nature in the mountains, which are his favorite habitat. One finds many of them who have hardly anything human about them except the human form, and even that is distorted and disfigured by goiter and other defects. In the open country, in towns and villages of other nationalities (for they fill the Principality and constitute the largest part of its population), they have indeed been offered the opportunity to acquire all possible accomplishments, but they are not educated; they remain rude and savage. An inexplicable obstinacy sets them against almost any culture. Natural mother wit and innate understanding have to replace everything that schools and education give to other peoples. A common mistrust of all other nationalities in the country and a common attachment to their own traditional ways and habits link them to one another in a common hatred of all. Thanks to this quite peculiar national feeling there is nothing more dangerous than an irritated and offended Wallach. He will, indeed, fawn and crawl where he sees a stronger party, but he keeps his eyes open, as one says, watches for his opportunity, lurks in the darkness and misses no chance to avenge himself, and his revenge always degenerates into cruelty. They seldom figure in history, and when they do, the pen of the historian shrinks from recording their acts. Enough proof can be found in Daska's rebels,[1] in Michael's inhuman reign,[2] in the recent revolt led by Horia.[3] A description of them should mention also that owners of cattle and horses have to have them insured through Wallachs if they do not want them to be stolen. I know village pastors who have to pay one or another Wallach a regular annual tribute to save their barns from being burnt to the ground after the harvest. Coupled with this natural savagery is their propensity to drunkenness and sensual excess. Even the children are soaked in wine and brandy, and lascivious desires are awakened in them equally early. If they abstain so long, the youths marry in their seventeenth and eighteenth years and girls in their twelfth, and a young man of twenty-five or twenty-six has already six or seven children. They used to be thought good soldiers, but, strictly speaking, they are at best good with the cudgel. Their boldness is ebullient rage, and their courage sinks if the danger grows. They possess cunning enough, and make good guerrillas, but it is exceedingly hard to accustom them to order and discipline. One would hardly credit how much labor it cost to put their frontier militia on a certain regular footing.[4]

Industry and diligence are equally foreign to them. Most of them loaf about behind the sheep, others trundle round the country as carriers. A very few of them take the trouble to cultivate fields or vineyards and then seldom more than is needed for their meager food, clothing, and rent. In the Talmacs district a few of them work in the tanneries, but they are clumsy and maladroit. All their actions are marked by laziness and carelessness.

Their whole outward appearance betrays their propensity towards every kind of excess. A low, prematurely wrinkled forehead, brown, uncombed hair hanging over their eyes and cropped on the nape, strong, bushy eyebrows, small, rolling eyes, haggard faces covered with beards and mustaches, thickset, bony bodies, entirely reflect the uncultivated spirit which dwells in them.

Their clothing makes them even far more unpleasant still. The

[1] A reference to a peasant revolt of the sixteenth century.

[2] "Michael the Brave." Voivode of Wallachia, 1593, invaded and for a time occupied Transylvania. He was captured and executed by the imperial general, Basta, in 1601.

[3] Horia, leader of a bloody revolt of the Rumanian peasants in 1784.

[4] Joseph II organized a sort of Military Frontier in the chief Rumanian districts bordering the frontier.

head is covered by a cap of raw fur or a flat felt hat. On the body they wear a coarse shirt open at the neck, with short, wide, open sleeves, hanging down over the trousers and girt round the loins with a leather belt studded with many buttons. They always carry a few knives in their belts and in their hand a strong staff, which they know how to wield with extraordinary skill in fights. They fight duels with these in a fashion as artful as it is terrible. The trousers are of coarse homespun cloth, roughly cut, and reach to the ankle, Hungarian fashion. On their feet they wear slippers, wrapped round with many rags and straps. This is all they wear in summer. The dress of the more genteel among them is the same, only that instead of sandals they wear a sort of shapeless boot of goatskin, which reaches only to the ankle. In winter they affect leather jerkins and furs or fur coats, sometimes full-length, but usually only half-length.

Their womenfolk are massively built but often endowed with quite surprising charms, almost in every way the opposite of the men. Their hair is properly combed, braided into plaits or cut off short round their heads. They wear earrings and necklaces of coral, but otherwise dress equally simply. A long shift, sometimes with red or blue embroidery on the neck and breast, with a leather belt around their waists and two narrow aprons, about half an ell wide, one tied on in front, the other behind, and a linen or muslin coif on their heads is their whole adornment. On their feet they wear slippers or, at the most, shoes with flat, iron heels. The women usually make this dress themselves, and if it is fine, it can be worth ten to twelve gulden. They also make the clothes of their husbands and children.

Equally monotonous are their wooden, half-charred huts. Their beds consist of a few planks, nailed on the beams, usually covered with sacks of straw. It is a rich man who has a feather bed and bolster. Their chairs are benches of simple boards, put against the walls. Then a table, a few pots and dishes, wooden spoons, and rude daubs of pictures of Greek saints. Not one house in a hundred contains any better furniture.

Their favorite dish is a broth of maize flour, bacon, milk, onions, garlic, green vegetables and beans, usually very simply prepared and generally only boiled in water. They eat little meat.

Their dances are noisy and wild. They make all sorts of great leaps and violent twists of the body.

Their musical instrument is a coarse pipe of oak or elder, which they fashion themselves, and out of which they produce very touching, plaintive notes. At a pinch they use also a fiddle or a bag-pipe.

To be distinguished from the Wallachs proper are the Bulgarians, who have immigrated here quite recently from Bulgaria proper. They are to be found in Kronstadt, Alvinz, Karlsburg, and a few other places. They are a somewhat more cultivated race, some of them Roman Catholics, but otherwise there is little real difference between them and the true Wallachs, who have long been here, and mostly profess the Greek Church, and know extremely little of God, religion, or morality. Yet they have the greatest respect for their clergy, who for the rest are such rude and stupid people that they are often unable either to read or write.

The Gypsies of Transylvania

. . . There are two kinds of gypsies. One kind is somewhat more cultivated and settled than the other, who wander about in tents up and down the whole country, like the nomads of old. But that they are one people is proved by their common speech, certain common features of their characters, and even some physical re-semblances. Their speech is quite different from the other local languages; but its character and affinities are unknown, because no one has taken the trouble to learn it. The speed and the loud, harsh tone in which it is spoken would suggest that it is akin to Hungarian, and it is possibly the original Scythian language. The characteristic common to all gypsies is a remarkable skill in all kinds of handicrafts, which they learn, one may say, at sight. They are workers in wood, iron, copper, tin, and other metals, and copy anything, roughly, but they never put finishing touches, and are content if their products have a modicum of form and shape. All gypsies are also uncommonly agile and light on their feet; they have a dancing gait and flit over the ground as though hardly touching it. They are obstinate and timid, have a threatening air, flare up easily, and create an enormous uproar over the smallest trifle. But they do not easily come to blows. When they have shaken their fists twenty times under one anothers' noses, they withdraw them twenty times under one anothers' noses, they are also, in general, prone to fraud, begging, and other low and childish actions; so much so that a man who possesses little or no *point d'honneur*, who is immodest in speech and act, hangs on everywhere and cannot be shaken off, is simply called "a gypsy." Equally uniform is their physical appearance. They are all slender of body, of medium height, with slight limbs. The complexions of them all, especially the men, are very dark, rather brown than olive; their eyes are small, but black and fiery. Their hair, too, is black and curly, their teeth dazzling white—a contrast to the rest of their faces that has led some to believe them to be of African origin. For the rest, they have very regular features, with nothing Negroid about them. Even their coloring is not really African but either that of sunburn or an Asiatic brown.

But the difference between them is only one of degree. The settled, or more cultivated, gypsies are in advance of the vagabonds in many respects. They work in the towns and villages as ordinary blacksmiths, locksmiths, tinkers, cobblers, old-clothes merchants, horse ropers and swine traders, seal engravers, musicians, etc. They have regular huts or cabins, but without courtyards or fences, and dress like the people round them; they like draping themselves in clothes of blue or red cloth, even if only rags. A gypsy never, or hardly ever, puts on a new garment, unless slippers, for which they prefer a red color. But they buy, steal, or beg all worn-out clothes from noblemen, burghers, or peasants and throw them on.

Their women, especially those living in towns, are by no means to be despised. One finds among them beauties who could vie with those of many other nations. They are all sturdy, stout brunettes, with full, beautiful bosoms. Their features are regular. One finds among them beautifully arched noses, fine black eyes and eyebrows, high, unwrinkled foreheads, full cheeks, often with a dimple in them. Round their heads they wear, a little awry, a muslin scarf, which sets off the charm of their black hair. In summer they wear a close-fitting, tight bodice, many coral ornaments in their ears and round their necks, and on their breasts, many rows of coins, which are not always legal currency, but are mostly of considerable value, being of good gold and silver. Then tight, close-fitting petticoats, and red slippers, with or without heels. This, however, is the only article of their clothing which looks at all unfashionable or coarse.

This kind of gypsy also possesses some religion. Most of them belong to the Greek Orthodox Church, but a few are Greek Catholics.

The vagabonds are, on the contrary, the most hateful and repulsive dregs of humanity. Their nomadic, idle life under a smoky tent, wretched and miserable as it may be, has for them a special charm. Whole families of human beings squat summer and winter on Mother Earth, naked except perhaps for a rag over their privy parts. The man tinkers at an old kettle, fashions troughs, platters, or wooden spoons, or forges fire irons out of old iron. Meanwhile their women—the dirtiest human insects—go round the villages begging and stealing, their youngest child slung in a sack on their backs, tell fortunes and cut indecent capers. The elder children of both sexes squat naked under the tents, bay at every traveler, dance and turn cartwheels for a kreuzer; until they get it, not even blows can drive them away. But they have a regular term for which they keep up their jumping and yelling. If they have received nothing by the end of it, they turn away, but with mocking laughter, curses and jeers, and throw themselves down again in the grass, where they bake all day in the sun. In brief, the Indians found by Columbus when he discovered America were probably not so wild and repulsive. No one can abide them. The law of the land forbids them to stay more than three days in one spot; but it depends on the village whether it will put up with them for longer. One could forgive them all their dirt and filth, but their extraordinary thievishness makes them intolerable anywhere. They steal anything they can carry away, poultry, pigs, horses, utensils of iron and copper, even children. In their food they are less fastidious than many animals. They devour without hesitation animals which have been strangled or have died of disease, even several days old. Extreme need forces them to this; but a vagabond endures need much more easily than order and culture.

Joseph II's intention to uniformalize the various peoples of Transylvania (as a philosopher, he distinguished only two kinds, the good and the bad) ran on many reefs, but it foundered completely when he tried to make the vagabond gypsies settled and more cultivated.

20. Leopold II's "Political Credo"

Leopold wrote this document at the moment of extreme crisis in which the Hapsburg monarchy stood when the year 1790 opened. Joseph II's arbitrary attack on their institutions and his violation of their religious feelings had already driven the Austrian Netherlands into open revolt, forcing the *Statthalter*, Joseph's sister Marie Christine, and her husband, Albert of Saxony-Teschen, to take refuge in Bonn. Similar revolt seemed imminent in Hungary. Joseph already knew himself to be dying and had been begging his brother and successor designate, Leopold, up to that time grand duke of the family secondogeniture of Tuscany, to come to Vienna and share the burden of government with him. Leopold had evaded complying with the request because he felt that for him to figure as Joseph's partner would identify him with his brother's policies, which he thought mistaken. He proposed to follow a different line on his accession, and believed that if reassured to that effect, even the Netherlands might be induced to return to their allegiance. He had written to Marie Christine (who was in any case his favorite sister and close political sympathizer and confidante) for an exact account of the situation in the Netherlands and on receiving her reply, had penned to her a statement of his own political beliefs, which would inspire the line which he proposed to follow on accession. The letter, which was actually written in invisible ink, was to be kept a close secret from Joseph and his advisers, but Marie Christine was to communicate the gist of it, at her discretion, to leading persons in the Netherlands.

The letter was thus no piece of pure self-analysis, but a bid for favor, and it is legitimate to ask whether the picture which it gives of its author's convictions and intentions had not been touched up for the benefit of its addressees. Historians do, indeed, admit that the account that occupies the opening paragraphs, of Leopold's recent conflict with the episcopate of Tuscany, which had, in consequence of his actions, accused him of "Jansenism," is slightly slanted. But the slant is no more than slight, and perhaps venial, and the deepest students of Leopold's political philosophy, and of the policy by which he expressed it in Tuscany, are able to maintain that the description of it that occupies the end of his letter is sincere and faithful. It was a tragedy for Austria that the storms conjured up by his brother made it impossible for this, the wisest and most truly enlightened of all the Habsburgs, to do more, on his accession, than carry through hurried emergency operations, and that his untimely death prevented him from expanding and modifying these into a definitive system.

The text from which the appended translation was taken was published by A. Wolf in his *Leopold II und Maria Christine. Ihr Brief-wechsel* (Vienna, 1863), pp. 80ff. It was reproduced also in German translation in A. Wandruszka's *Leopold II* (Vienna, 1965), Vol. II, pp. 215ff., which gives an excellent commentary on it and an account of the circumstances in which it was written. Marie Christine's letters to her brother were published, with commentary, by A. Schlitter in the *Fontes Rerum Austriacarum,* Series II, No. XLVIII (1896). We omit here the opening paragraphs, the allusions in which refer exclusively to Tuscan affairs, and reproduce only the last lines of this section, in which Leopold sums up his own attitude towards religious questions, followed by the second part of his letter, in which he gives his political credo.

My PROFESSION of faith is that I will uphold the Catholic, Apostolic, and Roman faith, and in it I will live and die; I will in no wise persecute persons who have or profess to have no religion, but will also not promote or distinguish them, that I will support the Bishops whose duty it is to supervise the disciplinary affairs of the Church. . . .

I believe that the sovereign, even the hereditary sovereign, is only the delegate of the people for whom he is appointed, and he should devote to it all his cares, efforts, and night watches; that every country should possess a fundamental law or contract between the people and the sovereign which limits the authority and power of the latter; that if the sovereign in fact does not keep that law he has *de facto* abdicated from his position, which was conferred on him only on this condition, and that his subjects are no longer bound to obey him; that the executive power resides in the sovereign, but the legislative in the people and its representatives and that the latter can make new conditions each time the occupant of the throne changes. That the sovereign may not intervene, directly or indirectly, in the processes of law, civil or criminal, alter its forms or sentences or issue any instruction, delegate power, etc.; that the sovereign is due to render the people every year an exact statement of the employment of the public revenues and finances, that he is not entitled to impose arbitrarily any taxes, duties, and fees; that only the people itself has the right to do this, after the sovereign has expounded to them the requirements of the State, and the people, through its representatives, has recognized these to be just and reasonable; that they are not to be granted except as subsidies, for the period of one year, and after their necessity has been recognized, and that the nation is not bound to prolong them before the sovereign has submitted an exact, detailed, and satisfactory report on how they have been used. That the sovereign must render account and secure consent for all changes of system, new laws, etc., and of pensions and gratuities which he wishes to grant, before he publishes them; that the sovereign's enactments only acquire legal force and binding authority after the Estates have consented to them; that the military may be employed only for the national defense and never against the people. That no person may be arrested or condemned except by order of the regular magistrates and by the regular forms and publicly, never by any arbitrary order, not even the sovereign's. Finally, I believe that the sovereign should rule only through the law, and that the author thereof is the people, which can never renounce this, nor can be robbed through any desuetude or tacit or forced consent of an inalienable right that is a natural right, and that on the basis of which it has consented to have a sovereign, that is, to confer on him a special position, in order that he may bring about its happiness and prosperity, not as he wills it, but as the people itself wills and feels it. For the only purpose of societies and governments is the happiness of their individual members. These, approximately, are my principles. I could expand myself on them in more detail, to give proofs of them, but that would be too long and too tedious.

II

The Hohenzollern Dynasty

Introduction: The Rise of the Hohenzollerns, 1600-1790

He would have been a bold man who had prophesied in 1600 that less than two hundred years later the Hohenzollerns would be challenging the Habsburgs for the leadership of central Europe. The dynasty was still, by comparison with the other, one of parvenus. It had only been in 1411 that the Emperor Sigismund had founded its real fortunes by sending the then head of it, Frederick—who at that time was occupying only the modest dignity of burgrave of Nuremberg, but had commended himself to the emperor as an energetic and efficient man—to take charge of the distant and unruly Mark of Brandenburg. Frederick had established his authority over the local nobles in a series of campaigns in which he had reduced many of their fortresses by artillery bombardment, then something of a novelty, and he and his successors had enlarged the boundaries of the original donation considerably, but in 1600 it was still only a medium-sized principality, hardly larger than Mecklenburg or Hanover, and its rulers were still no more than margraves. The Mark, was, moreover, singularly unblessed by nature, a featureless country of thin, sandy flats, scourged by an inclement climate, a hard land for farming, yet barren of non-agricultural resources; remote, and landlocked to boot. The domestic authority of the margraves was still limited by the wide powers which the Estates had enjoyed since the Middle Ages.

There were, however, features in the margraves' position which made it stronger, at least in potentialities, than it looked. Sigismund had made the first of them, and his successors, one of the Electors whose voice determined who should wear the imperial crown, and the vote could be sold for a high price in a contested election. At home, the nobles had never fully recovered from the first elector's repression of them; the knights collectively could put up a strong front against the margraves, but there was in Brandenburg now no great magnate class comparable to that of Poland, Bohemia, or Hungary; further, the Elector Joachim II (1535–71) had greatly strengthened the position of his house, when, on accompanying his subjects in their adoption of the Lutheran faith, he had seized the lands of the Catholic monasteries and converted them into crown domains, making the crown owner of something between one-quarter and one-third of the whole area of the country.

Most important of all were the family dispositions now established in the house. On the first elector's death his heritage had, as was then customary, been partitioned between his sons, but the fortunate early extinction of most of the lines had reunited the bulk of the heritage in one hand, and in 1473 the Margrave Albert Achilles had issued the so-called *"Dispositio Achillea,"* which, anticipating by nearly 250 years the Austrian Pragmatic Sanction, had laid down that the family possessions were thereafter to pass undivided to the male line in primogeniture. In 1599 the Margrave Joachim Friedrich, who had himself been obliged to invoke the *Dispositio* against his father's testamentary dispositions on succeeding to the margravate in the previous year, had, under the family Compact of Gera, extended the principle of primogeniture to all lands which might ever come under the rule of the house, and these were numerous, for the family had been prolific, and Hohenzollerns of one or another branch were then ruling over a considerable number of German principalities, while one cousin was reigning as vassal of the king of Poland over the secularized duchy of Prussia. Further, Joachim's son, John Sigismund, had, in 1594, married the duke's eldest daughter (he had no sons), who was also heiress in her own right to the five duchies or counties of Jülich, Berg, Cleves, Mark, and Ravensburg, in West Germany.

Thanks to these dispositions, even the first Hohenzollern with whom this sketch is directly concerned, John Sigismund, enlarged the family heritage considerably. He succeeded to the undivided Mark of Brandenburg when his father died in 1604, and when the reigning duke of the five duchies died in 1608, he claimed his wife's heritage. In 1614 he had to cede Jülich and Berg to a rival claimant, the duke of Pfalz-Neuburg, but he retained the other three, and in 1618 he also followed his father-in-law as duke of Prussia, although still only as vassal of the king of Poland.

The value of these acquisitions was, of course, much diminished by the absence of territorial contiguity between them—Prussia far away in the east, the three duchies, themselves not mutually contiguous, as far in the west. And neither John Sigismund nor his successor, George William (1620–40), possessed either the energy or the political insight to draw profit out of the troubles which tormented Europe during their reigns. When the Thirty Years' War broke out, George William simply watched helplessly while hostile armies invaded, ravaged, and squatted on his territories. When he died, he was actually a refugee in Prussia; Brandenburg, except for Berlin and a few fortresses, being in Swedish occupation. His rule in Cleves-Mark was only nominal. All his territories were dreadfully devastated and depopulated.

In addition, John Sigismund had adopted for himself and his family the Calvinist faith, an act which gave rise to an estrangement between him and the bulk of his subjects which he had great difficulty in smoothing over, and his successors in keeping the sore from reopening.[1]

Historians usually date the upturn of the family fortunes from the accession of the Elector Frederick William, who ruled from 1640 to 1688. The non-Prussian may feel that the epithet "Great" by which he is known (and which in fact came to him somewhat fortuitously: a poet bestowed it on him after one of his by no means regular victories, and it stuck) does him more than justice. What he did undeniably possess were singleness of purpose—purpose of self-aggrandizement—strength of will, unlimited pushfulness, and a realistic appreciation of the truth that a ruler living in an armed world and wishing even to defend himself, much more to expand his power, must himself be armed (his deathbed message to his privy council was to this effect). It probably also made for success that his standards of international morality, as expressed in terms of fidelity to his alliances, were exceptionally low, even for his age. But his foreign policy showed little perspicuity. He often overreached himself: some of his en-

[1] See Document 2.

terprises, such as his attempt in 1661 to seize Jülich-Berg, and his stillborn intervention in favor of Holland against France in 1672, were humiliating fiascos, and others brought in much less reward than he had hoped; thus, his repeated changes of side at the end of his reign, and heavy fighting, in itself brilliantly successful, brought him in only a small strip of land on the Oder. He owed most of his successes abroad to the fact that it happened to suit others that he should have them, but from the point of view of results, this fact was irrelevant, and it is a historical fact that his reign brought his dominions big advances in both area and status. The Peace of Westphalia of 1648 brought him the considerable territorial acquisitions of Lower Pomerania and the episcopal sees of Halberstadt and Minden, with the reversion of Magdeburg (finally incorporated in 1680). It also enhanced the relative importance of the German princes at the expense of the emperor, besides leaving the elector of Brandenburg the natural leader of Protestant North Germany. Equally important, the Treaty of Wehlau (1657), confirmed by that of Oliva (1660), brought him full sovereignty over Prussia.[2] His gain on the Oder has been mentioned.

The elector's domestic policy was essentially simply a function of his foreign ambitions, although the indirect effects of his steps in this field went far beyond their original purpose. His great objective was to establish a standing army, with assured funds for its upkeep, to be at his own disposal, in place of the *ad hoc* grants from the Estates on which his predecessors had had to depend for any major undertakings. His first attempts in Cleves-Mark and Prussia were defeated by the resistance of the Estates, but in 1653 he induced the Estates of Brandenburg to agree to pay a regular tax for the upkeep of a *miles perpetuus*, to be maintained in peace as well as war.[3] Later, he got the same concession from his other provinces. The standing army, which Frederick William welded into a unitary force and by the end of his reign had expanded to the extraordinary figure, for his age, of 30,000 to 35,000 men, made him the real master of his dominions, as was shown by the relative ease with which he crushed two revolts (in 1661 and 1672) in Prussia, and by more peaceful developments elsewhere. Frederick William seems not to have aimed consciously at de-

[2] See Document 4.
[3] For a summary of the Brandenburg Recess at which this concession was granted, see Document 3.

stroying the Estates; indeed, he rewarded them for their consent to his tax by confirming many of their privileges—heavily to the disadvantage of the poorer classes, especially the peasants, whose condition deteriorated during his reign. But first a central organization, the *Generalkriegscommissariat*, with a network of provincial and Kreis commissariats, was established for the administration of the army and the collection from the Estates of the *contributio*. Since the yield of the *contributio* was insufficient, a new tax, the excise, was imposed on the towns,[4] and presently, crown officials (*Steuerkommissäre*) were introduced to collect and pass it on to the treasury, and they gradually became masters of the towns. Simultaneously, the Cameral (crown) domains were reorganized, the local "*Aemter*," each consisting of three to six crown domains under a "*Beamte*,"[5] being placed under a "*Kammer*" for each province, and the whole set under a central "*Geheime Hofkammer*." These three services gradually developed into a centralized and authoritarian bureaucracy, whose activities left little for the Estates' old self-governing institutions to do.

Frederick William was a hard master. He taxed his subjects unmercifully to provide for his army. But he was sensible enough to realize that the milch cow must be fed, and towards the end of his reign he made considerable efforts to increase the wealth of his dominions. Peasant colonists were brought in from abroad to settle empty places. Other immigrants, including the Huguenots driven to leave France by the revocation of the Edict of Nantes, were imported to develop industry,[6] in the interest of which cause various protective measures were introduced.[7] Perhaps because he had been educated in the Netherlands, Frederick William was particularly interested in trade, especially waterborne. One of the most lasting achievements of his reign was the construction of the great canal which bears his name, from the Oder to the Spree, and he even had a seagoing fleet built and founded a company to trade with Africa.[8]

[4] See Document 5.

[5] *Amt* and *Beamte* were thus technical terms in Brandenburg-Prussia, and in the documents which follow we translate the latter term as "Crown agent," in preference to the general word "official" by which it is usually rendered today.

[6] See Document 9 for the edict admitting the Huguenots.

[7] For one of these, the edict establishing a wool monopoly, see Document 8.

[8] See Document 7.

When he died, after a reign of little under fifty years, he left a heritage still territorially not comparable to those of the great European powers, but yet a force to be reckoned with internationally, while at home he had laid the foundations on which his successors were to construct the efficient edifice of the Prussian military-bureaucratic state.

The Great Elector's son and successor, Frederick (1688–1713), advanced the prestige of his house by persuading Emperor Leopold to allow him to take the title of king—only, indeed, "King in Prussia," where he had himself crowned with great pomp on January 18, 1701.[9] He did not, however, succeed in augmenting his heritage territorially, his wars, although numerous, being uniformly unprofitable; nor did he carry through any important internal changes: if the power of the central services continued to grow during his reign, this was due chiefly to the *vis momenti* imparted by his father. He, or more properly, his wife, the Hanoverian Princess Sophia Charlotte, must be credited with raising cultural levels in Brandenburg through the refined and luxurious court which the royal couple maintained in Berlin, and through the foundation of the University of Halle (1694) and the Academy of Sciences in Berlin (1700), of which Leibniz was the first president. But the king's luxuries cost a lot of money, and on his death he left the exchequer heavily indebted, presenting another difficult situation to his son, Frederick William I (1713–40), who, however, coped with it with courage and resource.

Like his grandfather and namesake, Frederick William was an unadroit diplomat; moreover, unlike his predecessor, he was conscientiously opposed to aggressive wars, so that his gains in land —a number of small territories in the west acquired in 1714 and the small but important Hither Pomerania up to the Peene, wrested from Sweden in 1720—were rather windfalls shaken down in the European tempests of the day than anything garnered by his own planning. He again attempted to obtain the disputed heritage of Jülich-Berg, and again failed. But his achievements at home were remarkable. Uncouth and almost unlettered—he knew hardly any foreign languages, and spoke and wrote his own as ill as any peasant, and his attitude toward the arts in general is to be described, according to taste, as puritan or philistine—he was highly intelligent

---

[9] For a description of the ceremony, see Document 10.

and animated by a single-minded will to power, which was justified in his own eyes by the belief that it was God's will he should possess and exercise it, as a trust from God: a true despot, although it would be difficult to call him an enlightened one. "I ruin the Junkers," he wrote in a famous passage, when signs of resistance appeared in Prussia against his new taxes: "I come to my end and stabilize the sovereignty as a *rocher de bronze*." No less characteristic is a phrase in the "Instructions" for his creation, the Directorate General.[10] The ministers were to consider all questions, and report to him in writing, with their recommendations; but the decision lay with him. "We remain King and Lord, and can do as We please."

In accordance with what was now the family tradition, Frederick William put the army first, and for him it was even more an end than a means. He raised its strength to the enormous figure of 90,000 men, out of a total population of 2.25 million, parading and drilling it so that all Berlin seemed a barracks square. To finance it he extended taxation, subjecting the nobles in Prussia to a land tax (the *Generalhufenschoss*) and their colleagues elsewhere to a disguised equivalent of it. He combined and co-ordinated the work of the War and Finance Commissions in a great single Directorate General,[11] which supervised almost every aspect of public life, except foreign affairs and defense, reporting in writing to Frederick William, who took the operative decisions himself, through his secretariat. Unsparing of others as he was of himself, Frederick William kept this machine working at full capacity, disciplining and exacting, but also constructing, further broadening the agricultural basis of the economy and promoting industry.[12] All this was carried through with a strict economy which his contemporaries found distasteful and even ludicrous, but which enabled him to pay off the debts left by his father and to accumulate a substantial reserve against emergencies.[13]

An important feature of this militarization and bureaucratization was that it was not only administrative but also social. The nobles, their economic power weakened by the new taxation and their

[10] See below, Document 10.
[11] Extracts from the "Instructions" for this body are given in Document 10.
[12] For specimens of his work in this field, see Documents 11 and 12.
[13] See his remarks on this subject in his Political Testament, Document 14.

political functions usurped by the State services, were yet preserved as a social caste, but with a new function, for Frederick William insisted that they should regard it as a duty themselves to enter the services of the State, especially the army. He provided facilities for them to do so, especially by the establishment of a corps of cadets for young nobles, and he kept a careful check on who used this. The identification of the Prussian upper classes with the State, and especially the army, thus became far closer than was the case, for example, in Austria, whose officers were at this date still largely recruited from abroad. For the rank and file, especially for the giants of whom it was Frederick William's special pleasure to form his regiment of guards, he had, indeed, still largely to depend on foreigners enticed or kidnapped into his service.

The profit from Frederick William's work went to his son, Frederick II ("the Great," 1740–86), the last Hohenzollern with whom this sketch will be concerned, for his successor, King Frederick II, had been on the throne only three years when the French Revolution swept away the old world of Prussia, as well as that of France.

Frederick II is a strange and contradictory character, of whom anything can be said except that he did not leave his mark on history, for good or ill. He had, indeed, a childhood which was of a nature to breed in any man whole ganglia of complexes. Encouraged by his Hanoverian mother, he learned to react violently against all the ways of his rude, beer-swilling father, to affect foreign modes and pass his time in flute-playing and clever conversation, to speak cynically of religion and to ape the catchwords of the "enlightened" writers of the day, especially those of France. His father in return despised him for an effeminate fop, and treated him with such unmerciful harshness that on one occasion the hapless youth tried to flee the country and was punished by a term of solitary confinement, succeeded by hard labor learning the business of government.[14]

Released from this and partially reconciled with his father, Frederick returned, in appearance, to his *Feingeist* life, but his meditations were not so abstract as they seemed. They had given him an acute appreciation of European affairs and a conception of *raison d'état* which was totally free from any moral inhibitions

[14] See Document 15.

whatever. He showed this in one of the first acts of his reign, for his father's eyes had been closed only a few months when the sudden death of the Emperor Charles VI, leaving as sole heiress to his dominions a young, inexperienced, and apparently helpless girl, presented Frederick with what he saw as a unique opportunity to invade and grab Silesia from her.[15] He had, in fact, underestimated Maria Theresa's spirit, and the strength of the centripetal forces in her dominions, so that this act, the decisive one of his life, cost him twelve years of war—five before the first struggle against Austria was ended, and another seven later. (It has been argued that the act of aggression with which he opened that war was a preventive measure to forestall a coming attack, but it is indisputable that that attack would never have been planned but for the seizure of Silesia.) These years cost his dominions terrible sacrifices, and Frederick was often in danger of losing his loot; but he defended himself, and it, with a determination and resource that can truly be called great,[16] emerging still in possession of practically the whole of Silesia. A few years later he acquired as much territory again, at the expense of Poland, under the "First Partition" of that unhappy country.[17] With these acquisitions, plus that of East Friesia (inherited peacefully in 1744) Frederick had doubled the size of his dominions and fully doubled their wealth; for if the Polish provinces were sparsely populated and backward, Silesia was the opposite of these things. He had also established territorial contiguity between Brandenburg-Pomerania and Prussia. Further, his gain in Silesia had been Austria's corresponding loss, which the acquisition of Galicia under the Partition was far from compensating. Frederick had thus jumped Prussia into the position of a near-equal power, able to meet Austria on near-equal terms, as, indeed, she did toward the end of his reign, thanks to the apprehensions awakened among the lesser German princes by Joseph II's unwise ambitions.

Frederick retained through his life his early literary and philosophic interests, and he made not unsuccessful efforts to irrigate, mainly with French waters, the cultural desert to which his father had reduced Berlin. He is also to be credited with a valuable reform of the judicial system, a field which his father had neglected. Otherwise, once he had taken the decisive step, his activities at

[15] See Document 16.
[16] See Document 21.
[17] See Document 23.

home were, inevitably, largely governed by his doings abroad and
their effects. As a boy he had sneered at his father's military pre-
occupation; now he, too, had to devote most of his efforts to
enlarging and keeping up his army, and to making his country an
efficient supply base for it, a task the difficulties of which were
greatly enhanced by the devastation which his ambitions had
brought on it. He himself admitted that at the end of the Seven
Years' War his "once so flourishing provinces" presented "a terrible
spectacle which . . . resembled that of Brandenburg after the end
of the Thirty Years' War." But he worked hard and intelli-
gently to repair the damage. If his description of himself as "the
first servant of the State" contained a fallacy, in that his State
was for him simply the instrument of his own ambitions, his
service was unremitting, although not novel either in its directions
or its methods. He carried on his predecessors' work on the land,
devoting particular pains to the reclamation and settlement of such
desolate areas as the Warthe Marshes,[18] and he continued the promotion of industry and of trade, to the importance of which he was
more alive than his father. He was no great innovator in respect of
his methods. The overdimensioned Directorate General was relieved by the creation of some new ministries, which took over part
of its work, but otherwise little was changed. His rule, like that of
his predecessors, was despotic, but not egalitarian; the nobles were
left in possession of their caste privileges. Even more than his father,
he exercised his rule personally, through his secretariat, trusting no
one and often taking important decisions behind a minister's
back. Under his rule the Prussian bureaucracy emerged more
universally active and efficient than before, but his system also led
to a further exaggeration of that preference for disciplined obedience over initiative which became a notorious feature of the
Prussian State.

The selection of documents which follows is, like its Austrian
counterpart, rather a selection of illustrations than a "list" of the
most important documents of the period. Three (1, 3, and 5)
record what may be regarded as landmarks in the establishment of
the central monarchic authority over the older provincial and
class institutions. Documents 4 and 10 record other stages in the
rise of the Hohenzollerns—their acquisition of full sovereignty over

---

[18] See Document 20.

Prussia and their promotion to royal status. Documents 16, 18, 21, and 23 throw light on the mental outlook of the man who brought the dynasty its later possessions of Silesia and West Prussia.

The religious issues in Brandenburg-Prussia having been relatively easy, we have given only two documents (Document 2A and B) directly concerned with it, although 6 and (in part) 14 bear on it. Documents 5 to 9 illustrate aspects of the Great Elector's administrative activities, especially in economics. Documents 11, 12 and 13 are similar pieces from the reign of King Frederick I, and 14 gives in his own words that remarkable man's conception of his duties. Documents 19, 20 and 22 show Frederick the Great at work in the same field, while 15 and 17 have been chosen for the further light that they throw on the personality of that extraordinary man.

1. The First Brandenburg Privy Council

This enactment was issued by the Elector Joachim Friedrich towards the end of his reign. The body established under it was the first single political organ concerned, although only in an advisory capacity, with all the elector's territories, and in fact remained the chief organ of government in nonecclesiatical matters (which fell under the slightly older Consistory) until the reforms of a century later, to which reference is made elsewhere. For that reason alone, this, its birth certificate, can claim a considerable interest, from which its slightly naïve wording does not detract and which justifies us in giving it the opening place in this collection. The text is translated from the *Acta Brandenburgica*, ed. M. Klinkenborg, 3 vols. (1932ff.), Vol. I, pp. 91–6.

ORDER ESTABLISHING A PRIVY COUNCIL; CÖLEN ON THE SPREE, DECEMBER 13, 1604

WE, JOACHIM FRIEDRICH, by Grace of God Margrave of Brandenburg, Lord High Chamberlain of the Holy Roman Empire, Elector of Prussia, Duke of Stettin, Pomerania, of the Cassubians and Wends and of Crossen in Silesia and Jägerndorf, Burgrave of Nuremberg and Prince of Rügen, hereby make known:

Having not only recalled and laid to mind that Almighty God has set Us in a position of authority and high electoral dignity, and blessed Us with great and spacious lands and people, for which We render Him due and heartfelt thanks, but having further considered that We are beset with very high and difficult problems, particularly in Prussia, Jülich, Strasburg and Jägerndorf, each and all of which are so important that we truly need good, mature counsel and loyal men, We have thought it most necessary for the better consideration of the said questions of state to order certain dispositions such as exist in other well-ordered polities and governments, whereby the same may in the future be advised in orderly fashion and more speedily expedited in the confident hope that the Almighty will multiply His rich blessings toward Us, that We may in all things come to a desirable and fortunate conclusion; and further that Our faithful Councillors, in whom We repose absolute confidence, may play their part the more diligently and be studious, not only to see what is best for Us, but also to labor more assiduously in this, Our difficult situation, to relieve it for Us, and that in general, all things may redound, first to the honor of God and also to the salutary prosperity of Our Electoral House, and We master these most difficult problems of such moment for Us and Our Electoral House which do beset Us now, which are nearly all at their most acute and must be treated with discretion and secrecy, without delay or interruption.

To these ends We have thought it advisable—following the example of other well-ordered governments—to appoint a Privy Council for these and other similar secret matters of moment to Us, to wit Our High Chamberlain Hieronymus Schlick, Count of Passau, Lord of Weisskirchen, Otto Heinrich von Pielandt, Lord of Reith and Prembtt, Johann von Loeben on Blaunberg, Our Chancellor, Christoff von Wallenfelsen on Lichtenberg, Hieronymus von Diesskawen on Quess, Doctor Christof Benckendorf, Our Vice-Chancellor, Doctor Friedrich Pruckmann, Messrs. Joachim Hubner and Simon Ulrich Pistoriss of Seusslitz, all of whom hereby take solemn oath constantly to attend this Privy Council and besides the duty and obligation of loyal and discreet Privy Councillors, which duties We hereby enjoin them to perform with all diligence, also to take into consideration the following points:

1. Since confusion of councils leads to every kind of disarray, to the great detriment of the State, it is Our will that (hereafter) all proceedings in this Our Privy Council shall be conducted in

good order, in the following manner: when each matter comes to be considered, a formal motion shall be made by Our Chancellor, if present, or by the Councillor presiding, according to the nature of the problem, and the Councillors shall be asked their opinions, beginning with Our Chancellor, by Our High Chamberlain, Count Schlick, if present, or in his absence by Herr von Reith, or in the absence of both, by whoever is presiding under this Our order. And during the deliberations each Councillor shall give his vote freely and unobstructed by the others, and none shall attack or molest another, but shall cast his vote once and then sit silent until the others have voted also; unless some further consideration occurs to him, when he shall be allowed to revert to it when the round of questions is over. If, however, one member has particular knowledge of a question, We graciously permit him to begin by expounding the case and saying how he will vote, so that the others may be better acquainted with the merits of the case and each may have more solid grounds for his opinion; but he must regard first what the situation requires and propound and vote what lies in the best interest of Our service and that of Our Electoral House, without respect of persons and not according to the opinion of those voting before him.

2. Although it is right in principle, and advantageous, that votes should be rather weighed than counted, yet it is Our will that for better order's sake, the conclusion should be reached by majority vote, but with the qualification that when the votes differ and no unanimous conclusion can be reached, the secretary shall record the different opinions, with their arguments and bases, in a written memorandum, which shall be submitted to Us, signed by the Councillors.

3. And in order that the proceedings of the Council may be better preserved for reference and for future information, Our Privy Secretaries Augustin Hildesheimb, if he can release himself from other duties, and Julius Hasse (whom We hereby command to occupy no other post but this, for the time and until Our further orders) shall keep regular Minutes of all proceedings: of how each question was moved, and then a complete record of each opinion and shall place this, with the conclusion, with the other secret papers, in a separate cupboard, and bring it out again when the matter comes up for decision.

4. And that all undue delays may be avoided, the Master of

Our Posts shall always take all letters addressed to Us to Our secretaries, who shall first pass them to Us unopened. We shall read them, and according to their contents and substance either at once deliver Our decision, or else call our Councillors to us and deliberate thereon; but if we transmit them to the Privy Council, they are to read them round the table, as they shall all reports rendered to Us by envoys, and none shall be permitted to take anything to his home without the consent of the others, unless he needs to do so in fulfillment of a special commission, when he must always give the registrar a receipt for it. And to enable all Councillors to consult the documents easily, files of matters not yet discussed are to be kept together in the Council Chamber until finished with. But if We are absent from the Court, the Master of Our Posts shall hand all letters addressed to Us, as described, to Our Chancellor or the President of the Privy Council, who shall then lay them before the Privy Council, where they shall be read out and dealt with round the table, as provided above; and in-coming letters shall always be answered without delay; and Our Privy Council shall be most studious to advance the honor of God and the maintenance of religious peace; it being most particularly necessary to meet all threatening evil with good council, because the dangerous activities of the Papists and the persecution of Our true religion make themselves increasingly felt and seek to impose themselves by force.

But should discords over questions of religion, and the like, arise and come before the Privy Council, Our Privy Council shall not concern itself with them, but pass them immediately to Our spiritual Consistory, where all such questions are to be discussed and decided, under Our Consistorial and other similar Orders (which are based on Our true Augsburg Confession, as delivered to the Emperor Charles V in the thirtieth year of his reign).

5. They shall further be particularly studious that in Our correspondence We use the proper forms of address towards everyone and especially to Our closest friends, in order to confirm the good will of those who may give Us support and fellowship in matters of high policy. And Our Master of Posts shall keep a true and compete register of all incoming and outgoing documents, recording everything that comes in or goes out, and shall submit this monthly to Our Privy Councillors for their better information, and shall be specially sworn to perform this duty, which is not covered by his previous terms of appointment.

6. Sixthly, Our Privy Council shall consider what measures are conducive to the preservation of the public peace, and shall always call Our attention to any emergency, that We may fulfill the duty incumbent on Us by virtue of Our high Electoral Office to maintain the welfare of the Empire, to the satisfaction of the Imperial Deputation and the Circle representatives.

7. And since We are also rightly anxious to keep proper control over Our Cameral properties, which We must regard as the sinews vital not only for the maintenance of Our state and dignity, but also for other enterprises near to Our heart, this, Our Privy Council shall render good help to Our Cameral and administrative Councillors, and shall help them with advice in matters in which they require it, especially when money is needed for the conduct of Our high policy, or for domestic improvements, and on all other occasions when it may be needful to call on Our Cameral resources; and in such and similar important cases touching Our Cameral property the two Councils shall meet and reach an agreed conclusion and submit it to Us, whereby they shall also in general see that the figures are set out in intelligible fashion, and also correctly and faithfully set down, and all trivial argumentation avoided.

8. We also admit frankly that with all Our natural advantages and many navigable rivers, the state of trade in Our lands is very bad; it has, indeed, almost died out. It is therefore Our will and order that Our Privy Council shall not only consider without delay the establishment of a good administrative system, but also, how trade and enterprise are to be re-established, how the domestic commodities, such as cereals, wood, etc., are to be handled to the best advantage of the inhabitants themselves, the blocked navigation routes to Stettin and Hamburg opened, new businesses founded, and, in brief, the development of the country promoted; to which end they are to consult Our principal towns and instructed members of the Order of Knights and further to list and submit to Us the most necessary measures.

9. Since it is necessary to think of war in time of peace, Our Privy Council shall, in consultation with Our Colonels and military commanders, consider carefully what are Our chief needs, and especially see to it that Our fortresses are maintained and supplied with the necessary buildings, munitions, stores, and other essentials for defense, and the recruiting and whatever else is required for the defense and security of Our land carried through.

10. Finally, since it is impossible to remember and set down

every particular point, We do in general most graciously request and require Our Privy Council to keep in mind and regard what is best for Us in every case, that each and all of them shall faithfully dispatch all matters remitted to them, keep all these things most closely secret, speak no ill of each other, but confer together faithfully and in all amity; and if any one of them has a proposal which he thinks would be to Our benefit, he shall be empowered to bring it forward for discussion even if the Presidents have not put it on the agenda, and the President shall not prevent its being debated according to the regular procedure.

And although the nature of Our important affairs would call for daily sessions of Our Privy Council, yet, since Our Chancellor and others have to attend the Cameral Court, and look after Our Cameral business, We do hereby graciously command that except in case of necessity and of matters which brook no delay, Our Privy Council shall ordinarily meet only twice weekly, on Tuesdays and Thursdays, and thereafter report to Us on their deliberations, and on the other days, preoccupied as We are with so great cares and business, shall spare Us as far as possible.

But while Our Head Chamberlain, Count Schlick, cannot, on account of his other duties, always attend these meetings, Our other Privy Councillors shall nevertheless appear without fail in the Council Chamber on the said days and as often as necessity requires it, even if few in number, but as the importance and nature of the business require, and none shall excuse himself by the absence of the others.

Given under Our Electoral Hand and Seal, in Our Court at Cölln on the Sprew, December 13, in the Year of Our Lord 1604.

2. The Religious Issue Between the Elector John Sigismund and His Subjects

When, on Christmas Day, 1613, John Sigismund transferred his own and his family's spiritual allegiance from the original Lutheran to the "reformed" (Calvinist) version of Protestantism, he expected his country to follow him, sincerely believing as he did that there was no essential difference between the two forms. Instead, there arose an enormous outcry from his people. At first he protested in all innocence against this, exhorting the clergy to preach the "reformed" doctrine and denouncing those who refused to do so as troublemakers; we reproduce these injured exhortations in the first of the two following documents. The opposition proved, however, too strong for him, and a year later he was obliged, as shown in the second document, to give way to it and to allow anyone wishing to do so—and the overwhelming majority of his subjects did so wish—to continue to profess the "unchanged" Augsburg Confession, i.e., Luther's original version. Later Electors repeated these reassurances on many occasions (e.g., at the "Brandenburg Recess," proceedings given below[1]), and it must be said that John Sigismund's successors proved themselves, in general, well aware of the importance of refraining from alienating their Lutheran subjects. It must also be said for them that while they did not, in principle, extend their toleration outside the circle of Lutherans and Calvinists, they regarded themselves as bound to respect the faith of their Catholic subjects where they were under international obligation to do so, so that generally speaking Prussia was, after 1648, spared the horrors of the religious conflict that even after that date inflicted such devastation in the Habsburgs' dominions.

Both the texts that follow are translated from Christian Otto Mylius's *Corpus constitutionum Marchicarum*, Vols. I, 1. 12 and VI, 1. 79 respectively. The former is given complete; Mylius's second document is the record of a "Recess" which was concerned with a great number of questions; from this we have extracted only the passage which deals with the religious issue.

A. John Sigismund Deprecates Fanaticism from the Pulpit

ORDER THAT, to the avoidance of scandal, confusion of conscience, and detriment to the Church, seemly modesty and moderation be everywhere observed and used by preachers in the pulpit and elsewhere. Given at Cöln on the Spree, February 24, 1614.

We, John Sigismund, by Grace of God Margrave in Brandenburg, High Chamberlain and Elector of the Holy Roman Empire, etc.:

Offer Our greetings to all Reverend, high and learned Doctors and devout, Our dear subjects, and to all General and Special Superintendants, Inspectors, Ministers, and in general, to all servants of the Church of the Electorate and Mark of Brandenburg, on both sides of the Oder, and hereby make known to them that not only have pious and God-fearing persons in authority in every place regarded it as a real part of their office to see and ensure that

[1] See below, Document 3.

unnecessary controversy in the pulpits be silenced and banished from the Churches, but especially when certain persons arrogantly make bold and presume, contrary to Christian charity, to attack with sharp, acid, and bitter words, yea, often with all kinds of lewd and offensive expressions, other Churches over which no man has set them up as judges—inside and outside the Empire, abusing them and calling them heretics and damnable; whereby the common man is only offended, the Church only damaged and its edification visibly impeded.

In which respect, not to mention earlier examples, a praise-worthy example and memorial was left to be followed by others by the late Elector Augustus of Saxony in the year 66 [sic], the Dukes of Brunswick and Lüneburg in the names of all churches of Lower Saxony in the year 1652; the Elector Christian I in Saxony and Duke Joachim Frederick of Lignitz and Brieg in 1601, all of most glorious memory. And We are guided also by the comparison We make in this respect with other Electors and Estates, although there are very many of them who profess the teaching of Luther, Ourselves further to enact and provide in Our own lands that seemly modesty and moderation shall be observed and used by preachers in the pulpits and elsewhere, to the avoid-ance of scandal, confusion of conscience, and detriment to the Church. Any man can therefore easily understand how painfully it has affected Us that for some considerable time past now there has been heard from some (for We do not impute this to the whole body of you), being those who are impelled thereto, not by any special zeal for God's truth, but rather by ambition, pre-sumption, and arrogance—those who, if things came to a con-frontation, would assuredly have the least to say, or if they saw the slightest advantage in it, would probably even declare them-selves Papists—because they look for honor among men rather than honor with God, so much immoderate and indecent shouting, damning, cursing, storming and scolding, whereby they often heed little whether the things they say are true or untrue, fit to be uttered from the pulpit or not, only to vex pious Christians, hurt them and give full vent to their own little tempers, assuredly to the delight and amusement of our common enemies, the Jesuits and Papists—regardless of the fact that thereby they only draw down on themselves and their listeners the wrath of God and His judgment.

For the teaching of God's Holy Scripture is very different. It does not wish that those should be shut out from the brotherhood of Christ who are at one with us on the fundamentals of faith and firmly believe that they will be saved only through the mercy of God and by the merit of our only Redeemer, Interceder, and Savior, Jesus Christ, rejecting and casting away all other intermediaries and helpers; who also work, struggle and fight at our side in the Gospel of Christ, and for this have endured and suffered persecutions without number at the hands of the common enemies of our true religion, the Pope and his following, and still suffer and endure them today, yea, have often most joyfully shed their blood for this testimony. No less does it admonish us, very earnestly, that what is controversial should be overthrown and refuted, not by twisting of words and calumnies (which are a special device of the Devil's), not out of hearsay and false reports in crafty and perverse wise, but out of the sufficient word of God. It commands us further that all this shall be done and effected with Christian love, mildness of spirit, friendliness, patience, and heartfelt compassion towards those who are in error, not with brawling and calumnies, defamatory words, to the destruction and ruin of those strayed sheep. Therefore, any man can easily see how far these noisy clamorers of whom I have spoken stray from the true path and what a dreadful judgment they will one day have to suffer because they have cared more to rule over the minds of men than to set a good example to God's Church. But on Us, Whom God has set in authority over this land and Who have the right and the duty to see to the observance of both the first and the second of God's commandments, there lies the duty—lest We make Ourselves accomplices in such grievous sins—to use Our authority. We therefore enact, ordain, and declare Our will (following the injunctions already given to some of you personally, but little heeded) that you preach the Word of God to the congregations entrusted to you pure and undefiled, out of the prophetic and apostolic Books, the Four Chief Symbols[1] of the Reformed Augsburg Confession and its Apologies, without any distortion and without the self-devised glosses and doctrinal formulae of certain idle, ingenious and presumptuous theologians who have sought and claimed thereby the primacy in the Church

---

[1] The "four symbols" were those of the four great Councils of the primitive Church.

and the lay arm, that you thereby lead many souls to Christ and zealously devote yourselves, better than before, to advancing the honor of God and the blessedness of man. On the other hand, you are to cease, eschew, and avoid all berating and abuse of other Churches, which are not in your charge, even if they have not yet overcome certain generally recognizable errors, nor are you to brand them with the name of sectaries. For We cannot in conscience any longer watch this, nor hold Our peace on the subject; but if We learn that one or more of you, whosoever he or they may be, with no exception, continues to disregard this, Our strict command, which accords with the word of God (and it will not remain hidden from Us), such persons may be well assured that they will soon be summoned to Court and there be suitably admonished by Us. And if then no improvement is perceptible, he shall be deposed, removed from his office, or visited with other strict penalties appropriate to his offense and his deserts. And that person or persons who, being summoned by Us, does not appear shall be apprehended, in order that he or they be brought to obedience. We may allow it—and We have no objection—if some of such unseasonable fanatics and zealots as may be found among the crowds who believe that their consciences are constricted too narrowly by this Our benevolent Christian edict, that the same look round them for other posts and settle outside Our Electorate and territories in places where such un-Christian raging, ranting, scolding, rating, cursing, and damning of other Christian faiths and their followers is tolerated and allowed and there await their reward for this from God in due season. Further, We do enact and will that if any of Our clergy be molested by other peace-hating persons, attacked in sermons or writings, provoked and irritated, that he shall not, without Our special foreknowledge and leave, take any steps or enter into any quarrel with anyone, but rather rest satisfied with the testimony of his conscience and the knowledge that he is innocent of the imputations leveled against him by other, unquiet spirits.

And We would suffer no doubt that as We publicly announce and make known to all and sundry this Our open command, with the guidance of God's word, solely in order to seek and to ensure peace, tranquillity, unity, and the edification of the Church in the lands entrusted to Us by God, in this recent and most dangerous atmosphere and days in which the Roman Antichrist thirsts

more than before for the blood of true Christians, so shall also
every one among you, for the maintenance of peace and unity,
for the prevention of all offense and in due obedience, in accordance with the word of the Apostle Paul, when he warned and
enjoined all men to obey those set over them, lest they learn
that they do not wear the sword for nothing, show yourselves
diligent and do not move Us to disfavor and to use severity
against you. Therefore carry out what is Our gracious and also
honest intention, will and opinion, which We hold towards you
in sure and firm confidence in your due obedience, willingly
rendered. In token whereof We have ordered Our Privy Seal to
be appended hereto. Done at Our Court at Cöln on the Spree on
the twenty-fourth day of February, 1614.

B. EXTRACTS FROM JOHN SIGISMUND'S REVERSE IN THE MARK, 1615

The representatives present of the Estates have further most submissively requested and petitioned His Electoral Highness that He
and His well-beloved elder son, the Margrave George William,
should confirm to them, word for word, the previous Reverses
and Privileges. Since His Electoral Highness has regarded this
request and petition of the Estates as just and equitable, the said
Reverses and Privileges are hereby, and in virtue of this declaration,
renewed, confirmed, and ratified in their entirety, and in particular,
in respect of religion, to the effect that whosoever in the land
wishes it may remain attached to the doctrine of Luther and the
unchanged Augsburg Confession, as it was presented to the
Emperor Charles V in the year [15]30, and also to the book of
Concordia.[1] Such persons shall not be subjected to any pressure
or compulsion to relinquish it. For His Electoral Highness in no
way arrogates to Himself dominion over consciences and therefore does not wish to impose any suspect or unwelcome preachers
on anyone, even in the places in which He enjoys the right of
patronage, whether towns, communes, or villages (although He
could avail himself of all His rights to introduce a religion, freely
and without limitation, in virtue of His supreme sovereign rights).
Should it occur that any preacher should during his term of office
show that he was departing from the terms of his ordination, and

---

[1] The *Formula Concordiae* of 1577, for resolving differences in the
Lutheran Church.

therefore become disagreeable to his patrons and congregations, this shall be reported to His Electoral Highness, who will then make enquiry into the matter, carefully weigh all the circumstances, and order such dispositions to be taken as are equitable and just, that His Electoral Highness's Reverse may be honored and no one be therefore given cause for complaint. Accordingly, at the request of the Collators of the Estates, the examinations, ordinations, and confirmations of the Ministers shall take place in the manner that was usual in the days of the Elector Joachim Friedrich of most pious memory.

The composition and form of the Spiritual Consistory shall therefore remain under His Electoral Highness such that there shall at all times be sufficient members to deal competently with matters of transitory importance, but, should questions of special importance arise, the procedure customary under the Electors Hans George and Joachim Friedrich shall be followed, in that on such occasions the lay and spiritual Consistories shall sit together and give their decision jointly. Alternatively, one or two members of the Estates shall, if necessary, be invited to attend when such controversial questions come up.

3. The Brandenburg Recess of 1653

The Brandenburg Recess of 1653 was the momentous occasion on which Frederick William, then still a young man and feeling his way forward against strong opposition, extracted from the representatives of the Brandenburg Estates their consent to a tax for the upkeep of a *miles perpetuus*, a standing army to be kept together in time of peace, as well as war. The event proved the concession to be all-important for, although the tax was at the time voted for six years only, it proved to be permanent—it was, indeed, recognized at the time that this would be the case—so that the Estates, by granting it, surrendered a large part of the influence over public policy which their power to vote or refuse subsidies had previously given them. That they nevertheless consented to it was partly because the sum for which the elector now asked—530,000 thalers, spread over six and a half years—was substantially less than what he had in practice been levying during the previous ten years (this had averaged 150,000 thalers a year), and partly because, in return for it, he met the Estates halfway on a large number of points. It was not a complete surrender to their wishes, for almost every point agreed was the fruit of hard bargaining in which the Estates by no means always got all they wanted, but the general result was to affirm their position at least *vis-à-vis* that part of the population not represented at the negotiations, namely, the unfree populations.

These agreements covered every point on which either party felt a definition of its position to be necessary. They went into great detail, and a mere transcription of them would burst the bounds of this volume, while a full elucidation of and commentary on the questions involved would amount to a full-length study of the political, social, and economic conditions of the Brandenburg of the day. We have therefore translated verbatim only the most important of the articles, but have given an indication of the subject of the others, since even so much has its interest, and have added a few brief notes on the nature of the problems involved and the significance of the solutions reached.

That the agreement was reached at a Recess, i.e., a meeting of a comparatively small number of men representing their colleagues (*Deputationstag*)—two Knights from each of the fifteen Kreise of Brandenburg and a few burghers—and not at the full diet, was because the diet proper, when convoked in the previous year, had proved so obstructive that the elector, after adjourning it seven times, had in despair tried his hand again with the smaller body. The Diet of 1652 was, as a matter of history, the last ever held in Brandenburg, but no great weight should be attached to this; full diets had been great rarities in Brandenburg history even before this, and the *Deputationstage*, which were the normal channels for the transaction of business, continued to meet for another century.

The text from which the following extracts are translated may be found in Mylius's *Corpus constitutionum Marchicarum*, Vol. VI, pp. 118ff.

THE BRANDENBURG RECESS OF 1653 (GIVEN JULY 26, 1653)

Preamble

WE, FRIEDRICH WILHELM, by Grace of God Margrave in Brandenburg, Lord High Chamberlain and Elector of the Holy Roman Empire, Duke in Magdeburg, in Prussia, Jülich, Cleves, Berg, Stettin, Pomerania, of the Cassubes and the Wends, also in Crossen and Jägerndorf in Silesia, Burgrave in Nuremberg, Prince in Halberstadt and Minden, Count in Mark and Ravensberg, Lord of Ravenstein, etc., do hereby profess and make known in Our name and that of Our heirs and successors, Margraves and Electors of Brandenburg that after Our loyal and obedient Estates of Prelates, Lords, Knights, and towns of Our Electorate and Mark of

Brandenburg on both sides of the Oder and the Elbe have at the Diet now convoked and held most loyally and obediently declared their consent to pay —— thalers and even more, as specified hereafter,[1] and have in return submissively requested Us not only to confirm all the articles signed and sealed to them heretofore by their Electoral Highnesses, Our most noble ancestors, but also graciously to remedy their grievances:

We, having regarded and maturely considered the good will and most submissive loyalty they have always displayed toward Us and Our Electoral House, and have also shown, by action and in truth, at the present Diet, have most graciously acceded to their most submissive request.

We therefore pronounce, take oath, and declare in the name of Ourselves, Our heirs, and successors, that We will leave Our said loyal Estates in uncurtailed and undisturbed possession, enjoyment, and use of their privileges, liberties, and good and ancient rights and in particular of the former Electoral Reverses, and especially the Reverses of the years 1572, 1602, and 1615, and will protect and guarantee to the Estates of the Neumark and the incorporated Estates their Reverses of 1611 and 1614, and will always maintain these undiminished and unimpaired.

And whereas they have also most submissively begged Us to consolidate Our most gracious decisions on their petitions and grievances in a Reverse, and to confirm and ratify them of Our Electoral authority, We have most graciously acceded to this request also, and graciously make to Our loyal and obedient Estates the following declaration:

[Arts. 1 to 10 of the Recess are concerned with the religious question, on which, as we have already seen, a difference existed between the Calvinist Electors and the majority of their subjects, who had retained the "unchanged" Lutheran doctrine. The main purpose of these articles is to assure the Lutherans against encroachments by their rivals, while a digression confines the benefits of any such concessions exclusively to the two main branches of the Protestant faith. The protection enjoyed by Catholics in Cleves under the Treaty of Westphalia and in Prussia under that of Wehlau did not extended to Brandenburg.]

1. Firstly, We will have taught and professed in all Our Lands, in

---

[1] The sum is not named in the text.

Our University of Frankfurt, Electoral schools, and everywhere else, nothing but what is contained in the pure Word of God, in the Prophetic and Apostolic writings, and in conformity with the Four Chief Symbols.[2] The Holy Sacraments shall also be administered as appointed by Our Lord Redeemer and Savior, Jesus Christ, without any human addition and corruption. We further confirm the former Reverses of the country that whoever in the land wishes to do so may continue to profess the doctrine of Luther and the Augsburg Confession, as presented to the Emperor Charles V on June 25, 1530, at the Grand Imperial Diet of Augsburg, in the presence of His Imperial Majesty and also of the Electors and Estates of the Roman Empire, signed by the Protestant Electors and Estates, and as it has thereafter been used in Lutheran churches, particularly in the churches of this Electorate, and as Our loyal Estates have hitherto confessed it, and do now do so, and which is generally called by the Lutheran Churches "unchanged," and that each and all of their symbolical books shall remain inviolate, and everything is to remain as disposed by the Recesses of 1611 and 1615.[3] No compulsion or pressure shall be put on them to abandon it, as We have never thought to arrogate to Ourselves the dominion over consciences. Neither shall any person who is suspect to Our subjects be intruded in Our agencies and in places the patronage of which belongs to Us.

The majority of offices and benefices in the leading Colleges, and in the most reputed of them, have hitherto been occupied and enjoyed by more Lutherans than Calvinists. We are most graciously resolved to follow the existing practice and to confer Our grace and promotion on both Lutherans and Calvinists without distinction of creed.

[The remainder of this article promises that certain schools for the children of nobles shall be reopened and re-expanded as soon as circumstances allow and that preference in admission to them, fees, etc., shall be given to natives of Brandenburg, without distinction between Lutherans and Calvinists.]

2. Secondly, We will not permit the practice of their religion, in public or private, to Papists, Arrians, Photinians, Weigalians, Anabaptists, and Minists, and should it come to Our knowledge that conventicles of this type have, unknown to Us and contrary to

[2] See above, fn. 1, p. 225.
[3] See above, pp. 227–228.

Our will, been established in Our Electoral Lands, due visitation and punishment shall not fail.

We have had a special contract concluded with Jews, in virtue whereof all traffic of any kind is forbidden to them in Our Electoral Lands, except only on public and solemn festivals, on which, however, they must report themselves to the local magistracy, against which arrangement no one will have any cause to complain. For the rest, We will not permit to them any fixed domiciles or synagogues, and if they should offer inferior goods for sale or practice illicit usury, We will not fail to punish this severely.

3. Thirdly, We will leave the patronage of parishes to Our Estates, free and unrestricted as heretofore, and persons having the patronage or right of nomination and presentation shall further be empowered to install in them fit and qualified persons, and also to remove them, for serious reasons, as appropriate to the nature of the offense, but only by due process of law. We will also graciously protect and maintain persons who have the right of nomination and presentation.

[Candidates for ordination are to be examined by the Superintendant General in Frankfurt, and must satisfy certain standards laid down in the remainder of this article.]

4. Fourthly, parishes, churches, and their appurtenances are to be left in enjoyment of their old privileges, resources, and rights.

[The rest of this article and Arts. 5 to 10 are concerned with details of pastors' stipends, fees, etc. Art. 11, which is included in the Recess in the articles concerned with religion but is of wider application than the purely religious, since it deals also with nonecclesiastical appointments, is concerned with the important question of "*indigenat*," or nationality. There was at this time no single nationality for all the Elector's subjects; a man was a Prussian, Cleves-Mark, or Brandenburg national. The article represents a compromise, for the Elector's wish was to employ in any of his dominions anyone whom he thought fit, even if not a national thereof, but his hands were tied because in previous negotiations with the diets of Cleves and Prussia he had been obliged to promise to employ in those provinces only natives of them, so that he was now forced to accept the same principle for Brandenburg, but reserved his right here to depart from it in special cases:]

11. Eleventhly, as We have hitherto given preference before others to natives, especially nobles, in the conferment of prelacies

and canonries, this system shall be retained also in the future. Yet persons of burgher origin are not to be excluded, but protected in accordance with the customs and statutes traditional in each locality. We will, however, particularly maintain Our preference for natives over others, and will also promote them to prelacies, ecclesiastical benefices, dignities, Councillorships, and high public offices before any non-natives and foreigners who may with advantage be employed in Our business and the common business of the realm, in consultations, legations, and similar questions, and who have rendered or may in future render good service to the country. So also the sons of deceased persons, if they are capable, shall be given due consideration and admitted before any foreign nationals, not so much as their parents' heirs, by virtue of succession, since positions of responsibility cannot be made hereditary, but in their personal capacities and by virtue of choice. We cannot, however, so far allow Our hands to be tied as to renounce the right to confer benefices and offices of State on well-qualified non-natives and foreigners who have done notable, good and useful service to Us and to the State, or could do so; We hereby expressly reserve this right to Ourselves, Our heirs and successors.

In order, however, that the Estates of the Land may have even greater token of the special gracious love and affection which We constantly bear toward them, We further graciously declare that since Our subjects of Electoral Brandenburg are in Our Lands of Cleves, Prussia, and the Lands appertaining thereto, excluded from offices, benefices, Captaincies, and other services of those Lands, so the same principle shall be applied reciprocally, and natives of those Lands shall be treated similarly in these Lands of Electoral and Mark Brandenburg, and held incapable of enjoying any of the benefices and services to which Brandenburgers are not admitted in Prussia and Cleves, and further, in the future, shall not be promoted so long as the said Prussians and Clevelanders adhere to their present decisions. And the same rule shall apply in all Our Provinces which may make the same demand regarding the employment of natives.

[Art. 12 provides that all cloisters, except one, which is to be turned into a school, shall be left in possession of their statutes, and the number of their inmates may return to the prewar figures as soon as circumstances allow.

Art. 13 promises not to increase the obligations by which Chapters and their subjects were traditionally bound to provide food, lodging, and horses for certain categories of travelers, and to make moderate use of such rights in these respects as the Elector is unable to renounce. For instance—to take one example out of a long list—cooks and Electoral employees are not to be given special tips when quartered on a Chapter, "because they are not employed in the service of the Chapter, but in Ours."

Art. 14, which binds the Elector to consult with the Estates before taking decisions on questions of major importance, should by modern standards have been the most important of the entire document. In fact, it was a dead letter from the first, and that not solely of the Elector's fault; the Estates had already long ceased to attempt to influence foreign policy, except in the sense of objecting to the taxation made necessary by wars. But such as it is, it runs:]

14. Fourteenthly, We will make no decisions nor take steps in important questions crucial for the welfare of the country, or its reverse, without the foreknowledge and advice of Our loyal Estates, and will also conclude no alliances that would or might involve Our subjects or peoples, without the advice and consent of the Estates in general. In such important cases We will convoke the Estates to meet for consultation and will set out on the agenda the points of Our proposals.

We will at all times willingly listen to Our loyal Estates if they have any submissive request to make of Us, hear this with due attention, and deal with it with gracious good will.

[Art. 15 stands apart. It seems, like Art. 13, to have been an answer to complaints from the Electors' own subjects (on his crown domains), with which the Estates were not concerned:]

15. Fifteenthly, We will, as earlier Reverses stipulate, not sell or pledge any more of Our Electoral estates and domains, but will buy back and redeem those pledged as soon as possible.

[The next articles, a very long series, deal with questions which are treated here as matters of law. They range over a very wide field, and many of them are purely technical, providing for more Courts of Justice, eliminating conflicts of competence, etc. Others, however, are of great political and social importance, especially those which confirm the legal domination of the privileged Knights and burghers over their subjects. Conspicuous among these are Arts. 20, which confirms the lords' jurisdiction of the first instance, and 22, the opening of which provides penalties against a "subject" appealing against his lord's decision without sufficient cause, while the concluding paragraphs, among other things, expressly reaffirm the condition of serfdom where it already exists and place the onus of proving his freedom on the subject. Other articles favorable to the lords are 28 and 31.

In Art. 16 the elector promises to enlarge the personnel of the *Kammergerichte* of Sollin and Küstrin, and lays down principles to be followed in the appointment of judges. Art. 17 restricts the competence of the Consistorial Court, and Art. 18 extends and safeguards the right of appeal. Art. 19 lays down that Reverses have the force of law and must be so treated.]

20. Twentiethly, We are graciously pleased to protect in every way the Prelates, nobles, and town Councillors in their privilege of "first instance," and every case shall be first remitted to the immediate authority, and no case shall be irregularly taken out of his hands, except where the issue is one of justice denied, but the case shall be rejected and simply remitted back to the competent Court and immediate authority, as is expressly provided in earlier Reverses. We are, however, graciously prepared to allow aggrieved persons not only the right of appeal but also the possibility of a sentence's being quashed.

[The rest of the Article deals with special applications of or exceptions from this rule. Art. 21 amends the law against debtors. Previous enactments cannot be repealed, but all reasonable excuses or pleas for delay will be considered.]

22. Twenty-secondly, with reference to complaints that Knights are often taken to Court by their peasants and involved in unreasonable expense, the following procedure shall be followed for the avoidance of vexatious complaints: When a peasant brings an action against his lord and his complaint proves not to be well founded, he shall be punished with imprisonment in accordance with Our revised *Kammergericht*, in order that others may refrain from similar mischievous complaints; and should it be recognized that a townsman has accused the Council rashly, frivolously, and maliciously, he is to be punished, according to the degree of his disobedience and contumacy, either with imprisonment or with a fine, to be applied to pious causes.

The buying out of peasants is, under the Reverses of 1540 and 1552, again permitted to persons who inhabit their own properties and have no other seat or habitation, in which case, however, the peasant must be paid the value of his property, after valuation, in hard cash. The manorial authority in which the jurisdiction of the first instance is vested cannot be deprived of the right of evicting contumacious persons for grave and important offenses, but this must be done for cause stated, at an enquiry regularly appointed, and after report on the legal position.

Total expulsion of a delinquent from the country can, however, be ordered and executed only with the consent and ratification of Ourselves, Prince of the Land. We may also, given good and sufficient reason, reduce or modify a penalty imposed.

Remissions granted by manorial Courts on compassionate grounds to poor subjects in time of war are not to be taken as creating permanent situations, and shall in no way affect or invalidate the right of the lord to collect his normal rents and services.

Serfdom [*Leibeigenschaft*] remains in being where it has been introduced and is the custom. Should any person contest this by arguing possession of a prescriptive presumption of freedom, length of time alone is not sufficient to prove his case, but good faith, title, or the cognizance and acquiescence of his lord must also be shown, and even this shall be without prejudice to exceptions, particularly to those arising out of wartime conditions.

[Art. 23 orders a more careful procedure when civil cases are conducted before a municipal council. The Crown does not wish to interfere with the free election of aldermen, but desires them to carry out their duties in such fashion as to give the burghers no cause for complaint. Arts. 24 to 30 are of minor or local importance, except 28, which rules that a law officer of the Crown cannot proceed directly against a noble nor imprison his subjects, but must send the documentation of the case up to the Supreme Court. With Art. 31 we come to the question, of great importance to the Knights, of the succession of fiefs. This is solved in a way very favorable, on balance, to the petitioners.]

31. Thirty-firstly, in respect of new fiefs, We are graciously prepared to include the feoffee's brothers and the children of his brothers in the donation and will also not object to including more remote agnates if they apply to Us and fulfill the conditions. Similarly, while it is the practice of Our Court of Appeal that when a noble fief is distrained it is passed to a noble purchaser and

when a fief falls vacant it is always bestowed on a noble, sufficient evidence of which is to be found in the registry of fiefs,

Yet We cannot renounce the right to escheat vacant fiefs which are suitable for Our domains and to incorporate them in Our domains and estates, especially in the present condition of the country, in which so many noble estates are lying derelict and empty, with little prospect of getting reclaimed.

We are, however, always graciously prepared, but with reservation of Our rights, to bestow vacant fiefs on nobles and other native families. We cannot, however, completely exclude servants of Ours of burgher quality who have rendered useful and loyal service to Us and to Our Electoral House, and we cannot recall any instance when a vacant and ownerless fief has been incorporated in Our domains; on the contrary, many large and valuable properties have been detached from the Electoral domains and conferred and bestowed in fief on certain nobles.

[Art. 32 deals with the legal position of agnates succeeding to a heavily indebted estate; Art. 33, with the position of the creditors of a bankrupt. Art. 34 deals with the provision to be made for the daughters of a noble landowner whose estate is inadequate to provide proper dowries for them. If a noble's daughter marries below her station, but to an honorable man, decent provision should be made for her; but those who live dishonorably, or marry dishonorably, forfeit their dowries. Art. 35 limits the obligation of a depopulated Kreis to pay in full debts contracted by it when it was more densely inhabited.]

36. Thirty-sixthly, landlords cannot demand rents for years in which a farm was derelict, nor can persons who remained on their farms be subject to writs or distraints, but they must be granted substantial reductions, especially for those years in which Our lands were visited and ravaged by the scourge of war. In token whereof We are graciously conceding to Our own subjects and tenants not only a proper and substantial reduction, but total remission for most of these years. [The Church is to allow similar remissions of tithe.]

[Art. 37: nobles or Crown agents occupying derelict holdings are liable to taxation on them. Art. 38: how prices are to be calculated when rents are paid in kind. Art. 39: nobles retain their privilege that only their properties in towns are liable to quit-claim duty, not those lying outside the jurisdiction of the municipality. Art. 40: a subject under obligation to resume possession of his holding and return to his lord's jurisdiction and offered a temporary holding *ad interim* while his own is being put in order is bound to accept it.]

41. Forty-firstly, subjects and peasants who have remained on their holdings throughout the war, endured the great hardships, and helped to carry the common burden, are not to be evicted, nor are persons of totally unknown origin and conduct to be put in their places, but the Estates cannot object, seeing that it is to their advantage, if, besides natives, foreigners also are accepted in the places of those who have gone away and the derelict localities settled with them or new places established and brought under cultivation.

We have, of grace, allowed six tax-free years to persons prepared to settle in and bring under cultivation certain derelict places on Our Electoral domains; thereafter they are without fail to pay their dues and to help carry the general national burden like other subjects. Meanwhile, however, the new settlers cannot be exempted from the dues in kind which the priests and sextons receive in lieu of stipends; they must deliver these, or else allow the priests and sextons the use of sufficient land from their holdings to make up the outfall in their dues.

[The rest of this article deals with the special difficulties of certain towns. Arts. 42 to 44 are directed against restrictive practices by blacksmiths, carpenters, bell-founders, and dealers in hops. Art. 45 promises an early delimitation of the frontier with Poland. Art. 46 approves arrangements made by the Knights and towns to discuss certain difficulties that had arisen between them. Art. 47 lays down the procedure for settling disputes between the Crown officials on the one hand and Knights and towns on the other. Art. 48 deals with the appointment of commissioners to collect certain taxes. Art. 49: where possible, persons against whom prosecutions are pending are not to be kept in custody.

The articles which follow are, in the main, concerned with economic questions. The chief interest in them lies in the efforts made by the Knights and towns to retain old privileges of exemption from taxation. As a rule, the Elector admits these, but insists on safeguards against abuse. The most important articles dealing with this question are 52, 62, and 65. An article of a different interest is 63. While the right of coinage was at this date a Crown prerogative almost everywhere, and the practice of making a profit out of it by debasing the currency almost a regular one, Frederick William had been carrying this so far that the level of prices had been badly affected.

Under Art. 50, a general ban on exports, especially of corn, hops, cattle, and hemp, is not to be enacted except in cases of urgent necessity, and then only after consultation with representatives of the Estates. Art. 51 deals with the abolition, total or partial, of certain emergency levies.]

52. Fifty-secondly, except for the new duty on corn exported abroad by land or water, which is to be paid by all exporters, but only at a place which We shall designate, We are willing to confirm those Knights and towns which are exempted from the payment of duty in their traditional privileges and exemptions from cartage duty, and Prelates, Lords, and Knights shall be absolutely free to export by land or water corn grown by themselves and their tenants, also wine so much as they have above their own needs, and also cattle, wool, and any other produce from the Knights' estates that may be for sale, and to import in return, duty-free, wine, victuals, cooked articles, and other commodities needed by them. [Precautions must, however, be taken against abuse of this privilege.]

[Art. 53 lays down various rates of export duty on beer. Art. 54: duties on corn exported from certain localities. Art. 55: further safeguards against abuse. Art. 56: customs and excise officers must report to the local authority before distraining on any noble estates. In Art. 57 the Elector promises to continue, as best he can, the supply of cheap timber. Art. 58: Crown employees entitled to fell timber on nobles' estates must not take mast-bearing trees in bearing. Art. 59: certain types of iron may be imported, but duty must be paid on them. Art. 60: the shepherds and drovers of lords are not to be required to pay toll when making short journeys. Art. 61: anyone may buy millstones wherever he pleases, at home or abroad, but the traffic in them is declared a Crown monopoly, and everyone except the Knights and duty-free towns must pay import duty on them.]

62. Sixty-secondly, on the purchase of salt. Since certain Prelates, Lords, and Knights have their own transport services to Lüneburg and think that they can get salt cheaper there, at Stettin, or at other places on the frontier, We are willing, as pro-

vided by previous Reverses, to exempt and relieve the Prelates, Lords, and Knights of all Our Electorate, and also owners and holders of knightly estates, from the salt tax insofar that any of them may, as heretofore, buy the salt necessary for their own households and for their sheep and dairy farms, without let or hindrance, wherever they will, and have it conveyed by land or water. [The carriers must, however, be provided with papers showing the destination of the salt, which must not be in excess of the buyer's own needs, nor may it be resold, under pain of loss of the privilege for life. A noble's privilege extends to his widow, orphan children, their guardians, etc.] For the rest, We retain the Crown monopoly of salt in all Our Lands of the Mark on both sides of the Elbe and Oder, with no exception in favor of any locality or Circle, in such fashion that henceforward no person shall presume to import salt into Our Lands nor to sell it, under pain of the penalties laid down in Our Edict, and if these prove inadequate to stop smuggling, We reserve the right to impose an exemplary punishment, to be determined on each occasion as appropriate to the gravity of the offense. In respect of the preparation and retail of salt, We shall negotiate with the towns and graciously concede the traffic to them, to be used for the benefit of the municipal Councils or their foundations, as they may agree between themselves, but on condition that they buy the salt only from Our agents, do not overcharge the public when selling it, and take care to suppress all smuggling, and also provide neighboring Circles with salt for certain periods. [If Knights prefer to buy their salt from the Crown agents, they may do so. The price to be fixed annually and notified publicly.]

Art. 63. Sixty-thirdly. Whereas Our obedient Estates have most submissively represented that Our Land is now sufficiently provided with all currency at present needful, and that there is no shortage any more, We will stop the mint next Michaelmas, unless it should have been forced to stop before for technical causes and the full quota not minted, in which case minting must go on up to the end of October. But at the end of February of the coming year, 1654, We will again call together a Committee of Our obedient Estates, most graciously listen to their proposals and submissive representations, and give them satisfaction, and also take the appropriate decisions and give the orders how the issue of currency in Our Lands is best to be regulated.

[Art. 64 deals with the case of travelers who enter the country by certain routes to avoid paying customs at the regular place of entry. Art. 65: The Estates have asked for the abolition of the new duties on corn introduced by Sweden during the Thirty Years' War. The Elector quotes back at them, as justification for maintaining it, an old edict to the same effect issued by the Emperor Frederick III in 1456. He promises, however, not to increase the tax, unless on the new Oder-Spree canal then under construction;[1] he reserves his right to levy any dues he wishes on this canal, when completed. Arts. 66 and 67 are of local interest. In Art. 68 the Elector promises not to extend his hunting rights in the Altmark at the expense of those of the Estates. "Subjects" are not to be impressed into service at wolf hunts, but are to be encouraged to assist in them. Those whose duty obliges them to help in such hunts will be treated "civilly" and not kept overlong at the task. Art. 69: The preparation of saltpeter is prohibited; the nitrous earth is to be buried in peasant farms.

With Art. 70 we return to politics, and miscellanea. Art. 70: nobles and Knights of the Neumark are entitled to signed themselves "Edler von."]

Art. 71. Seventy-firstly, in respect of the memorial presented to Us by Our loyal Estates concerning the appointment of a Regent [*Statthalter*, i.e., during the Elector's absence from the country], all We know is that during the whole period of Our reign, so often as We have had occasion to leave the country, We have always made dispositions satisfactory to Our loyal Estates, and We again graciously offer to make such gracious dispositions in similar cases that the Estates shall have no cause for complaint.

[Art. 72 promises the towns remedy against a complaint made by them of excessive requisitioning of horses by servants of the crown. Next follows approval and ratification of an agreement concluded between the Knights and the towns on certain points of detail. The final paragraph again registers the Estates' promise to pay "—— thaler of 24 groschen each," in good money, over six and a half years.]

---

[1] See above, p. 211.

4. The Treaty of Wehlau, 1657

The Treaty of Wehlau, bringing as it did to the Elector of Brandenburg the coveted prize of full sovereignty over the Duchy of Prussia, marked a major stage in the upward progress of the Hohenzollern dynasty toward European importance. It was not, however, either to the fact of this acquisition or to his manner of obtaining it that the Great Elector owed his honorific soubriquet. The Treaty was really an almost secondary by-product of a much larger multilateral conflict, the beginning and ending of which lay elsewhere, and the part played by the Elector in that conflict was almost inglorious, marked neither by good faith nor by diplomatic skill; it was the ambitions and fears of others that finally threw Prussia into his lap. For our purposes, we may take as the beginning of the conflict in question the great revolt of the Cossacks against Poland which broke out in 1648. The Cossack leader, Bogdan Chmielnicki, was heavily defeated by the Polish armies in July, 1651, but then transferred his allegiance to the Grand Duke of Muscovy, who thereupon, breaking his truce with Poland, invaded that country. Next (June, 1654) came the abdication of Queen Christina of Sweden. The new king of Poland, John Casimir, unwisely put in a claim to the succession (it will be noted that in the treaty, John Casimir styles himself, *inter alia*, King of Sweden), and Christina's designated successor, Charles X, seized on this as a pretext to renew Gustavus Adolphus's expansionist ambitions in the Baltic. He suggested to the Elector of Brandenburg that he should join him but, far from promising him any reward, even demanded concessions of him. Frederick William refused these, and his first moves—a defensive treaty with the Netherlands and another with the Estates of Polish Prussia—were rather directed against Sweden, although he also made no move to help Poland. Meanwhile, in the summer of 1655, Charles had overrun Poland with sensational speed. The Polish fortresses surrendered to him, the King took refuge in Austria, the army swore allegiance to Charles. Charles now led his armies into Prussia and forced Frederick William to sign the Treaty of Königsberg (January 17, 1656), under which the Elector received, indeed, the episcopal enclave of Ermland, but had to accept Swedish suzerainty, in lieu of Polish, in Prussia, and to make further concessions.

Now, however, the Poles rallied, unexpectedly and sensationally, and drove the invaders back to the Baltic. The help of Brandenburg, with its intact army, was now worth buying—by either side. Brandenburg itself had fixed its price, full sovereignty over Prussia; but which bidder would, and could, pay it? Councils in Brandenburg were divided, but the Swedish party prevailed. After signing the Treaty of Marienburg (June 25, 1656), which promised him, not his price, but other Polish territory, Frederick William joined the war and sent a force to Warsaw, and in a further treaty (Libau, November 20, 1656) was able, after all, to extract from Charles renunciation of his suzerainty over Prussia and Ermland.

But Charles had made these concessions out of weakness, for now he was in difficulties. Denmark attacked him, and Austria entered the war on Poland's side. Charles moved his troops to Denmark, leaving Brandenburg to face the incensed legitimate suzerain of Prussia alone.

Fortunately for him, Austria was concerned that Sweden should not grow overpowerful and therefore wished to detach Brandenburg from her. Moreover, the Emperor Ferdinand III had just died, and his son Leopold needed Brandenburg's vote for the forthcoming election. Austria's most capable roving diplomat, Lisola, whose name figures justly in the preamble to this treaty, undertook the mediation, and after difficult negotiations secured the conclusion of the treaty that follows. Frederick William thus re-ceded Ermland, but received after all, from the hands entitled to give it, the coveted full sovereignty over Prussia; and the developments of the following years, which, after anxious moments, saw the defeat of Sweden at the hands of a coalition composed of Brandenburg, Poland, Austria, and Denmark, made the acquisition permanent, for in the Treaty of Oliva, concluded through French mediation on May 3, 1660, which terminated the war, all its signatories acknowledged his sovereignty in Prussia.

The allusions in the Treaty of Wehlau require little elucidation, with the exception of those in its twentieth article. The great Lithuanian family of Radziwill played an obscure part throughout the war. Prince Janusz Radziwill, Hetman of Lithuania, pacted with both the Russians and the Swedes, and after his death in November, 1656, his son Boguslaw signed the Pact of Radnóth (December 6), under which Poland was to be partitioned between Sweden, Brandenburg, Transylvania, the Cossack Ukraine, and a Lithuanian Principality ruled by the Radziwills. When the tide turned, Boguslaw made submission to John II Casimir.

The text is translated from J. Dumont, *Corps Universel Diplomatique du Droit des Gens* (8 vols., Amsterdam–Hague 1726–1731), Vol. VI, No. 2, pp. 191ff.

Treaty of Peace Between John Casimir, King of Poland, and Frederick William, Elector of Brandenburg, Done at Wehlau in Prussia, September 19, 1657

Be it made known to all men, that when in earlier years, and in that time in which the most Serene and Puissant Prince and Lord, John Casimir, King of Poland, Grand Duke of Lithuania, of Russia, Prussia, Masovia, Samogitia, Livonia, Smolensk, and Chernigov, and Hereditary King of the Swedes, Goths, and Vandals, and the glorious Kingdom of Poland and Grand Duchy of Lithuania, were involved in Muscovite war and Cossack incursions, the Swedes similarly assailed Poland with hostile armies and at last penetrated into Royal and Ducal Prussia, so that the most Serene Prince and Lord, Frederick William, Margrave of Brandenburg, Head Chamberlain of the Holy Roman Empire and Electoral Prince of Magdeburg, Prussia, Jülich, Cleves, Münster, Stettin, Pomerania, the Cassubians, and Vandals, and also Duke of Crosna and Carnovia in Silesia, Burgrave of Nuremberg, Prince of Halberstadt and Minden, Count of Mark and Ravensberg, Lord in Ravenstein, and his dominions and subjects, was so harrassed and pressed by the enemy armies of the Swedes and by the concentration against him of Swedish forces on all sides, that he was forced by the pressure of necessity to conclude certain pacts with them, and consequently certain hostilities arose and were perpetrated between the Most Serene King of Poland and the Most Serene Elector of Brandenburg. Yet at last, by the singular grace and clemency of God, the Most Serene and Puissant Prince and Lord, Leopold, King of Hungary, Bohemia, Dalmatia, Croatia and Sclavonia, Archduke of Austria, Duke of Burgundy, Styria, Carinthia and Carniola, having intervened and brought about mutual agreement through the mediation of his Privy Councillor and Plenipotentiary, the most illustrious and Excellent Lord Francis of Lisola, Lord of Tysen and Marienfeld, the plenipotentiaries both of His Sacred Royal Majesty and of His Electoral Serenity [the names and titles of the plenipotentiaries follow . . .] being duly accredited, have agreed and established perpetual peace, concord, and friendship between the said Most Serene and Puissant King and Grand Duke of Lithuania and his successors, and the Kingdom of Poland and Grand Duchy of Lithuania, on the one hand, and His Electoral Serenity of Brandenburg as Duke of Prussia and his successors, on the other, on the following conditions:

1. Seeing that the said peace is to be perpetually true and sincere, all hostilities between the two Parties and their forces, soldiers and subjects shall cease immediately. Neither Party shall attempt, nor suffer to be attempted, anything to the damage of the other, but each shall study in every way to promote the glory, welfare, and

security of the other. And whatsoever loss, injury, or damage has been inflicted during these wars on one or the other Party, either in the Kingdom of Poland or the Duchy of Prussia and on their inhabitants, by the other Party, either through violence and military forays or by exactions, looting, or in other ways, shall all be buried in perpetual oblivion and never revived. Neither shall His Sacred Royal Majesty and the State of Poland, nor any Province united thereto, nor any of their subjects, of whatever rank, dignity, or condition, nor His Electoral Serenity or his subjects, soldiers or Ministers, be entitled to cite or sue the others, or their heirs or lands, dominions, soldiers or subjects, much less extort anything from them by force, but all these things shall be mutually wiped out, and henceforward each shall promote the welfare of the other and avert loss from it, saving in respect of personal and civilian debts contracted between the inhabitants of the Kingdom, the Grand Duchy of Lithuania, and this Duchy during or before this war, which each shall be bound to pay; neither to those who were under Electoral occupation in this war, or in any way agreed with His Electoral Serenity or his officers in the Kingdom of Poland— all this shall, in token of friendship and of the intercession of His Electoral Serenity, be forgiven them by His Royal Majesty, and shall in no way be held against them to the detriment of the rights and liberties of any description previously enjoyed by them, without any exception or reservation.

2. Prisoners of war taken by the Polish and Electoral forces shall be restored to their previous liberty without ransom or confiscation of their chattels; but if any have joined the colors of the other Party and enlisted in his forces, they shall be left with that Party and their extradition not claimed. Real property and documents which were seized or put under sequester by either Party in consequence of this war shall be restored to their lawful owners, irrespective of any deeds of gift made by any person, under any title.

3. Each Party shall in these present times of war strive diligently to promote the common welfare and security against any disturbers thereof; and shall combine with united councils, forces, and efforts for the stabilization of peace and mutual security and the expulsion of enemies from the Kingdom of Poland, the Grand Duchy of Lithuania and the Duchy of Prussia; notwithstanding any other

obligation or connection that might seem contrary to this most equal intention and reciprocal obligation, but shall be regarded as rescinded in virtue of this Treaty.

4. His Electoral Serenity shall immediately, and, so soon as this Convention shall have been ratified by His Royal Majesty and the Senators and Dignitaries of the Realm and Court officials assisting him, restore fully and without any reservation all territories throughout the Kingdom of Poland and the Grand Duchy of Lithuania and the Bishopric of Ermland occupied under any title or *de facto* held by him. The evacuation of these places shall be supervised by Commissioners of each Party, in concert, in accordance with the customary laws of war, with no injury or molestation to the inhabitants and without demolition of fortifications, old or new, unless in any place both Parties should agree that this is expedient; artillery belonging to the Bishopric shall be left *in situ.*

5. In consideration whereof and of other returns enumerated below, and for other just causes, he and the male heirs of his body, legitimately begotten, and thereafter all his descendants, so long as any male descendants of His Electoral Serenity shall survive, shall possess and rule the Duchy of Prussia, within the limits within which H.E.S. held it as a fief before the beginning of this war, in full and absolute sovereignty, free of any servitudes previously attaching to it.

6. But although the Most Serene Elector and all his male descendants shall be freed of the whole nexus of vassalage by which they were formerly bound to the King and State of Poland, and everything deriving therefrom, yet the fief shall not thereby be alienated in perpetuity, but on failure of male descendants in the said legitimate Electoral line, the full rights of the Most Serene Kings and State of Poland to the said Duchy are reserved, and the said Duchy is not by this agreement detached from the State of Poland; which reservation shall in no wise prejudice the sovereign rights of H.E.S. and his descendants before the situation arises. And H.R.M. promises in his own name and that of his descendants that should his line become extinct, they will pay special consideration to the agnates of H.E.S., to wit, the House of Culmbach and Onelsbach, and will use their influence in the assemblages of the Kingdom, that in case of extinction they shall be preferred to others and admitted to the succession to the said Duchy, under the

same conditions and obligations of vassalage under which H.E.S. and his predecessors possessed it in virtue of their investiture.

7. H.R.M. and the State of Poland hereby release the Estates, officials, and all subjects of the Duchy of Prussia from the earlier oath by which they were previously bound. In place whereof the Most Serene Elector shall bind himself and all subjects of Prussia to observe these Pacts and Perpetual Treaty on exchange of ratifications. And, further, all Estates, magistrates, officials, and commanders of fortresses, ports, strong places, and cities shall take oath that should the line become extinct they will recognize the Most Serene King and State of Poland as their sole and immediate lords and will render them all obedience and due loyalty and will repeat this oath when doing homage to each Duke of Prussia, in the presence of representatives of the Most Serene King of Poland and of the Polish State, according to the special form of oath herewith appended. The day on which the said oath shall be taken shall be agreed with H.R.M. or His representatives.

I, N.N., swear that in the event of extinction, under which ownership and full sovereignty over the Duchy of Prussia shall belong to H.R.M. and the State of Poland, according to the Treaty concluded on September 19, 1657, between H.R.M. and H.E.S., I will recognize the most Serene King of Poland and His successors, and State of Poland, as my sole, legitimate, and immediate lords and will render them due loyalty and obedience, so help me God, through Jesus Christ, Amen.

8. In the event of extinction of the male line of the present Elector, the surviving Margravines of the line or, should there be none such, the nearest agnate of His Electoral Serenity and his descendants, whoever shall then succeed in the Duchy of Prussia, shall pay out the sum agreed between H.R.M. and H.E.S. and set out in the ratification. And until this is liquidated, the said Margravines or the said nearest heirs shall be allowed to retain the Prefecture of Fusterburg, with all land and Cameral Domains, commonly known as Kammer-Ampter, appertaining thereto, and to possess and enjoy them, but on condition that whatever they receive from the fruits of the said Prefecture shall be counted toward the payment and amortization of the said sum; after liquidation whereof they shall be bound to cede that Prefecture to the legitimate owners of Prussia and shall have no further claim thereon.

9. H.E.S. and his male descendants will preserve and maintain

the Barons, nobles, cities, and magistrates and all subjects of Prussia, of whatever rank and condition, in their ancestral and recognized privileges, statutes, legal rights, and liberties, where not contrary to this Convention, and will not attempt any infringement or modification of them, nor suffer others to do so. And they shall see that justice is administered according to the customary and received law of Prussia and its other statutes and customs. If any person shall claim to have suffered injustice in a lower Court, he shall be entitled to appeal to the Supreme Court of Appeal to be established by H.E.S. in the Duchy of Prussia, and there to seek his rights in proper fashion. There shall be no room for further appeal, ordinary or extraordinary, or however called; the President and Assessor of this Court of Appeal shall be appointed by H.E.S. and his male descendants from natives and citizens of the Duchy of Prussia, and they shall take oath to him; neither shall subjects be in any way entitled to carry their disputes before the King and Kingdom of Poland, nor admitted by them. Similarly, H.R.M. and the State of Poland promise, in case of reversion, that they will in the future preserve, whole and entire, the said liberties, privileges, statutes, customs and acknowledged laws of the Estates of Prussia and will maintain them in quiet and tranquil possession of them all and will introduce nothing new in any of them.

10. In place of the previous vassalage, H.E.S. and his descendants shall be joined to the King and State of Poland by a perpetual and inviolable treaty, through which the security of each Party shall be assured for ever, in the following fashion:

11. H.E.S. and his descendants will cultivate true friendship and union with the Most Serene Kings and Kingdom of Poland and the Grand Duchy of Lithuania, and will never, directly or indirectly, enter into any treaty with the enemies of the Most Serene Kings or of the Kingdom, to the prejudice of the King and the State; they will refuse such enemies transit through their dominions, ports, and fortresses, and also supplies and commissariat and any kind of help, neither shall they hand over to them their ports or strong places in any way or under any title.

12. The subsidies which H.E.S. will be required to pay to the Most Serene King and State of Poland in the present war are specifically set out and delimited in the special treaty concluded on this point, which Convention shall be observable in all points by virtue of the present Treaty. But whenever, after the close of this

war, any new war arises against the M.S.K. and S.P., H.E.S. and his descendants will be required to supply to the M.S.K. and S.P. 1,500 foot soldiers and 500 horse soldiers, who shall be at the charges of the King and State of Poland after they have left the Duchy of Ducal Prussia.

13. In return, the Most Serene King and his successors and the State of Poland and Grand Duchy of Lithuania will keep reciprocal friendship with H.E.S. and his successors and will not permit any of his enemies entry into the lands of H.E.S. but rather be bound to pay heed in every way to the defense, preservation, and security of the Duchy of Prussia; especially, if any person shall, now or in the future, be minded to make war against H.E.S. and his successors on account of this Convention or despatch of auxiliaries (whereof above), the Most Serene King and the Kingdom of Poland shall be bound to send an adequate force to his succor.

14. The King's forces shall have free passage whenever the need arises through Ducal Prussia, but without causing damage, loss, or harm to any of its inhabitants; and H.E.S. and his descendants shall arrange their march routes, etc., and, that this may be done aright, early notification of the arrival of the Polish army or troops shall be given by H.R.M. or his Generals, commonly called "Feldherren," to H.E.S. or his descendants or, in their absence, to the persons to whom the government of the Duchy has been entrusted; and the Polish army and its commanders shall be required to follow the march route designated. Similarly, H.E.S. and his descendants, the Dukes of Prussia, shall be free to convey troops through Poland and Royal Prussia, subject to the same restrictions and precautions.

15. The ships of either Party shall enjoy complete freedom and security of entry into and passage through the ports lying in the dominions of the other Party, irrespective of their cargoes and freights and with every security for the same, as shall be agreed in due course between the Parties. And each Party shall be free to buy provisions, supplies, and all necessaries of war in the territories of the other; and each Party may recruit soldiers in the territory of the other Party, but shall first address to him a friendly request, and then the two Parties shall agree conformably with the present Treaty and the circumstances of the day, and this procedure shall always be observed, that no inconvenience to the Parties or loss to their subjects be involved.

16. The practice of the Roman Catholic religion, as it was, or ought to have been, enjoyed in Ducal Prussia before this Swedish war, under old and more recent treaties, shall be maintained or restored. Those who wish shall be free to profess it, nor shall any subject of the Duchy professing it now or in the future be molested on that score; and their chapels and oratories and all ecclesiastical properties appertaining thereto, anywhere, either in the confines or elsewhere, shall be kept whole and safe, and they shall be allowed to profess therein the doctrines and institutions of the Roman Catholics. No one shall be molested on that account, no one shall suffer any violence, injury, insult, or molestation because of his Catholic religion, and any person injuring them in any way shall be severely punished. Catholics who are qualified shall have free admission to gifts and honors, and any Catholic Barons, nobles, or cities who have legitimately acquired rights of patronage may use and enjoy them without impediment or obstacle in places where such rights are in their hands; but if other co-patrons not of Roman religion have anywhere been introduced and question arises regarding the said rights and exercise thereof, the issue shall be composed and decided by Commissions to be constituted by H.E.S. of an equal number of each religion, as laid down in Canonical Law. And the [Catholic] Church in Königsberg, with its cemetary and places appertaining to it and charters and other admitted rights shall be kept in the same state as it was, or ought to have been, before this war. Ecclesiastical personages shall enjoy in the future the same immunities and privileges as they enjoyed, or ought to have enjoyed, under earlier treaties. The spiritual jurisdiction of His Most Excellent Reverence, the Bishop of Ermland, over his See and all other ecclesiastical personages professing the Catholic religion shall be preserved intact and entire, as the treaties provide. Finally, they shall enjoy all rights, prerogatives, and liberties contained in ancient and in recent treaties and charters, which are here again confirmed in this point, and are regarded as specifically expressed and declared. Similarly, they shall retain the calendar hitherto officially used and accepted. Similarly, the King and State of Poland promise in their own names and in those of their successors that in case of reversion they will not attack or infringe either the Augsburg-Lutheran or the Augsburg-Reformed religion.

17. Commerce shall be free and secure between the inhabitants of the Kingdom of Poland, the Grand Duchy of Lithuania, and

the Duchy of Prussia; and if any disputes arise relating to commerce or to questions connected therewith or deriving therefrom, or in any way relevant thereto, a Commission shall be constituted at the instance of the complainants, and all matters shall be amicably composed by Commissioners drawn from both Parties in equal numbers, appointed within the space of two months on the initiative of either H.R.M. or H.E.S. And no new tolls, by land or water, that did not exist before this war shall be imposed in the dominions of either Party to the detriment of either, and, if it seems necessary in the common interest to impose or increase any such, this shall be done by agreement between the Parties.

18. As to the frontiers and subjects as allocated by the frontiers, should any doubt or dispute arise between H.R.M., his successors on the throne, the Kingdom of Poland, and the Grand Duchy of Lithuania on the one hand and H.E.S. on the other, regarding the observation and execution of this Treaty and Convention, or for any other reason, it shall be resolved and settled amicably, on the instance of either Party, by Commissioners appointed in equal numbers by the two Parties within the space of three months, who shall, if necessary, meet on the spot.

19. Amicable agreement shall be reached as often as necessary by delegates from each Party on the price, value, and assessment of currency and its free circulation.

20. On the intervention of His Serene and Most Puissant Majesty, the King of Hungary and Bohemia, made through his said delegate, and also of His Serenity the Elector of Brandenburg, who pressed strongly for the full restitution and complete security of the said Prince, the Plenipotentiaries of the Most Serene King of Poland, having observed and taken note of the benevolence shown by H.R.M. and testified in more than one document toward all others who have returned to obedience and especially toward the Most illustrious Prince Boguslaw Radziwill, Duke of Birza,[2] Dubnica,[3] Slucia[4] and Repislia,[5] Prince of the Holy Roman Empire, have agreed and consented that the said Prince, seeing that he, with all his following, has indeed returned with due submission to his

[2] German Birsen, Lithuanian Birzai, in the District of Kowno (Kaunas).
[3] Dubnica, Russian Dubinki, north of Vilna.
[4] Slucia, i.e., Slutsk, Russian Sluzk, in the District of Minsk.
[5] Probably a misprint. The fourth place usually named in Prince Radziwill's titles is Copita = Kopyl, north of Slutsk.

former obedience, faith, and allegiance, has renounced all commerce with the enemy, and has sworn faithful allegiance in the future to the Most Serene King and State, shall not only enjoy and benefit by the general amnesty, but shall in virtue of the present transaction be understood to be restored and reinstated in full form, with all that is his, in the patrimony of his Duchies and in all benefits and rights legitimately accruing to him therefrom, nor shall anyone be entitled to cause him or his followers any trouble or molestation on account of the injuries, losses, and hostilities inflicted *de jure* or *de facto* in this war either by him or by his soldiers or servants, but all these things shall be regarded as buried in true amnesty and forgetfulness of the past, in virtue of this settlement, saving personal and civilian debts, which must be paid.

21. Each Party shall swear that this Treaty and all contained in this instrument shall be faithfully copied and the Most Serene King of Poland and the Senators attendant on him shall solemnly ratify and confirm by oath this Agreement and shall promise that all contained therein shall be transmitted for ratification to the next competent assemblage or Diet; similarly H.E.S. will likewise ratify it and confirm it by oath. And whenever a new King of Poland is elected, and a Duke of Prussia succeeds in the Duchy, it shall be renewed and confirmed on the above oath by Delegates swearing on the souls of their Principals. And if either Party contravene this Convention and Treaty, and fail to make proper amends, the injured Party shall be held to notify the mediators and Most Serene Kings and Estates named in the following Article and enlist their offices to procure satisfaction, and each Party shall adhere strictly to this procedure of conciliation that all disputes may be composed amicably and equitably.

22. That they may also pledge their faiths to the security and affirmation of these Pacts, the Most Serene and Puissant Kings of Hungary and Bohemia and also of Denmark and Norway and the Estates General of the United Netherlands shall be requested, in case of injury or violation of this Convention, to take all good counsel together and procure due satisfaction therefor.

23. Two identical copies of this Pacification and Treaty have been made by the Plenipotentiaries named above, to be ratified and affirmed on oath within six weeks from the below date by His Royal Majesty of Poland and the Senators attendant on him and by H.E.S. of Brandenburg, and the ratifications shall be exchanged. One copy shall be given to the Plenipotentiaries of H.R.M. and the

other to the Plenipotentiaries of H.E.S., and for greater faith and greater strength shall be furnished by the said Plenipotentiaries of both Parties with the signatures of their own hands and affixing of their seals.

Done at Wehlau in Prussia, on the nineteenth day of September, in the year of grace 1657.

VENCESLAS DE LESNO, Bishop of Ermland, Plenipotentiary of H.R.M. of Poland and Sweden.

VINCENT CORVINUS GOSIEUSKI, Grand Treasurer and Field Marshal, Plenipoteniary of H.R.M. of Poland and Sweden.

F. DE LISOLA, Delegate of the King of Bohemia and Hungary for the mediation of this Treaty.

OTTO, Baron of Schwerin, Electoral Plenipoteniary.

LAURENCE CHRISTOPHER SOMNITS, Electoral Plenipotentiary.

5. Introduction of the Excise Tax in Brandenburg, 1667

The excise tax—a copy of an institution already in existence in France, the Netherlands, and some of the smaller German principalities—was a device for increasing crown revenues, which had consisted solely of the yields from the crown properties, plus what could be wrung from the Estates as a *contributio*, and of putting the burdens equitably on the shoulders of those most easily able to bear them. On its introduction it had, indeed, to be confined to the towns because the land-owning nobles could not be induced to renounce their privilege of exemption from taxation—this distinction between town and country was maintained into the nineteenth century—and it was consequently found necessary to introduce it only very cautiously and tentatively (see para. 10 below), but it was, in fact, well enough received, the towns realizing that if they did not pay more in this way, they would have to do so in some other; the representations made against it in the months following its introduction all related to points of detail.[1] The excise was developed in time into one of the pillars of the State's financial structure.

The text that follows is translated from Mylius, *Corpus constitutionum Marchicarum*, IV, III.2.

[1] Consideration was given to these in an amending enactment dated November 15, 1667. This is printed in Mylius, *op. cit.*, pp. 96ff.

ORDER ESTABLISHING A CONSUMPTION OR EXCISE TAX IN ALL
TOWNS OF ELECTORAL AND MARK BRANDENBURG, FOR THREE
YEARS, BEGINNING JUNE 1, 1667 (DATED APRIL 15, 1667)

WE, FRIEDRICH WILHELM, by grace of God Margrave in Brandenburg, Chamberlain of the Holy Roman Empire and Elector, etc.,
in Prussia, etc.: Do hereby proclaim and give notice to all and
sundry: Inasmuch as most lively representations have on various occasions been made to Us concerning the poor and needy condition
of Our towns in Our Electorate and Mark of Brandenburg, and
We have accordingly considered all kinds of ways and means to
restore them and to save them from final ruin and complete destruction, it has seemed to Us that it would be particularly conducive to the improvement of their condition and promotion of their
prosperity if the public burdens were somewhat more evenly distributed, not all laid only on the poor, nor levied exclusively on
land and houses, for which purpose we can think of no means
more convenient and equitable than the introduction of a fixed and
moderate excise, toward which all inhabitants without distinction
shall contribute, each contributing much or little, according to
whether his consumption is large or small.

1. And it is therefore, firstly, Our most gracious and strict
will and command that as from the first of June, by which date the
Patent can be brought to the public notice in all towns of Our Electoral Mark of Brandenburg including also the Episcopal, Crown
Agents', and Knights' towns, and in particuar also in Storchow and
Beesekow, and similarly, so far as brewing is concerned, in all
alehouses and breweries that engage in the sale of beer in cloisters,
liberties, suburbs, villages and hamlets, the following tax shall
be placed on the commodities hereafter specified and included in
the *contributio*, but the contribution towards this excise from the
Episcopal, Crown Agents' and Knights' towns shall count toward
the quota of *contributio* paid by each place.

1. Locally brewed beer
    Per 3 sacks   3 thaler
    Per sack   1 thaler
    Per bushel,[1] where
    brewing is done by the bushel   2 groschen

[1] The Prussian "bushel" was, strictly, 54.96 liters, and thus about 1 1/2
English bushels.

2. Foreign beers, such as Zerbster, Brühau, Mumme, etc.

Per cask of 3 tuns	1 thaler	12 groschen
Per tun		12 groschen

3. Foreign wines, Alicante, Malvoisie, mead, or other heavy wines imported for consumption

Per firkin[2]	2 thaler	
Rhine wine, per firkin	1 thaler	
Franconian or French wines, imported for consumption, per firkin	1 thaler	6 groschen

4. Local wines

Local wines pressed on the spot or dispatched from the country into a town, per tun (to be paid by the buyer)		6 groschen
The same wine drawn from the cask		9 groschen
Foreign wines such as Guben or Meissen wines, per tun		10 groschen

5. Brandy

Home-distilled, per quart		6 groschen
Rhenish, Polish, and other foreign brandy, per quart		9 groschen

6. Flour

Per bushel of wheat[3]		2 groschen
Per long ton[4]	2 thaler	
Per bushel of rye		1 groschen
Per long ton of rye	1 thaler	

7. Meat slaughtered in a public slaughterhouse

Per ox so slaughtered and exposed for sale by the butcher	1 thaler	
Per cow		15 groschen
Per hog		6 groschen
Per sheep		2 groschen
Per calf		2 groschen
Young lamb or goat		1 groschen

8. Slaughtered domestically

Per ox		12 groschen
Per cow	7 groschen, 6 pfennigs	

---

[2] *Eimer.*
[3] See above, fn. 1.
[4] *Winspel:* 1 *Winspel* = 24 *Scheffel* = 36 bushels.

Per hog fattened		3 groschen
Per hog unfattened	1 groschen,	6 pfennigs
sheep		1 groschen
suckling young lamb or goat		6 pfennigs

9. Cattle

Per milch cow (annually)	6 groschen
Per 25 sheep or goats milch or for breeding	6 groschen

10. Salt

Per ton	4 groschen

11. Seed corn

Per bushel of hard corn		1 groschen
Per long ton	1 thaler	
Per bushel of soft corn		8 pfennigs
Per long ton		16 groschen

12. Craftsmen and skilled artisans, fishermen, boatmen, carriers, etc., quarterly

Master	1 thaler	12 groschen
A worker hired by the year [*Michel-handwerker*]	1 thaler	
A worker hired by the day [*Taglöhner*]		12 groschen
A journeyman		2 groschen

2. The local magistrate shall apportion the taxation exactly and equitably; but it shall not be imposed on craftsmen and unskilled workers until a real improvement can be expected out of the general funds, whereafter they, with the merchants and keepers of shops and stalls, must contribute, as above, to the general tax on all transactions and commodities, but the journeymen must pay their contribution as from June 1.[5]

3. The State agents or magistrates in each place are therefore to be vigilant that the taxes on the specified articles are duly paid, and that there is no evasion; and any article on which the excise has not been paid is to be confiscated forthwith and one-fourth of the value given to the informer, while the remainder is set toward the exchequer.

4. The magistrates of each town shall, with the help of committees of the burghers, make proper arrangements to ensure that

---

[5] This seems hard on the journeymen, but they were a particularly unruly section of the community whose disorderly conduct had been causing much trouble in many German states.

no evasion is practiced when livestock is slaughtered in the public slaughterhouses or domestically or by the bakers in the towns and suburbs or in connection with any other specified articles, and the brewers, retailers of liquor, slaughterers, and bakers shall obey these regulations exactly.

5. For which purpose the collection and administration shall everywhere be entrusted and assigned by the magistrates and burghers' committees to established, respectable, and diligent persons who are already under attestation and acting as collectors of the *contributio*, thus avoiding expense and the creation of new salaried posts.

6. For the rest, no person whatsoever, whether resident in noble manors, Colleges, Episcopal liberties, on the Werder[6] or in other liberties, in suburbs or outlying districts, whether he be cleric or noble, employee of the Court or army, higher or lower official, or of any other quality, shall under any pretext whatever, be exempt from this tax, nor shall any exemption or liberty be given contrary to this rule, either by Us or by any other person, and anything of the sort that shall inadvertently occur shall be regarded as null and void and no regard whatever paid to it; the magistrate shall, however, not pretend to any other jurisdiction over any houses or localities which are exempt or otherwise not dependent on him.

7. Immediate inspection shall be made of all places retailing wine and beer, and the owners shall be required to pay the excise in full on their stocks.

8. And the magistrates of each locality shall pay due heed and attention that the innkeepers, slaughterers, bakers, and handworkers do not make this small excise a pretext to raise their prices excessively, and shall fix equitable prices and see that they are observed.

9. All towns are to render to Us quarterly a true account of what this excise has yielded, in order that we may issue further instructions how and in what way the yield from it is to be applied to the welfare and best interests of the town, for which purpose alone it is to be used, and not touched in any other way or employed for any other purpose.

10. This excise is to remain in force for three years from the above date. After the expiration thereof and after it has been ascer-

---

[6] The "Werder Island" outside Berlin; it was being laid out as a pleasure ground, and enjoyed special privileges.

tained whether the towns have been improved thereby and whether much reclamation has been carried through, further instructions will be issued to promote the welfare and best interest of the country. This interim introduction of the excise is, indeed, itself not disadvantageous to the liberties and privileges of the towns, and they shall be free to cancel and annul this operation as they think fit, immediately or even before the expiration of three years.

11. We hereby graciously and strictly command all Our Governors, Commanders, and others in places where garrisons are kept or Our soldiers quartered to render all assistance to magistrates and excise employees and not to permit anything conducive to the diminution or evasion of the excise. Given under Our Hand and Electoral Seal in Our residence in Colln on the Spree, April 15, 1667.

FRIEDRICH WILHELM

6. The Readmission of Jews into Brandenburg

All Jews had been expelled from Brandenburg in 1573, during the great wave of intolerance which had swept over the Electorate with the coming of the Reformation. When Frederick William decided to readmit a limited number, it was probably due to his belief that the measure would be conducive to that promotion of commercial activity in which he took so keen an interest. He had, as we have seen,[1] announced his intention to take the step at the Brandenburg Recess of 1653, but various preoccupations had delayed its realization for nearly twenty years. As pattern for the treatment to be accorded them, he took the arrangements in force in the recently acquired Halberstadt, in which a small Jewish community had survived the Reformation. A year after issuing the edict which follows, Frederick William further appointed a rabbi to be in charge of interconfessional and similar disputes throughout the Electorate. Thereafter, the Jews were not again molested, although King Frederick I had, as we shall see, strong views on the inadvisability of admitting more of them.[2]

The text that follows is translated from Mylius, *Corpus constitutionum Marchicarum*, Vol. V, (3), in which it constitutes No. 2 of

---

[1] See above, p. 232.
[2] See below, p. 318.

the series; the whole of this chapter of Mylius is devoted to enactments relating to Jews, most of them concerned with cases of Jews who had infiltrated over the Polish frontier.

EDICT ON THE ADMISSION OF FIFTY FAMILIES OF PROTECTED JEWS; BUT THEY ARE NOT TO HAVE SYNAGOGUES (DATED MAY 21, 1671)

WE, FRIEDRICH WILHELM, by Grace of God Margrave in Brandenburg, High Chamberlain and Elector of the Holy Roman Empire, etc., hereby make public announcement and graciously notify all whom it may concern that We, for particular reason and at the most submissive request of Hirschel Lazarus, Benedict Veit, and Abraham Ries, Jews, have, for the furtherance of trade and traffic, decided to admit a number, to wit, fifty families of Jews from other places into Our Land of Electoral and Mark Brandenburg and most graciously to extend to them Our special protection. We hereby do this, under the following conditions:

1. We declare the admission of the said fifty Jewish families, whose names, their numbers, and the place in which each has settled are most shortly to be made known by Us in a regular announcement, into Our said Land of Electoral and Mark Brandenburg, also into Our Duchy of Crossen and the incorporated Lands, in the following fashion: that they are authorized to settle in the places and towns most convenient to them, and there to hire, buy, or build rooms or whole houses and residences, but under condition that anything they buy shall be sellable again, and what they build must be left to Christians again, perhaps after the expiration of a certain number of years, their expenses, however, being refunded to them.

2. These Jewish families shall be free to trade and traffic, conformably with Our Edicts, in the whole Land of this Our Electorate and Mark of Brandenburg, Duchy of Crossen and incorporated Lands, whereby We further expressly permit them to keep open stalls and booths, to sell cloths and similar wares by the piece or the ell, to keep large and small weights (but they are not to overreach anyone in buying or selling), without payment to the public scales or the magistracy where it keeps the heavy weights, to deal in new and old clothes, and further, to slaughter in their houses and to sell what is above their needs or forbidden to them by their religion, and finally, to seek their subsistence in any place where

they live, and also elsewhere, especially in respect of wool and spices, like other inhabitants of this Land, and to sell their wares at the annual and weekly markets.

3. But as We have reminded them, above, of Our Edicts, so they must continue to conduct their traffic in accordance with the Imperial Statutes relating to Jews, and consequently abstain from all forbidden traffic, especially, as far as possible, traffic in stolen articles, not to injure the inhabitants of this country, nor anyone else, by unfair dealing, not intentionally to defraud or overreach any person, not practice usury with their money, but content themselves with the rate of interest which We have sanctioned to the Jews of Halberstadt, as also the Halberstadt procedure shall be followed with them if they have purchased stolen goods.

4. They are to pay customs duties, excise and milling fees like Our other citizens, without any preference, but since they are resident in Our Land they shall be exempted from the body-tax paid otherwise by all Jews in transit, but, lest other Jews who do not belong to their number pass through tax-free under this pretext, each family is to pay one Reichsthaler a year protection money, and one golden gulden, like the Halberstadt Jews, whenever one of them marries; as to other taxation, they must reach an equitable agreement with the local magistrate, and, should this prove impossible, they are to report the case to Us, and We will then take suitable steps.

5. Although, however, We have taken the said fifty families under Our special protection, they must submit themselves in civil cases to the jurisdiction of the Burgomaster in charge of each place, whom We particularly and personally charge with this office, but if anyone has a complaint against any of the Jews, this is always to be made in writing. But should criminal cases arise among them, these are to be brought immediately to Us; the magistrate of each place is to see that this is done.

6. They are not to be permitted to have synagogues of their own, but may meet in one of their houses and there conduct their prayers and ceremonies, but without giving offense to Christians, and shall abstain from all offensive language and blasphemy, under pain of severe punishment, and they are hereby permitted to keep a slaughterer, and a schoolmaster to instruct their children, under the same conditions as in Halberstadt.

7. For the rest, they shall everywhere behave and conduct them-

selves honorably, peaceably and soberly, and above all, they shall take good heed that they do not take any good coinage out of the country and bring bad in. Similarly, they are not to take gold or silver church plate to other places, but to sell it for the proper prices in Our currency, and should anyone bring them for sale silver stolen from one of Our subjects, or should they learn in any other way of the existence of any such silver, they are bound to report, not only the silver, but also the persons concerned, and meanwhile to take charge of the person bringing it to them for sale.

8. The magistracy of every place in this Our Electoral Mark of Brandenburg, Duchy of Crossen, and incorporated Lands in which any Jews of the above fifty families wish to settle is not only hereby graciously and earnestly commanded to receive the said Jews willingly and readily, to give them all friendly assistance in establishing themselves and also all protection, in Our name, but also to treat them equitably in respect of their allocation of taxation, not to permit anyone to abuse or ill-treat them, and to treat them like any other citizen and in accordance with the tenor of this, Our Letter of Protection, and, in particular, to assign to them a place for the burial of their dead, against payment of an equitable fee.

9. Insofar now as the above Jews fulfill all the requirements made of them, as above, and all their promises, We will afford them Our gracious protection and patronage for twenty years from the above date, and We also graciously promise, in Our name and that of Our heirs, if We think fit, to continue this also after the expiration of the said period, but, if not, We reserve to Ourselves and to them the right to withdraw Our protection from them after due enquiry even before the expiry of the said twenty years.

10. Should—which may God forbid!—war break out in Our Lands in these twenty years, the said Jews shall be free, like Our other subjects, to take refuge, with their families, in Our fortresses, and they are to be received and tolerated there.

Accordingly, We command all Our subjects and servants of whatever rank or status that they shall for twenty years from this date on allow the said Jews to pass freely and securely everywhere in the whole of Our Electorate and other lands, to attend the public fairs, depots, and places of trade, to offer all their wares for sale publicly, and to give them facilities without let or hindrance for honorable trade and such traffic as is not forbidden, and not to molest them. Furthermore, all magistrates and officers of law are to give them all due assistance for which they ask and to offer them the same hospitality as they give to others, under pain of Our highest displeasure and also of a fine of fifty gulden in gold, and more if We think fit. In token whereof We have signed this Privilege and Letter of Protection with Our own hand and confirmed it with Our Seal of Grace.

Potsdam, May 21, 1671

FRIEDRICH WILHELM

7. The Great Elector's Venture into Overseas Commerce

We have referred elsewhere to the Great Elector's particular interest in the development of his country's trade. His inspirer and adviser-in-chief in this field was an enterprising immigrant from the Netherlands, Benjamin Raulé, for whom he created the post of Directeur-Général de Marine. On Raulé's initiative, colleges of commerce were founded in Berlin, Königsberg, and Kolberg, and a seagoing fleet was built, which in 1681 actually fought a successful engagement against a Spanish squadron off Cape St. Vincent. The chartered company whose foundation charter is reproduced below was established in the following year, in which an expedition to the Guinea Coast founded a base there, the "Feste Gross-Friedrichsburg."

The enterprise, like the Emperor Charles VI's Ostende Company, proved, indeed, a failure. Only the Elector himself and Raulé put much money into it, and, after stagnating for forty years, it was sold by King Frederick William I to the Dutch West India Company, for a small sum, in 1721.

The text translated below is taken from Mylius, *Corpus constitutionum Marchicarum*, Vol. VI (1), p. 156.

EDICT OF 7/17 MARCH, 1682, ON THE CHARTER FOR THE TRADING COMPANY TO BE ESTABLISHED ON THE COASTS OF GUINEA, ETC.

WE, FRIEDRICH WILHELM, by the Grace of God Margrave in Brandenburg, High Chamberlain and Elector of the Holy Roman

Empire, Duke in Prussia, Magdeburg, Jülich, Cleves, Berg, Stettin, Pomerania, of the Cassubians and Wends, also in Silesia, Duke of Crossen and Jägerndorf, Burgrave of Nuremberg, Prince of Halberstadt, Minden, and Camin, Count in the Mark and Ravensberg, Lord of Ravenstein and of the Lands of Lauenburg and Bülau, etc., do hereby convey to all and every man who may wish, or need, to know these presents, Our greetings, according to his rank, and make known to them as follows:

That, having considered that Almighty God has blessed some of Our Lands with well-situated seaports and being consequently minded, among other measures which We are resolved to introduce to improve shipping and commerce, which are most conducive to the prosperity of a country, to set up and establish, with God's help and blessing, a Company trading with the so-called Guinea Coast in Africa; which shall conduct trade in free places there under Our flag, authority and protection, and furnished with Our credentials.

It is Our will to grant the following Privilege and Charter to the said Company:

1. Any person, foreigner or native, shall be free to bring to and deposit with the Company, by the thirty-first of December of this year, any capital sum, not smaller than 200 thalers, for which purpose he shall apply to Our Councillor and Directeur-Général de Marine, Benjamin Raulé.

2. Both those who have invested much and those who have invested little shall share in the profit, so often as it is distributed, proportionately to what they have invested; but those who have invested less than 1,000 thalers shall not attend the meetings of Directors, but their share shall be paid out to them or their representatives.

3. As soon as the first ships are ready to sail, which, God willing, will be next May, all shareholders who have invested 1,000 thalers or more shall be convoked to a meeting in a place of which they will be notified in advance, there to appoint and elect from among their number two or four Commissioners to receive the accounts for the equipment and cargoes.

4. Similar meetings or *conventus* shall be held whenever one or more ships return from Guinea, and there consideration shall be given as to how the goods that have arrived are to be sold and

placed to the best advantage. Should, however, one or another of the shareholders be unable or unwilling to attend in person, he may entrust another with his vote; those present shall nonetheless continue with their deliberations.

5. Every year a balance sheet of the Company shall be drawn up, with an inventory of all its assets, and after this, a distribution made, so that each may know how it stands with his capital.

6. The Company shall be managed by four Directors or trustees, who shall, where possible and necessary, live in different places and shall be elected by the shareholders at the first meeting.

7. We, as Founder and Protector of this Company, wish, whenever a meeting is held, to send one of our Ministers to preside over it, that We may be kept regularly informed of everything that goes on there.

8. The capital of this Company shall, if God grants it His blessing, be increased yearly by as much as the assets will bear; but in such fashion that all shareholders always receive some profit (or interest, as much as possible).

9. Should any shareholder observe that the Company is not being managed by the trustees honestly, rightly, and diligently, he may bring the matter to Our notice or to that of the person presiding at the last meeting, and We will then provide equitable remedy or, if We think fit, call a meeting at which the complaints may be heard and the abuses eliminated and redressed.

10. We promise to protect and maintain the Company by all lawful means and to the best of the power given Us by God against all and any person who may presume to molest or damage it in any way in its activities in free places on the coast of Guinea, Angola, and on the high seas, and, to that end, to furnish the ships with efficient soldiers, so many as are needed on each ship, besides the sailors given by the Company; but the Company must provide the soldiers with food and drink, the same as the sailors'. And We will, in general, do and undertake everything necessary for the maintenance of the Company and its trade.

Anyone wishing to enter the Company under these conditions and invest in it has to apply to Our Councillor and Directeur-Général de Marine, Raulé, and register his name, with the amount of capital he is investing.

Given under Our Hand and Electoral Seal at Colln on the Spree, March 9/19, 1682.

8. Protection of the Brandenburg Woolens Industry

The edict that follows is among the most important of the Great Elector's measures to foster home manufactures. Wool was at this time perhaps the chief of Brandenburg's native products, and, as the text mentions, both the Elector himself and his father made many attempts, of which this was the last and the most thorough, to keep the profits of turning it into cloth at home by founding a native woolens and cloth industry. Similar import prohibitions were imposed on salt and articles manufactured from glass, iron, copper, and brass. The text is translated from Mylius, *Corpus constitutionum Marchicarum*, Vol. V.

EDICT ON THE PROHIBITED PURCHASE AND SALE OF WOOL IMPORTA-
TION OF CLOTH AND STUFFS FROM ABROAD, AND IMPROVEMENT OF
THE WOOLENS INDUSTRY (MARCH 30, 1687)

WE, FRIEDRICH WILHELM, by grace of God Margrave in Brandenburg, Imperial High Chamberlain and Elector, etc., do hereby convey and make known to all and every of Our loyal subjects, to the Prelates, Counts, Lords, Knights, Captains and Crown Agents, Commissioners, assessors, tax collectors, clerks, Burgomasters and Councillors in towns and villages, directors of customs and collectors of excise, also receivers of customs and mounted police, also employees, clerks, and bailiffs on the lands of nobles and others, and to all and every inhabitant of Our Electorate and Mark of Brandenburg whom it may concern:

Although Our forefathers now at rest and in particular His Highness, Our father of glorious memory did, in reply to the repeated submissive representations and complaints of the cloth-makers and wool weavers of Our Electorate and Mark of Brandenburg over the pre-emption and buying up of wool which has for a considerable time gone on there, to their great detriment and loss, in that certain merchants, tailors and others, and even in part persons without fixed abode who do not even bear part of the national burden, and also speculators possessed of foreign currency and likewise Jews, have presumed to journey about the country and to pre-empt the wool, even before the shearing, from nobles, priests, village mayors and clerks, peasants and shepherds and afterward to smuggle it illicitly out of the country, strictly forbid this, as long ago as the Monday after Trinity, 1611, by Edicts published throughout the land, and afterwards issued all manner of other salutary enactments for the improvement and development of the cloth industry, which We also, being desirous that such malpractices should cease, have on various occasions, such as on the twenty-fourth of May, 1641, the thirtieth of May, 1660 and the sixth of May, 1676, expressly repeated and ordered to be brought to the universal notice—

Yet since We have experienced that the application of such paternal solicitude has not achieved the desired end, but that the buying up and pre-emption of wool has steadily increased, through the connivance and negligence of Our officials appointed to control it, in particular the customs officials, controllers, and police, the wool has been sorted, the best taken out of the country, and the bad sold to the clothmakers, in consequence whereof the cloth made out of it has been unserviceable, and the merchants have turned to neighboring countries, the cloths maufactured in foreign towns out of the exported wool has been reimported into Our Lands, and very great sums of money have gone out in return, unaccompanied by any other commodities, and further, the previous number of clothworkers (especially up to 1680) has gradually and perceptibly diminished and dwindled, to the patent detriment of Our towns, and this branch of manufacture totally ruined.

Consequently, We, out of paternal solicitude for the conservation and promotion of Our subjects, have considered such measures as We feel Ourselves entitled to take in virtue of natural and other right, and first must find means whereby the good wool, wherewith Divine providence has so richly endowed Our Land, may as far as possible be processed in Our Electoral Lands, and the cloths, fabrics, and stuffs made out of it consumed and used not only there but also in Our other Duchies, Principalities, Provinces and Lands, and also that other foreigners may be encouraged by its good quality to purchase and export it.

Accordingly, We do hereby most graciously and earnestly command, enact, and will, of Our sovereign Power and Highness, that none of Our subjects, military or civil servants, burghers of towns or landsmen, but in particular no merchants, pedlars, tailors, clothworkers, or any other persons who have hitherto had any dealings in foreign cloth, shall as from the beginning of next

July bring into the land or the towns any cloths manufactured in neighboring or other foreign places of which they cannot at once prove that the ell cost them to buy more than 1 thaler, 12 groschen, under pain of confiscation of the cloth for the first offense and a further punishment at Our discretion, in case of repetition. We do not, however, wish free trade in such cloths between foreigners and foreigners, or between Our subjects and foreigners, wholesale, or if the purchasers collect a quantity of pieces and have them made up into bales—this only at the fairs—to be in any way prohibited or impeded, but wish it to go on unimpeded as heretofore, but subject to the condition that the merchants report all foreign cloths to Our tax officials, have them made up into bales by a sworn packer, and sealed on the spot at which the bales or packages are made up with a seal of lead bearing a scepter and round it the words, "Foreign cloths in transit"; neither foreigners nor Our subjects may then open such bales in Our Lands, and Our customs officials—and in the case of native merchants, the tax collectors—are to see carefully whether the seals have been broken or opened.

With the same regard for the public welfare, We further equally forbid the importation of all foreign-manufactured serges, baizes, etc., for cutting or consumption in this country, under pain of confiscation, and with the same possibility as above of further penalties.

And since it is highly necessary to supplement the above prohibition with careful and adequate provisions for making good the exclusion of foreign cloths under this prohibition by improving the manufacture of them in this country and providing the tailors, drapers, and others of Our subjects with good cloths, baizes, etc., of various grades, We not only repeat all the above-mentioned Edicts published by Our father of glorious memory and confirmed by Ourselves, but also extend, precise, and elaborate them in the following respects:

[There follow thirty detailed enactments, providing:

1. Every year before the shearing an official warning is to be given to all sheepfarmers that they are not to export their wool, nor to sell it except at annual fairs to any person not directly engaged in the woolens-manufacturing industry.

2. No wool is to be offered for sale at the annual fairs before 11 A.M. After that it can be bought by all weavers, tailors, etc., who have registered with their guild; but not for export.

3. Crown agents and nobles may still export their own wool, but it must be weighed and provided with a permit before export. Foreign buyers may not buy directly from nobles, etc., but only from merchants in the towns, after the wool has paid excise.

4. Traders authorized to sell abroad may for that purpose buy wool from nobles, but not from other growers, and must keep registers of what they buy.

5. Villages, etc., where no weavers' and tailors' guilds exist must take their wool to a place where there is such a guild.

6. A clothworker who has bought more wool than he needs may not sell it abroad; he must distribute it to other members of his guild.

7. Wool must be washed and cleaned before being offered for sale.

8. The wool of wild rams must not be mixed with that of the farm sheep; the animals are to be destroyed.

9. Similarly, goats' hair is not to be mixed with sheep's wool. To ensure this, goats are to be pastured with swine.

10. Growers may spin, full, and weave cloth for their own consumption only, not for sale.

11. They may not sell homespun wool to anyone except tailors and clothworkers.

12. No one may sell clothes manufactured out of cloths, etc., the importation of which is prohibited.

13. An inspectorate of cloths is to be established.

14. Special attention is to be paid to promoting the manufacture of types of cloth formerly imported.

15. Cloth weavers must not sell inferior goods.

16. Deals with relations between cloth weavers and tailors.

17. Forbids the peddling of cloth.

18. Merchants must provide weavers with materials on credit, and, where necessary, cash advances; the terms are to be left to free bargaining, but must not be oppressive.

19. On the other hand, weavers, clothworkers, etc., must not, as has notoriously been their habit, spend the sums received by them as payment in advance on their cloth in gorging and carousing. The paragraph lays down safeguards to ensure that the advances are used properly.

20. Deals with details of the procedure to be followed in importing and exporting cloths.

21. Loose-living and unattached journeymen who refuse to take employment with the spinning mills, and attempt to work independently, are to be compelled to take wool from the weavers and clothmakers and to spin it properly; they must, however, be paid a regular and adequate wage.

Paras. 22 to 25 lay down provisions for ensuring the supply of dyestuffs, and of livelihoods for dyers. Native clothworkers may not send cloths out of the country for dyeing. Paras. 26 to 29 deal with details of guild organization.

30. The order is to be given the widest publicity, and any infringement of it or failure by customs officers, etc., to enforce it is to be severely punished.]

9. The French Huguenots Made Welcome in Brandenburg

The practice of inviting skilled persons from abroad to fill gaps in a national economy was very common in the seventeenth and eighteenth centuries. No rulers followed it more extensively than those of Brandenburg-Prussia, and, among these, none favored it more than the Great Elector. The French Huguenots driven to leave their homes by the revocation of the Edict of Nantes in 1685 would have been a welcome windfall to him on economic grounds alone, but he had additional reasons for extending to them a particularly warm welcome. He was genuinely attached to Protestantism and concerned for the fortunes of his co-religionists, yet he might have expressed his feelings less demonstratively in a different political situation. But the alliance with France into which he had entered in 1679 had proved a deep disappointment to him: he was already meditating another change of sides (such as he, in fact, effected a few months later), and there is little doubt that when Louis turned on his Protestant subjects, the elector grasped at the chance to demonstrate his resentment.

It may be added that, from the mercantilist point of view, the reception of the Huguenots proved extremely successful, the considerable sums which it cost being repaid many times over by the fresh life which the refugees injected into the commerce and industry of Frederick William's dominions.

The text is translated from Mylius's *Corpus constitutionum Marchicarum*, Vol. II (1), pp. 65ff.

EDICT RELATING TO THE RIGHTS, PRIVILEGES, AND OTHER BENEFITS
WHICH HIS ELECTORAL HIGHNESS OF BRANDENBURG HAS MOST
GRACIOUSLY RESOLVED TO GRANT TO THE EVANGELICAL-REFORMED
CITIZENS OF FRANCE WHO PROPOSE TO SETTLE IN HIS TERRITORIES,
IN RESPECT OF JURISDICTION, ETC.

(OCTOBER 29, 1685)

WE, FRIEDRICH WILHELM, by Grace of God Margrave of Brandenburg, High Chamberlain of the Holy Roman Empire and Elector,
Duke in Prussia, Magdeburg, Jülich, Cleves, Berg, Stettin, Pomerania, of the Cassubians and Wends, also in Silesia, of Crossen
and Jägerndorf, Burgrave of Nuremberg, Prince of Halberstadt,
Minden, and Camin, Count of Hohenzollern, the Mark and Ravensberg, Lord of Ravenstein and the Land of Lauenburg and Bülow,
etc.,

Do hereby proclaim and make known to all and sundry that
since the cruel persecutions and rigorous ill-treatment in which
Our co-religionists of the Evangelical-Reformed faith have for
some time past been subjected in the Kingdom of France, have
caused many families to remove themselves and to betake themselves out of the said Kingdom into other lands, We now, out of
the righteous sympathy which We must in justice feel toward
these, Our co-religionists, who are oppressed and assailed for the
sake of the Holy Gospel and its pure doctrine, have been moved
graciously to offer them through this Edict signed by Our own
hand a secure and free refuge in all Our Lands and Provinces,
and further to announce to them what justice, liberties and
prerogatives We are most graciously minded to concede to them,
in order to relieve in some measure and make more tolerable the
great need and tribulation with which it has pleased the Almighty,
according to His only wise and inscrutable counsel, to afflict so
important a part of His Church.

1. In order to make it easier for all those who may resolve to
settle in Our Lands to reach and move there, We have commanded
Our Envoy Extraordinary to the States General of the United
Netherlands, von Diest, and Our Commissioner in Amsterdam,
Romswinckel, to procure for all Frenchmen of the religion reporting to them ships and other necessaries, and to transport them and
theirs from the Netherlands to Hamburg, where Our Aulic Coun-

cillor and Resident in the Circle of Lower Saxony, von Gericke, will give them all further facilities and help needed by them, that they may be conveyed to the place in which they have chosen to establish themselves in Our Lands.

2. In respect of those who wish to proceed to Our Lands via Sedan, from Champagne, Lorraine, Burgundy, and the southern provinces of France, without going through the Netherlands—such persons are to travel to Frankfurt am Main and there to report to Our Councillor and Resident, Merian, or to Our agent Lely in Cologne on the Rhine, and We have instructed both to provide them with money, passports, and ships and to send them down the Rhine to Our Duchy of Cleves, where Our Government will see to it that they are either established in Our Lands of Cleves and Mark or, if they wish to go further into others of Our Provinces, are provided with all necessaries therefor.

3. Since Our Lands are not only well and amply endowed with all things necessary to support life, but also very well-suited to the establishment of all kinds of manufactures and trade and traffic by land and water, We permit, indeed, to those settling therein free choice to establish themselves where it is most convenient for their profession and way of living, in Our Duchy of Cleves, in the Counties of Mark and Ravensberg, the Principalities of Halberstadt and Minden, or in the Duchy of Magdeburg, the Electoral Mark of Brandenburg and the Duchies of Pomerania and Prussia; but since We consider that in Our said Electoral Mark of Brandenburg the towns of Stendal, Werben, Rathenow, Brandenburg, and Frankfurt, and in the Duchy of Magdeburg the cities of Magdeburg, Halle, and Calbe, and in Prussia the town of Königsberg, will be the most convenient for them, both because they can live there very cheaply and on account of the facilities they will find there for living and practicing a trade, We have made provision and do hereby announce Our command that so soon as any of the said Evangelical-Reformed Frenchmen arrive there, they are to be well received and helped in all possible ways to establish themselves. Whereby We leave it to their free choice to choose for their place of settlement any other place in Our Provinces outside the towns enumerated above, wherever they find it most convenient to practice their professions and trades.

4. The personal property which they bring with them, including merchandise and other wares, is to be totally exempt from any taxes,

customs dues, licenses, or other imposts of any description, and not detained in any way.

5. And whereas the towns and villages in which numbers of the said Protestants will be settling and establishing themselves contain certain disrepaired, abandoned, and ruinous houses, whose owners have not the means to repair them and restore them to good condition, We do confer and assign the same in freehold to Our said French co-religionists, their children, and their children's children, and also provide that the former proprietors shall be compensated to the value of the said houses, and the same shall be totally released and made free from all liens, mortgages, arrears of taxation, and all other similar debts. We further order that they be supplied gratis with timber, lime, and other materials necessary for the repair of the said houses and grant them six years' exemption from all taxation, billeting, and other public charges of any description and further ordain that for the said six years the occupants shall not be required to pay any taxation except the normal excise tax on consumption.

6. We similarly provide that in towns and other places in which there are certain empty places and sites, these shall not only be assigned, with all gardens, fields, meadows, and pastures appertaining thereto, to Our said Protestant co-religionists of French nationality in perpetual freehold, but also that the same shall be totally released and liberated from all charges and servitudes attaching to them, and further, they are to be provided gratis with all materials required by them for the cultivation of these sites, and the new houses built by them and their inhabitants are not to be liable to any charges except the said excise, for the first ten years. And since We are also graciously minded to provide all possible facilities for the reception and establishment of the said people in Our Lands, We have had orders conveyed to the magistrates and other officials in these Our Provinces to hire certain houses in each town in which the said Frenchmen may be received on their arrival, and the rent thereof for them and their families is to be paid for four years, on condition, however, that they be required in due course to bring under cultivation the sites made available to them, as above.

7. As soon as these Our French co-religionists of the Evangelical-Reformed faith have settled in any town or village, they shall be admitted to the domiciliary rights and craft freedoms customary

there, gratis and without payment of any fee; and shall be entitled
to the benefits, rights, and privileges enjoyed by Our other, native,
subjects, residing there. We also declare them totally exempt from
the so-called *droit d'aubaine*[1] and other similar charges commonly
imposed on foreigners in other Kingdoms, Lands, and Republics
and, in general, wish them to be regarded and treated on the same
footing as Our own native subjects.

8. Not only are those who wish to establish manufacture of cloth,
stuffs, hats, or other objects in which they are skilled to enjoy all
necessary freedoms, privileges and facilities, but also provision
is to be made for them to be assisted and helped as far as possible
with money and anything else which they need to realize their
intention.

9. Those who settle in the country and wish to maintain themselves by agriculture are to be given a certain plot of land to
bring under cultivation and provided with whatever they need
to establish themselves initially, and in other respects helped as has
previously been done with sundry Swiss families who have entered Our Land and settled there.

10. In respect of jurisdiction and settlement of suits and disputes
arising between the said French families, We graciously consent
and hereby concede that in towns where there are several French
families they shall elect one of their own number who shall be
competent to bring about amicable settlements of such differences,
in summary fashion. But should such disputes arise between Germans on the one side and Frenchmen on the other, they shall be
investigated jointly and in common by the magistrate of each
locality and by the person chosen by the French to be their
spokesman, and a summary judgment delivered, which shall also
be done when the differences arising between Frenchmen among
themselves cannot be settled by the above procedure of conciliation.

11. Our said French co-religionists in each town shall be provided
with their own pastor, and Divine Service shall be conducted in
the French language with the same rites and ceremonies as have
hitherto been customary in the Evangelical-Reformed Churches
in France.

12. And just as those French nobles who have previously sought

[1] The Escheat to the Crown on the property of a deceased alien.

admission to Our protection and Our service enjoy the same honors, dignities, and prerogatives as Our other noble subjects, and We have also in fact employed sundry of them in the highest offices and posts of honor at Our Court, and also in Our armed forces, so We graciously consent to confer the same grace and promotion on French noblemen settling in Our Land in the future, and to admit them to all charges, services, and dignities for which they are qualified; similarly, if they buy and acquire fiefs and other noble estates in Our Lands, they shall also in like manner enjoy the rights, privileges, freedoms and immunities enjoyed by Our subjects born.

13. All rights, privileges and other benefits mentioned in the above points and articles accrue not only to those who arrive hereafter in Our Lands, but also to those who escaped from France before publication of this Edict and took refuge in these Our Lands, before previous religious persecutions; but those who are devoted to the Roman Catholic faith have in no way to presume to like favor.

14. We propose to set up Commissions in each and every one of Our Lands and Provinces to which the said Frenchmen may apply both on their arrival and afterward, and receive from them counsel and assistance; whereby We most graciously and earnestly enjoin all Our Governors, Governments, and other Servants and Commanders in towns and in the country, in all Our Provinces, through this public Edict and also through special orders, to take Our said French Evangelical-Reformed co-religionists, all and sundry, as many of them as shall come to Our country, under their special care and protection, to maintain and keep them expressly in all the Privileges hereby graciously conceded them, and in no wise to suffer that the least harm, injustice, or vexation be done them, but rather that they be shown all help, friendship, and good treatment. We have signed this Edict for record with Our own hand and have had Our Seal of Grace imprinted on it.

Given at Potsdam, October 29, 1685

FRIEDRICH WILHELM
Elector

10. The First King in Prussia

The coronation of Frederick I; translated from J. von Besser, *Preussische Krönungsgeschichte*, Cölln an der Spree (1712), pp. 23ff.

. . . ON JANUARY 18, [1701], the day of the coronation, service was held quite early in all the city churches; but in the Castle church it was not to start until about ten. The Master of Ceremonies, who some days before had issued tickets stamped with His Majesty's seal to those who were to be admitted to see the ceremony, now had to allocate to them, and also to all those taking part in the procession, their places, which Captain von Cosander arranged with particular skill, having made all ready.

The great upper chancel which spans the three parts of the church, was for the onlookers; the lower part, from which all chairs had been removed, had been made ready for Their Majesties and their suites and for the foreign Ministers. Since the altar was not in the usual position, at the end of the church, but in the middle, on one side, under an arch resting on two pillars, it was difficult to arrange the place for the anointment and the two thrones, for the King and the Queen, without overcrowding, and to arrange the baldachins and canopies so that they did not obstruct the view, but allowed the whole to be seen. To achieve this, a dais, two feet high and as wide as the altar arch, had been erected in the middle of the church, in front of the altar, and the two thrones placed on it, raised on three steps, one against each pillar, half-facing each other and the altar, and the canopies shortened and drawn in on the side of the spectators.

The bearers of the insignia and the other crown jewels had their places on the dais with the ladies of the Court, the King's on the right and the Queen's on the left; all other persons who had taken part in the procession were placed in the same order on the two sides of the dais, on tiers of benches; and obliquely opposite them, under the great chancel, and beyond the broad passage through which the church was entered, were seated the Royal trumpeters and livery servants and the courtiers; the trumpeters

placed under the great chancel, at the two ends, the liverymen
and pages in stalls in the two small aisles, while for the courtiers
a great semicircle of rising seats had been put up immediately
opposite the altar and behind the two thrones.

The sides and floor of the dais were covered with crimson velvet
with very broad edgings of gold; the amphitheater and the other
benches and balustrades, and also the wide passage of entry, with
red velvet; and the whole church, with the altar arch under which
the preachers stood, was draped with the richest carpets. The altar
itself, and the floor in front of it, was covered with a massive
Persian carpet, laid over the velvet, and had in front of it a
footstool with a handstool covered with the same velvet and with
cushions; the footstool for Their Majesties to kneel on and the
handstool for the crowns and scepter.

The canopies over the two thrones were round, and also of
crimson velvet. In front they bore a shield with Their Majesties'
monogram and the wings and trumpets of *renommée*, or fame,
and behind, a so-called *"queue royale"* or hanging piece of the
same crimson velvet with alternate strips of golden brocade and
white damask, with many tassels, fringes, and embroideries, and
studded, like the baldachin, with golden eagles and crowns. Over
each canopy hung a great eagle in flight, not unlike the living bird,
that over the King's throne holding a lightning bolt in its right
claw, and that over the Queen's, a scepter; in their left claws they
held two great cords of gold, which, with the tufts attached to
them, held up the rears of the two canopies to allow a view, and
hanging as they did, quite loosely, made everyone doubt and
wonder to what the eagles, which were always in motion, could
be attached.

The thrones beneath the canopies were equally sumptuous, with
figures and reliefs of heavily gilt metal; on the back of the King's,
Wisdom and Strength, and of the Queen's, Piety and Justice,
held golden crowns over their heads, through these symbols
expressing in most noble form both Their Majesties' qualities and
also the means by which they had attained to their dignities. So
that wherever one turned one's eyes, they were struck and delighted to see always something new, without confusion or repetition; always something meaningful and appropriate to the
coronation, and always a most gorgeous spectacle with the wealth
of scarlet, velvet, and gold. Especially when Their Majesties en-

tered the church with their purple, jewels, canopies, guards, and
their great trains, and took their places, while the Royal livery
servants under the great chancel and the courtiers in their amphitheater, dressed, like them, in richly braided and embroidered
coats, took their places, one row above the other, so that the
brilliant shimmer of the dense array of silver and gold lighted
the whole place as with a mirror, or at least, threw a great reflected
light on the thrones and altar opposite them.

At eight in the morning, as soon as the service in the city
churches was over, the Estates and all other bodies which were to
take part in the procession assembled in the antechambers of the
Castle designated for them. Meanwhile, the burghers were to assemble and take their places in the streets, partly to enhance the
splendor of the day, partly in order to give the common people
something to do, and to prevent the crowds, which were already
overdense, from making the press in front of the Castle church
greater still.

His Majesty had himself dressed and robes of royalty put on
him by his High Chamberlain in his sleeping apartment; but in
the audience chamber he put his crown on his head with his own
hands and also himself took the royal scepter in his hand, as the
independence of his realm required. The other insignia, which
would lie before the throne on a table, each on a cushion of
crimson velvet, were handed by the High Chamberlain to the
Prussian High Councillors: the Seal of State to the Chancellor, the
Globe of State to the Comptroller of the Household and the
Sword of State to the Supreme Burgrave; one of the insignia
to each, according to his rank. For although otherwise the Comptroller of the Household is the first of the High Councillors and
takes precedence of the Supreme Burgrave, yet on this occasion
he had, as Comptroller of the Realm, to take the globe, and to
leave the sword to the Supreme Burgrave as Justiciary of the
Realm; this symbol being carried immediately behind the royal
couple, as denoting the sovereign power. But the Banner of State
was given to Count von Dohna, to follow His Majesty's canopy
with it; not only because it is customary to give this place to the
Banner of State, as was done at the funeral of King Francis I of
France, and recently at the coronation of the present King of
Sweden, but also because this is the only appropriate place for it,
that the Field Marshal or Constable should go with it behind

His Majesty as a symbol of his sovereignty and especially his supreme authority in a war, and as representing all the other regalia, just as, when arms are carried, it is right for the Blood Banner to wind up the procession of regalia and, as it were, to cover them with its shield.

Then His Majesty went to place the Queens' crown on her, having his own crown on his head and his scepter in his hand, and accompanied by the whole Court and all the other insignia of royal majesty; whereby His Majesty wished to exercise, by crowning the Queen, one of the very highest of his royal prerogatives. The crowns of Kings are their kingdoms; but the crowns of Queens are the Kings, who are not only, like all other husbands, called the crowns of their wives, but also, by the setting on of a crown, truly make their wives participants in the glory and majesty of their rank; even as—as the Holy Writ testifies—Ahasuerus of old set the royal crown on the head of Esther, and made her, lowly as she was, Queen. The Lord High Chamberlain, Count von Wartenberg and his attendant chamberlains bore the train of the King's robe, and the High Commissioner of War, Count von Döhnhof, walked immediately before the King, bearing the Queen's crown on a velvet cushion.

All the Queen's apartments were filled with courtiers, who naturally thronged forward to see so rare a ceremony, and when His Majesty, with the Crown Prince and his brothers, reached the Queen's apartments, she came to meet him as far as the outermost antechamber, followed by all her ladies in waiting and herself dressed in royal robes; where His Majesty took back the crown from Count von Döhnhof, set it with a loving joy on the head of the Queen, who had made obeisance before him, and afterwards conducted her, crown on head, into the innermost apartment. The Duchess of Holstein, with the two head ladies in waiting, von Steenland and von Bülau, fastened the Queen's crown on her head; and when this was done, the King went back to his audience chamber, and the Queen followed with her attendants and, conducted by the two Margraves, took her seat on the throne in the audience chamber by the side of His Majesty the King.

Insofar as the rule of Papal ceremonial is true, that the degree of majesty is to be judged by the nature of the adornments, it is necessary to describe at this point Their Majesties' royal attire, not to prove the advantage they beyond doubt enjoyed on this day above many kings and queens, but at least to give a better idea of the deep impression Their Majesties' splendor made on all present. The robe of the King was of cloth of scarlet richly embroidered with gold, and with great buttons of diamonds, each worth three thousand ducats, and his cloak was of purple velvet, embroidered with crowns and eagles, lined with sable and fastened in front with a brooch consisting only of three linked diamonds, but of the value of a ton of gold. The scepter was of gold, encrusted with diamonds and rubies, and on its tip an eagle with spread wings, and further adorned with two vast rubies, one of which, being round, symbolized the globe or the throne, and the other, which was oblong, the body. One circumstance also made them priceless, that His Majesty the Emperor of Russia had presented them from his own scepter to His Majesty, then still an Elector, and had thereby presaged the coming of his Kingdom, as Poland did later, when surrendering the insignia of royalty to His Electoral Highness.[1] The crown, like the scepter, was of pure gold, but the usual foliage pattern was replaced by a solid mass of diamonds, which seemed to have been cast on the circuit and the cap as from one mold, and not to be distinguished from each other except by their different sizes; for some were of a weight of 80, 90 or 100 grains, some actually of 130, and the fire which they gave out varied accordingly.

The Queen was dressed in gold brocade embroidered with pansies, with an adornment of diamonds, which covered all the seams of her dress and the whole breast between the embroideries. Her cloak and crown were like the King's, only that her crown was set on her bare head and shone out the more brilliantly among the thick waves of her naturally curled coal-black hair. On the right side of her breast she wore also a spray of pure pearls, one of which in particular must well have been unique, for no one had been able to find its match in many years; as the viewer can easily see for himself, for these pearls and also all the other priceless jewels are daily on show to visitors in the Royal Castle.

Adorned with this indescribable wealth, Their Majesties took their seats on the throne, on the two silver armchairs placed on it; and as the seating and reception of the throne constituted the real enthronement, just as the previous setting on of the crowns

[1] This had been done in 1700, in accordance with Article 4 of the Treaty of 1699 between the Elector and the King of Poland.

had constituted the true and proper coronation of Their Majesties, the courtiers standing on both sides, and the corporations of the Estates and other bodies now entered here in their order, made their most submissive obeisance, and saluted Their Majesties as King and Queen for the first time with deep bows.

All were almost overcome by emotion at the first sight of so great splendor. Soon, however, it was apparent that neither the King's splendor nor his crown could increase in the smallest measure that majesty of his person which his subjects had revered with the greatest respect and obedience during the whole of his reign; and as for the Queen, that the gifts bestowed on her by nature easily outdid the treasures of her adornment and even of her crown. The President of the High Court of Prussia, Court and Tribunal Councillor Pauli, expressed this well the next day when, speaking in the name of his College, he congratulated, not the Queen on the crown, but the crown on the Queen; for certainly the royal crown has never during long ages sat on a nobler head, nor one from which it derived so much grace, as from this Queen.

Now the procession had to go to the church for the anointing, which ordinarily takes place before the coronation. The church selected was, as we have said, that of the Castle, which, although it serves as a Lutheran place of worship, had been chosen, partly as being near and convenient, partly owing to the peculiar circumstance that it was here that His Majesty had received the sacrament of baptism. His Majesty wished to be anointed in spirit where he had been anointed in the body; he further wished to show his desire for harmony with the Lutheran confession, and to that end had not only chosen a Lutheran Court preacher to participate in the anointing, but also, instead of having the altar and its cross removed from the church, as some had feared, had, on the contrary, presented it with new vessels and a cross all of silver, for keeping; and he even several times attended the Lutheran service in this church during this stay in Königsberg.

In order to lend more solemnity to the ceremony of anointing, His Majesty had, by special letters, called the two seniors of the clergy and had nominated them Bishops: for the Reformed Church, the senior Court preacher and Consistorial Councillor, Master Benjamin Ursinus, and the Lutheran senior Court preacher and Consistorial Councillor, Dr. von Sanden; the two were, as is usual with kings, to carry through the ceremony together, as

Bishops, the one as Consecrator and the other as Assistant. For although the title of Bishop has, for well-known reasons, generally fallen out of use in the German Evangelical Church, yet it was an easy matter for His Majesty to confer the title of Bishop on his senior Court preachers, the easier, because the ceremony of anointing required it; since on the one hand, all senior Court preachers (Superintendents and Inspectors) of the Evangelical persuasion in His Majesty's Lands are already such in office and name, and bear a title which is the translation of the Greek word *bishop*—that is, superintendent and inspector of the congregations in their charge; and further because, even were this not so, His Majesty would unquestionably be entitled to nominate and install new bishops, in virtue of his complete supremacy in matters both religious and profane, after the example of other kings, especially evangelical kings; seeing that the enclosed tops of their crowns signify nothing else than that they include in them all authority, the spiritual with the temporal.

The stormy weather, with snow and hail, which had raged all the night, cleared up completely at about the hour of the procession, and since Their Majesties wished to make the journey on foot, a very broad path of planks covered with red cloth had been laid from the royal palace to the church. Guards, mounted and on foot, kept watch on both sides: the bodyguards, under Colonel and Chamberlain von Grote on the right, and the foot-guards, under Lieutenant-Colonel von Borck, on the left. The hundred Swiss, on the other hand, stood in two files on the cloth-covered path, and created no small sensation with their officers in brand-new uniforms, which, like those at French coronations, were in the old Frankish mode, in white satin and silver braidings, with split doublets, knee breeches and short cloaks covered with gold and silver lace, pointed silk hats with roses, shoe buckles, silken pearl-colored stockings and round Swiss ruffs. Not to mention the other troops distributed outside the Castle: a battalion of Holsteiners on the ice of the moat, a battalion of the Dohna regiment in the stable square and horsemen of the Schlippenbach regiment on the Stone Dam; who, with the thirty-two cannons placed behind the Castle were also (with the guards) to contribute to the later salvoes and *feux de joie* from the walls of the fortress and the city.

The two canopies, for the King and Queen, were held on the

square by twenty young Counts and nobles until the arrival from the Court of the twenty persons designated to bear them: for the King's canopy, Commissary of War, General Count von Döhnhof, Lieutenant-General du Hamel, Lieutenant-General von Gröben and Master of the Hunt von Pannewitz at the four cords, and at the six poles, Chamberlain Count von Blumenthal, Chamberlain von Bären, Chamberlain von Tettau, Jr., Chamberlain Count von Solms, Chamberlain von Flemming and Major-General Count von Truchses; for the Queen's canopy, at the four cords, Major-General de la Cave, Privy Councillor von Osten, Chancellor von Bolswing and Colonel Count von Döhnhof, and at the six poles, Titular Chamberlains von Creutz, von Ostau and von Eichstadt, with Colonels von Canitz, von Bredau and von Wobser. In the church, then, the twenty young Counts and nobles took over the carrying of the two canopies again.

At ten o'clock, when the procession was ready to start, a signal was given by the hoisting of a flag on the Castle tower; whereupon all the bells in the Castle and the town began to ring, and the first herald, Chamberlain-Quartermaster Holzendorf, read out the names of the assembled corporations in the order laid down by His Majesty himself; whereupon all filed off, one after the other, to the church, all bareheaded except the guards, in the following order.

1. Two heralds with their crowned staves and in their armorial coats.
2. All the Royal livery servants and pages, in their rich liveries.
3. A Royal drummer, before whom the silver army drums were carried, with the new drum colors, all worked in gold, and the arms of the Kingdom embroidered on them.
4. Twelve Royal trumpeters, with similar flags worked in gold on their trumpets, who during the procession blew alternately with the singing of the choir.
5. The Marshal of the Court and the Cupbearer, their marshals' staves in their hands.
6. Then the Corporations:

   The Chamber of the Exchequer
   The Chancellery
   The Chamber of War
   The High Court of Justice

The Consistory

The representatives of the University

The Councillors of the Court of Justice, all dressed in blue velvet, as were the four High Councillors; only that their coats were, unlike the others, adorned with very rich gold lace, while those of the others had no lace

The Tribunal

The representatives of all the Estates: the towns, the Knights and the Lords.

7. The members of the Court and the Ministers, including Privy Councillors von Fuchs and von Schmettau

8. Two more heralds

9. Another drummer (with silver army drums), and

10. Twelve Royal trumpeters with silver trumpets and small flags, like the first twelve

11. The two High Marshals, with marshals' staves all of silver and tipped with the crowned eagle of Prussia

12. Chancellor von Cruetz with the Seal of State, which he carried on a cushion of crimson velvet

13. Comptroller of the Household von Perband with the Globe of State, also carried on a cushion of crimson velvet. This was enameled in sky-blue and set with diamonds and rubies, as also was the scepter.

14. The Supreme Burgrave with the Sword of State, unsheathed

15. His Royal Highness the Crown Prince, in an embroidered coat of gold; and behind him, to his left, the Comptroller of his Household, Count von Dohna

16. His Majesty the King, the crown on his head and the scepter in his hand, under a canopy of crimson velvet, on the outside of which, round the central chaplet, was a massive coverlet of gold with wide golden fringes, and at the four corners four golden eagles with thick golden cords and tufts and inside another heavy golden fringe with a ground of cloth of gold: eagles and crowns worked on it, and carried by the ten persons named above by four golden cords and six poles covered with velvet and tassels of gold. The hundred Swiss marched on either side, in two files, as they had stood, with flags flying and instruments playing, while they entered the church. Their officers marched in front of His Majesty, also in two files, and between them went the bearers of the

insignia and His Royal Highness the Crown Prince. Beside the canopy marched, on His Majesty's right, the Commander of the Bodyguard Major-General and Chamberlain von Tettau, as First Captain of the Guard, and on his left, Colonel du Rosey, Captain of the Swiss Guard, in the same uniform as his officers, only that on his breast he wore a plate of silver instead of the silver braid, and the lace on his coat was all gold, instead of gold and silver. Behind His Majesty walked his High Chamberlain with the two chamberlains who helped him carry the train of the royal cloak; and behind them walked Field Marshal Count von Barfuss, as High Constable or Commander in Chief of the army.

17. Two bodyguards, who walked behind and at the side of the canopy, and between them

18. Count von Dohna of Reichertswald, with the Banner of State of cloth of silver, to match the color of the heraldry, with golden fringes, and the grand coat of arms of the Kingdom.

19. His Highness, the Duke of Holstein, by His Majesty's command leading the Queen's suite.

20. Her Majesty the Queen, wearing her crown, conducted by the two Margraves and under a canopy similar to the King's. On her left hand walked the Comptroller of her Household, von Bülau; behind her walked the Duchess of Holstein and the two ladies in waiting in chief, carrying the train of her robe, and behind them, von Mirop, lord in waiting, carrying the train of the Duchess.

21. Two bodyguards at the rear corners of the royal canopy.

22. The Princess of Holstein, conducted by Messire von Grumkau, lord in waiting to the Queen; Her Highness the Duchess of Courland with her Princes and all her Court were, on the other hand, not able to take part in the procession but only watched it, and the ceremony of the anointing, from His Majesty's stall in the great chancel of the church.

23. The ladies of the Queen's Chamber, and lastly,

23. The noble ladies of the town.

Of the two doors of the church, that on the left was closed; that on the right had been enlarged and heightened to allow the canopies to enter; also, instead of the usual steps, a ramp of planks had been laid, leading up from the path. The two Bishops, in long black gowns of velvet over undercoats of damask, stood by the door on the left side of the entry with six other pastors (three Reformed and three Lutheran), and when the King and Queen, under their canopies, entered the church, the Consecrator addressed them as follows: "Enter, ye blessed of the Lord, our King and Queen, in the strength of our God. May the Lord bless your comings in and your goings out from this time forth for evermore, through Jesus Christ Our Lord, Amen!"

Meanwhile, the leaders of the procession took up the places shown them by the heralds: the trumpeters in the two transepts, the livery servants in the stalls below the great chancel, the Estates and the Ministers on the benches on the right of the royal throne and the members of the Court in the amphitheater; all the rest remained standing until the Consecrator had ended his address, whereupon the organ at once sounded and the pastors passed by the marshals' staves and placed themselves on the dais before them: the two Bishops immediately in front of the altar, the six others on its two sides.

Their Majesties took their seats on their thrones. The High Councillors with the insignia and the bearers of the King's canopy took up places beside the King's throne, down the length of the dais; the ladies of the Court and the bearers of the Queen's canopy, opposite them. The two Head Marshals with their staves placed themselves between the two thrones, the Marshals of the Court on the back step of the dais; and the Royal Banner was placed between the four staves. The twenty young Counts and nobles with the two canopies remained at the entry to the dais, as did the hundred Swiss with their officers, drums and banners; and on the benches at the Queen's side sat the noble ladies of the city, immediately opposite the benches of the Ministers and the Estates.

The Crown Prince sat on the King's throne, a little to the rear, and behind him the Comptroller of his Household. Behind His Majesty sat the High Chamberlain with the two chamberlains, and behind them the Constable of the Kingdom. On the lowest step, on each side, stood the two bodyguards, on the upper step the two Captains of the Guard, again one on each side, and on the same step stood the Master of Ceremonies, to receive His Majesty's commands.

On the Queen's side, Their Highnesses the two Margraves and

the Duchess of Holstein sat behind the Queen's chair. Behind Their Highnesses sat the Duke of Holstein with the Princess his daughter and behind them, the Queen's Master, Messire von Bülau. The two ladies in waiting in chief sat with the ladies of the Court, while the two lords in waiting, von Grumkow and von Mirov, stood on the uppermost step of the throne, at the back, and the two bodyguards on the lowest step, in front, as with the King. So that even not counting the organ and the choir above the altar, on which stood the members of the Royal choir and the chamber musicians, all places round the whole church were occupied. The reader can gather some idea of the scene if he can think of the many various pictures of groups in a well-arranged gallery, all, with all their figures and backgrounds, directed only toward one object, and yet, owing to the multiplicity of themselves and their positions, always presenting some particularity to the eye and thus causing it to turn restlessly now hither, now thither.

The hymn "God Be Gracious unto Us" was sung, and when it ended, the Consecrator went into the sacristy, but the Assistant remained in front of the altar, and turning his face to His Majesty, delivered himself of the following prayer:

Almighty and everlasting God, Who alone art wise and great, Thou Who art our refuge in all things, God of Gods, King of Kings, Lord of Lords, and father of mercies in Jesus Christ Thy beloved Son; we most humbly acknowledge that Thou alone canst make any man great and strong; and it is Thy grace and truth when Thou makest Kings to be the fosterers of Thy people and Queens to give them suck: and now too Thou hast set before our eyes, in all their royal adornment, our most dear sovereign Thy Prince and servant, the Lord Frederick, King in Prussia, and Thy Princess and servant, Sophie Charlotte, Queen in Prussia; who in Thy sanctuary do here most heartily commend and dedicate to Thee, O most high God, their Royal Majesty and royal thrones, crowns, scepters, globe, sword, seal and banner; even as they have received all these from Thy hand. And because Thou hast especially moved them now to receive publicly the unction which Thou, Lord, didst ordain of old for the Kings of Thy people Israel: so do Thou, O God, Thou Holy One in Israel, bless this holy act in the bodies and souls of our King and Queen! Be it to them a sure sign that Thou wilt anoint them with the oil of gladness, Thy Holy Spirit! Pour therewith Thy love into their hearts, that on them may rest the spirit of wisdom and understanding, the spirit of counsel and strength, the spirit of recognition and of the fear of the Lord! May they draw from it strength in all kingly virtues to the honor of Thy Name, the comfort of Thy

Churches and the joy and welfare of their Royal House and of all
their lands and peoples! Forgive us all our trespasses, for Thy dear
Son's sake! Lend Thy blessing to the preaching of Thy word! Let all
our undertakings now be hallowed through Word and prayer,
and bless Thou us, O God! thoroughly that all our spirit, soul and
body be kept unpunished for the coming of our Lord and Savior,
Jesus Christ! Amen.

After this prayer the anthem "Glory Be to God on High" was
sung and after this the Consecrator delivered a short discourse on
the text, "Who honoreth Me, him will I honor," during which
time the other pastors remained standing in their previous order,
the Assistant in front, and the other six beside the altar. The Consecrator showed "the reward of godliness" from his text, and was
able to apply this to His Majesty with the greater assurance because
from his youth up he had had the honor of holding the office of
a preacher and chaplain to the Court; and for the listeners, was
able to apply this with full certainty to their daily experience; of
which the act of anointing was now to give fresh proof.

When the sermon was over the choir sang some verses out of
the twenty-first Psalm, and then the anthem, "Come, O God,
Creator, Holy Spirit": then the Consecrator rejoined the Assistant
in front of the altar, and when the anthem was finished, came
forward with him to the anointing stool; before which His
Majesty the King stepped to the sound of trumpets and drums
and accompanied by his suite.

The Head Marshals, after bowing deeply, led the way and
placed themselves on either side. The bearers of the insignia followed, and placed themselves to the right of the altar. His Highness the Crown Prince moved to His Majesty's right; the Constable,
the guards and their captains, with the Banner of State, remained
behind His Majesty, and the High Chamberlain, who, besides the
train of the King's robe, which he was carrying, also held in his
hand the consecrated oil, stepped to the left and poured it into
a very costly vial of jasper on the golden salver which the Consecrator held before him.

His Majesty took the oil, since no one but he could confer on
the Consecrator the power to anoint him; and he brought with
him all the insignia; for His Majesty was not first attaining through
the unction the royal dignity expressed by them, but only pro-
claiming and confirming it, or rather, showing that he received it

from the Lord God alone. The heathen have pretended that Jupiter sent their ruler crown, sword and scepter down from Heaven: the crown through the Goddess of Dominion, the sword through the Goddess of Justice and the scepter through his messenger, the eagle; which may be the reason why they represented Jupiter's scepter as tipped with an eagle, and the old Etruscans used a similar scepter to show that their power derived from Heaven. But what the heathen fabled of their false Gods, His Majesty believed and knew of the only true and living God, Who verily has power over all the kingdoms of mankind and can confer them on whom He will and has in fact given his to His Majesty. Therefore as soon as he reached the altar he laid aside crown and scepter, knelt down, and prostrated himself and cast them down as the four and twenty elders cast down their golden crowns. This did he himself do, with all his greatness, before the throne of Him who has created all things; thus to show and openly to confess that he received all this only from His hands, owed all to His grace and therefore returned all to Him, dedicating all the treasures of his Kingdom before His altar.

The High Chamberlain pushed His Majesty's wig up a little to leave the forehead free for the unction, and the Consecrator, who had given the Assistant the oil and the plate to hold, took the vial from the plate, dropped a little oil on the two first fingers of his right hand and anointed His Majesty in the shape of a circle or a crown, first on his head, then on both his wrists, saying:

> May Your Royal Majesty receive and take this unction as a Divine sign wherewith God of old gave testimony through His priests and prophets to the Kings of His People that He Himself, God Most High, had made, set and ordered them to be Kings: and the Lord our God anoint thee hereby with the Holy Spirit Your Royal Majesty! that ye, as the Lord's anointed, may rule and reign over your Kingdom and people with cheerful, brave and willing heart and may serve the counsel and will of your God in all royal prosperity for many years. Through Jesus Christ our Lord, Amen.

The choir answered in the name of all, all instruments, drums and trumpets joining in: "Amen, Amen! Happiness to the King! Happiness to the King! Happiness to the King! God grant him long life!" thereby representing the popular acclamation otherwise customary. Meanwhile the High Chamberlain wiped the oil off the King's forehead and hands with a soft kerchief of linen, which he handed to the Consecrator, and took back from him the vial with the oil; and His Majesty again set the crown on his head, took the scepter again in his hand, and betook himself with his suite to his throne.

Trumpets and drums continued their jubilant music; and thereupon the Queen also went to the altar for anointing, followed by all her suite. Their Highnesses the two Margraves conducted her and the two High Marshals went ahead with their staves; coming and going Her Majesty made deep obeisance before the throne of the King: not alone out of common courtesy, but especially in testimony that the dignity which was about to be conferred on her came from no other source (after God) than from the wellpleasing sharing of this throne.

The High Chamberlain followed with the oil; and when he had again (as before) set it on the golder salver, Her Majesty knelt down on the footstool and was anointed by the Consecrator, in the same fashion as the King, on forehead and hands; only her crown, being fastened to her head, could not be taken off for the anointing. The Consecrator addressed her:

> May Your Royal Majesty receive this unction as a Divine sign that you owe your anointing and ordination to Kingly majesty and dignity from God, Who has made you partner with your King that he may have his joy and delight in you: and the Lord our God anoint you ever more with His Holy Spirit that you may serve God with a cheerful and willing heart and honor Him. In Jesus Christ our Lord, Amen.

The choir answered again, "Amen, Amen," and sang with equal jubilation, "Happiness to the Queen! Happiness to the Queen! Happiness to the Queen! God grant her long life!" Meanwhile, the Duchess of Holstein wiped off the oil and handed the cloth to the Consecrator, who handed back the vial with the oil to the High Chamberlain. The Queen returned with her suite to her throne, and the Lord High Chamberlain to the throne of the King. This concluded the whole solemnity of anointing, whereby both Their Majesties now enjoy the name and dignity of "anointed"; unanointed Kings having formerly been held for something lesser, and called only "common Kings."

At other coronations the oaths of fealty and that of most submissive loyalty, formerly known as the "salutation" or "adoration," were usually taken at this point, whereby the King's vassals either

—the form differed among different peoples and nations—made a deep obeisance before the new King or cast themselves on their knees, and kissed either his cloak, his hand, his foot, or, as is the custom in France and England, his face, to show that they recognize the newly crowned King for a true King and hold him to be God's representative on earth, crowned and anointed by God Himself; and must thereafter be regarded with all honor and love as God's Anointed and Vicar after the pattern of the spiritual King of whom the Psalm says, "Kiss the Son, that he be not wroth."

As regards the oath of fealty, this was simply impossible on this occasion, because the duty of the subjects had been not so much altered and interrupted by His Majesty's new dignity as rather enhanced and strengthened; but precisely for this reason, their duty to honor Their Majesties most submissively was the more imperative; and this oath was indeed taken, partly already in the audience chamber, at the enthronement, by the courtiers and Estates, partly, by all the clergy, now, after the anointing.

First the Consecrator stepped before the altar with the Assistant, and afterwards, accompanied by all the other pastors, bowed himself to the earth before His Majesty's throne and said: "Good fortune to King Frederick, King in Prussia, and may the Lord, the God of our King, say it also! As the Lord has been with him unto today, so may He continue to be with him that his royal throne be ever greater and greater, Amen!"

In the same way he advanced to the throne of the Queen, with the Assistant and the other pastors, bowed himself and said: "Fortune to the Queen Sophie Charlotte, Queen in Prussia! May the Lord our God establish you as a blessing to His people, that you see the prosperity of your Royal House and of your children's children in the peace of Israel, Amen!"

The choir answered each address with "Amen, Amen, Fortune to the King! Fortune to the Queen!" and closed the whole rite with that acclamation and angel's song of praise, "Glory be to God on high, and on earth, peace, goodwill towards men"; during which the pastors retired again, with deep obeisances, and took up their previous places before the altar. And the Consecrator, as soon as all was quiet, addressed the people as follows:

Fear God! Honor your King and your Queen! Their help cometh from the Lord, Who hath made Heaven and earth. May the Lord not suffer their foot to slip! May He be their guardian and their shade over their right hand, so that the sun shall not burn them by day, neither the moon by night! The Lord preserve them from all evil! The Lord keep their souls! The Lord guard their goings out and their comings in, from this time forth for evermore, Amen!

The choir now sang alone: "Lord, make ready to bless the House of Thy servant, Frederick, King in Prussia, that it may be for Thee forever, for that which Thou, Lord, dost bless is blessed for evermore." Then they sang, with the congregation, "Praise and honor of great price," from the familiar hymn, "Salvation Is Come Down to Us," after which the Assistant lifted up his voice in the following prayer for the welfare of Their Majesties and their House:

Almighty and everlasting God, merciful and true Father in Jesus Christ our Lord and Savior! We praise and extol Thy holy name, not only that Thou hast given to us Thine only begotten Son Jesus Christ to be our eternal King, and hast in Him made known and bestowed Thine everlasting Kingdom of Heaven to be the heritage of the saints in light, but hast also, besides this, conferred on us this peculiar grace to see before our eyes Thine Anointed, our King and Queen, in Thy holy place. As now Thou hast lent Thy Grace to this holy sacrament of the royal unction, and hast here established his realm to our King, so be pleased, O God, to fortify and establish the same, for it is Thy work. We commend to Thee His Royal Majesty, Frederick, our most gracious King and sovereign lord, to be as the apple of Thine eye, together with his royal consort, Her Majesty the Queen, our Crown Prince their heir, the Royal Princess, their royal Highnesses the brothers and sisters and all the royal family and household. Preserve them from all evil and bless them with all good of body and soul! Bless also the House of Thine anointed that it be ever for Thee; for what Thou, Lord, blessest is blessed for evermore. Graciously hear us, Heavenly Father, for Jesus Christ's sake, Amen."

Then he spoke the blessing; then came the anthem, "Lord God, We Praise Thee," sung by the congregation with accompaniment of drums and trumpets, and finally, in testimony of the royal grace, a general pardon was proclaimed, read out by the Supreme Burgrave, who lowered the Sword of State held in his hand as though it should now be at rest, as follows:

His Royal Majesty in Prussia, our most gracious King and Lord, has, in token of his royal clemency and grace, most graciously resolved on this his coronation day that all and every prisoner in this

his Kingdom and other Lands be hereby graced, pardoned and set at liberty; excepting only those who have blasphemed against Divine and human majesty, wilful murderers, and those imprisoned for debt.

God save the King!

God save the Queen!

During the anthem the cannon on the walls and behind the Castle were fired; the bells of all churches and towers and the salvoes of the regiments from the squares in which they had been posted made a joyful noise. Meanwhile, the procession filed gradually out of the church. And great as was the throng of onlookers who had come in from the surrounding towns, Provinces and Kingdoms, yet its members found their places in their former order, without jostling and so quietly that one was hardly aware of their leaving the church, and they were able to follow His Majesty after the reading of the pardon unimpeded and with none missing; which was observed with particular pleasure—as they remarked —by the Ministers of the Imperial, English, Dutch, Danish, Polish, Hanoverian, and Casselian Courts seated on the front benches. And both the great quiet and the clearing up of the weather were taken as good omens that His Majesty would possess his crown in peace.

11. Frederick William I on Colonization in Lithuania

Like other monarchs of his age, Frederick William attached importance to increasing the population of his dominions, particularly where there were large areas of unpopulated or sparsely populated land that contributed nothing to his revenues and might excite the acquisitive interest of neighbors. Such was, conspicuously, the condition of "Lithuania" (the western portions of Prussia), the more so after it had been grievously devastated by plague over the years 1709 to 1713. In 1716 he had sent a commission to the area, and the document translated below reflects the decisions taken by him in the light of the commission's report.

In this particular case, the crown had a double interest in establishing peasant colonies here, since local nobles had squatted on many vacant areas. They had been rudely evicted, but it was politically— as well as economically and militarily—inadvisable to leave the spaces quite uncared for, and the document shows that the experiment of establishing State farms on them had proved something of a failure.

The text is translated from R. Stadelmann, *Preussens Könige in ihrer Tätigkeit für die Landeskultur, Friedrich Wilhelm I* (Berlin, 1882), No. 7.

CABINET ORDER BY KING FREDERICK WILLIAM I ON THE CAMERAL AND CROWN PROPERTIES AND LAND SETTLEMENT IN LITHUANIA (1718)

WE HAVE received the report of the Commission appointed by Us on the condition of Our Cameral organization in Lithuania. And whereas We have most graciously determined to place the same on a sounder footing, and We also recognize that the Chamber cannot possibly be brought into proper order unless the local land offices [*Aemter*] are put in better order and good agents [*Beamte*] appointed, We do enact:

1. That, in order that Our peasant subjects may be led toward God and thus achieve blessings and prosperity, schoolmasters shall be appointed in all considerable villages, and each one shall be given for his maintenance a half hide from Our unoccupied farms, free of rent, land tax [*contributio*] or billeting duty. We have also written to Our Samogitian Consistory to make the necessary further arrangements, and have also instructed Our Court Preacher, Dr. Lypsius, and Master Franke in Halle to find the necessary personnel, toward which you and all serving under you are to contribute, in order that Our most gracious purpose may be realized.

2. Further: since it is indispensably necessary for the realization of Our purpose in this and other respects that efficient agents shall be appointed to the local offices, who are good farmers and experienced in accountancy, We wish that they shall receive adequate salaries, and therefore graciously command you to send in a schedule of the salary each should be paid, proportionate to the size of his district and the work involved, and then, on receipt of Our further instructions, to seek out and enlist good, experienced, efficient and upright officials, and We will also send such men to you from Pomerania and the rest of Our Province of Kurmark and Neumark.

3. And although it is not in principle advisable that either members of the Cameral staff or local agents should rent farms from the Crown, yet under the exceptional circumstances We authorize your Department to permit this practice, if thereby you secure good officials; but this is only a temporary provision, and We will go into the question further when the shortage of man-power has been made up.

4. And since We do not find it consonant with Our interests to allow many new demesne farms to be established, in default of tenant farmers or for other reasons, since those established to date, as hitherto administered, and not leased, are not nearly re-paying the capital invested in them and are consequently of little profit, it is Our will not to go beyond those already established and in operation; and We are totally resolved, instead of demesne farms, to have the deserted villages rebuilt and repopulated, to which end you and the agents are to devote every effort and care to repopulating the country—building up one village after an-other, not beginning all of them at once. Each peasant in the new villages is to be given two hides of land, and for livestock, since We have observed that with the livestock hitherto allocated to them the peasants cannot farm their holdings properly nor plow their arable land as it should be done, he is to be given four horses and four oxen, besides the other stock, all to be given him at once on his entry into possession. Colonists of the same origin are to be brought together as far as possible, and, when the annual report is rendered, it shall state clearly how many villages you pro-pose to construct in the year, how many farms they are to contain, how they are situated, and how much money will be needed for the purpose. We shall then take the necessary action and arrange for the money to be budgeted.

5. We further wish to have this, Our most gracious purpose, proclaimed by Patent, of which you are to prepare a draft, stating clearly what each settler is to receive and what he will have to pay in the future. You will submit this for Our most gracious approval. The new settlers must, as already stated, be given all stock punctually and complete, and also given stock books with accurate inventories, the winter crops sown and the fields ready for the summer crops, and, generally, they must receive very good and friendly treatment, to prevent them from becoming discon-

tented at the outset, and to that end, none of the new settlers is to arrive before the spring, for so We save their keep for six months and they also find pasturage for their livestock at once. This is to be stated in the Patent. On the expiration of a year, then, you are to report fully to Us, and Our future enquiries will be based on the facts as stated in your reports.

6. You are to see that the agents are attentive to their duties, and carry through the settlement of the peasants as speedily as possible, but you must never treat them otherwise than fairly, nor differently from how they are treated by other Chambers. If one of them is slack, he should be fined or, if the circumstances require it, and after report to Me, dismissed, and another put in his place.

7. And whereas the colonists so far established have, owing to a series of misfortunes, fallen into difficulties and the "free years" they have been granted can be little or no help to them, We are not disinclined graciously to remit what they owe at present and are unable to pay without ruin, if this is sufficiently attested by the priests, village mayors, Captains, and agents and also, for a few years, to allow you to accept half rents from those in real distress, again if this is sufficiently well attested, but you must first send in an exact calculation of how much this will cost; We shall then decide.

8. And although We do not doubt that so much grace will attract new men to Lithuania and also deter persons already there from emigrating to Poland, where they are, We hear, being promised extensive liberties, yet it is absolutely indispensable that the agents, while they must be instructed to supervise the peasants' work closely and see that they deliver what is due from them, without shortage, must yet be most expressly enjoined not to treat the newly arrived settlers roughly in any way, and especially not to harry them at once—as they have been doing—by ruthless executions, which only cost a lot in fees and thereby impoverish the peasants, but first to let them strike their roots, and keep them under control and alive to their obligations in kindly fashion, by unhostile supervision and regular visits and, if all else fails, to follow no other procedure than that of official distraint. You must order the agents, in Our name, to observe these instructions exactly, and you must set them a good example.

9. And whereas it has been reported to Us that Our peasant subjects are at present, under Our previous orders, required to pay for half the timber used by them, and We plainly see that as conditions now stand in Lithuania this will not always be practicable and will result in the peasants' letting their buildings fall into disrepair, We have graciously resolved that peasants of small means shall be given their timber altogether free of charge. But their houses are not, as hitherto, to be built of timber alone, but half-timbered; you are to take the necessary steps.

10. In respect of the outstanding sums still owed by agents and tenant farmers, which make up part of the debt of 145,000 thalers reported by you, you must first demand regular settlements, providing for this in the case of the tenant farmers in their leases; the whole of every liquid debt to be paid within six months, and accurate monthly statements are to be sent to Us of what has been paid and what is still outstanding.

11. And whereas, unless proper accounts are rendered, it is impossible to put the Cameral affairs straight and see how they stand, two Cameral accountants shall within the next six months go through all accounts not yet audited with the Master of the Chamber, but under the supervision of yourself, the President, and, in the presence of the Cameral Councillor from whose Department the account is taken, shall rectify them and see to it most strictly that in future the regulations governing the drawing up and despatch of accounts to the General Audit Chamber are punctually observed. The two accountants and the Master of the Chamber shall make this their principal business and not allow themselves to be diverted from it by any other task; for which purpose you, the President, are to choose the persons whom you judge fittest, and to speed up the work. We have most graciously resolved to appoint two new accountants and to give them the same salaries as the others, to which end either We shall send you two efficient men from Berlin, or if you know of any suitable persons, you may propose them.

12. In connection wherewith, the official accounts are not to be left, as hitherto, open, on account of the outstanding debts, but the said debts and sums are to be carried over from one account to the next; but must be claimed and called in as soon as possible.

13. We wish that the reliefs which have so often been permitted

to tenants and promised in their leases shall so far as possible cease, and your duty is to see that in the future, when new leases are drawn up, the tenants are allowed no reliefs except in cases of general failures of the harvest and for the stock, of general cattle mortality, but in other cases of cattle mortality only against wastage, as is customary in the Kurmark and elsewhere. To facilitate this We graciously consent, in respect of wastage of sheep, that whereas a sheep was previously valued at 24 Polish groschen after deduction of expenses, in future it shall be valued at only 21 Polish groschen, the reliefs being abolished, and We trust you to make every effort to get this set on a correct footing.

14. As moreover the achievement of the necessary exactness in the agents' offices is greatly facilitated if the Captains and administrators also pay attention to the economy, We have written to this effect to Our Prussian Government, as per the enclosed copy.

15. Although We should in general like to see the taxation put on the footing of the Mark, as We have ordered Our German Chamber, yet We think that at present this would not be advisable in Lithuania; it would, in particular, probably frighten away the tenant farmers by imposing on them a system unfamiliar to them. Things are therefore to remain as before, until further notice.

16. Nevertheless, in order that there should be some basis for taxation, the fields of the demesne farms are to be measured, where this has not already been done, and local sworn men are to be present at the sowing for three or four years in succession, according to the number of the fields, and to make an accurate register of all the different crops sown.

17. And as it would appear contrary to Our interests if the persons at the head of the Chamber turned out their horses to feed and graze on demesne farms not rented by them, you, the President and the Chamber, shall keep no horses on demesne farms not rented by you.

18. We also desire the repeoplement of the land and the introduction of good cultivation to be carried forward with all imaginable diligence and care; it is your duty to submit to Us your respectful ideas on the subject.

Finally, We command you to obey all the above most strictly, and also to carry into execution without delay all agreements and undertakings conducted by you with Our Commission, as minuted. As We also expect periodical progress reports from you.

To the Lithuanian Chamber
Tilsit, July 2, 1718

Fr. Wilhelm
C. B. v. Creutz

12. Frederick William I Wants Untinted Spectacles

The document which follows calls for no elucidation. The date is 1722; the source of the original, the *Acta Borussica* (Deutsche Akademie der Wissenschaften, Berlin, 1892 ff.), Vol. III, p. 267.

Rescript to the Commissariat of Pomerania; Berlin, July 20, 1722

For some time past We have on various occasions remarked with particular displeasure that the reports rendered to Us, especially on matters concerning Our Provinces and towns, often contain statements that are unfounded, or, at least, not based on the necessary conscientious and mature examination of the true circumstances involved, and afterward, after closer scrutiny and examination, show that the event did not occur at all, or at any rate, not in the way in which it was represented, so that in the end We have not known what to believe, and what not. We wish therefore that this improper practice, which is directly contrary to the duty and obligations of Our servants, shall for the future cease absolutely, and no reports be rendered that do not rest on correct and truthful foundations and on mature precedent investigation of all and every attendant circumstance, as their authors have to answer for it before God, Us, and their consciences, under pain of Our extreme disfavor and most severe and active displeasure toward those who do not obey exactly this, Our express command, but continue to send in superficial reports in the belief that they are carrying out their duty if they simply put down something, whether founded on fact or not; which is, however, not to be interpreted as meaning that Our Colleges and servants should thereby be frightened into concealing and keeping secret from Us the true state of affairs. Our most gracious intention remains, as before, that complete information should be rendered to Us periodically on everything that occurs in the country and the towns, and on the true situation, particularly when there is any deficit in the land tax or the town excise, or any incident in the commercial field; and similarly when, as often occurs in connection with recruiting and billeting, excesses have been committed —real, not hearsay, but actual and demonstrable facts which have not been remedied by the commanding officers, to whom the complaints must, by regulation, be first addressed, detailed reports of all such and other similar cases must be sent to Us personally under seal, duplicates to be sent in every case to the General Commissariat of War. We hereby make known to you this, Our considered wish, and command you, not only yourselves to obey it in the future, but also to make it known to the magistrates and other persons whom it may concern, in order that each one may safeguard himself against trouble and certain punishment.

13. Frederick William's "Directorate General"

Frederick William's decision to set up what amounted to a single administrative service for all his dominions is supposed to have been taken on the advice of his friend, Prince Leopold of Anhalt-Dessau, but was most likely forced on him by the inevitable rivalries and jealousies between the two older bodies, the line between whose functions had, in fact, not always been easy to draw. Provincial separatism also no doubt played its part in the decision (see the careful provisions in Art. 1, para. 11, for the staffing of the commissariats and chambers of each province by persons not natives of it).

Centralization is also served by the curious arrangement under which each of the four departments into which the Directorate is divided is at the same time competent for the local problems of one of the four "Provinces" of the monarchy, and for one aspect of general policy.

The "Instructions" are much too voluminous to be given in their entirety; we have selected for translation only those which show the central structure and purposes of the new body, and some others which are especially characteristic of Frederick William's mentality.

Drafted at the end of 1722, in Frederick William's hunting lodge of Schönebeck, the "Instructions" were promulgated in January, 1723. The text is contained in the *Acta Borussica*, Vol. III, pp. 575ff.

INSTRUCTIONS AND RULES FOR THE DIRECTORATE GENERAL
(HUNTING LODGE OF SCHÖNEBECK, DECEMBER 20, 1722)

I. ON THE employees of the Directorate General, also the Provincial Commissariats and Chambers and the instructions for them.

1. Since We have become convinced of the supreme necessity of making changes in respect of Our present Commissariat General of War and Directorate General of Finance, and of winding up and abolishing entirely both these offices and establishing in their place a Supreme Directorate General of Finance, War, and Crown Properties, and of entrusting to that body most graciously the conduct of all business hitherto dealt with by the former Commissariat General of War and Directorate General of Finance, We hereby declare that We propose Ourselves to assume the Presidency of the said Directorate General, in order to give it more prestige, authority and weight and at the same time to demonstrate the special and most particular attention which We propose to devote, unremittingly and untiringly, to the affairs falling within the competence of the said Directorate, conformably with their extreme importance. . . .

[Para. 2 lists the names of the persons appointed to the Directorate: five "Vice-Presidents and Directing Ministers" (Lieutenant General von Grumbkow and Real Ministers of State von Creutz, von Krautt, von Katsch and von Görne), and fourteen councillors or assessors.]

3. Even as We now show hereby that We repose special gracious confidence in the said Ministers and Assessors appointed by Us to the Directorate General, so We also lay down that the five Directing Ministers [the names follow] . . . shall be responsible to Us for all proceedings whatever of the Directorate General.

4. The Privy Councillors of Finance, War, and Crown Properties are, on the other hand, responsible only for what belongs to the Department to which each of them is appointed.

[Para. 5 deals with questions of precedence. In general, mem-

bers of the Directorate take precedence immediately below Privy
Councillors.]

6. When vacancies occur in the staff of the Directorate, the
five Ministers are to propose candidates to fill them.

7. But they must be men as able as can be found in the length
and breadth of the country, of Evangelical-Reformed or Lutheran
religion, loyal and honest, with open minds, who understand
agriculture and have themselves practiced it, are well informed
on commerce, manufacture and kindred subjects and also able to
express themselves on paper, and, above all, must have been born
Our subjects, although, as regards the last point, if someone were
proposed who was a foreigner but very able, we might allow one
or two such persons admission to Our Directorate. But to put the
above and other necessary qualities in a nutshell, they must be
men capable of carrying out any duty entrusted to them. . . .

[Paras. 8 and 9 list the qualifications required of presidents and
councillors of the provincial commissariats and chambers.]

10. Employees of the Provincial Chambers must be good agriculturalists, who have themselves been farmers and local agents[1]
and themselves substantial leaseholders, also capable of expressing
themselves on paper and of keeping accounts, wide-awake and
sound men.

11. Further, the following system shall be followed in the
making of new appointments to fill vacancies occurring in the
Provincial Commissariats and Chambers. When a vacancy occurs
in Prussia, the persons proposed to Us by the Directorate General
to fill it shall be natives of Cleves, the Mark, or Pomerania, but
not Prussians.

In the Commissariats and Chambers of Cleves, natives of Prussia,
the Mark, or Magdeburg, but not of Cleves.

In Pomerania, Prussians or natives of Cleves or Magdeburg, but
not Pomeranians.

In Magdeburg and Halberstadt, natives of the Mark, Cleves, or
Prussia, but not of Magdeburg or Halberstadt.

In a word, Our most gracious intention is that no person shall
be proposed for a vacancy in a Provincial Commissariat or Chamber
who is a native of the Province in which the vacancy occurs. . . .

---

[1] See above, fn. 5 to p. 211.

15. For all excisemen, inspectors of mills, police patrols, messengers, and other similar services, We wish no one to be employed except disabled ex-N.C.O.'s and soldiers, whose names must always be put forward by Our Adjutant General for Our most gracious approval. . . .

17. We also most graciously command the Directorate General to examine carefully and closely whether some retrenchments cannot be made in the Commissariats and Chambers where there are many employees, and whether other services cannot be combined, and the cost of their maintenance thus reduced. For example, in towns where customs are levied, the excisemen can at the same time receive the customs, and the salaries of the customs officers be saved.

If the Directorate sets itself to look into this point with due regard for Our service and interests, it will render Us considerable service, profit, and savings. . . .

19. Instructions to the Provincial Commissariats must in particular lay down that the Provincial Presidents are to visit the towns under their charge frequently, and inform themselves exactly of their conditions in respect of their trade and traffic, commerce and manufactures, the citizens and inhabitants and their conditions of living and employment, so as to become as closely acquainted with the towns in their Departments as a Captain in Our army must—as We insist—know his company; he must be exactly acquainted with the morale, intelligence, and physical qualities of every soldier belonging to it. . . .

[II.] 7. The drafts of all communications sent out from the Directorate General, judicial matters alone excepted, are revised by all five Directing Ministers.

8. The originals are to be countersigned simultaneously by Our Lieutenant General and Real Minister of State von Grumbkow and by Councillor von Creutz.

9. Should one of these two Ministers be absent, the countersignature shall be given in his place by von Krautt, and so on, the countersignature being in every case appended by the two senior Ministers present.

10. Councillor von Katsch revises and countersigns judicial papers alone.

11. The Directorate shall meet every Monday, Wednesday,

Thursday, and Friday at the place designated by Us, and all business coming before the Directorate shall be transacted by it in joint session and not, as hitherto, by its members in their own homes.

12. Mondays are the departmental days of Lieutenant General, etc., von Grumbkow. On them all matters relating to Prussia, eastern and western Pomerania, and the Neumark shall be considered, also frontier questions and matters relating to clearance and drainage of swamps shall be submitted and decided, but no others, even if urgent, because three, four, or eight days make no difference to Commissariat and Chamber business.

13. Wednesdays are the departmental days of the Real Minister of State and Councillor von Creutz. On them reports will be made and decisions taken on the affairs of Minden, Ravensberg, Tecklenburg and Ling and on questions of audit and forage, but no other.

14. Thursdays are the days of Real Minister of State and Councillor von Krautt. On them the affairs of the Kurmark, Magdeburg, and Halberstadt are to be treated, also matters concerning movements and supply of Our army, but no other.

15. On Fridays Our Real Minister of State and Councillor von Görne has his departmental days. On them matters will be debated which concern Guelder, Cleves, Meurs, Neuchâtel, the Orange Succession, the postal services, and the currency, but none other.

16. Judicial questions have no special departmental day, but shall be reported and settled on the day set for the Province in which the question originated.

17. The Directorate shall meet at 7 A.M. in summer and 8 A.M. in winter.

18. It is not to break up until every question in the Department whose day it is has been settled down to the last small detail.

19. If members can deal with the business in an hour, they are free to disperse, but if they cannot finish in the morning, they must continue to sit without a break until 6 P.M. or until they have finished all the business. We therefore instruct Our Head Marshal and Real Privy Minister of State von Printz that if the Directorate remains in session till after 2 P.M. he is to have a midday meal of four good courses, with wine and beer, brought up from Our kitchen. Half the heads and members of Departments are to eat while the other half work, and afterward those who worked while the others ate shall eat in their turn, and the

others work, that Our service may be carried on efficiently, diligently, and truly. . . .

[IV.] 2. The Directorate must watch with all diligence that the
regiments of Our army always receive their pay punctually and
in full, and that there are never any arrears. . . .

VII. On maintaining the welfare of the unfree population.

1. Everyone knows how important it is to every Power that
the condition of its unfree population should be satisfactory and
what dangerous consequences can ensue when the unfree population is exhausted by a bad economic system and excessive burdens,
and is reduced to a state in which its members are unable to fulfill
their ordinary obligations toward their master at all, or at any
rate, not completely. The Directorate is therefore to devote its
attention, with great diligence and application, to maintaining the
welfare of all Our unfree populations, so that they be always
maintained in a flourishing and prosperous state, and that neither
the war tax nor the landlords' dues, etc., be fixed at an unsupport-
able level.

2. The Directorate must not confine itself to keeping the
towns in a flourishing condition but must also pay special attention to the conditions of the peasants, the villagers, and the rural
districts. . . .

VIII. On the war tax (contributio).

1. The Contribution is a matter of the utmost importance, to
which the Directorate General must devote tireless application
and pains, and on this point both the entire said Directorate and
all Ministers belonging to it, and also the members of every Department, but as regards the latter, only so far as it falls within
their competence, and not where they are not competent, are
to be individually responsible.

2. The Directorate General is to pay especial attention to seeing
that the Contributions are paid punctually and in full, and that
there are no deficits. . . .

4. In particular, the Directorate General is to take good care
that Our immediate subjects[2] are not unduly burdened in respect

---

[2] I.e., the peasants, etc., on crown land.

of taxes and billeting, since in many places they are unfairly burdened in both respects by comparison with the mediate subjects,[3]
and the said Directorate must investigate this point exactly and
immediately make any changes and reforms which are found
necessary.

5. The taxation due from Our immediate subjects is to be collected by the agents and paid into the Provincial Circle account,
which will then pay it into the war chest, so that the peasant is
not harassed twice and delays are avoided. . . .

X. The excise.

1. In respect of the excise, one of the points to which the
Directorate General must pay the greatest attention is that the
tariffs must be well and accurately fixed, and under them all
foreign woolen and other goods must be subjected to heavy duties,
in such fashion that Our own native products and manufactures
can be cheaper and sell better than foreign ones. . . .

7. No man in Our Kingdom, Provinces, and Lands shall be
exempt from the excise, and for the further prevention of all
evasion We Ourselves and Our Royal House will pay the excise,
and great care shall be taken that no one shall in future presume
to defraud the excise under the pretext that these or those commodities or goods are destined for Us or Our Royal House. . . .

11. The Directorate General must also use every means to prevent persons domiciled in Our Lands from transferring their money
or capital abroad. And the said Directorate will have to consider,
in full session and maturely, how this may best be prevented, and
how capitalists may be given the opportunity to place and invest
their money in Our Lands. . . .

XII. Manufactures.

1. The Directorate General is already aware of the importance
to Us and Our Lands of the establishment of good and well-organ-
ized manufactures, and must therefore take all pains to ensure that
all kinds of manufactures of woolens, iron, wood, and leather, and
the craftsmen for them which are not yet established in Our
Lands be, as far as possible, introduced into them.

2. In order to achieve this most useful objective, the Directorate

[3] The unfree population whose "immediate" masters were their manorial
lords.

General must import the necessary manufactures, according to the methods adopted by Us for the musket factory in Potsdam. . . .

XIV. On arresting deserters.

1. In order that desertion from Our army be checked and deserters more easily apprehended, the Directorate General shall issue and publish, as from Us and in Our name, in Our Kingdom and also in all Provinces and Lands, a severe Edict, which shall afterwards be read out on the first Sunday of each month in towns in which there are no fortresses, and similarly in all villages with churches, to the effect that burghers and peasants shall not allow any soldier, N.C.O., grenadier, musketeer, cavalryman, or dragoon, man on furlough, or orderly who cannot show a regular pass to pass through any town or village, but shall immediately arrest him and hand him over to the nearest regiment, which shall then send the deserter on to his own regiment, which will then defray the expenditure incurred.

If a soldier deserts from a regiment or company and the officer announces this in the town or country district, the burghers and peasants shall immediately sound the alert, ring the alarm bells, occupy the exits, and institute further search for the deserter.

When they apprehend him the nearest excise office shall pay the peasants, burghers, or agents who have caught and handed in the deserter the sum of twelve thalers, which Councillor Schöning is to deduct from the money paid to the regiment. . . .

A person helping a deserter to escape has earned the gallows and shall, as soon as he is convicted of the crime, be hanged, without waiting for Our confirmation.

XVIII. Leasing of agents' leaseholdings, demesne farms, and other Crown properties.

1. The Directorate General shall work with tireless diligence, fidelity and application, and shall always keep in mind that Our Crown estates and leaseholdings are to be improved and set in better order every year, and, where new demesne farms can with advantage be established, or new dairy farms, or where wild and uncultivated fens can be cleared and drained, they are to set about the work at once, without fail, and in every way to see how, through industry and expertise, the yields of Our Crown properties can be increased without equal or greater loss to Our war or other

revenues. If, for example, the Commissariat for Crown Properties improved the "Amt" of Potsdam by 400 Reichsthaler a year, and this brought Us a corresponding loss of 400 thalers on the Potsdam excise, this would be no real improvement. . . .

3. The Directorate General is to apply these principles in all improvements and to act at once where We find a real advantage, no matter into which of the accounts the surplus goes, so long as We get real advantage out of it. . . .

[XVIII.] 29. The Directorate will be able to see from the above instructions as clearly as man could desire that it is Our will that reports and queries submitted to Us from the said Directorate shall and must always be in such form that We can rely on them confidently and without misgivings, and be satisfied that everything contained in the reports corresponds exactly to the facts and has been previously well examined and thrashed out. And as We shall be dependent on the Directorate, if it should report any matter to us erroneously, it follows that it must keep many spies in the Provinces to guide it aright.

Nor is it admissible that the Directorate General should try to put the blame on the Provincial Commissariats and Chambers by saying that they reported so and so and the Directorate trusted them and consequently submitted the matter to Us as it was reported to them. We shall not accept such excuses nor recognize them as valid. The Directorate General must personally inform itself of the matter and examine it in full, to see whether the reports from the Provinces are not partial and whether human considerations and intrigues, etc., have not colored them, for under these instructions Our said Directorate must be collectively responsible, each for all and all for each, in such and all other cases. . . .

[XXXIV]. 2. We have already (above) ordered that the Directorate shall correspond diligently with the Commissariats and Chambers, and the members of each Department with the private informants and spies to be organized in the Provinces, in order that they may be informed in minutest detail of what goes on in the Provinces, either in the Commissariat, Crown Property, financial, Provincial, or political fields; also new journals and all sorts of particulars of Provincial events. For example: in Prussia a good winter and heavy frost. Big quantities of provisions, etc., being brought into the towns. Large supplies of timber for the new constructions are coming in from the forests. The construction is going on well. A good harvest is anticipated. Commerce, shipping, and manufactures are looking up. Were Your Royal Majesty to come here, you would—we hope—deign to be satisfied with the way things are progressing.

This or that town or village has been burnt down. There is a secret movement among the nobles to get rid of the general tax on holdings, strong resistance to this or that edict. This or that nobleman is objecting to the land tax.[4] This or that regiment is buying fodder from neighboring foreign countries. The Chamber will pay its quarterly dues in full, or it will fail to do so, but will be able to give reasons so valid that H.M. will, under the instructions, be obliged to accept them; or, it will be necessary to put strong pressure on the Chamber, to force it to pay. The Chamber works very diligently, as does the Commissariat. The Royal Edicts and the substance of the instructions are carried out, or not. Twenty new houses are being built in this or that town. The attendance in the Commissariats and Chambers is regular, or not. This or that regiment has carried out forced requisitions. The Commissariat has asked the officer commanding the regiment to pay compensation for such requisitions, without effect, etc.; also, in general, any new developments.

As now the Directorate General has been instructed by Us to summarize all such and similar information reaching it from the Provinces in a short report and to submit such report to Us weekly, so it is also permitted, should any matter be contained therein on which it regards it necessary to ask for Our gracious opinion and command, to request the same from Us.

3. The questions must, however, be framed as shortly and clearly as possible, concisely and to the point, and accompanied by the Directorate's own recommendation and the reasons on which this is based.

4. A quite short extract must be made on the same day from the record of all discussions and decisions in the Directorate General and sent to Us in the evening, so that We can see and read it the next morning and can also deliver Our most gracious decision if there are any questions in it. . . .

---

[4] *Generalhufenschoss*, a general tax on all land, introduced between 1715 and 1719.

In every case, the Directorate's own recommendation must be added, with the reasons on which it is based; We remain King and Lord, and can do as We please.

If, however, they submit their recommendation with the question, firstly, We know that they have examined the question thoroughly before reporting; secondly, We are convinced that if the question has been examined by so many honest and capable men, We can never be cheated; and thirdly, We profit from the fact that they must be responsible to Us for their recommendation that they have represented the matter as it is and not otherwise, and also cannot answer to Us otherwise than to the best of their knowledge and consciences.

14. Frederick William's Political Testament

The composition of "political testaments" or other reflections for the benefit of their prospective successors was something of a family tradition among the Hohenzollerns. Several of the rulers mentioned in our introductory sketch indulged in it, but considerations of space preclude more than a reference to the earlier of these productions.[1] It is, however, impossible so to pass over the "testament" of Frederick William, although it is too long to be given in its entirety. Frederick William's "Instructions for His Successor" would qualify for the title of a curiosity of the first order by its spelling and grammar alone, in which respects Maria Theresa herself was a Walter Pater in comparison with the Prussian king; but it has also a more serious and very real interest. It is, in essence, a description of the peoples, resources, governmental machinery, etc., of the writer's dominions, with special reference to problems and weaknesses, and accounts of the steps taken by the writer to remedy these and his recommendations to his successor. Considerations of space have necessitated the omission of a few passages which deal with small personalia or trivialities, or simply record facts the substance of which can be found by today's reader more easily, more fully, even more accurately, in modern textbooks. But Frederick William's comments on peoples and individuals are uniquely refreshing, and, the entertainment value of these apart, the Instructions are a valuable and illuminating historical source, for their author takes most of his pet hobbyhorses out for a ride through these pages, which, con-

[1] They have been collected by G. Küntzel and M. Hass in *Die Politischen Testamente der Hohenzollern*, 2nd edn. (Leipzig, 1919) Vol. 1.

sequently, not only convey a most vivid picture of the personality of this extraordinary man, but also show, from his own mouth, what were the principles—very serious and considered ones—on which he governed his dominions.

He wrote the Instructions, as he says himself, in the opening weeks of 1722 (thus at a time when the "dear successor" whom he apostrophizes was still a child and had not yet incurred his displeasure). The original text can be found in G. F. Schmoller, *Das Politische Testament Friedrich Wilhelm des Erstens* 1722 (Berlin 1896) or in Küntzel and Hass, *op. cit.*, pp. 94ff.

EXTRACTS FROM KING FREDERICK WILLIAM I's INSTRUCTIONS FOR HIS SUCCESSOR

INSTRUCTIONS HOW my successor to the throne of Prussia is to shape his conduct, and the necessary information on the whole state of the army and Provinces. I have written this in Potsdam on January 22, 1722.

Since I clearly perceive that my health is growing worse year by year, and I know that by human expectation my life cannot last much longer, I have set down the following instructions that my dear successor may model his conduct on them.

I begin with a few words on my own life. I stand well with Almighty God. From my twentieth year I have put all my trust steadfastly in God, Whose gracious hearing I have ever invoked, and He has also constantly heard my prayer, and I am assured of salvation through the grace of Jesus Christ and His bitter passion and death.

I heartily repent all grievous and inner sins which I have committed and pray to God to forgive them for Jesus Christ's sake. I have always labored to make myself better and to live a godly life so far as I was humanly able to do so, and with God's help I will so persevere until my end. So help me the Holy Spirit, through Jesus Christ, Amen.

Let my dear successor be well assured that all successful rulers who keep God before their eyes and have no mistresses or, rather, whores, and lead a godly life—on such rulers God will shower down all worldly and spiritual blessings. I therefore beseech my dear successor to lead a godly life and to show a good example to his lands and army, not to tipple and gorge, which lead to a dissolute life. Neither must my dear successor allow any comedies, operas, ballets, masks, or redoutes to be held in his Lands and Provinces, he must abhor them because these are godless and devilish things, whereby Satan, his temple, and kingdom are increased.

Therefore, we true Christians must destroy the temple of Satan. It is the duty of a God-fearing ruler—rather, your duty—to repress and not to tolerate the temple of Satan, that is, mistresses, operas, comedies, redoutes, ballets, and masques, and yourself to lead no such ungodly life, which has never been tolerated in our House, and from the day of John Sigismund[1] no such sins have flourished in the House of Brandenburg. Read the history of our House; you will find there that this is true, and for that reason, God has continually blessed our House. Be assured that the blessing that still rests most constantly on our House comes from our godly conduct. So I beeseech my dear successor, keep no mistresses nor follow any other such scandalous pleasures, and do not allow such abominable sins to flourish in your Lands and Provinces, but punish them, and I enjoin you to follow my example, and beseech you, in considering the constitution of my land and army, to remember that I have always begun with God. Do likewise. Do so, and God will certainly bless you and will not forsake you.

Beware of flatterers and toadies; those are your enemies who always agree with you, and they are capable of leading you astray into all sorts of mischief. You must not listen to them, but reject them flatly, for by their imperceptible flatteries they seduce you into many evil sins which can damage the well-being of your lands and army, for flatterers are your greatest enemies, but those who tell you the truth are your friends, and it is they who love you, be assured of that. . . .

[The writer now enters into certain budgetary details, recommending economy in the payment of all servants of the State, beginning with the ministers. Then:]

You must manage your finances personally and alone and order the command of the army personally and alone and dispose of the two main points alone; then you will have authority in the army through the command and the love of all your officers and civil employees, because you alone hold the pursestrings, and you will be respected and admired by the whole world for a sage and good ruler—may Almighty God help you to it!

[1] I.e., since the adoption by the Hohenzollerns of the Calvinst faith.

I beg my successor most earnestly to impose no cuts in the pay of the regimental commanders, junior officers, and rank and file, and to leave their commissariat as he will find it after my death. Insofar as you do that, I give my dear successor my blessing, that God may prosper him in all his enterprises and make him formidable, that God may bestow on him more blessings than He did on Solomon. But if you act otherwise and cut down the commissariat, I withdraw my fatherly blessing from you and call down on you the curse that God sent down on King Pharaoh, that it may go with you as it went with Absalom.

[Next follows a list of Frederick William's regiments, their pay and the sources of it. This section ends:]

My dear successor, what will the world say of the increase in the army when you mount the throne? That you are a formidable Power in the face of your enemies, of whom our House has very many, and your friends will hold you to be a clever and sensible ruler; may Almighty God help you to be it, I wish it from my heart, Amen.

I must make my dear successor acquainted with all my Provinces, the Lands and their inhabitants.

Prussia is a very fine and big land and very fruitful. The people make good servants of the State for they are very intelligent, but my successor must keep his eye on them, for the nation is false and cunning. But with good words you can do what you will with them. They understand nothing of accounts or economics, so you must not employ them in those departments.

But they make excellent employees in the army, in negotiations, and in the judicial services. The previous organization of my domains was unsuccessful, but this year I have taken it in hand seriously and begun building and improving. If this can be kept up for four or five years more, it is certain that the revenues from the domains will be at least doubled. May God bless and preserve Göhren,[2] because he has a thorough understanding of how to organize and improve the domains. If he should die, my successor can find no better men than Privy Councillors Thile[3] and Rocho.[4]

[2] Friedrich von Görne, director of economic affairs in the Directorate of Finance.

[3] Friedrich von Theile, Privy Cameral Councillor since 1722.

[4] Friedrich Wilhelm von Rochow, Privy Councillor in the General Directorate of Finances since 1720.

As to the Contribution, my successor must not raise it, but leave it at the single land tax [*Generalhufenschoss*][5] and by no means reintroduce the old Provincial funds [*Landkasten*], for it cost me a great deal of trouble to get things as far as I have. For it is a big infringement of the privileges of the Province, which are very detrimental to the Prince's sovereignty, and the Prince used to depend on the nobles, and now everything depends on me, without argument; is that not better?

As to Königsberg, my successor must introduce the Berlin excise tariff. This country is lacking in small towns; my successor must establish new ones in Lithuania, and in the Prussian towns there are no manufactures, but manufactures are the true backbone of a land, and of the Prince of a land, so my successor must establish manufactures in Prussia and in all his other Provinces where there are none, especially manufactures of woolens; for that purpose my successor must forbid the importation of all foreign woolen goods into Prussia and all his Provinces under pain of confiscation of all the offender's assets, and if they come a second time, they must go into the cart forever [sic]. My successor must also keep to my edict that no raw wool shall be exported from any Province, under pain of forfeiture of life and limb, and my successor must protect the manufactures in all his Provinces, then you will see how your revenues will increase and your lands and subjects will flourish. God grant it! If you make the beginning, this will certainly be the result. As to the nobles, they had of old great privileges, which the Elector Frederick William broke down through his sovereign power, and I brought them to obedience in 1715 by the single land tax. If my successor wants to be ceremonially installed in Prussia he must tell Ilgen and Kniphausen secretly to arrange for you to receive the homage in Prussia quickly, so that no Polish magnates appear, and the homage is done in the same form as I received it, but if a Polish magnate is present that will have bad consequences. You will find out about this in the archives. Look up the installations of my father and grandfather, you will see how important it is, not just a ceremony. In Prussia there is also a powerful nobility; the Counts' Estate is the most considerable. My successor must keep a watchful eye on the families of Finck and Dohna or they will share the rule with my successor,

[5] See above, fn. 4, p. 308.

and both families still cherish the old Prussian Polish privileges in their hearts, be assured of this. My successor must make it a policy, and direct his efforts thereto, that the nobles and Counts of all his Provinces, and especially Prussia, are employed in the army and their sons put into the cadet school; this gives strength to his service and army, and more tranquility in his lands. My successor must also grant only to very few of them permits to travel abroad, for first they must stand in your service. But if they are really in your service and you are not at war, you can allow a few to travel abroad. It is good that my dear successor should enjoy the advantage that the whole nobility is brought up in your service from youth up, and know no lord except God and the King of Prussia, but if my successor does not act so and takes heaps of foreigners into his service as senior officers he will not be served so well by the foreign officers, and his own vassals [s.c., holders of fiefs from the crown] will serve abroad, for as to those who serve abroad, be assured that they are all recalcitrants with little respect for their Prince. If all your officers are children of your own land, be assured that you will have in them a reliable army and good, reliable officers, and no potentate has better than that. You must be courteous and gracious in your behavior toward all nobles, from all Provinces, and sort out the good from the bad and distinguish the true among them, then you will be loved and feared.

As to West and East Pomerania, this is a good, fertile land. The domains are in better condition than in Prussia, and there is no derelict land, but they can be improved in many respects, and if you re-lease them and improve the economy, the Cameral revenue from the domains in Pomerania can be brought up to 50,000 to 70,000 thalers a year. My successor must employ Göhren, Thile, and Rocho on this and other similar economic tasks. The Pomeranian vassals are as true as gold, they kick up a bit of a row at times (*Resonnieren wohl bissweilen*), but if my successor says "this is how it is to be and you must make the best of it," none of them will move against your orders.

As to the New Mark, it is in all respects like Pomerania. There are many improvements to be made in the domains, but the vassals are always complaining, especially those from the Circle of Crossen, but you must not take any notice of the New Mark complaints, for they are mostly groundless, but that is their national habit.

For the Middle and Uker Mark, the vassals are the loyalest of all and whatever you command them, they gladly and readily obey your orders. The domains in the whole Kurmark Chamber are in fairly good condition, but a revision, Amt by Amt, is most necessary, for it would be possible to effect a very big improvement, more than 100,000 thalers. For the forests, you must appoint a commission to go into their condition thoroughly, get rid of all abuses and arrange for a better sales service, so that the Dutch and Hamburg merchants pay better and higher prices than now for the timber. There is much to be done there, and a great deal of fraud is being practiced by the hunters. The vassals of the Altmark are bad, disobedient men who do nothing with a good grace but are obstinate and treat their sovereign right lightly. My successor must keep a very watchful eye on them and not be soft with them, for there are elements among them who take their duties altogether too lightly. When you issue any order, important or trivial, to the Provincial Councillors and the Councillors resist and kick up a shindy and the order is not carried out, you must at once dismiss any Councillors who have not obeyed the order and yourself appoint new ones from the Province—do not let the Knights choose them. This will show them that you mean to be master and that they have to be vassals. The families of Schulenburg, Alvensleben, and Bismarck are the most distinguished and the worst. You must not appoint any native of the Altmark to its Provincial government; send them to Pomerania and Prussia, but not to Magdeburg, for Magdeburg has many connections with the Altmark.[6] The Knesebeck family is a bad one, too. The vassals of Prignitz are much better, the same type as those of the Neumark.

The land and cities of Magdeburg are fine ones. The vassals are like those of the Altmark, but almost worse still. You must not appoint any Magdeburger to the Provincial government of Magde- or Halberstadt, nor to the Altmark; they can be sent to Prussia, Pomerania, Mittelmark, Minden, or Cleves. The domains are in a very good state; improvements are possible, but at the outside they could be made to produce 30,000 to 40,000 thalers more.

As to Halberstadt and Hohenstein, the vassals are like the Magde-

[6] For the principle Frederick William recommends to his successor, of appointing non-natives to the central posts of authority in each province, see also paras. 2 to 14 of his instructions for his Directorate General (above, pp. 300–301). For the earlier constitutional rules, over which this advice rides roughshod, see pp. 232ff.

burgers. You must not appoint natives to the Provincial government, but take them from other Provinces. As to the economy, it is very good, but there are still many improvements that could be made, especially in Hohenstein.

As to the salt mines and other mines in Magdeburg, the salt mines are in a good condition. My successor must set to work and find ways of improving the sales, then they will be excellent. As to the Wettin coal mines, I now draw 20,000 thalers a year from them; if you go into things there carefully you must be able to get another 10,000 a year, above the 20,000, that is sure.

As to Minden, Ravensberg, Tecklenburg, and Lingen, the vassals are stupid and opinionated, you cannot employ them much, for they are too easygoing to make good employees, but they are not so bad as the Altmarkers, for if you put on a gracious face and manner toward them they will do what you want. The domains are in good condition. Some reorganization is necessary, then you can well get another 10,000 to 20,000 thalers a year more, here and there.

As to the County and Mark of Cleves, the vassals are stupid oxen but malicious as the Devil. They are very tenacious of their privileges, but meanwhile they will do and give what my successor demands of them. As to the Provincial government, follow the same rule with them as with the Altmarkers. The people are great intrigants, and false into the bargain, and soak like beasts, that is all they know to do. If a Clevelander comes from home very young and is brought up in Berlin, he can be made into a good, sound, clever fellow, whom my successor can well use. In their private lives they are bad managers, for they consume more than their revenues produce. The domains are in right good condition, but could be improved to yield at least 40,000 thalers a year, if not more.

As to Mörs and Gelder, the Mörser are like the Clevelanders but very good Dutchmen, as the Clevelanders, too, are better Dutchmen and Emperor's men than Prussians. The revenue from the Mörs domains could be raised by improvements from 5,000 to 6,000 thalers. As for the Gelder, the vassals are Emperor's men through and through. My successor must keep a sharp eye on the Marquis de Honsbrug, who is a godless fellow toward his sovereign and would place himself under the allegiance of the Emperor at once if he only had a chance and is only waiting for the opportunity. As to the domains, they could well be improved. The annual revenue is 10,000 thalers.

So I have been through all the Provinces and given a general idea of the chief points and have left this description to my successor, to give him a general idea of his realm.

My dear successor must visit his Lands and Provinces each year, as I have done, then he will learn to know his regiments and army, his lands and peoples, and will see for himself that good improvements can be made in the domains of all Provinces and at least 600,000 to 800,000 thalers a year more revenue got out of them without oppressing the subjects. The revenue from domains can certainly be increased by good application and economy if my dear successor puts his mind to it and prays diligently to God and himself works diligently, then it will certainly succeed, may Almighty God help him to it, Amen!

. . . As to finances: when I am dead, my dear successor must not go back into past history, to see whether this or that person has robbed me, for while you are distracting yourself with old matters, the new will fall into the greatest confusion, and while you are occupying yourself with old history your servants will rob you. This is how I acted, and got on very comfortably, but your servants will tell you that so and so has robbed the late King of 1,000 or 20,000 thalers. They will try to divert your attention to old history, so as to keep it from their own doings, and the reason why they want to let everything fall into disorder is that troubled waters are good to fish in. . . .

. . . It is true that I am leaving you a treasury in which there is quite a pretty sum of money, but it is indispensable for a Prince to have ready money; for—while may God preserve you from war and plague—if some Provinces fail, war costs a terrible lot of money, but if you have a good, well-larded treasury, you can support this misfortune, so you must add at least 500,000 a year to the present treasure for a formidable army, and a big treasure to mobilize the army in case of need can give you a big standing in the world and you will be able to make your voice heard, like other Powers.

As to religion, I am a Calvinist, and with God's help I shall die one, but I am assured that a Lutheran who lives a godly life will achieve blessedness as well as a Calvinist, and the difference has been created only by quarrels between the preachers; so hold Calvinists and Lutherans in equal honor, do good to both religions and make no difference between them—God will bless you for it, and you will be beloved on all sides. . . . Do good to the poor and let no poor man in your land suffer want and help as much you can, God will requite you ten thousand fold. . . . My dear Successor must not let the preachers of either religion meddle in worldly affairs, for they like meddling in worldly affairs and have to be kept on a tight rein, for the clergy would like to be the Popes in our faith, for with the Papacy the priests decide everything. . . .

[Catholics must be tolerated as stipulated in international agreements—the Peace of Westphalia and the Treaty of Wehlau] but . . .

You must not tolerate Jesuits in your lands. They are devils who are capable of much evil and intrigue against you and the whole community, so you must not allow them to settle in your lands, under whatever pretext they try to do so.

As regards the French, or refugees, my Successor must confirm the privileges granted by the Elector Frederick William, but you can with a good conscience cut and economize 22,000 out of the 44,000 that I give them every year out of the exchequer, for many people are drawing pensions out of the 44,000 who do not need them at all, being very well off. For the rest, the French are very industrious people who have made the towns in our country capable of producing manufactures, for fifty years ago no fine cloths, stockings, crepe, velvet or woolen goods were manufactured here, and we had to import these from England, France, the Netherlands, now our lands export considerable quantities all over Germany. . . .

The Jews. As to the Jews, there are, unfortunately, very many in our lands who have no letters of protection from me. Those you must chase out of the country, because the Jews are locusts in a country and ruin the Christians. I beseech you to issue no new letters of protection, even if they offer you large sums for them, because it will be a great damage to you and the ruin of your subjects. . . .

My dear successor, I beseech you for God's sake to preserve your army well and to strengthen it more and more and not to split it up, as my father Frederick, King in Prussia, did in the last French war,[7] but always keep your army together, then you will see how you are sought after by all Powers of the world and will be able to hold the balance in Europe, for it will depend on you, for if one can hold the balance in the world there is always some profit to be got for one's lands, and you will be respected by your friends and dreaded by your enemies.

My dear successor must therefore not split up his fine army and give no troops for money and subsidies to Emperor, England, Holland, but must return the Powers the answer that I have given them: if you want to have troops, I will march myself with my whole army but not for subsidies, but give me land and men, which is what I want, then I will march, but not before. No country, no Prussian [*Paing de Pais Poing de Prussien*] is what best serves the interest, welfare, and glory of you and the land. You must draw the bow tight; if they need you they will have to give you what you ask, if they don't need you you sit quiet with your army, and wait for a good opportunity, for your affairs are in order. What does it profit you to sacrifice your army for a bagatelle for the benefit of Englishmen, Emperor, or Dutchmen, this would be the greatest folly in the world, but you have too much sense to cut such a caper. . . . Your Imperial contingent consists of 14,000 men. These you must provide, but not from your army. You must recruit foreign troops—ten squadrons and ten battalions—against annual subsidies from small German principalities, Gotha, Darmstadt, Breitensbach, Eisenach, they must do for the 14,000 men. You must send one of your Generals with them as commander. The Ministers will do everything to split your army up, but take my advice, it is good, and I have learned all this by experience, and what do you get from it if you let your army be sacrificed, you always get money again, but if your country is depopulated, that is difficult to make good. The welfare of a ruler is if his land is well populated, that is the true riches of a land. If your army marches outside the country the excise will not bring in a third as much as

[7] King Frederick I had not only sent troops to help in the Imperial campaign against the Turks, but between 1688 and 1690 had also supplied troops, in return for subsidies, to help William of Orange in the Netherlands and West Germany against France. The other partners of the "Grand Alliance" had, however, treated Brandenburg simply as an "auxiliary," and the Peace of Ryswyck had brought Brandenburg no advantage whatever.

if the army is in the country. The prices of commodities will fall, then the Crown agents will not be able to pay their rents in full, it is total ruin.

I beseech my dear successor in God's name not to start any unjust wars and not to be an aggressor, for God has forbidden unjust wars and one day you will have to give account for every man who has fallen in an unjust war. Consider that God's judgment is sharp, read history, there you will find that unjust wars have come to no good end, you have for examples King Louis XIV in France, King Augustus of Poland, the Elector of Bavaria, and many others. The two last were expelled from their lands and dethroned into the bargain because they started an unjust war. Be assured that God gives an army its heart, and also takes it away from the soldiers, for when King Augustus began a very unjust war, his Saxon army was so frightened of the Swedes that in many battles and encounters the Saxons were beaten by the enemy even when they were twice as strong as the Swedes, for the Saxons were always in fear in this unjust war, so that they refused to stand and fight. There my dear successor can see the hand of God, the Saxons are otherwise brave people and have always served bravely in Brabant and the Reich, but as soon as their King engaged in an unjust war the heart was gone out of them. I therefore beseech my dear successor not to begin an unjust war, then dear God will always bless you and your army and will give courage. You are, indeed, a great lord on earth, but you will have to render account before God for all unjust wars and blood that you have caused to be spilled, that is a hard thing, so I beseech you, keep a clear conscience before God, then you will enjoy a happy rule.

You must be very cautious in entering into alliances with great lords and promise nothing that you cannot keep and nothing that is against the word of God and against your country's interests. [Here follow counsels on what relations the recipient of these instructions should follow with other powers: close friendship with Russia, good relations with Poland—but everything must be done to ensure that it remains a republic. "Always be on your guard against the House of Austria and the Emperor, who is very jealous of Prussia and its army," etc. Frederick William is not opposed to Brandenburg's sending troops against France, if properly rewarded, "but not to Italy or Hungary, this is against your interest and total ruin of your army and too far away from your own country."]

I beg my dear successor to take no decision in affairs of State until you have considered everything well with your Ministers for Foreign Affairs. For if you spend a year listening to your Ministers speak and report on affairs you will soon learn and understand the subject and will learn to understand where your interest lies.

My dearest successor will think and say, why did my late father not act in all things as is written here? This is the reason. When my late father died in 1713, I found the land of Prussia practically a dead country, from human and cattle plague, all the Crown lands in the whole country, or most of them, pledged, or let under hereditary leases all of which I had to redeem, while the finances were in such a state that we were on the verge of bankruptcy. The army in so bad a condition and so small in numbers that I cannot even describe all that was wrong. It is certainly a masterpiece that in nine years, by 1722, I have gotten everything back into such good order and condition, and your estates are unencumbered with debt, your army and artillery in such a state as to count in Europe, and I assure you that I have had little help from my servants, but have rather been impeded by them, directly and indirectly. So I have not been able to do more in these nine years, but my dear successor will certainly be able to achieve everything that is written here in the instructions after my death. I wish my dear successor all good fortune and Divine blessing in this, and should God grant me a few more years of life, I shall myself be able to achieve much, as it stands here. Should I live longer I will write a supplement to these instructions, meanwhile I commend all to God and beg you to read it through often with reflection and attention; I am persuaded that you will find use in it and will follow me, for I have myself learned everything through experience, and in my time I have myself tried many experiments.

My dear successor, if you have loved me during my life, so after my death you can show your love to me by making the King's Regiment your regiment and leaving it with its present pay and distinguish it for my sake; secondly, continue to enlarge the town of Potsdam and give it the name of Wilhelmsstadt, for which God will give it His blessing.

Meanwhile I commend my soul to God and herewith give you once again my paternal blessing and wish you to keep God before your eyes and to rule your lands justly and in fear of God, and may you always have loyal servants and obedient subjects and a strong arm and a victorious army against all your enemies, and I pray that you, my dear successor, and those that come after you, may prosper as Kings and Electors to the end of the world, and that your provinces may prosper from hour to hour. May Almighty God help you to this through Jesus Christ!

Your true father, till death
F. WILHELM

Potsdam, the 17th February, 1722

15. Frederick William and His Son

We have mentioned elsewhere[1] the extraordinary persecution to which Frederick William subjected his son during the latter's adolescence. The exchange of correspondence that constitutes the first two of the following three pieces took place when Frederick was sixteen. They are translated from F. Foerster's *Friedrich Wilhelm I*, pp. 362ff. The third document (taken from the *Acta Borussica*, Vol. V, 3 Vols., Potsdam 1894–5, Vol. I p. 79) shows the sequel to Frederick's attempted flight. After being forced to watch the execution of his confidant in the enterprise, a certain Lieutenant Katte, Frederick had for a while been kept in close confinement in the fortress of Küstrin, and his father for a time thought of disinheriting him, but relented and instead sent him to undergo an intensive course of instruction in the local chamber of war and crown properties, the directors of which were given the instructions translated in the third document below. Von Hille, incidentally, proved an excellent and understanding mentor.

FREDERICK TO FREDERICK WILLIAM (WUSTERHAUSEN, SATURDAY, SEPTEMBER 11, 1728)

MY DEAR PAPA

For some time past I have been unable to nerve myself to go to my dear Papa, partly because I was advised not to, but chiefly

---

[1] See above, p. 214.

because I feared an even worse reception than usual, and, fearing that my present prayer would annoy my dear Papa more, I preferred to put it in writing. I therefore beg my dear Papa to be gracious to me, and after long reflection I am able to assert that my conscience has not accused me of the smallest thing for which I should reproach myself. But if I should, without wishing it or intending it, have done anything to annoy my dear Papa, I herewith beg most humbly for forgiveness, and I hope that my dear Papa will discard that cruel hatred which I have had sufficient cause to observe in all his treatment of me. Otherwise I could not bear it, for I have always hitherto supposed that I had a gracious father, and now I should have to believe the contrary. I therefore have the fullest confidence and hope that my dear Papa will think all this over and be gracious to me again; I assure him meanwhile that I will not willingly allow my time to be wasted and, in spite of his disfavour, I remain, with the most submissive and filial respect, my dear Papa's most obedient servant and son,

FRIDERICH

FREDERICK WILLIAM TO FREDERICK

That self-willed, evil disposition, which does not love its father, for when one does everything that is necessary and especially when one loves one's father, one does what he wishes, not only when he is present, but also when he does not see what is being done, and also knows well that I cannot abide an effeminate chap who has no manly leanings, who, to his shame, can neither ride nor shoot, and at the same time is personally unclean, wears his hair long and curled like a fool. I have reprimanded all this a thousand times, but all in vain, and there is no improvement in anything. Into the bargain haughty, arrogant as an upstart, speaking to no one, except a few individuals, not popular or affable, grimaces as though he were a fool, and does nothing as I wish it until he is driven by force, nothing out of love, and takes no pleasure in anything except following his own way, as though nothing else were of any value. This is the answer.

FR. W.

INSTRUCTIONS TO PRESIDENT VON MUNCHOW AND DIRECTOR VON
HILLIE ON HOW THE CROWN PRINCE IS TO BE KEPT TO HIS WORK
IN THE CHAMBER OF WAR AND STATE PROPERTIES IN CUSTRIN.
(WUSTERHAUSEN, NOVEMBER 14, 1730)

His Royal Majesty hereby informs President von Münchow and
Director von Hille that He has resolved, with good and sufficient
reason, that His Highness the Crown Prince is to attend the sessions of the Chamber of War and State Properties in Cüstrin for
instruction in agriculture, finance, administration, excise, and other
subjects.

At first, until further orders from His Majesty, he shall only
sit in, and have no vote, thus attending only as an observer; he is
therefore to be given a small table, at the foot of the room, with
a chair, and ink, pen and paper laid on the table. One of his two
Gentlemen of the Bedchamber is always to be with him, and to sit
at the same table. Since one of them, von Rohwald, has already for
some years been a member of the Chamber of the Kurmark, he is to
have a vote and seat in the Chamber of Neumark, but not to be
placed in charge of any Department.

Since the Crown Prince does not yet understand any of the
business transacted in the Chamber, and has not the least compre-
hension of it, President von Münchow and Director Hille are to
impart to him thorough information on the nature and mutual
connections of questions of excise, manufacture, administration,
agriculture, etc. In order that this may be done profitably and in
proper order and the Crown Prince not confused by the mass of
material, President von Münchow and Director Hille are to proceed systematically and first draw up a proper plan of how they are
to go through one subject after another each day with the Crown
Prince, so that he is always taken on from the easier subjects to
the more difficult. They should thus begin by seeing that he first
learns to write and to despatch files fluently and quickly; they
are therefore to put him in the registry and have a skilled secretary
show him the procedure, also make him do much copying every
day.

After this they are to show him customs questions, then agricultural questions, and instruct him in revenues and the drawing up
of valuations: how many acres go to a holding, how it should be

composed; how to judge its yield and make a valuation of it; how the pastures, livestock, breweries and distilleries, etc., can be used; in short, everything to do with revenue and correct valuations, not in general terms or superficially, but in detail, and thoroughly. They are then to give him specimens of valuations of leaseholds and the balance sheets of offices, and explain everything to him so clearly that he gets a complete understanding of it, and they are to take all imaginable pains to ensure that the Crown Prince understands it through and through. When doing this, President von Münchow and Director Hille are to show him how valuable are a well-ordered household and agriculture, and what it takes to earn a thaler.

They are then to give him documents to read, and to attach someone to him to show him how to read them with profit and make clear summaries of them. Also, in the evenings or when the Crown Prince has some leisure, they are to send one or more Councillors to him to entertain him with clever conversation on all sorts of business connected with the Chamber and out of the instructions for it, and show him the reasons why His Majesty has given this or that order.

When Departmental Councillors have to render accounts, the Crown Prince is to be present, as soon as he understands anything of the matter, and is to be shown the procedure for drawing up and rendering accounts.

When any agricultural, administrative, etc., development takes place in the town of Cüstrin, President von Münchow and Director Hille are to inform the Crown Prince and take him with them, that he may inform himself the better on every point.

The Crown Prince is to write out every week two or three of the reports sent to the Directorate, so that he gets thoroughly used to writing quickly, and a skilled secretary is therefore to give him instructions so that he learns to write quite fluently.

Should, however, the Crown Prince have any doubt why he should not put his name to a report or order, His Majesty will be most particularly pleased if he raises the question at a session and has it explained to him.

To which end the Crown Prince is also to put his signature to all reports and orders of the Küstrin Chamber, but not in one line with the members, but after them, in the middle, as shown on the attached plan.

President von Münchow and Director Hille are further to render His Majesty every two weeks a dutiful and conscientious report whether the Crown Prince is practicing diligently and learning to write fluently and quickly, whether he is getting an idea of economic questions, and whether he is taking pains, or not. But it is His Majesty's will that they shall report the pure truth, with no dissembling or evasion, for His Majesty will, after all, learn the whole truth through other channels, and if He finds that President von Münchow has not written the whole truth, He will make His displeasure felt unsparingly. They are therefore to write the pure and exact truth, and, if they are speaking to and instructing the Crown Prince, they are to tell him courteously that if he is diligent and applies himself properly to learn everything thoroughly, that is the only way in which he can hope one day to enjoy the complete favor of His Majesty. Should he, however, not prove himself diligent and industrious, they are to say to him that they are in duty bound to report to His Majesty to that effect, and that in that case his disgrace will certainly be greater and severer.

His Majesty therefore orders President von Münchow and Director Hille to pay heed to these instructions and to spare no care, pains, or diligence in observing them.

16. Frederick the Great Plans His Coup

These notes, which are in Frederick's own hand, were presumably jotted down immediately on the arrival of news that the Emperor Charles VI had died, on October 20, 1740; but the ideas expressed in them must have been in Frederick's mind before that, for a day or two later he was writing to a friend that "Everything has been foreseen, all arrangements made; it is simply a question of executing plans I have long had in my head." In fact, the first Prussian troops left Berlin on December 4; Frederick led them across the frontier on the sixteenth, and the whole of Silesia was in his possession a few weeks later, except for three fortresses, which were invested. He was thus able to conduct the "negotiations" according to program.

The French original of the jottings is to be found in the *Politische Correspondenz Friedrichs des Grossen*, 43 vols., Ed. J. C. Droysen and others (1879ff.), Vol. I, pp. 90–1.

IDEAS ON POLITICAL PROJECTS TO BE FORMED IN CONNECTION WITH THE DEATH OF THE EMPEROR

SILESIA IS the part of the Imperial succession on which we have the best claims,[1] and that which would suit the House of Brandenburg best; it is right to maintain our claims and to seize the opportunity of the Emperor's death to take possession of the areas concerned.

The superiority of our troops over those of our neighbors, the promptitude with which we can act, and, in sum, the advantage which we possess over our neighbors, is complete, and gives us, in an unforeseen occasion such as this,[2] an infinite superiority over all other European Powers. If we wait to act until Saxony and Bavaria have made the first hostile moves, we shall be unable to prevent Saxony from enlarging her territory, which, however, is entirely contrary to our interests, and in that case we have no good pretext. But if we act at once we keep Saxony down, and by preventing Saxony from acquiring remounts we make it impossible for her to make any move.

England and France are at loggerheads; if France interferes in the affairs of the Empire, England can never allow it, and in this way, each of the two opposed parties will always offer me an advantageous alliance. England can never be jealous of my acquisition of Silesia, since that can do her no harm, and she can, on the contrary, hope for advantages in the present state of her affairs, which require alliances.

Holland will look on indifferently, especially if one guarantees the merchants of Amsterdam the capital which they have invested in Silesia.

---

[1] Brandenburg's "claims" were, in fact, virtually nonexistent. The dynasty had concluded pacts with some of the Piast rulers of Silesian principalities under which the reversions should fall to it, but the Habsburgs had always contended these pacts to be contrary to their own rights both as emperors and as kings of the Lands of the Bohemian Crown, and in 1686 the Great Elector had traded them for possession of the enclave of Schwiebus, which the Emperor Leopold afterward made his son restore, as part of the price for helping him to the title of king. The most that Frederick's own advisers had been able to argue had been that the price was inadequate, and had been extorted "fraudulently."

[2] Charles's death, the result of food poisoning while out hunting, had been very sudden and quite unexpected. He had only just completed his fifty-sixth year.

If we fail to reach satisfactory agreement with England and Holland, we shall certainly be able to do so with France, which in any case will be unable to thwart our designs and will regard with satisfaction the blow to the Imperial House.

There remains Russia. None of the other Powers of which I have spoken are in a position to give us trouble; Russia alone might be able to cause difficulties for us.

Next Spring, we shall not find anyone in our way; thus, if Russia wants to attack us, she can be assured that she will have the Swedes in her rear, so she would be putting herself between the hammer and the anvil. If the Empress is alive, the Duke of Courland,[3] who has very rich estates in Silesia, will court my favor in order to keep them; furthermore, we must shower down among the leaders of the Council the rain of Danae, which will make them think as we want. If the Empress is dead,[4] the Russians will be so occupied with their internal affairs that they will have no time to think about foreign questions; and in any case, it is not impossible to procure the entry into Petersburg of an ass with a load of gold.

I conclude from all this reasoning that we must put ourselves in possession of Silesia before the winter, and negotiate during the winter; then we shall always find cards to play, and we shall negotiate successfully when we are in possession, whereas if we act otherwise, we shall sacrifice our advantages, and we shall never get anything out of simple negotiation, or else the others will impose burdensome conditions on us, for granting us trifles.

FEDERIC

17. Frederick the Great as Others Saw Him (1751)

The following sketch of Frederick's personality and technique of government constitutes the opening of a *"Tableau de la Cour de Berlin,"* sent to Paris in 1751 by Lord Tyrconnell, who had gone to Berlin as minister of France in the previous year. Tyrconnell died suddenly in 1752; the paragraph marked with an asterisk was added by his

[3] Empress Anna's husband.
[4] The empress died on November 28, 1740.

successor, the Chevalier de Latouche. The *"Tableau"* was first printed in 1836 in Paris, in the *Journal de l'Institut Historique* (Vol. V, pp. 13ff.); it has subsequently appeared in German translation in the *Forschungen zur Brandenburgschen und Preussischen Geschichte* (1894) Vol. VII, pp. 88ff., and in G. B. Volz, ed., *Friedrich der Grosse im Spiegel seiner Zeit*, 3 Vols., Berlin, 1934.

The King of Prussia is compact of contradictions. He loves greatness, fame, and, especially, anything that can increase his fame abroad. Nonetheless, he is the shyest, most undecided creature, without a spark of courage or nerve. He always sees the future black and has a mighty dread of it. He is sluggish by nature, and abhors everything known as the art of war. Nonetheless, he overcomes his disposition, and he must be seriously ill if he does not personally command the parade of the guard which he has held daily and does not occupy himself with the details of the service. He is convinced that by this he is impressing Europe and maintaining strict discipline in his army and exactness in all ranks up to his brothers, the Princes. The King rightly regards this as necessary for his reputation in Europe and as the foundation of his power. But for these strong reasons he would perhaps abandon himself to his natural inclination toward solitude and devote himself entirely to literature, poetry and music.

The King is naturally mistrustful and in general thinks ill of all men. He consequently gives his confidence to none and often plays his own Ministers false by misinforming them on the few subjects which he leaves in their hands. He transacts all his business himself, and seldom allows his Ministers to make representations, especially in foreign affairs. He only suffers them from the Ministers of his Directorate General when it is a question of scaling down a few acts of grace granted by him.

*He tells his brothers, the Princes, nothing and places no confidence whatever in them. Consequently, the Royal family is often the witness of disagreements, which are sedulously fostered by the Princess Amalia, a creature of very uneven character.

His heart is not sincere. His first impulse is always to deceive or at least, to leave open a back door, to avoid fulfilling his obligations. As, however, he is very clever, he often perceives that he is seen through, and, since he fears to have his all too well-founded bad name confirmed, he masters himself and goes to work sincerely, particularly in his dealings with Powers which he thinks it his interest to handle with kid gloves. At the present moment this applies only to France. His Majesty certainly feels that France is the only Power on which he can rely for support, and that at the moment when that Power leaves him in the lurch, he will be dropped also by all the other Powers allied with her, and immediately overpowered by the House of Austria, by Russia, England and even by the Court of Dresden. This truth appears to the King of Prussia so obvious that the belief is that it must have the effect of chaining him most closely to France. It is, however, only fair to say that if he has any inclination or attachment, these are for France alone.

The eternal conflict between all the contradictions that make up the King's character makes him impetuous and rash, and sometimes leads him to undertake several mutually irreconcilable enterprises at the same time. But he perceives that they are irreconcilable only on later reflection, and when he has committed himself too far to draw back. Then he tortures his brain to find a way of reconciling them all and hurting no one. His own spirit then often suggests to him such a way, which for the moment he thinks good. He embarks on it without mature consideration, and thus succeeds in heaping embarrassment on embarrassment and making every single person believe that he meant to play him false, whereas his only intention at first had been to unite incompatible things, which, however, thanks to his not having considered them closely, he had not thought to be incompatible.

He is naturally indiscreet, and in this respect commits mistakes which are unforgivable in so talented a man. If one has the chance to observe him frequently and long in a series of *tête à tête* conversations, it is not quite impossible to see through him or even partially to entice his secret out of him by drawing him on to talk, of which he is very fond. But the difficulty is to discover his true mind out of the mass of contradictory things which, mentally lively as he is, he says, especially when he realizes that he has let something drop that he ought not to have said. The person who has the honor of speaking must be very careful not to hesitate or give the appearance of considering what answer to give him; for with his innate mistrust, the King at once imagines that you are trying to deceive him. For the rest, it is his principle to press any who hesitate, and this throws them into such embarrassment that they often speak unguardedly and thus let their secret slip out. He regards this method as infallible, and maintains that it has never failed him.

18. Frederick the Great's Political Testament (1752)

Frederick the Great carried on the family tradition of composing "political testaments" for the instruction of his successor; he even improved on his father in this respect, for he left two of them, a first written in 1752 and a revised and expanded version put down in 1768. The revisions in the latter documentary are, however, simply adaptations to meet changed circumstances; the two do not differ essentially in plan or even in outlook, and we have taken the extracts which follow from the earlier version, as the better known and, in the general opinion, the more characteristic.

Frederick followed fairly closely the general pattern of his father's work, down to the detailed factual descriptions of various conditions and institutions, and even to the comments on the national characteristics of the inhabitants of his different provinces. We have omitted the purely descriptive passages for the same reason as we did the corresponding parts of Frederick William's production (incidentally, an inordinate number of Frederick's pages are taken up with military technicalities). It has also seemed unnecessary to record twice what their rulers thought of the peculiarities of their subjects' characters, and, if one of the two versions was to be left out, there was no question but that it had to be Frederick's, which is far the less entertaining of the two: the strong ale of the older man's pragmatic but robust German somehow turns to milk and water in his son's finicking French. From his chapters on internal administration and on political statecraft in general we have selected only the two relatively short sections below (each of these is given *in extenso*).

The chief interest in Frederick's testament is to be found in his chapters on foreign policy. In these, Frederick departs from his father's model with a vengeance, to give, instead of the other's simple and honest exhortation to eschew aggressive war, a *machtpolitisch* homily of a cynicism so naked that for many years the world was not allowed to see it in its entirety. When the testament was first discovered in the archives, Bismarck forbade the worst parts of it to be published, lest they should damage Prussia's relations with other states, and they saw print only after the fall of the German monarchy.

We, too, omit certain parts of this chapter, but not for Bismarck's reasons; the passages left out by us are either repetitive or of secondary or ephemeral interest. Our text is translated from that published by G. B. Volz, *Das Politische Testament Friedrichs des Grossen (Ergänzungsband* to the editor's *Politische Korrespondenz Friedrichs des Grossen*), in 1920, the first edition to reproduce the censored passages. The extracts given here range through pages 37 to 67 of Volz's text.

Extracts from Frederick the Great's Political Testament of 1752

On Certain Maxims of Policy Relating to the Nobility

An object of policy of the sovereign of this State is to preserve his noble class; for whatever change may come about, he might perhaps have one which was richer, but never one more valorous and more loyal. To enable them to maintain themselves in their possessions, it is necessary to prevent non-nobles from acquiring noble estates and to compel them to put their money into commerce, so that if some gentleman is forced to sell his lands, he may find only gentlemen to buy them.

It is also necessary to prevent noblemen from taking service abroad, to inspire them with an *esprit de corps* and a national spirit: this is what I have worked for, and why, in the course of the first war, I did everything possible to spread the name of "Prussian," in order to teach the officers that, whatever province they came from, they were all counted as Prussians, and that for that reason all the provinces, however separated from one another, form a united body.

It is right that a nobleman should prefer to devote his services to his own country, rather than to any other Power whatever. For this reason, severe edicts have been published against nobles who take service elsewhere without having obtained permission. But since many gentlemen prefer an idle and degraded life to service under arms, it is necessary to draw distinctions and to give preference to those who serve, to the exclusion of those who do not serve, and from time to time to collect together the young gentlemen, in Pomerania, in Prussia, and in Upper Silesia, to put them into cadet schools, and after, to post them to units.

On towns and burghers

I have left the towns in the old provinces the privilege of electing their own magistrates, and have not interfered with these elections unless they were misused and some families of burghers monopolized all the authority to the prejudice of the rest. In Silesia I have deprived them of the franchise, for fear of their filling the councils with men who are devoted to Austria. With time, and when the present generation has passed away, it will be possible to restore the electoral system in Silesia without danger.

On the peasants

I have relaxed [on the Crown estates] the services which the peasants used to perform; instead of six days labor service a week, they now have to perform only three. This has provoked the nobles' peasants, and in several places they have resisted their lords. The sovereign should hold the balance even between the peasant and the gentleman, so that they do not ruin one another. In Silesia the peasants, outside Upper Silesia, are very well placed; in Upper Silesia they are serfs. One will have to try to free them in due course. I have set the example on my Crown lands, where I have begun putting them on the same footing as the Lower Silesians. One should further prevent peasants from buying nobles' lands, or nobles, peasants', because peasants cannot serve as officers in the army, and if the nobles convert peasant holdings into demesne farms, they diminish the number of inhabitants and cultivators.

That a Sovereign Should Carry on the Government Himself

In a State such as this it is necessary for the sovereign to conduct his business himself, because he will, if he is wise, pursue only the public interest, which is his own, while a Minister's view is always slanted on matters that affect his own interests, so that instead of promoting deserving persons he will fill the places with his own creatures, and will try to strengthen his own position by the number of persons whom he makes dependent on his fortunes; whereas the sovereign will support the nobility, confine the clergy within due limits, not allow the Princes of the blood to indulge in intrigues and cabals, and will reward merit without those considerations of interest which Ministers secretly entertain in all their doings.

But if it is necessary for the Prince to conduct the internal administration of his State himself, how much more necessary is it that he should direct his own [foreign] policy, conclude those alliances which suit his purposes, form his own plans, and take up his own line in delicate and difficult situations.

Finance, internal administration, policy and defense are so closely interlinked that it is impossible to deal with one of these branches while passing over the others. If that happens, the Prince is in difficulties. In France, the kingdom is governed by four Ministers: the Minister of Finance, who is called *Contrôleur-général*, and the Ministers of Marine, War, and Foreign Affairs. The four "kings" never harmonize or agree; hence all the contradictions which we see in the government of France: the one pulls down out of jealousy what the other has put up with skill; no system, no planning. Chance governs, and everything in France is done according to the pleasure of Court intrigues: the English know everything that is discussed in Versailles; no secrecy and, consequently, no policy.

A well-conducted government must have a system as coherent as a system of philosophy; all measures taken must be based on sound reasoning, and finance, policy, and military must collaborate toward one aim, the strengthening of the State and the increase of its power. But a system can be the product of only one brain; it must consequently be that of the sovereign's. Idleness, self-indulgence, or weakness are the causes which prevent a Prince from working on the noble task of creating the happiness of his peoples. Such sovereigns make themselves so contemptible that they become the butts and laughingstocks of their contemporaries, and in history books their names are useful only for the dates. They vegetate on thrones that they are unworthy to occupy, absorbed as they are in self-indulgence. A sovereign has not been raised to his high rank, the supreme power has not been conferred on him, to live softly, to grow fat on the substance of the people, to be happy while all others suffer. The sovereign is the first servant of the State. He is well-paid, so that he can support the dignity of his quality; but it is required of him that he shall work effectively for the good of the State and direct at least the chief affairs with attention. He needs, of course, help: he cannot enter into all details, but he should listen to all complaints and procure prompt justice for those threatened by oppression. A woman came to a King of Epirus[1] with a petition; he snubbed her, telling her to leave him in peace. "And why are you King," she replied, "if not to procure justice for me?" A good saying, which Princes should always keep in mind.

We have here the Directorate General, the Colleges of Justice,

---

[1] A mistake; it was Philip of Macedon (see Plutarch, *Demetrius*, c42).

and the Ministers of the Cabinet, who daily submit their reports
to the sovereign with most detailed memoranda on the questions
which call for his decision. In controversial or difficult questions,
the Ministers themselves set out the pros and cons, which makes it
possible for the sovereign to take his decision at a glance, provided that he takes the trouble to read and understand the matter
in question. A sound intellect easily grasps the essential point of
a question. This method of dealing with business is preferable to
the conciliar system practiced elsewhere, because it is not from
big assemblages that wise advice comes, for Ministers are mutually
divided by intrigues, private hatreds and passions intrude into the
affairs of State, the system of debating questions by dispute is
often too lively, casting shadows instead of bringing light, and,
finally, secrecy, which is the soul of business, is never well kept
by so many people.

It may be well for a Prince, when uncertain, to consult the
Minister whom he judges to be the wisest and the most experienced;
if he wants to consult a second, this should be done separately so
as to avoid sowing the seeds of an ineradicable jealousy by pre-
ferring the advice of one man to another's. I shut up my secrets
in my own mind; I keep only one secretary[2] (of whose loyalty I
am satisfied); without corrupting me personally, it is impossible
to guess my designs. The Ministers here are charged only with
Imperial [sic] affairs; all important negotiations, treaties, or alliances pass through my hands.

On Foreign Policy

[When he turns to foreign policy, Frederick points out that "by
our geographical position, we are neighbors of the greatest Princes
of Europe; all these neighbors alike are jealous of us and secret
enemies of our power. The geographical situation of their countries, their ambitions, their interests, all these different combina-
tions determine the principles of their policies, which are more or
less hidden according to time and circumstance."

Frederick then surveys the list of Prussia's enemies: Austria—
by far the most ambitious, and also "of all the European Powers
the one which we have offended most deeply, which will never forget either the loss of Silesia or that part of her authority which we

---

[2] August Friedrich Eichel, Secretary of Cabinet to Frederick.

divide with her in Germany"; England, via Hanover; Russia—only "an accidental enemy" through the personal policy of her chancellor, Bestuzhev (if he could be gotten rid of, "things would revert to their natural condition"); Saxony—"a vessel without a compass; the Netherlands—"without sufficient discernment to know whom they should love and whom hate." Against these, Prussia's natural allies are headed by France, but Frederick includes among them also some other minor powers, principally those which feel themselves threatened by Austria. He goes on:]

In view of the present situation, you can easily see that Prussia will never lack for allies. To choose them, one must divest oneself of any personal hatred and of any prejudice, favorable or unfavorable. The interest of the State is the only consideration that should decide the counsel of a Prince. Our present interest, especially since the acquisition of Silesia, is to remain united with France, as with all the enemies of Austria. Silesia and Lorraine are two sisters, of whom Prussia has married the elder and France the younger. This alliance forces them to follow the same policy. Prussia could not watch unmoved while Alsace and Lorraine were taken from France, and Prussia's diversions in favor of France are efficacious, because they carry the war immediately into the heart of the Hereditary Provinces [of Austria]. France, for similar reasons, cannot suffer Austria to recover Silesia, because that would weaken too greatly an ally of France, which is useful to her for the affairs of the North and of the Empire and whose diversions (as I have just said) provide certain safety for Lorraine and Alsace, in case of acute and unforeseen danger. . . .

I should add one thing to these considerations: if we were allied with England and the House of Austria (not to mention that it would be against our interests), we could not promise ourselves any aggrandizement from that side, whereas, united with France, we can hope for acquisitions in case of war, if good fortune attends the efforts of our arms.

Whatever we might expect from war, my present system is to prolong the peace, so far as this is possible, without shaking the majesty of the State, because France is in a condition of complete lethargy, the maladministration of her finances having rendered her almost incapable of presenting herself on the scene of Bellona [i.e., battle] with the power and dignity that become her, because Sweden is a name without power behind it, because France has been so neglectful as to lose her hold on Spain,[3] which prevents us from making a diversion in Italy.

There are also other reasons. It is not in our interest to reopen the war; a lightning stroke, like the conquest of Silesia, is like a book the original of which is a success, while the imitations of it fall flat. We have brought on our heads the envy of all Europe through the acquisition of this fine Duchy, which has put all our neighbors on the alert. There is not one who does not distrust us. My life is too short to restore them to a sense of security advantageous to our interests.

For the rest, would war suit us while Russia stands powerfully armed on our frontiers and only awaits the moment to act against us (which, however, she could not do without help from English subsidies), and a diversion by that Power would upset all our plans at the very beginning of our operations? In such circumstances, the safest course is to let the peace run on and to await developments in readiness. For these developments to favor our enterprises, it would be necessary for Bestuzhev, that Minister-Emperor of Russia in the pay of the Austrian Court, to fall into disgrace, and for us to be able to win over his successor by corruption; for the death of the King of England to plunge England into the dissensions of a minority; for there to be a Suleiman on the throne of Constantinople and an ambitious and all-powerful Minister-President in France. Then, in such a conjuncture, is the time to act, although it is not necessary to be the first on the stage. My advice would be to let the belligerent parties fire their first shots and to take up arms only when the others have exhausted themselves by the struggle. This would suit us the better because we should by this circumspect conduct have put ourselves in a more advantageous position, and, while our financial resources would be unequal to a long war, we should still be able to last out the three or four final campaigns, following the maxim of Cardinal Fleury: he remains the master of his adversary who has the last crown in his pocket.

There are two kinds of war: those made out of vanity, and those made out of interest. They are madmen who undertake wars of the

---

[3] Under the Treaty of Aranjuez (June 14, 1752) France had concluded a Treaty of Neutrality for Italy with Spain and the king of Sardinia. Austria and Spain had concluded a similar treaty immediately before. The result of these was to free Austria from the fear of attack in Italy.

former kind; to engage in those of the latter it is necessary to have made the right preparations and not to divulge one's secret and one's objectives until peace becomes inevitable. He who reveals his designs prematurely renders them abortive, because he gives his enemies and his enviers time to oppose them. He who knows how to keep silent can make fine acquisitions, or at the worst, he does not lose prestige by being forced to make a peace less advantageous than he had hoped.

We must constantly watch Russia and the Austrians, Russia with respect to Polish and Swedish affairs and to the alliances which she might plan between Poland and the Court of Vienna. Austria, equally, calls for close attention, as the chief of our enemies, who is planning to place the Prince of Lorraine on the throne of Poland[4] and would like to play the despot in the Empire, all things which we could not suffer. It will be asked—how prevent this? The means dictated by good sense are these: to ally ourselves with the enemies of our enemies, that is, with France, Sweden, some Princes of the Empire, if possible, with the King of Sardinia, and the Turk himself; to work to break up the Polish Diets, dispensing some sums in the right quarters; to insinuate to the Poles that the Queen of Hungary and the Empress of Russia are dangerous enemies, whose ambition it is to dispose of the throne of Poland without taking heed of the Republic and to make the Duke of Lorraine sovereign, after having placed him on it; but above all, to make the Turks feel that it is contrary to their policy to allow Hungary and Poland to be united in the same family.

Of the conduct to be adopted toward the European Powers

A man well-versed in policy must have a conduct which is always different and always adapted to the circumstances in which he is placed and the persons with whom he has to deal. It is a grave political fault always to act haughtily, to want to decide everything by force, or, again, always to use softness and suppleness. A man who always follows a uniform conduct is soon penetrated, and one must not be penetrated. If your character is known, your enemies will say: "We will do this and that, then he will do that," and they will not be deceiving themselves; whereas if one

---

[4] Charles of Lorraine, brother of Maria Theresa's husband, Francis Stephen, and husband of her sister Marianne.

changes and varies one's conduct, one misleads them and they deceive themselves on issues which they thought to have foreseen. But so prudent a conduct requires that one watch oneself constantly, and far from abandoning oneself to one's passions, follow slavishly the line which one's real interests dictate. The great art is to conceal one's designs, and for that one must veil one's character and reveal only a firmness measured and tempered by justice.

[After these words, Frederick describes in considerable detail the line of conduct he had followed in previous years in his negotiations with the various powers. 'Thus," he ends this section, "each occasion, each person, calls for a different line of conduct. If it is time for a rupture, it is well to explain oneself firmly and haughtily; but the thunder must not growl unless the lightning falls at the same time. If one has many enemies, one must divide them, segregate the one which is the most irreconcilable, concentrate one's fire on him, negotiate with the others, lull them to sleep, conclude separate peaces, even at a loss, and, once the principal enemy has been crushed, there is always time to turn back and fall on the others, under the pretext that they have not fulfilled their engagements."

Political Projects

Now follow chapters on "the qualities of negotiators," on "corruptions which must be made and how to guard against them in one's own circle," and on "great political projects." This last ends:]

All this shows that great projects undertaken prematurely never succeed, and that policy, being too much at the mercy of chance, does not allow the human spirit to control events unborn and all that falls within the field of future contingencies. Policy lies in profiting by favorable conjunctures, rather than in preparing them in advance. This is why I advise you not to conclude treaties formed in anticipation of uncertain events, and to keep your hands free, so that you can take your side according to the hour. the place, the situation of your affairs, in a word, as your interest then dictates to you. I served myself well by acting in this way in 1740, and I am doing the same at present in the Polish situation.[5] I have warned France of the designs of the House of Austria,

---

[5] The Austrian plan to put Charles of Lorraine on the throne of Poland.

I have urged her to awaken the Turk, but I am taking care not
to tie my hands by treaties, and I am waiting on events before
taking up my line.

Political Pipedreams (Rêveries Politiques)

So much for the substance and basis of the line that should be
followed in this State. Let us pass to the world of fantasy. Politics
has its own metaphysic, and just as there is no philosopher who
does not amuse himself by constructing his system and explaining
abstractions according to his own genius, so it is permissible for
statesmen, also, to divert themselves in the spacious field of chimeri-
cal projects, which may sometimes become real if one does not
lose sight of them, and if successive generations, marching toward
the same goal, are sufficiently skilled to hide their designs deeply
from the curious and penetrating eyes of the European Powers.

Machiavelli says that any disinterested Power which might be
found among the ambitious Powers would certainly end by perishing.[6] I regret it, but I am forced to admit that Machiavelli is
right. Princes are bound to have ambition, but it must be prudent,
measured, and illuminated by reason. If the desire of self-aggrandizement does not procure acquisitions for the prince-statesman,
at least it sustains his power, because the same means which he pre-
pares for offensive action are always there to defend the State if
defense proves necessary, and if he is forced so to use them.

There are two ways by which aggrandizement is achieved:
rich successions or conquests. . . .

Successions Which Could Revert to the Royal House

[This section enumerates the territories which the head of the
House of Hohenzollern could claim as of hereditary right, on the
extinction of the previous ruling line: these are the margravates
of Bayreuth and Anspach, Prussia's claim to which is described
as "incontestable" (in fact, they were united under one hand in
1769 and reverted to Prussia in 1791), and Mecklenburg, where
Frederick admits his case to be more arguable, but the question
is not urgent, as the line is in no apparent danger of extinction.

---

[6] Presumably Machiavelli's dictum in Chap. 15 of *Il Principe:* "*Un uomo,
che veglia fare in tutte le parti professione di buono, conviene che rovini
infra tanti, che non suono buoni.*"

This section is followed by the much more controversial one which was the chief victim of Bismarck's blue pencil:]

Acquisitions by right of interest (*par droit de bienséance*)

Of all the provinces of Europe there are none which would suit the State better than Saxony, Polish Prussia, and Swedish Pomerania, because all three round it off.

But Saxony would be the most useful: it would set the frontier back furthest, and would cover Berlin, that seat of empire, the residence of the Royal family, and the site of the treasury, the High Courts of Justice, the financial administration, and the mint, that capital which is too extensive to be defended, and the fortifications of which were dismantled, mistakenly, by my father.[7] Saxony remedies the weakness of the capital and gives it double coverage, by the Elbe and by the mountains which separate it from Bohemia. If one were master of Saxony, it would be necessary to fortify Torgau, to build a fortress in the style of Hüningen[8] near Wittenberg, but closer to the Elbe, to work on the height beyond Zittau and on the other height this side of Peterswald; by these two great forts one would block those two roads into Bohemia: there would remain to be defended only those leading to Carlsbad, Teplitz, and Gera, but those places would be harder for an Austrian army to pass because it would have to bring its supplies by cart along terrible, long, and almost impassable roads. A competent general would find it easy to defend these three last adits, and the Electorate would be covered and surrounded by a double barrier.

If it proved impossible, after all, to annex the whole of Saxony, one could content oneself with Lusatia and take the course of the Elbe for frontier, which would fulfill the desired purpose, partly by rounding off the frontier, and by three fortresses and a river, presenting a formidable obstacle covering the capital against enemy assault.

You will no doubt think that it is not enough to indicate which are the countries which we should like to have: one must also suggest the means of acquiring them. Here they are: you must dissemble and hide your designs, profit by junctures, wait patiently for those favorable to us, and, when they arrive, act vigorously. What

[7] The greater part of the defenses of Berlin on the Kolln side had been dismantled between 1734 and 1737.

[8] The fortress of Hüningen had been built by the famous French military engineer, Vauban.

would facilitate this conquest would be if Saxony were in alliance with the Queen of Hungary and if that Princess or her descendants broke with Prussia. That would be a pretext to march into Saxony, disarm its troops, and establish oneself in force in the country. You could even tranquilize France by representing to her that it is contrary to good policy (when one is at war) to leave in one's rear an enemy so powerful as Saxony. It would be easy to disarm the Saxons. . . .

[The next paragraphs consist of a purely technical plan of campaign to achieve this end. Then Frederick goes on:]

For this plan to be completely successful, it would be necessary for Russia to be at war with Turkey while we are at war with Austria and Saxony, and it would also be necessary to incite as many enemies as possible against the Court of Vienna, so as not to have all its forces against us.

After having subdued Saxony, it would be necessary to carry the war into Moravia. A decisive victory won in that province would open the gates of Olmütz and Brünn and carry the war near the capital. It would be well, before the campaign is over, to raise 40,000 men in Saxony, to hire troops from the Princes of the Empire, and to procure new forces. During the following campaign one would work to raise Hungary. Twenty thousand men would enter Bohemia and would easily conquer that undefended kingdom. If, at that juncture, England was governed by an indolent King, it would be unnecessary to bother about the Electorate of Hanover; but if it happens to be a warlike Prince, one will have to persuade France to make a diversion (using auxiliary troops) in the Electorate, which will free Prussia's hands. This Hanoverian expedition would force England to accept the conditions imposed by France and its allies, and, under the peace, France would acquire Flanders, and Prussia would restore Moravia to the Queen of Hungary and would trade Bohemia against Saxony with the King of Poland.

I admit that this plan cannot be realized without a great deal of good luck; but if one fails in it, one has lost no prestige, provided that one has not divulged one's secret, and even if one did not gain the whole of Saxony at the first stroke, it is certain that it would be very easy to cut off part of it. The chief points would be that Russia and the Queen of Hungary would have to be engaged in a war against the Turks, France, and the King of Sardinia.

The province which would suit us best after Saxony would be Polish Prussia. It separates Prussia from Pomerania and prevents us from sending support to the former by the difficulties presented by the Vistula and by fear of inroads the Russians that might make through the port of Danzig. You will see this more plainly if you consider that the Kingdom of Poland cannot be attacked except by the Muscovites, that if they descend on Danzig, they cut the army of Prussia off from any connection with this country, and that, if that army was forced to retire, it would be necessary to send them a considerable force to help them cross the Vistula.

I do not think that the best way of adding this province to the Kingdom would be by force of arms, and I should be tempted to say to you what Victor Amadeus, King of Sardinia, said to Charles Emmanuel: "My son, you must eat the Milanese up like artichokes, leaf by leaf." Poland is an electoral Kingdom; when one of its Kings dies it is perpetually troubled by factions. You must profit from these and gain, in return for neutrality, sometimes a town, sometimes another district, until the whole has been eaten up.

Those who are fortunate enough to achieve this acquisition will no doubt fortify Thorn, Elbing, and Marienwerder, and will even strengthen the smallest places along the Vistula, which would frustrate all enterprises which Russia might launch against us. Their regular troops are certainly not to be feared, but their Kalmuks and Tartars bring fire and destruction, devastate countrysides, carry away peoples into captivity, and burn all the places of which they make themselves masters. This is how they behaved in Finland, and this should make you try to avoid war with Russia so far as your reputation allows it.

The acquisitions which one makes by the pen are always preferable to those made by the sword. One runs fewer risks, and ruins neither one's purse nor one's army. I think that in making the pacific conquest of Prussia, it would be absolutely necessary to reserve Danzig for the last mouthful, because this acquisition would raise a great outcry among the Poles, who export all their wheat through Danzig, and would fear, with justice, being made dependent on Prussia by the taxes which Prussia could put, through the Vistula and the port of its discharge, on all the commodities which the Sarmatian lords sell to other countries.

Swedish Pomerania is the province that would suit us best after those of which I have spoken. This acquisition could only be made by treaties. I think that the plan is even more chimeric than the others. It could, however, be brought off in the following way: Russia, as the most considerable northern Power, might bring Sweden into alliance with Prussia, to establish a counterweight in the balance of power. If, then, in a happy conjuncture when Russia had a war on her hands, and Sweden conceived the plan of recovering Livonia, why should Prussia not promise her help on condition that, when the operation had been carried through, Sweden ceded Prussia the part of Pomerania that lies beyond the Peene? The difficulty of attacking Russia from the side of Livonia and Estonia is that it is necessary to have superiority at sea. The Swedish fleet is weak, and we have not a single galley. It would thus be impossible to besiege Reval, Narva, and the other fortresses, not to mention that the problem of supplies might be entirely insuperable, and, even supposing Prussia to succeed in conquering Livonia, has it not been practically proved that Sweden would be unable to advance through Finland, prevented as she would be by the Russian fortresses which their sitings render impregnable? Thus, after much blood had been spilt, the end would be a draw, and each party would remain in possession of what it had possessed under the *status quo ante*.

This is about all that I can say to you on the subject of acquisitions which would profit us. If this House produces great Princes, if the discipline of the army is kept up to its present level, if the sovereigns economize in time of peace, so as to have the money in hand for war if they understand how to draw profit from events with skill and prudence, and, finally, if they are themselves clear in their purpose, I do not doubt that the State will continue to grow and expand and that with time Prussia will become one of the most considerable Powers of Europe. . . .

Conclusion

[After this, Frederick again sketches the present weaknesses of Prussia and once more surveys "the changes that might occur in Europe" a chapter that is largely repetitive, but contains the admission that his conscience "was not easy about his behavior toward Maria Theresa." He ends this chapter with the following passage:]

You will perhaps ask how I advise you to act in the event of all these changes that I foresee? I am not rash enough to give you advice about distant and uncertain events. These things are too vague for me to be able to prescribe to you exact rules on what course you should follow. I content myself with repeating what I have already said to you in more detail. Keep a prudent control over your finances, so as to have money when you need it; make no alliances except with those who have exactly the same interests as yours; never make treaties binding you to act in contingencies which are remote, but wait for the case to arise before deciding on your line and acting accordingly; take good care not to place your trust in the number and good faith of your allies; count only on yourself; then you will never deceive yourself, and look on your allies and your treaties only as second strings. A large number of treaties harms more than it helps; conclude few of them, always to the point and of such nature that you have all the advantage from them and involve yourself in the least risks.

The policy of small princes is a tissue of cheatings; that of great princes consists of much prudence, of dissimulation, and of love of glory. It is a great mistake for a statesman to cheat always; he is soon seen through and despised. Keen-sighted spirits reckon on a consistent conduct; that is why one must, as much as one can, change one's game, disguise it and turn oneself into a Proteus, appearing now lively, now slow, now warlike, and now pacific. This is the way to confuse one's enemies and to make them circumspect in the designs they entertain against you. It is not only good to vary one's conduct: it must, above all, be framed to fit the situation of the moment, the time, the place, and the persons with whom one is dealing. Never threaten your enemies: a barking dog does not bite. Put pleasantness into your negotiations: soften down haughty or offensive expressions; never carry small disputes too far; count your own pride for nothing and the interest of the State for everything; be discreet in your business, and dissimulate your designs. If the glory of the State obliges you to draw the sword, see that the thunder and the lightning fall on your enemies simultaneously.

You must not break treaties except for important reasons. You may do so if you fear that your allies are making a separate peace, and if you have the means and the time to forestall them, if lack of money prevents you from continuing the war, or, finally, if important advantages demand it of you. Coups of this kind can be made once, or at most, twice in a lifetime, but they are not expedients to which one may resort every day.

19. Frederick the Great on Industrialization

The following instruction of 1752 from Frederick the Great to one of his privy councillors is given as an illustration of the importance which Frederick attached to industrialization, especially as a means of keeping the national balance of payments in equilibrium. The large sums spent by German states on the importation of silk and silk goods from France and Italy were a particular and constant grievance to their princes and their advisers (cf. on this point Hörnigk's outburst in *Austria Above All* above, Part I, pp. 70–78, and not least to Frederick, who spreads himself at some length on the subject in his *Political Testament* of 1752 (pp. 17–18, ed. Volz). A detailed account of the development of the silk industry in Brandenburg during his reign may be found in the *Acta Borussica, Die preussische Seidenindustrie im 18en Jahrhundert*, ed. O. Hintze, 3 vols., (Berlin, 1892). Frederick was not, however, the founder of the industry; the first beginnings had been made by the Great Elector.

The text which follows is translated from R. Stadelmann, *Preussens Könige in ihrer Tätigkeit für die Landeskultur, Friedrich der Grosse* (Berlin, 1882), No. 113, p. 306.

TO PRIVY FINANCE COUNCILLOR FAESCH

Since I have seen from your report of the ninth that you are of the opinion that except for the few factories listed by you, which in themselves are very good and necessary, we need no more factories in this country, but have more than enough, I cannot refrain from informing you that I must conclude that you can have made only a very superficial survey and examination of the extracts and balance sheets of imports and exports sent in by the Cameral; certainly, if you had looked attentively at the rubrics in them of imports from foreign countries, you would easily have seen from the details specified in them how very many objects there are which at present we have to get from abroad, and that we could spare ourselves that necessity by setting up our own factories here or sometimes by extending beginnings already made. The example of silk alone will make my ideas clearer to you. We have made a small beginning in setting up silk factories here, but they are still very far from sufficient to meet all our domestic demand for silken goods of all kinds, much less to meet the demands of neighboring countries; so that we are forced to use a very considerable quantity of foreign silks, importing them, and sending the money for them abroad. I cannot accept it if you object that you could not see this out of the Cameral extracts; if you had only taken the total or sum cost of the imported foreign silks and had reckoned out, taking approximate prices, how much this worked out to per piece and ell and then how many pieces can be made in a year on one frame and how many frames we are still short of, you would have seen that we are still lacking in a considerable number of such frames, which could be established here with assurance of success. The same attention would have shown you that we still have in our provinces no vellum factories, or not nearly enough, yet the consumption of vellum is so large that big sums of money have to go out of the country for it.

Besides these examples, you would have found a hundred more similar things for which we have at present no factories and will gradually have to establish them. I therefore require you to go through the extracts (which are being returned to you) again, with closest attention, and report accordingly. You must pay special attention to the question of which factories are particularly advantageous to each province and whether there are too many of any kind in some province, in which case they must be established in another, in which they are lacking. You appeal, indeed, to the order isued by the Cameral President that shortage of factories is the Camera's business; but when you consider with how many different questions the President is charged, whereas the Fifth Department has no other business, you will see yourself that it is its duty to work on the question with all attention.

FRIEDRICH

Potsdam, August 11, 1752

20. Abuses in the Kurmark

This document, dated 1755, is self-explanatory. The text is translated from Stadelmann, *op. cit.*, No. 139, pp. 326ff.

TO THE CHAMBER OF THE KURMARK
Remedy of abuses which have taken place in respect of conversion of peasant holdings; oppression of unfree subjects.

Whereas most humble reports and representations have reached His Royal Majesty that the Directorate of new establishments and enterprises in the Prignitz was, under Pfeiffer, conducted in such bad and conscienceless fashion, and so confusedly that:

1. Sundry nobles laid hands on many peasant holdings and messuages under the pretext of establishing new enterprises and converted them into demesne farms, sometimes settling small men of mean estate on them, most of whom, being treated and regarded as serfs, and no proper contracts of succession having been made with them, soon ran away;

In connection with this abuse His Majesty has further been informed that:

2. The greater part of the nobles in the Prignitz have neither any regular system nor fixed rules for the dues and services obligatory on the peasant and subject, so that the latter are pressed and squeezed dry. And finally,

3. That various of the Privy Councillors of the Prignitz have departed very far from their duties and obligations, so that instead of regarding the best welfare of the land and the maintenance of the subjects and the equal allocation of their burdens, they have simply worked for the destruction of the land, robbed the subjects in various ways, and freed their own properties from all haulage duties and saddled others, even subjects of the Crown Agency, with them,

His Royal Majesty therefore feels obliged to inform the Chamber of Kurmark of all these things and at the same time to reprimand them most sharply and severely for not having—as their oath and their duty required—kept a closer eye on these practices, which are so detrimental to the land and contrary to His Royal Majesty's paternal intentions, and either themselves remedied the same or reported them properly to His Majesty, the result of which, and of the fact that the said Chamber has, in particular, not paid better attention to the new establishments, is that His confidence in the said Chamber has been greatly weakened, and He is obliged to signify to them His extreme displeasure.

In order, then, to remedy these abuses, which are so detrimental to the land and its inhabitants, and to put all things back on a proper footing, His Royal Majesty hereby makes known His most solemn will and command that, seeing that edicts exist that no nobles shall convert any peasant holdings into demesne land, still less, turn them into home farms, and that the introduction of small day laborers and farmhands to replace the peasants is insufficient, and also forbidden, and further, that His Royal Majesty has many times told the Chamber, in connection with the new establishments, that no man shall be done violence and wrong thereby, and that the Chamber must see to this, the said Chamber shall now enact, and diligently enforce, that the peasant holdings converted by nobles to demesne farms shall be resettled in their entirety with peasants, and these shall not be taken as serfs, but proper contracts of succession—under no circumstances limited to one or a period of years—shall be concluded for the tenure of the holdings and messuages. The Chamber shall, under pain of the highest Royal displeasure, not only do this, but shall keep a watchful eye on it, continuously.

As to point 2, that the great majority of the nobles in the Prignitz, or at least very many of them, have no system of fixed rules for the dues and services to which the peasants are bound: His Royal Majesty wishes this point to be settled and determined once and for all, in such fashion that regular rules shall be drawn up and the nobles be told what services and dues they are entitled to receive in the future from their peasants and subjects, which rules shall be based on what is customarily accepted in the locality as equitable and tolerable, and, if no regular customary law exists, what is the law and custom in the circles neighboring to the Prignitz shall be adopted. Nor can the said nobles defend themselves by appealing to a historic right to levy dues from their peasants and subjects at their pleasure, for here the general welfare must simply be put ahead of private interests, and while His Royal Majesty is glad to protect His nobles in their rights, He will not allow the subjects to be oppresed and sucked dry thereby.

Finally, as regards point 3, regarding those Provincial Councillors who have grossly neglected their duties, as has been said of many of them: it would be most detrimental to the service of His Majesty and to the subjects if such persons were allowed to retain their offices further. The Chamber shall therefore, after a short, quite summary investigation, remove and cashier all such persons and replace them by others who are worthy and honorable.

Potsdam, November 1, 1755

21. Frederick the Great Before Leuthen

In the summer of 1757, a year after the outbreak of the Seven Years' War, Frederick's position was exceedingly serious. A Russian force had invaded Prussia; a Swedish, Pomeranian, and a French, the territory of his allies, Brunswick and Hanover. Austrian raiders had actually penetrated into Berlin, only, indeed, to retire from it after levying a tribute; but a large Austrian army was advancing into Silesia. Frederick was a prey to the worst forebodings; his correspondence from these weeks is full of desperate phrases such as: "I shall bless Heaven for its goodness if it grants me the grace of perishing sword in hand. . . . How can a Prince survive his State, his nation's glory, his own reputation?" Nevertheless, he rallied with great determination, and on November 5 routed a French force at Rossbach, in Saxony, then turned east to meet the Austrians, who by now had taken Breslau and were holding strong positions in front of it. Their force looked to be much stronger than Frederick's, for it numbered 60,000 men to his 40,000, but the superiority was more apparent than real, for a considerable proportion of the Austrian army was composed of levies from the Empire, many of whom were unreliable: Würtembergers, whose sympathies were rather with Lutheran Prussia than with Catholic Austria, or Bavarians, to whom Austria was a hereditary (and also a recent) enemy, whereas Frederick's force now consisted almost entirely of Prussians, his own least reliable auxiliaries having already deserted. Frederick had a superiority in heavy guns (78 pieces to 65) and, most important perhaps of all, the Austrian commander, Prince Charles of Lorraine, was conspicuously and notoriously incompetent.

The odds were, however, still so great as to make the venture of attacking in face of them seem most hazardous, and to inspire Frederick to compose one of his (not infrequent) "military testaments," directing what should be done if he fell on the field (see Doc. A, below). But he felt the situation to be such that the risk had to be taken, and on the night of December 3 he assembled his senior officers and addressed them in the terms reproduced below (Doc. B). In fact, the situation was changed the next day by the Austrians moving out of their positions into the open country round the village of Leuthen. Delighted at this move ("The fox," he cried, "has come out of its earth"), Frederick postponed his attack for twenty-four hours, opening it on December 5, with successful results. The losses suffered by the two armies in the fighting were, indeed, almost equal (about 1,500 dead and 5,000 wounded on each side), but the Austrians, confused by Frederick's successful tactics, retreated in disorder, losing, in addition to their dead and wounded, over 13,000 prisoners (almost all of them disaffected elements), and by a few days later, had re-evacuated Silesia.

The victory seemed so decisive that Frederick actually believed that it would bring peace. This proved not to be the case; the war was destined to drag on for more than five years more, and Leuthen proved to be no more than an episode in its checkered course. The two documents that follow have been picked, not because they were decisive, but because they are as characteristic as any that can be found in the long series of their likes. The address to the troops is, moreover, famous. The text is translated from G. B. Volz, ed., *Die Werke Friedrichs des Grossen*, 10 vols. (Berlin, 1913ff.), Vol. III, pp. 224ff., who himself took it from A. Retzow, *Charakteristik der wichtigsten Ereignisse des Siebenjährigen Krieges* (Berlin, 1802).

A. FREDERICK TO MINISTER COUNT FINKENSTEIN

I HAVE issued orders to my Generals concerning all matters which must be done after the battle, whether the fortune of it be good or evil. For the rest, as concerns myself, I wish to be buried at Sans Souci, without display or pomp, and at night. I desire that my body should not lie in state, but that I should be taken there without ceremony and buried at night.

As to public affairs, the first thing should be that an order should be issued to all Commanding Officers to swear allegiance to my brother. If the battle is won, my brother is nevertheless to send a messenger to France to carry the news, and at the same time, to negotiate terms of peace, with full powers. My will is to be opened, and I discharged my brother of all the money legacies in it, because the desolate condition of his finances will make it impossible for him to fulfill them. I commend to him my aides-de-camp, especially Wobersnow, Krusemark, Oppen and Lentulus. This is to be taken as a military testament. I commend all my domestic household to his care.

November 28, 1757   FREDERIC

B. FREDERICK'S ADDRESS TO HIS SENIOR OFFICERS

AFTER SUPPER the King ordered all Generals and Commanding Officers to come to his quarters, and there said to them, with mournful solemnity and, at times, with tears in his eyes:

"Gentlemen! I have had you brought here, firstly, in order to thank you for the loyal services that you have rendered to the Fatherland, and to me. I recognize them with feelings of deep emotion. There is hardly one among you who has not distinguished himself by great and most honorable feats. Relying on your courage and experience, I have prepared a plan for the battle that I shall, and must, wage tomorrow. I shall, against all the rules of the art, attack an enemy which is nearly twice as strong as ourselves and entrenched on high ground. I must do it, for if I do not, all is lost. We must defeat the enemy, or let their batteries dig our graves. This is what I think and how I propose to act. But if there is anyone among you who thinks otherwise, let him ask leave here to depart. I will grant it him, without the slightest reproach."

At this point Frederick paused. There was a dead silence, broken, we are told, only by some sobs; but no one moved. Frederick went on:

"I thought that none of you would leave me; so now I count entirely on your loyal help, and on certain victory. Should I fall, and be unable to reward you for what you will do tomorrow, our Fatherland will do it. Now go to the camp and tell your regiments what I have said to you here, and assure them that I shall watch each of them most closely. The cavalry regiment that does not charge the enemy at once, on the word of command, I shall have unhorsed immediately after the battle and turned into a garrison regiment. The infantry regiment which begins to falter for a moment, for whatever reason, will lose its colors and its swords, and I will have the braid cut off its uniforms. Now, gentlemen, farewell: by this hour tomorrow we shall have defeated the enemy, or we shall not see one another again."

22. Land Settlement and Amelioration in the Neumark

This document, dated 1766, again explains itself. The text is translated from Stadelmann, *op. cit.*, No. 176, pp. 353ff.

To Privy Councillor von Breekenhoff

Instructions for the reclamation of the Warthe Marshes

1. YOU MUST see to it that the villages and farms are sited, so far as possible, on hills and elevations, so that there is no danger of the farmers and their livestock drowning in cases of unavoidable flooding; also, the cultivators on the hills can employ their manure better than those in the marshes, and thus obtain larger yields.

2. The old Cameral villages near Landsberg have more arable and pasture than they use; much of that they lease to Poles and sell the hay from them. These tracts must be taken from them and settled with new families, in order that these areas in My country may be made productive and that I thereby get more manpower, and that the money may remain in the country.

3. Timber for the 1,370 large families [i.e., families on large holdings] who are farming their land at their own expense, in return for certain "free years," is to be supplied free of charge by the landlords on whose estates they have been settled, because they [the landlords] thereby get more subjects, and also more revenues.

For the settlement of the 1,369 small families, I am prepared to provide the timber gratis out of My forests, but only from the most outlying tracts on the Upper Drage, viz., Sabin, Balster and Regenthin; this is then to be floated down the river and the raftsmen's wages paid out of the sum set aside for the building costs.

4. When the uncultivated marshes outside Landsberg are allocated, 2,000 Magdeburg yokes of the so-called Great Burghers' Marsh are to be reserved for the town's timber. These 2,000 yokes are to be divided into 20 fellings, one of which shall be assigned to the town each year for its timber; for the town of Landsberg will be unable, given proper management, to consume this amount of

timber in twenty years, since as much will always grow up in the first felling areas.

5. Since the citizens of Landsberg are objecting so strongly against exchanging their present pastures—to their own advantage—they are to be left with their old pastures and the colonists settled on the new, virgin pastures.

6. Since the municipal and Cameral funds in Landsberg have fallen into such confusion and disorder that no one really knows what he has to collect or what really belongs to which fund, the two funds are to be separated and put in order. Half the surplus left after payment of the interest charges is to be allocated to the town and half to the Camera. This will result in increasing both funds substantially.

Berlin, December 23, 1766.   FRIEDRICH

23. Frederick II and the Partition of Poland

As shown by the quotation given elsewhere[1] from his first "political testament," the idea of enriching himself at the expense of Poland was early in Frederick's mind and was even something of a fixation there; he repeated the passage quoted in his second testament almost verbatim and had even been advocating the course earlier yet, while still crown prince. But, as his testament shows, he hoped to get the prize without fighting for it, and, when the question became present, he was nervous and hesitant, especially after a first, very tentative suggestion put forward by him (in appearance, simply the report of a suggestion made by another[2]) had been coldly received by the Russian minister. Then the suggestion was put to him again, this time by the Austrian minister, Count Nugent, whose idea it was that Prussia should restore Silesia to Austria, compensating herself in Poland. Frederick reported this to his brother, Prince Henry, who was then in Saint Petersburg, on the empress's invitation, and received in reply the uninhibited answer given below as Document A. Frederick was then in one of his timorous moods, and his reply, Document B, is cautious, although it may be remarked that his hesitations were due only to considera-

[1] See above, p. 343.
[2] Count Lynar.

tions of expediency, not of principle (also that neither brother, apparently, thought the idea of surrendering Silesia to merit even a word).

But in the autumn the empress's objections appeared to wane, and in January, 1771, she told Prince Henry that she did not see why other powers should not follow Austria's example. In fact, Austria had by now begun to set a dangerous precedent. When she had first occupied the Szepes (Zips) area in the summer of 1769, it had been at the invitation of the king of Poland himself (whose opponents were marshaling in the area), and Kaunitz had formally announced that the occupation was not to be permanent. But since then, Joseph II had been arguing that Austria ought not to miss the chance of formally recovering the Szepes, which was historically Hungarian and had never been ceded to Poland, but only pledged to her. Worse, Austrian troops had begun occupying areas of Galicia well to the north of the indisputable Hungarian frontier.

In this situation, when Prince Henry brought Catherine's message to Frederick, its reception brought about what Prussian historians have called "the decisive turn in Frederick's policy." This is shown in Documents C and D.

Documents A and B are taken from R. Koser's *Aus der Vorgeschichte der ersten Teilüng Poles"* (Sitzungsberichte [reports of sessions] der Königlichen Akademie zu Berlin, 1908), pp. 286ff; Documents C and D are Nos. 19687 and 19710 from the *Politische Korrespondenz Friedrichs des Grossen*, Vol. XXX. See also the commentary by G. B. Volz in the Academy's *Sitzungsberichte*.

A. PRINCE HENRY TO FREDERICK (SAINT PETERSBURG, JUNE 14, 1770)

I ADMIT that my imagination was struck by this idea, the first time that you have done me the honor of speaking of proposals made to you, however vague. But if it is a chimera,[1] it is such an agreeable one that I find it difficult to renounce. I should like to see you master of the coasts of the Baltic, sharing with the most formidable German Prince the influence that those Powers, united, might exercise in Europe. If it is a dream, it is a very gracious one, and you may imagine that the interest that I take in your glory makes me wish to see it realized.

---

[1] In the chapter of his first political treatment which deals with foreign affairs, Frederick first gives a factual survey of conditions in various countries, then writes: "*venons-en à présent au chimérique*"—it is in this section that he dreams of annexing West Prussia. The corresponding section in the second version is headed "*Rêves et projets chimériques.*"

B. Frederick to Prince Henry (Potsdam, June 25, 1770)

I see, my dear brother, that you are blessed with a hearty appetite in political affairs. But I, who am old, have lost that which I possessed in my youth. Not that your ideas are not excellent, but one must have the wind of fortune in one's sails for such enterprises to succeed, and I no longer dare, or am able, to flatter myself of this. It is, however, always good to keep these plans in reserve, to realize them if the occasion presents itself. We are placed between two Great Powers, Austria and Russia; it is certain that, to keep the balance between them without risk, we are too weak at present to acquit ourselves well; but the biggest evil is that neither Austria nor Russia is very anxious to contribute to our aggrandizement.

C. Frederick to Privy Councillor of Legation Count von Solms at Saint Petersburg (Potsdam, February 20, 1771)

I think it well to communicate to you the details which I have received of the occupation effected by the Austrians of territory along the frontiers of Hungary, which seems to me interesting enough to merit the attention of the neighboring Powers. I have just learned that not only the Starosty [District] of Zips, but also those of Novitarg, Czorstyn, and another area equally considerable have been surrounded by an Austrian cordon; that the territory so occupied is probably some 20 miles[2] in length, from the County of Sáros in Hungary to the frontiers of Austrian Silesia; that it contains in all several towns and up to ninety-seven villages; that the Court of Vienna has already exercised sovereign rights there several times; that in reply to the complaints made by the Republic of Poland, Prince Kaunitz has given replies which are vague, but clearly indicate an intention to assert ancient rights, and they are probably already at work in Vienna to make a case to justify and support these various seizures.

I have no doubt that Petersburg has already informed itself of

[2] About 95 English miles.

most of this. I even remember that the first news which arrived of the occupation gave rise in the minds of many persons at the Russian Court to the idea of an equal aggrandizement for all Poland's neighbors, and although I saw from one of your reports that that idea did not take general hold, and although I feel very strongly the reasons that could be adduced against it, I have yet thought well to write to you, because these reasons are always based on the assumption that the Court of Vienna will desist from its enterprise, whereas all the indications which I have just passed on to you make it plain that it is firmly resolved to persist in it.

If we thus look at the realities of the position, the question is no longer one of maintaining Poland intact, since the Austrians want to truncate it, but of preventing this dismemberment from upsetting that balance between the House of Austria and my own that is so important for me and of such interest to the Russian Court itself. But I see no other way of maintaining it than to imitate the example set me by the Court of Vienna, to assert, as it does, old claims which the archives will produce for me, and to place myself in possession of some little province of Poland, which can be restored if the Austrians desist from their enterprise or retained if they try to make good the pretended title alleged by them.

You will yourself feel that an acquisition of this kind could offend no one, that the Poles, who are the only party which would have a right to cry out, have by their attitude forfeited any right to be considered either by the Court of Russia or by my own, and that once the Great Powers are agreed, this could not prevent the work of pacification.

But I should like first to know the real feelings of the Russian Court on this question, and I leave you free to choose whatever means you regard as most proper and fitting to achieve this. If you succeed in getting the Empress and her Minister to adopt my views, you will be rendering me a service that will be the more agreeable because, as I see it, this is the only means of preserving equality between me and the Court of Vienna. I consequently have no doubt that you will employ all your tact to carry out this commission in accordance with my wishes, and that you will render me an exact and detailed account of how far you have been successful.

D. Frederick to Count von Solms (Potsdam, February 27, 1771)

Your dispatch of the twelfth of this month has duly reached me, and since it informs me that the postillion carrying the post of January 27 was robbed near Petersburg, I hasten to send you herewith a duplicate of my orders of the twenty-seventh of that month.

I also enclose a passport which the "Administrator" of the district of Poland occupied by the Court of Vienna issued on November 8, 1770, to the Staroste [Prefect] Pelilcancyk, which shows only too clearly that that Court already regards that district, with all its dependencies, as States incorporated in its Kingdom of Hungary.[3] This move proves clearly enough that it is determined to keep it, and I have every reason to suppose that it will never relinquish it unless obliged to do so by *force majeure*.

This idea naturally leads me on to another, and leads me to believe that the best course would be if Russia and I profited equally from this situation, and if, imitating the Court of Vienna, we looked to our own interests and derived some real and proportionate advantage from it. It seems to me, in fact, that it must be indifferent to Russia in which quarter she gets the compensation she is, as your despatch announces, so anxious to obtain. For although her present war[4] arose solely out of Polish affairs, I do not see why she need think only of gaining her compensation from the territory of that Republic, and for myself, if I want to prevent the balance from being tipped too far to the Austrian side, I could not renounce obtaining for myself, in the same way, some small part of Poland, if it were only as a token equivalent for my subsidies and the losses and damage that I have suffered during this war. Even more, I shall be greatly pleased if I am able to say truthfully that it is to Russia that I am chiefly obliged for this new acquisition, which will, at the same time, furnish a new

[3] The pass, issued by the Austrian "Administrator" of the territories in question, Hofrat von Török, described them as *"districtus neo-recuperatus Hungariae"* (recovered district of Hungary) and Pelilcancyk as *"fidelis sanctissimae caesareae regiae et apostolicae Majestatis subditus"* (loyal subject of her most sacred Imperial, Royal and Apostolic Majesty).

[4] The war declared by Turkey on Russia in October, 1768.

opportunity for us to reaffirm our mutual links and to render them more unbreakable than ever.

As to her peace negotiations, she may, on the contrary, rest well assured that I shall not cease to support her to the best of my power, and that I shall leave no stone unturned to procure for her a glorious peace; and on this point, I must inform you that her Minister at Vienna, Prince Galitzin, has already carried out the commission which he was ordered to perform with Prince Kaunitz. So far, however, he is still waiting for his answer, Kaunitz having only received his proposals *ad referendum*, pending Her Imperial and Royal Majesty's decision. He will soon be given his answer, and we shall see how it will run. . . .

[The rest of the despatch is concerned only with enjoining the completest secrecy.]

Bibliography

The Habsburg Dynasty

No even approximately adequate full-length account of the Habsburg monarchy, covering the whole period with which this volume deals, has appeared in the English language for over a century. Phases of it are covered in various chapters (of very unequal merit) in the two versions of the *Cambridge Modern History*. An excellent short sketch in German is H. Hantsch's *Die Entwicklung Oesterreich-Ungarns's zur Grossmacht* in Vol. XV of the series *Geschichte der Führenden Völker* (1933). See also the same author's *Geschichte Oesterreichs* (3rd edn., 1962). Other recent general histories are *Geschichte und Kulturleben Deutsch-Oesterreichs* by F. M. Mayer, R. F. Kaindl, and H. Pirchegger (Mayer's old work brought up to date; 3rd edn., 1964) and E. Zöllner, *Geschichte Oesterreichs* (2nd edn., 1961). All these works contain bibliographies, Zöllner's being the best, but the fullest bibliography of the subject is that by K. and M. Uhlirz, *Handbuch der Geschichte Oesterreichs* (4 vols., 1927ff., new issue, with later material in preparation), which also itself furnishes a good narrative history. Most of these works concentrate, outside the diplomatic, etc., history of the monarchy, on its German-Austrian provinces; the latest Mayer-Kaindl-Pirchegger has even cut out many pages on the other parts of the monarchy which were in the original Mayer. They are all more or less Germanic in sentiment. For views of the subject from the Czech-Bohemian angle, see Ernest Denis's monumental *La Bohême depuis la Montagne-Blanche* (2 vols., 1903) and R. W. Seton Watson, *A History of the Czechs and Slovaks* (1943, shorter). For Hungary, nearly all the serious work is in Magyar; but see C. A. Macartney, *Hungary, A Short History* (2nd edn., 1966).

Many of the sources have to be dredged out of the huge series, *Fontes Rerum Austriacarum*. There is also a series, *Die oesterreichische Zentralverwaltung,* ed. T. Fellner and others (1907; still in progress), with texts and narrative.

For individual periods and figures, the works on the seventeenth century are mostly either antiquated or slight. For the first half of the eighteenth, far the best is O. Redlich, *Das Werden einer Grossmacht* (1942); this, however, covers only the foreign-political side; Redlich died before completing his companion volume on internal affairs. The basic biography of Maria Theresa is still that of A. von Arneth (10 vols., 1863ff.), antiquated but still indispensable. Arneth also edited much of Maria Theresa's correspondence (for other editions, see Uhlirz) and wrote a life of Prince Eugene. The numerous later biographies of Maria Theresa are usually journalistic; an exception is that by H. Kretschmayer (2nd edn., 1938). The latest is C. A. Macartney, *Maria Theresa and the House of Austria* (1969). By far the most solid biography of Joseph II is still that by the Russian, P. Mitranov (German trans., 2 vols., 1910). The later works on Joseph are mostly shallow; the best is V. Bibl's *Kaiser Josef II* (1954). Leopold II had been neglected by historians until a full-length life of him was published by A. Wandruszka (2 vols., 1964).

The Rise of the Hohenzollerns, 1600–1790

The contribution by Dr. M. Braubach to the volume in the *Geschichte der Führenden Völker* (see above under Habsburgs) is an excellent short sketch, with an adequate bibliography. This omits, oddly, Christian Otto Mylius's *Corpus constitionum Marchicarum* (6 vols., 1737), an invaluable and comprehensive collection up to the date of publication, but lists the other main collections, the chief of which are the *Acta Brandenburgica*, ed. M. Klinkenborg (3 vols., 1932ff.); the *Acta Borussica* (1892ff.); the *Urkunden und Aktenstücke zur Geschichte des Kurfürsten Friedrich Wilhelm* (23 vols., 1864ff.); and the collections of Frederick the Great's writings, notably his *Werke,* ed. G. B. Volz (10 vols., 1913–14) and his *Politische Correspondenz* (42 plus 1 vols., 1879ff.). For a fuller bibliography, see Dahlmann-Waitz, *Quellenkunde der deutschen Geschichte* (9th edn., 1931). Fuller general histories: in English, S. B. Fay, *The Rise of Brandenburg-Prussia to 1786* (1937); J. A. R. Marriott and C. Grant Robertson, *The Evolution of Prussia* (1946); the relevant chapters in *The New*

Cambridge Modern History are also very useful. German works: L. von Ranke, *Zwölf Bücher Preussische Geschichte* (1887ff.), by a master; F. Holtze, *Geschichte der Mark Brandenburg* (1912); O. Hintze, *Die Hohenzollern und ihr Werk* (5th edn., 1915); W. Pierson, *Preussische Geschichte* (10th edn., 1911); and R. Koser, *Geschichte der brandenburg-preussischen Politik* (1913). There are two good special studies of the Great Elector: H. von Petersdorff, *Der Grosse Kurfürst* (1927; admiring) and F. Schevill, *The Great Elector* (1947; more critical). Frederick the Great is one of the most written-up figures in his history. A solid and relatively modern work in German in G. Koser, *Geschichte Friedrichs des Grossen* (4 vols., 1912–14); later, W. Hegemann, *Friedrich der Grosse* (1924), English translation by W. Ray, *Frederick the Great* (1929). Original works in English: W. F. Reddaway, *Frederick the Great and the Rise of Prussia* (1909), and N. Young, *The Life of Frederick the Great* (1919; hostile, but with a good bibliography).

"Austrian" Chronology, 1600-1800 A.D.

1576	Rudolph II Emperor. Onset of Counter-Reformation in Austrian lands.
1592	Opening of "Long War" in Transylvania.
1595	Ferdinand II assumes rule in Inner Austria.
1606	Bocskay Prince of Transylvania. Treaties of Vienna (Bocskay and Empire) and Zsitvatorok (Empire and Porte).
1608	Matthias King of Hungary and ruler of Archduchy of Austria and Moravia.
1609	Bohemian "Majestätsbrief."
1612	Rudolph d. Matthias Emperor.
1613–1629	Gabriel Bethlen (Bethlen Gabor) Prince of Transylvania.
1618	Ferdinand II crowned in Hungary and Bohemia. Defenestration of Prague.
1618 (ca.)–48	Thirty Years War.
1619	Matthias d. Ferdinand Emperor. Bohemian Estates elect the Elector Palatine.
1620	Battle of the "White Hill." Prague submits to Ferdinand.
1648	Peace of Westphalia.
1672–8	"Vernewerte Landesordnungen" for Bohemia and Moravia.
1634	Assassination of Wallenstein.
1637	Ferdinand II d. Ferdinand III Emperor.
1660–1	Transylvania reduced by Turks.
1662–4	War between the Empire and Porte.
1664	Peace of Vasvar.
1669	Betrayal of "Nadasdy conspiracy."
1672–9	War between Empire and France.
1673	Suspension of Hungarian Constitution.
1678	Thököly in Transylvania.
1679	Peace of Nymwegen, Empire and France.
1681	Hungarian Constitution restored. Thököly Prince.
1683	Turkish invasion; siege of Vienna.
1684–99	Recovery of Hungary, including (1687) Transylvania.
1687	Hungarian Diet recognizes Habsburg hereditary suc-

cession in male line. Joseph I crowned King in Hungary.

1699   Peace of Karlowitz.

              Charles II of Spain d. Leopold claims his throne.

1701   Outbreak of War of Spanish Succession. Charles VI (Emperor), III (in Spain and Hungary).

1703   *Pactum Mutuae Successionis.* Rakoczi Rebellion in Hungary.

1705   Leopold d. Joseph I Emperor.

1711   Joseph d. Charles VI (III) Emperor. Peace of Szathmar with Hungary.

1713   Promulgation of Pragmatic Sanction.

1714   Peace of Rastatt. Charles renounces Spanish succession, but receives Austrian Netherlands, Milanese, etc., Naples and Sardinia.

1716–18   War with Porte.

1718   Peace of Passarowitz. Remainder of South Hungary recovered and Serbia acquired.

1717   Maria Theresa born.

1720   Sardinia exchanged for Sicily.

1722–3   Hungarian Diet accepts Pragmatic Sanction in return for constitutional guarantee.

1733   Outbreak of War of Polish Succession.

1735   Preliminary Peace of Vienna (confirmed 1738). Charles loses Naples.

1736   Maria Theresa married to Francis Stephen of Lorraine.

1737–9   War with Porte.

1739   Peace of Belgrade; Serbia lost.

1740, Oct.   Charles d. Maria Theresa succeeds him in Austria.

    Dec.   Frederick of Prussia invades Silesia. Outbreak of War of Austrian Succession.

1741, March   Joseph II born.

May–October   Coronation Diet in Hungary.

1742   Treaties of Breslau and Berlin.

1745, October Francis Emperor.

December   Peace of Dresden. Austria cedes Silesia.

1748   Peace of Aix-la-Chapelle.

1747–56   Maria Theresa's "First Reform Period" (administrative and financial reorganization).

1752–3   "Renversement d'alliances."

1756   Outbreak of Seven Years' War.

1763   Peace of Hubertusburg. *Status quo ante bellum* restored.

1765	Francis d. Joseph II Emperor and co-regent in Austria.
1767	Maria Theresa's "Second Reform Period" (social, cultural, reforms).
1772	First partition of Poland. Galicia to Austria.
1775	Bukovina to Austria.
1778–9	War of Bavarian Succession.
1780	Maria Theresa d. Joseph II sole ruler.
1780–90	Decade of Joseph's "enlightened absolutism."
1778	War with Porte. Revolt in Netherlands. Unrest in Hungary.
1790, Jan.	Joseph repeals majority of his decrees in Hungary.
February	Joseph II d., Leopold II succeeds him.
1791	Convention of Reichenberg (with Prussia). Treaty of Sistovo (with Porte). Pacification of Hungary.
1792, March	Leopold d. Francis II (later I as Emperor of Austria).

Chronology of Brandenburg-Prussia, 1600-1796

1598	Joachim Frederick Elector of Brandenburg. Compact of Gera.
1604	Establishment of Privy Council.
1608	Joachim Frederick d.; John Sigismund Elector.
1609	Duke of Jülich d. Dispute for his heritage, ending in 1614 in Agreement of Xanten; Brandenburg allotted Cleves, Mark and Ravensburg.
1613	John Sigismund adopts Calvinist faith.
1618	Duke of Prussia d. John Sigismund Duke, as vassal of the King of Poland.
1618 (ca.)–1648	Thirty Years' War.
1619	John Sigismund dies. George William Elector and Duke (1620).
1620	Brandenburg tries to preserve neutrality.
1627	Brandenburg occupied by Swedes.
1640	George William d. Frederick William (the "Great Elector") Elector and Duke.
1644	Truce with Sweden. Sweden agrees to evacuate Brandenburg.
1646	The "miles perpetuus."
1646–47	Abortive hostilities with Neuburg.
1648	Peace of Westphalia. Brandenburg acquires Lower Pomerania, Halberstadt and Minden, with reversion of Magdeburg.
1651	Invasion of Neuburg. Reorganization of Privy Council.
1653	Treaty of Stettin with Sweden. Brandenburg Recess.
1654	Outbreak of Swedish-Polish War.
1657	Treaty of Wehlau (confirmed in Treaty of Oliva, 1660); Hohenzollerns receive full sovereignty over Prussia.
1660	Domestic and military reforms. Definitive recognition of Brandenburg's claim to Cleve, Mark and Ravensburg.
1672–4	Revolts in Prussia crushed.
1672–9	Wars with or against France and Sweden.

1675	Battle of Fehrbellin. Institution of Generalkriegs-commissariat.
1685	Edict of Potsdam (Admission of French Huguenots).
1688	Frederick William d. Frederick III Elector and Duke. Wars with France.
1700	Foundation of Berlin Academy.
1701	Frederick crowned King in Prussia (as King Frederick I).
1712	Frederick (later Frederick II) born.
1713	Frederick I d. Frederick William I King. Financial and administrative reforms.
1713–15	Territorial enlargements in Gelderland and Pomerania.
1722–23	Establishment of Directorate General.
1730	Attempted flight and imprisonment of Crown Prince Frederick.
1732	Crown Prince re-instated and gradually reconciled with his father.
1740, May	Frederick William I d. Frederick II King.
December	Frederick invades Silesia, opening War of the Austrian Succession.
1742, July	Treaties of Breslau and Berlin, which leave Frederick holding most of Silesia.
1744, May	Frederick re-invades Austria.
1745, Dec.	Peace of Breslau. Provisions of 1742 Treaties reaffirmed.
1746–56	Internal Reforms.
1756, Jan.	Convention of Westminster between Prussia and Great Britain.
August	Frederick invades Saxony.
1756–63	Seven Years' War. Prussia at war with Austria, France, the Empire (officially), and at times Sweden and Russia.
1763, February	Treaty of Hubertusburg, restoring *status quo ante bellum*.
1764	Alliance with Russia.
1773	First Partition of Poland. Acquisition of West Prussia and Poland up to the Netze.
1775	Creation of the "Fürstenbund" (league of German Princes under Prussian leadership).
1778–9	War of the Bavarian Succession.
1776	Frederick d.; Frederick William II King.

The Austrian Habsburgs

B = King of Bohemia   E = Holy Roman Emperor   H = King of Hungary

FERDINAND I d. 1564
m. ANNE of Hungary and Bohemia
B and H, 1526. E, 1556

MAXIMILIAN II d. 1576
m. MARIA of Spain
B, 1562 H, 1563 E, 1564

FERDINAND d. 1595
(Tyrol)

3 dau.

(Inner Austria)
CHARLES d. 1590
m. Mary of Bavaria

RUDOLPH II d. 1612
H, 1572 B, 1575
E, 1576

MATTHIAS d. 1619
m. Anne of Tyrol
H, 1608 B, 1611
E, 1612

3 s., 1 dau.

FERDINAND II d. 1637
m. Marie Anne of Bavaria
Styria 1595.
B, 1617 H, 1618
E, 1619

Mary
m. Philip III
of Spain

1 s., 2 dau.

FERDINAND III d. 1657 m. Marie of Spain
H, 1625 B, 1627
E, 1637

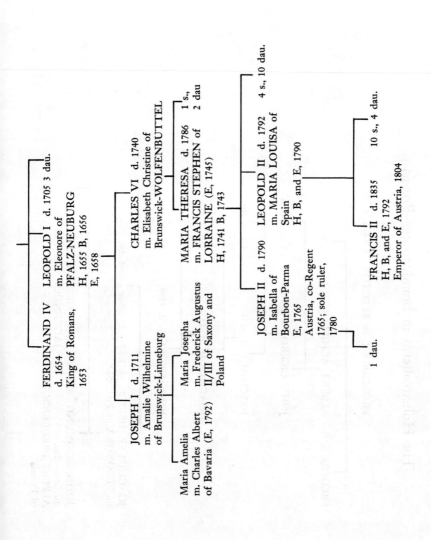

FERDINAND IV
d. 1654
King of Romans,
1653

LEOPOLD I d. 1705 3 dau.
m. Eleonore of
PFALZ-NEUBURG
H, 1655 B, 1656
E, 1658

JOSEPH I d. 1711
m. Amalie Wilhelmine
of Brunswick-Linneburg

CHARLES VI d. 1740
m. Elisabeth Christine of
Brunswick-WOLFENBÜTTEL

Maria Amelia
m. Charles Albert
of Bavaria (E, 1792)

Maria Josepha
m. Frederick Augustus
II/III of Saxony and
Poland

MARIA THERESA d. 1786 1 s.,
m. FRANCIS STEPHEN of   2 dau
LORRAINE (E, 1745)
H, 1741 B, 1743

JOSEPH II d. 1790
m. Isabella of
Bourbon-Parma
E, 1765
Austria, co-Regent
1765; sole ruler,
1780

LEOPOLD II d. 1792 4 s., 10 dau.
m. MARIA LOUISA of
Spain
H, B, and E, 1790

1 dau.

FRANCIS II d. 1835
H, B, and E, 1792
Emperor of Austria, 1804

10 s., 4 dau.

The Hohenzollerns in Brandenburg—Prussia

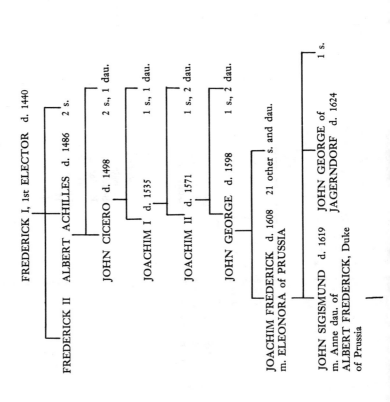

FREDERICK I, 1st ELECTOR   d. 1440

FREDERICK II

ALBERT ACHILLES   d. 1486   2 s.

JOHN CICERO   d. 1498   2 s., 1 dau.

JOACHIM I   d. 1535   1 s., 1 dau.

JOACHIM II   d. 1571   1 s., 2 dau.

JOHN GEORGE   d. 1598   1 s., 2 dau.

JOACHIM FREDERICK   d. 1608   21 other s. and dau.
m. ELEONORA of PRUSSIA

JOHN SIGISMUND   d. 1619   JOHN GEORGE of   1 s.
m. Anne dau. of   JAGERNDORF   d. 1624
ALBERT FREDERICK, Duke
of Prussia

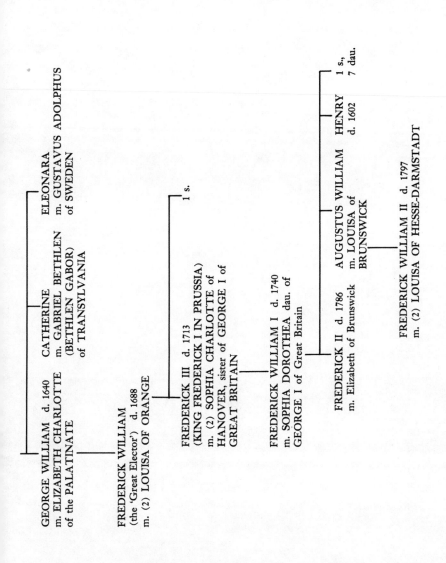

GEORGE WILLIAM d. 1640
m. ELIZABETH CHARLOTTE
of the PALATINATE

CATHERINE
m. GABRIEL BETHLEN
(BETHLEN GABOR)
of TRANSYLVANIA

ELEONARA
m. GUSTAVUS ADOLPHUS
of SWEDEN

FREDERICK WILLIAM
(the 'Great Elector') d. 1688
m. (2) LOUISA OF ORANGE

FREDERICK III d. 1713
(KING FREDERICK I IN PRUSSIA)
m. (2) SOPHIA CHARLOTTE of
HANOVER, sister of GEORGE I of
GREAT BRITAIN — 1 s.

FREDERICK WILLIAM I d. 1740
m. SOPHIA DOROTHEA dau. of
GEORGE I of Great Britain

FREDERICK II d. 1786
m. Elizabeth of Brunswick

AUGUSTUS WILLIAM
m. LOUISA of
BRUNSWICK

HENRY
d. 1602 — 1 s., 7 dau.

FREDERICK WILLIAM II d. 1797
m. (2) LOUISA OF HESSE-DARMSTADT

Index

69 70 71 72 73   12 11 10 9 8 7 6 5 4 3 2 1